The
WISDOM
SERIES

The
WISDOM

WISDOM
is the way
GOD
shepherds
us to
SHALOM

SERIES

A Bible Survey Curriculum For Adults

A Worship Approach to Education in 52 Sessions

Celia M. Hastings

**Sheepfold
Publishing**
Ellsworth, Michigan

The Wisdom Series is designed as a guide to studying The Bible. Every effort has been made to make this series as complete and accurate as possible. However, there may be mistakes, both typographical and in content. Therefore, this series should be used only as a general guide and not as the ultimate source of wisdom. You are urged to read other available material and learn as much as possible, tailoring the information to individual and group needs.

The purpose of this Bible survey series is to educate. The author and Sheepfold Publishing shall have neither liability nor responsibility to any person or entity with respect to any loss or damage caused, directly or indirectly, by the information contained in these books.

If you do not wish to be bound by the above, you may return this book to the publisher for a full refund.

 Published by Sheepfold Publishing
P.O. Box 72, Ellsworth, Michigan 49729

Publisher's Cataloging-in-Publication Data
Hastings, Celia, M.
    The wisdom series: a Bible survey curriculum for adults / Celia M. Hastings.—Ellsworth, MI:
Sheepfold Publishing, c1997.
        p. : ill. : cm.
Includes bibliographical references.
ISBN: 0-9656335-1-9
    1. Bible—Reading. 2. Bible—Study and teaching.
    3. Bible—Handbooks, manuals.
    I. Title.
BS617 .H37   1997
220' .07 dc–21   97-65081

PROJECT COORDINATION BY JENKINS GROUP, INC.
00 99 98 ❖ 5 4 3 2 1

Printed in the United States of America

Dedicated To
my husband, John
whose wisdom, love and partnership
have made this work possible
and
my son, Paul
whose insights of wisdom
have blessed my life and work
and
ecumenically
to all who use this series —
"SO THERE WILL BE ONE FLOCK,
ONE SHEPHERD."
(John 10:16c)

THE WISDOM SERIES • TABLE OF CONTENTS

The aim of this session
is to encounter wisdom as the way God shepherds us to Shalom.

FOREWORD

Hoping to follow the reading of the Old Testament Lesson in Sunday worship, a parishioner fumbles through the pages of the pew Bible in another futile attempt to find the correct place. In a Sunday school class, one adult learner who cannot name the twelve disciples avoids eye contact with her teacher so she won't be asked to answer this question from the day's Bible lesson. At home, a father is unable to help his child find the Lord's Prayer in the Bible. On a college retreat, a junior student turns red with embarrassment at not knowing the Ten Commandments.

These four scenarios are not unusual. In fact, they are happening with increasing frequency in Christian congregations throughout North America. The inability to locate a particular book of the Bible, or the lack of knowledge about the basic content of the Bible, or the absence of an overview of the central story line and major themes of the Bible are all examples of biblical illiteracy.

There are many kinds of illiteracy, including the basic inability to read with understanding and express oneself in writing. Edward D. Hirsch, Jr. speaks of "cultural illiteracy," by which he means that persons do not possess a knowledge of their culture's central stories, major customs, or core traditions. Others speak of "computer illiteracy," by which they mean that persons lack an understanding of computers and how to use them. Drawing on these examples, it could be said that biblical illiteracy is the lack of basic knowledge about the Bible and an inability to understand its meaning for faith and life.

Abraham Lincoln was not only a courageous leader, but also a gifted public speaker. His speeches included many allusions and quotations from the Bible. Most of Lincoln's listeners – even those who were not Christians – understood what he meant when he used a biblical allusion in one of his speeches. They recognized sayings that were quoted from the Bible. Today, a growing number of Christians would not recognize Lincoln's biblical allusions, nor would they be familiar with the Bible stories or characters to which he referred in his speeches. For too many Christians, it would be like missing the humor in a joke because they did not recognize the punch line.

Biblical illiteracy is a serious problem facing Christian congregations, regardless of denominational affiliation. Pastors, church educators, denominational education leaders, and curriculum designers have recognized the challenge of biblical illiteracy and have tried to respond to it. Pastors have taught Bible study classes, church educators have organized Bible studies, denominational leaders have developed programs, and curriculum designers have produced an impressive array of Bible study materials.

In spite of considerable investment of time, talent, and energy, some Bible study programs have done little to counter biblical illiteracy. There are a number of reasons for this situation. Some of the Christian religious education programs designed to provide adults with foundational knowledge of the Bible are very costly. These programs are often out of reach of many smaller congregations or congregations with limited financial resources. Other programs require a high degree of teacher training and preparation. Busy pastors soon find the demands of these programs overwhelming and eventually stop teaching them. Still other programs assume a basic Bible knowledge on the part of the learners. Those seeking to gain an entry level Bible knowledge soon become discouraged and drop out of class.

The Wisdom Series offers congregations with limited financial resources an affordable curriculum for adult learners with a limited knowledge of the Bible. The curriculum empowers pastors to become effective teachers by drawing on their knowledge of scripture and seminary training and by providing a user-friendly format. The curriculum encourages learners through the use of a rich variety of teaching methods and learning activities.

Several features of The Wisdom Series deserve particular attention. First, the accent is on active learning. Unlike traditional adult Bible classes where an "expert" teacher talks and learners listen and, perhaps, answer an occasional question, adult learners using The Wisdom Series become actively engaged with the lessons. Second, the series is ecumenical in scope. While the author's roots are in the Reformed and Methodist traditions, she does not impose denominational beliefs on the learners. Third, the curriculum reflects one of the emerging trends in biblical scholarship. The wisdom tradition of the Bible, often neglected, is the organizing principle around which the fifty-two lessons of this series have been shaped. Fourth, The Wisdom Series recognizes the importance of worship. Learning grounded in worship is less likely to be limited to acquiring information or memorizing facts and more likely to lead to transformation.

George Brown
Professor of Christian Education and Associate Dean
Western Theological Seminary
Holland, Michigan

Epiphany, 1997

PREFACE

The Native American ceremony of the "Peace Pipe" was celebrated with participants seated in a circle. A smoking pipe was held up to the four directions and then passed around the circle so everyone could receive the gifts of reconciliation and peace. The expression, "Put that in your pipe and smoke it" stems from the "Peace Pipe" ceremony, inviting consideration of a great truth, nugget of wisdom or even a differing opinion.

Four "nuggets" which have been "smoked" in my "Peace Pipe" are: 1) The Bethel Series, one of the first Bible survey courses, still widely used, which I had the privilege of learning and teaching, 2) My seminary journey which included a study tour of Israel, 3) Insights gained from daily scripture reading, and 4) Prayer. The result is a synthesis known as *The Wisdom Series*.

Why "Wisdom?" While "salvation history" has long been a major theme for biblical study, the focus has recently shifted to "Wisdom," a theme which incorporates salvation history. Wisdom is a complex subject, sometimes personified – in Proverbs 8 and 9 as a woman (Sophia) and in Matthew 11:19 as Jesus. Elsewhere, wisdom seems to be a vague and elusive entity that people struggle to grasp but which always seems just out of reach. It cannot be bought or possessed. It patiently waits for people to turn from foolish ways to seek it. Wisdom is mysterious and resists definition.

In The Wisdom Series, WISDOM IS THE WAY GOD SHEPHERDS US TO SHALOM. From Wisdom's perspective, the Holy One reaches out to people who are prone to wandering, calls them from their waywardness, leads them through dark and dangerous places, into relationships of wholeness and peace – like the Good Shepherd leads sheep – "SO THERE MAY BE ONE FLOCK, ONE SHEPHERD" (John 10:16c).

Since reading scripture via The One-Year Bible plan has played a major role in shaping The Wisdom Series, this daily reading plan is used throughout the series. Space is provided on the "Daily Scripture Reading" hand-out page for recording insights while reading through the Bible. Much awaits discovery!

ACKNOWLEDGMENTS

No project of this size comes about single-handedly but rather in community with those who follow the Shepherd with me. Everyone I've known, followed, led, worshipped with, talked with or studied with has influenced me (and thus this project) in some way. So my first acknowledgment, sheepishly, is to those not mentioned by name. I hope you will see yourselves and your influence in this work and find your enjoyment of this series enhanced because we have journeyed together.

I am especially grateful to Rich and Helen DeVos for their friendship and encouragement throughout my seminary journey and this project, and for providing a grant (and at times a research/writing haven) through The DeVos Foundation – a gift designed to go forward as an affordable blessing for all, especially for small groups, small churches and home study groups.

My heartfelt thanks to my friend and seminary classmate, The Rev. Mary Anne Evans-Justin, who has encouraged this project since its inception by telling me: "Ideas that don't go away deserve to be paid attention to." Special thanks also to her mother, Jeanne Wandersleben, an experienced curriculum writer, for reviewing an early manuscript, offering encouragement, guidance and affirmation.

Thanks to my mother, Wilma Bolhuis, for patiently listing the Daily Scripture Readings.

Thanks to the Petoskey United Methodist Church for assisting in research.

Thanks to Julie Keefer of Morningstar Retreat Center who first introduced me to the term "kin-dom of God."

Thanks to the Win-Some Women Retreat Intercessors and the Sacramentine Sisters for supporting this endeavor in prayer; thanks to Barbara Hubeny, O.P., for her hospitality and for providing a writer's haven at the Augustine Center.

Thanks to The Rev. Richard Smiley for sharing knowledge and insights into the publishing process.

Special thanks to Molly Scott for initial sheep, creation and garden illustrations, to Cynthia Linn Robson for initial layout and design, to Barbara Hodge for completing the layout and design, to Alex Moore and Mark Dressler of Jenkins Group, Inc., for shepherding the publication process.

Many thanks to Norwood United Methodist Church for administration of the DeVos grant, for providing a haven for research and writing, to Elizabeth Hoffmann, Grace Warner, Henrietta Weisler, Tony and Elaine Dvoracek for faithfully field testing the original manuscript with me, catching typos, glitches and irregularities – for learning with me.

Thanks to Tim and Linda Matchett for sharing their sheep and their practical shepherding wisdom with me.

Special thanks to my cousin and friend Mark Groenink for shepherding me in computer wisdom as I tackled the gargantuan task (as a computer novice) of putting this project on disk.

Thanks to Elizabeth Hoffmann for expert and timely assistance in the proofreading process.

Thanks to the following people from whom I learned the centrality of Psalm 23, the "Shepherd Psalm," in all of Scripture and thus of The Wisdom Series:

- My parents, Fred and Wilma (Groenink) Bolhuis, who owned and operated a family farm which provided much interaction with animals, and to my sister Ardith (Bolhuis) Tornga and brother Roger Bolhuis who grew up on the farm with me;

- Dr. Sonja Stewart, Professor of Christian Education and Director of the Master's In Religious Education Program at Western Theological Seminary, Holland, Michigan, especially for "The Good Shepherd" story in "Children and Worship" class;

- Dr. Charles R. Page II of the Jerusalem Center who led the seminarians' scholarship study tour (via Educational Opportunities of Lakeland, Florida) of the land of Israel as a classroom, showing how Israel's geography shaped its shepherding culture which shaped its faith; and

- My husband, John, with whom I work in funeral service — where Psalm 23 remains central for comfort in bereavement.

Last but not least, a heap of thanks to Louise Bass, biblical illustrator, for the shepherd and sheep, creation and garden illustrations used in The Wisdom Series.

Sheepish thanks to all!

Celia Hastings

How to use The Wisdom Series

Pacing The Journey — Although there are 52 sessions, it is not necessary to complete the series in one year. The pace of moving through The Wisdom Series can be adapted by leader and participants. The group may wish to spend additional time on some sessions. Special sessions may be included for questions and answers, sharing insights from Daily Scripture Readings or inviting a guest speaker. As with any curriculum, it is the task of the leader to adapt the material to the needs of participants so that leaders and participants weave their own creativity into the series.

The Worship Approach — Each session includes "The Approach To God." A worship approach to education is essential – not to "warm God up" before pressing for benefits – but to shift the focus from our own busy thoughts to God. In worshipping God we encounter the Living Word which transforms us so we can extend God's love to others.

Please do not skip the worship approach altogether – but feel free to adapt it to the group's likes and needs. For example, taped background music and/or candlelight as participants gather can transform ordinary time and space, creating sacred space where participants encounter God.

If the session takes place following a worship service, participants may be ready to encounter God without further preparation. An unhurried, quiet setting with a circular seating arrangement works best.

Answer Guides — Ideally, leaders should read and search the Scriptures as outlined for participants (shepherds cannot lead where they have not been . . .). Realizing that life is not always ideal and that my purposes may not immediately be clear, answer guides have been included. It is my hope that they will be used sparingly and flexibly – that God's Spirit may lead as you search the Scriptures to discover new insights and encounter WISDOM.

Delegating — Because some sessions (such as Session 1) involve learning stations, board games, etc., the leader may wish to delegate these tasks. Delegating prevents leader burn-out and enhances group ownership of the series. The whole group benefits from cooperative leadership.

Introductory Session — "An Introduction To The Bible" and "The Books Of The Bible" are provided as hand-outs for an introductory session. Following the introduction to the Bible, participants may wish to create a group contract which specifies:

- Time, place and length of sessions
- Scheduled breaks for holidays, Q&A or insight-sharing sessions, inviting guest speakers, etc.
- Confidentiality, commitment to pray for each other
- Other considerations important to the group

Copying Privileges — All rights reserved. No part of this publication may be copied or reproduced in any way without the written permission of the publisher. ("Copying and reproduction" includes recording, storage in an electronic retrieval system and transmission in any form or by any means, electronic or mechanical.) Exceptions to the above include the Search Sheets, Daily Scripture Readings, Hand-out Illustrations and certain in-session materials, which are marked with the **"open-book" symbol (📖)**. Such materials can be reproduced only in quantities necessary for use by the church or home study group purchasing this curriculum. Reproduction of any part of this curriculum for any other purpose is both illegal and unethical.

An Introduction to the Bible

The Wisdom Series covers the Bible (Protestant) which consists of 66 Books: 39 in the Hebrew Scriptures (Old Testament or First Testament), and 27 in the New Testament. The books are not arranged in chronological order. There is a 400-year gap between the Hebrew Scriptures and the New Testament. (This is where 1 and 2 Maccabees from the Bible (Catholic) provide important historical context.)

These 66 Books of the Bible contain a variety of writings: prophetic history, poetry, stories, parables, sermons, teachings, prophecies, wise sayings (proverbs), songs and prayers (psalms), letters (epistles), etc.

Take a look at "The Books Of The Bible" hand-out. You may wish to color-code your copy for easier reference.

Find the Index in your Bible. Open your Bible in the center and see which Book you find there. Then locate the end of the Hebrew Scriptures (Old Testament) and the beginning of the New Testament. Find Genesis 1, Matthew 1, Psalm 1 and Proverbs 1. Place bookmarks in these places. You are now ready to begin Daily Scripture Readings, a plan for reading through the Bible in one year.

There are many versions of the Bible. You can use a Bible you already have, or you may wish to purchase a new Bible for this purpose. The New Revised Standard Version is used throughout The Wisdom Series (except for Psalm 23 in the familiar King James Version) and will be needed for many assignments.

If you have not memorized the Books of the Bible, it would be helpful to do so. If you have memorized them, you may need a "refresher course." Your group may wish to make a contract and/or weekly check list to encourage and support one another in faithfully reaching the goal of reading through the Bible in one year.

A Special Note: Some adults may be unable to read due to learning disabilities, concentration difficulties, vision problems, etc. Cassette tape versions of the Bible are available for those who (for any reason) may prefer audio to visual learning.

The group can offer a "team approach" for those who need assistance in completing Search Sheets and in-class reading/writing assignments.

"Are you willing to be led?"

THE BOOKS OF THE BIBLE

The

WISDOM

WISDOM
is the way
GOD
shepherds
us to
SHALOM

SERIES

SESSION 1 • SHEPHERD WISDOM

The aim of this session
is to glimpse the relational wisdom of God as Shepherd and us as sheep.

MATERIALS NEEDED

Hymnals
Accompaniment for singing – piano, guitar, etc., or taped music
Flip Chart (provided at end of Session 1)
"Taking the Journey Materials" (listed below)
Copies for each participant of:
    Illustration 1-A
    Search Sheet 1
    Daily Scripture Readings for Week 1

Taking the Journey Materials

Five chairs and one small table or large box to be set up as stations in a large circle with enough room to move about easily.
Instruction cards, one for each station – 5x7 cards provided in "Taking the Journey" section

Station 1:	Pen Name tags (could be sheep-shaped) for each participant and one for yourself
Station 2:	Pieces of green felt or other fabric (as "pasture") Bowl of grapes and/or small pieces of other fruit Small circles of colored construction paper, pen or pencil
Station 3:	Pitcher of water with a glass for each participant
Station 4:	Scroll with *"Words of Wisdom"* written on the outside and *"Love God"* and *"Love People"* written on the inside
Station 5:	Pieces of navy blue or charcoal gray posterboard cut in "rock" shapes Pens, pencils, small pieces of paper, and transparent tape Blindfolds – *optional*
Station 6:	Use the small table or large box for this one Small container of oil Place cards with names of participants printed on them Individual candles with holders for each participant Matches, glass container for used matches Food for "table" experience – *Could simply be fresh fruit and water and/or crackers and cheese, grapes, juice and juice glasses*
Station 7:	No materials – see card to be used by leader

▣ ASSEMBLING

Allow enough time to prepare the area/areas you will be using and enough time for yourself, to sit quietly for a few moments before participants arrive. As they arrive, welcome each one by name.

▣ THE APPROACH TO GOD   (5 to 10 minutes)

❥ **Prayer:** Begin with a prayer which focuses on God's love and care for all people. Ask God to lead and guide this session.

❥ **Singing A Hymn:** Select *(or delegate someone else to select)* a familiar hymn based on Psalm 23. Check the Topical Index and/or the Scripture Reference sections in your hymnal. Some of the participants may be eager to sing; others may be shy and reluctant. Gently take the focus off "ability" by inviting everyone to "sing off-key, on-key, or in any key you wish"– focusing on the words and offering them to God as a prayer. Later, if the group enjoys singing together, offer them the opportunity to sing at a worship service. It's a good group bonding experience, and it lets the rest of the congregation know how enjoyable searching for wisdom can be!

▣ ENCOUNTERING THE WORD   (40 to 45 minutes)

⇨ Using "The Annual Cycle of the Shepherd" with enlarged illustrations, lead participants through the annual shepherding cycle. Following the presentation, invite participants to reflect on the cycle and Psalm 23: "Name something new you saw in Psalm 23 as we looked at the annual shepherding cycle."

⇨ Set up the learning center for "Taking the Journey." This can be set up in advance in another location if space permits. If only one room is available, invite participants to share in set-up. Arrange five chairs and one small table or large box in a circle with enough space in the center for participants to move about easily. Number the chairs 1 through 5, number the small table or box "6." Place items (as listed under "Materials") at various sections. Copy, cut, and place directions at appropriate stations. Proceed with the Journey.

⇨ After participants have taken the journey, invite them to "share something new you discovered about Psalm 23 as you took the Journey."

▣ GOING FORTH IN GOD'S NAME   (5 to 10 minutes)

❥ Sing an appropriate hymn based on Psalm 23

❥ Offer a closing prayer summarizing the session

❥ Distribute copies of:
  Illustration 1-A
  Search sheet 1 – *to be completed at home so that it may be used here next session*
  Daily Scripture Reading for Week 1

■ "THE ANNUAL CYCLE OF THE SHEPHERD"

A Lecturette with Flip Chart

The annual cycle of a shepherd begins in the springtime.

❧ *Open flip chart to show first picture*

"The Lord is my shepherd; I shall not want."

This is the springtime, a time when the shepherd establishes ownership. Before the shepherd leads the sheep to common grazing land where they mingle with other sheep, it is important to know which sheep belong to which shepherd. So the shepherd takes a hot branding iron and burns a symbol of ownership through the sheep's wool onto its skin. This is painful; but it is lasting proof of ownership.

A sheep must belong to someone – or go its own way. So it is with people. We can go our own way which leads to meaninglessness – or we can accept the ownership of the Good Shepherd who gave his life for us and longs to lead us to abundant life here and always.

❧ *Flip to second picture*

"He maketh me to lie down in green pastures;"

As the winter snow melts, the shepherd leads the branded sheep out from ranch headquarters to the slopes where the warmth of the sun uncovers the lush sweet grass of spring.

The One who shepherds our lives provides plenty for us. Our basic needs are graciously met so we are free to share with others, not needing to fight to get our fair share.

❧ *Flip to third picture*

"He leadeth me beside the still waters."

The sheep will not drink from moving waters, especially the rising streams of melting snow. So the shepherd has to find a place where the waters are still or make a place where the sheep can safely drink.

It is "beside the still waters" that our restless thirst for "something more" is quieted. We read or listen, taking in more and more of the Living Truth.

❧ *Flip to fourth picture*

"He restoreth my soul; he leadeth me in the paths of righteousness for his name's sake."

In the early summer, the shepherd shears the sheep – takes off the old thick wool they no longer need, setting them free to enjoy the summer's warmth. The shepherd counts the sheep frequently and watches them carefully; for if a sheep falls and gets onto its back, it is "cast" and totally helpless to get up on its own. Left alone, it will die in a matter of hours. The shepherd restores fallen sheep.

The shepherd has a pre-determined plan of action for the sheep. If they graze too long on the land, the roots of the grass are damaged so that pastureland becomes wasteland. A proper balance between grass growth and grazing is important (and environmentally sensitive). This usually means finding new grazing ground each week.

Like the sheep, we need shearing – the intentional removal of the old self-life, our masks and our pride. And we are helpless to fix our own fallenness (our sin, guilt, shame, stubborn pride, and wandering). God alone offers restoration.

Like the shepherd, God has a pre-determined plan of action for us, a plan that will move us on to new spiritual growth and graces. Since we cannot see or understand what lies ahead, we learn to trust and obey the Shepherd.

➤ *Flip to fifth picture*

"Yea, though I walk through the valley of the shadow of death, I will fear no evil; for thou art with me; thy rod and thy staff they comfort me."

To get the sheep from the lowlands to the highlands or tablelands – the rich grassy mesas of summer – the shepherd had to lead them through rugged valleys with treacherous rocks where they could get hurt, slip, or fall. In the valley, there were niches or caves in the rocks where wild animals or thieves could hide. There were poisonous snakes in the valley, and there was always the danger of flash floods. Here in the valley, the sheep needed the shepherd most. The shepherd used the rod to correct sheep who wandered or strayed, trying to avoid the valley. And the staff was used to keep the weaker sheep close to the shepherd to guide and protect them.

Like the sheep, we would rather not go through the "valley of the shadow of death" – the grief and pain that seem unending when we're in the midst of it. But our Good Shepherd (God in human flesh) did not avoid the valley. He went through it ahead of us to show us the way, revealing the valley as a passageway to new life on the other side. Now we can pass safely through the valley knowing we do not go alone; there is Someone who leads and guides us through.

➤ *Flip to sixth picture*

"Thou preparest a table before me in the presence of mine enemies; thou anointest my head with oil, my cup runneth over."

This is midsummer on the grassy mesa, the lush green grass of the highland or tableland beyond the valley of the shadow. It is a wonderfully beautiful and peaceful place. There is no hunger, for there is always plenty to eat. But there are enemies. Mountain lions lurk, and there are bears. The shepherd protects the sheep, keeping them close to himself so he can defend them from predators.

The sheep are plagued by nose flies and other insects which bite and irritate. The shepherd prepares a mixture of linseed oil, sulphur, and tar and anoints each sheep, carefully checking for wounds and bites. When the sheep get wet and cold, the shepherd gives them a mixture of brandy and water to ward off pneumonia – remedies for all their diseases.

Jesus, our Shepherd, prepares a table for us – communion and plenty in the midst of a materialistic and addictive world. As we share bread together remembering all God has done for us, we are mysteriously healed of our diseases. Life's irritations are gently soothed; our restless searching is satisfied. We are at peace with God, with ourselves, with each other and with nature.

➤ *Flip to seventh picture*

"Surely goodness and mercy shall follow me all the days of my life; and I will dwell in the house of the Lord for ever."

As summer turns into fall, the shepherd leads the sheep down from the highland pastures, back through the valley of the shadow, and into ranch headquarters before winter begins. The sheep have followed the shepherd through all the seasons. The shepherd calls each sheep by name, and the sheep know the sound of his voice. So they can trust that there will be plenty of food and water, oil and remedies for all their diseases. Wherever the shepherd is, there is protection, belonging, contentment, peace and plenty.

Our Good Shepherd has a plan for our lives, a way which leads to Shalom – wholeness, justice, and peace now and forever.

Sources:
- Keller, Phillip. *A Shepherd Looks at Psalm 23*, Zondervan (Daybreak Books), Grand Rapids, Michigan, 1973.
- *And lots and lots of funeral messages on Psalm 23*

The Shepherd Psalm

Psalm 23

"The Annual Cycle of the Shepherd" Flip Chart

The Lord is
my Shepherd;

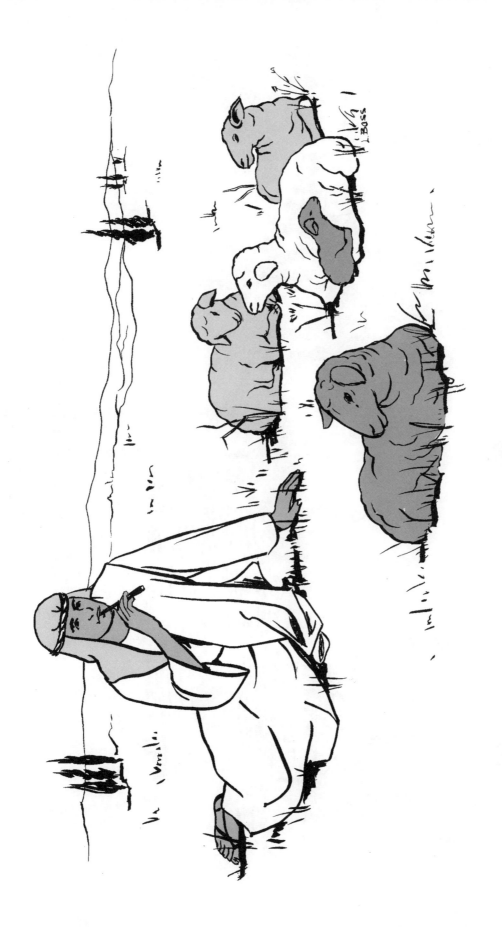

I shall not want.

He maketh me to lie down in green pastures;

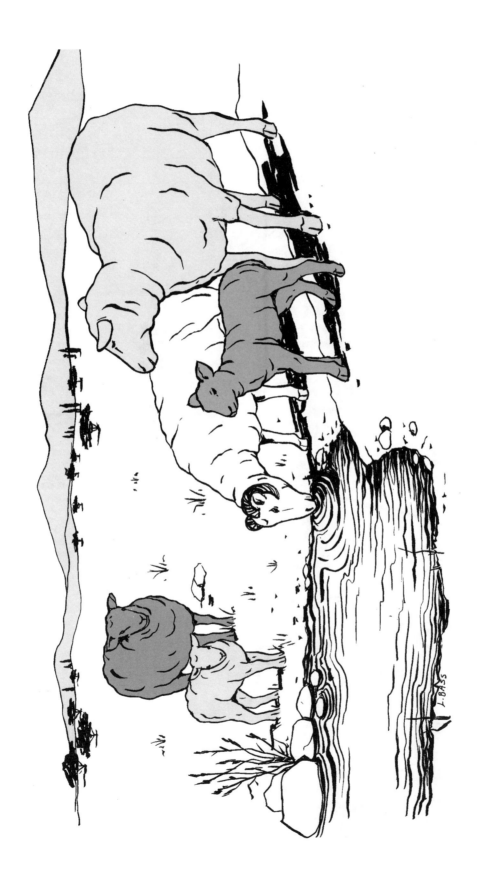

He leadeth me
beside the still waters.

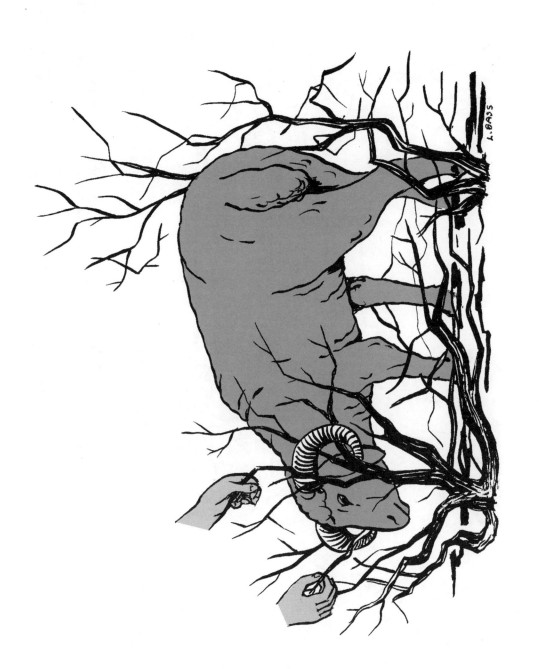

He restoreth my soul; he leadeth me in the paths of righteousness for his name's sake.

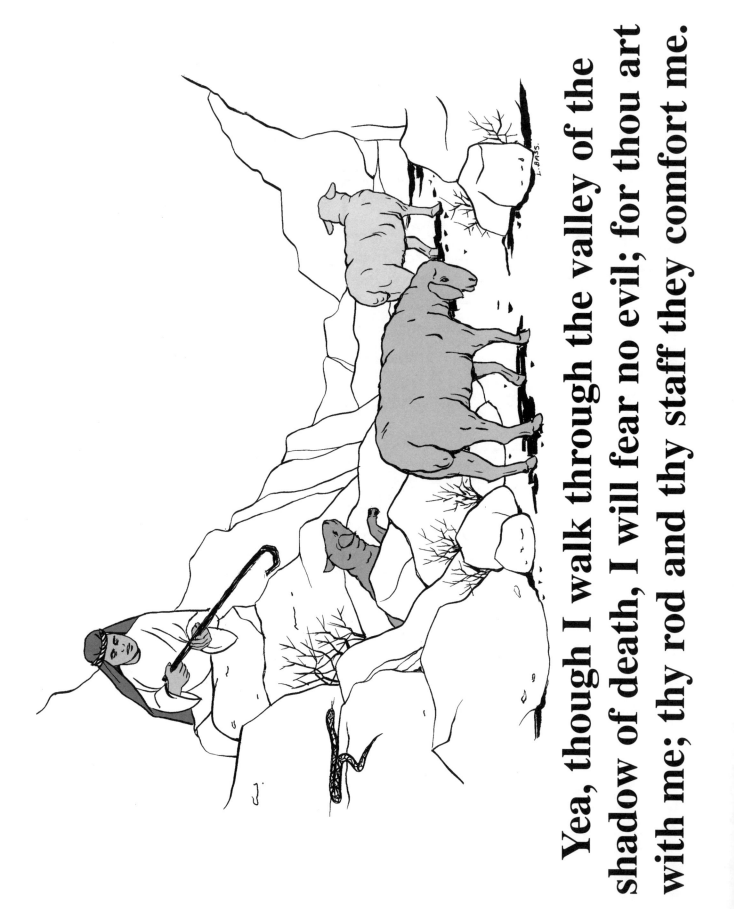

Yea, though I walk through the valley of the shadow of death, I will fear no evil; for thou art with me; thy rod and thy staff they comfort me.

Thou preparest a table before me in the presence of mine enemies; thou anointest my head with oil, my cup runneth over.

Surely goodness and mercy shall follow me all the days of my life; and I will dwell in the house of the Lord forever.

TAKING THE JOURNEY

We've explored Psalm 23 as the annual life cycle of Shepherd and sheep and of God to all people. There is a sense of progression from one place, through other places, to another place. Others, since the Psalmist, have looked at the life of faith as a pilgrimage, a progressive yet ever-circling journey. Since we learn best by the things we DO, let's experience the Twenty-Third Psalm in seven stations.

❧ *Leader invites participants to begin at any station and move through all the stations at their own pace ending in the center of the stations for participation in Station 7.*

STATION 1

"The Lord is my Shepherd;"

God calls each one of us personally by name, to follow the Good Shepherd. In our baptism, we are "branded" with the sign and seal of our belonging to God.

❧ *Write your name on a name tag and put it on.*

STATION 2

"I shall not want. He maketh me to lie down in green pastures;"

The green pastures of the Shepherd are places of plenty. In a time when we try to get more and more because we're afraid there may not be enough, the green pastures of the Shepherd announce that with God there is abundance. Every need is graciously met. We learn to trust.

❧ *Eat from the abundance provided for you.*
❧ *Then write on one of the colored circles something God has given you in abundance.*
❧ *Place the circle on the "green pasture."*

STATION 3

"He leadeth me beside the still waters."

We drink from the Source of Life enjoying the still waters. Water washes, cleanses, refreshes and baptizes us anew as people who belong to the Good Shepherd and to one another.

❧ *Pour some water into a glass.*
❧ *Listen and watch as the moving water from the pitcher becomes still in the glass.*
❧ *Taste the water.*

STATION 4

"He restoreth my soul; he leadeth me in the paths of righteousness for his name's sake."

There are so many voices in life telling us what to think and what to do. We can easily become confused, overly busy, trying to please too many voices. The Good Shepherd rescues us and saves us from the confusion and busy-ness with "Words of Wisdom," showing us the key to right living.

➤ *Open the scroll and read its message.*

STATION 5

"Yea, though I walk through the valley of the shadow of death, I will fear no evil; for thou art with me; thy rod and thy staff they comfort me."

Each of us has a "shadow experience," something that is or was difficult for us, something we fear or dread. There is power in naming these experiences, these "rocks."

➤ *On a small piece of paper, write one of your most difficult experiences.*

➤ *Tape it to a "rock."*

➤ *Option: you may put on the blindfold and ask someone to guide you safely through the "valley of the shadow."*

STATION 6

"Thou preparest a table before me in the presence of mine enemies; thou anointest my head with oil, my cup runneth over."

➤ *Find the place card with your name at the table.*

➤ *Light the candle at your place-setting, giving thanks for God's provision in the presence of the enemies of your faith.*

➤ *Dip a finger into the container of oil and make the sign of the cross on your forehead, giving thanks to God for the gift of belonging to the Good Shepherd.*

➤ *Eat from the food provided, remembering the gifts you are thankful for.*

STATION 7

"Surely goodness and mercy shall follow me all the days of my life; and I will dwell in the house of the Lord for ever."

➤ *When all participants have completed Stations 1 through 6, gather in a circle inside the circle of chairs, raise arms in a gesture of benediction, and announce this truth to one another.*

➤ *Sing The Doxology or sing a responsorial Amen.*

SEARCH SHEET 1

COMPLETE AND BRING TO CLASS FOR USE IN SESSION 2

1. **What was the lifestyle/occupation of the people to whom God offered a "forever" promise of grace and blessing?**
   Genesis 13:2-7 _____

   _____

   See also Genesis 47:1-3, Exodus 3:1, I Samuel 16:11-13 _____

   _____

   _____

2. **What role did women play in this lifestyle?**
   Genesis 24:10-21, Exodus 2:16_____

3. **How were people of this occupation regarded by others? What was their "social status?"**
   Genesis 46:34_____

4. **How did this lifestyle affect the people's understanding of their relationship with God?**
   Psalm 23, Genesis 48:15, Isaiah 40:11, Jeremiah 31:1-3,10, Ezekiel 34:11-16,30,31 _____

   _____

   _____

5. **What was the purpose of this covenant relationship?**
   Ezekiel 34:25-31 _____

   _____

6. **What was the responsibility of those who entered into this covenant relationship?**
   Micah 6:8_____

7. **What special people were chosen to announce the birth of Jesus?**
   Luke 2:8-12 _____

8. **How did Jesus describe his relationship to people?**
   John 10:1-18 _____

9. **How did New Testament epistle writers describe Jesus' relationship to us and all people?**
   Hebrews 13:20, I Peter 2:25,5:4 _____

10. **Why do you think God chose such people?**
    Luke 1:50-53 _____

    _____

11. **Describe one insight you gained from this Search which you can share in a group experience next session:**

    _____

    _____

    _____

    _____

    _____

    _____

    _____

SEARCH SHEET 1
ANSWER GUIDE

PARTICIPANTS SHOULD COMPLETE AND BRING TO CLASS FOR USE IN SESSION 2

1. **What was the lifestyle/occupation of the people to whom God offered a "forever" promise of grace and blessing?** (Genesis 13:2-7). *Wealthy shepherds/herdsmen with many flocks, herds, tents. (See also Genesis 47:1-3, Exodus 3:1, I Samuel 16:11-13) Jacob's family as shepherds in Goshen, Moses in Midian, David at Bethlehem*

2. **What role did women play in this lifestyle?** (Genesis 24:10-21, Exodus 2:16) *Rebekah, seven daughters, draw water for flocks*

3. **How were people of this occupation regarded by others? What was their "social status?"** (Genesis 46:34) *"Abhorrent to Egyptians"*

4. **How did this lifestyle affect the people's understanding of their relationship with God?** (Psalm 23, Genesis 48:15, Isaiah 40:11, Jeremiah 31:1-3, 10, Ezekiel 34:11-16, 30,31) *They knew God as their shepherd, the shepherd of all earth's families, one who seeks lost sheep, rescues and feeds with justice.*

5. **What was the purpose of this covenant relationship?** (Ezekiel 34:25-31) *The "covenant of peace," the security of relationship to God was meant to make Israel "showers of blessing" to all.*

6. **What was the responsibility of those who entered into this covenant relationship?** (Micah 6:8) *To do justice, love kindness, and walk humbly with God.*

7. **What special people were chosen to announce the birth of Jesus?** (Luke 2:8-12) *Shepherds*

8. **How did Jesus describe his relationship to people?** (John 10:1-18) *I am the Good Shepherd who lays down his life for the sheep.*

9. **How did New Testament epistle writers describe Jesus' relationship to us and all people?** (Hebrews 13:20, I Peter 2:25, 5:4) *Great Shepherd and Guardian of souls, Chief Shepherd*

10. **Why do you think God chose such people?** (Luke 1:50-53) *They fear/reverence God. God brings down the powerful and lifts up the lowly.*

11. **Describe one insight you gained from this Search which you can share in a group experience next session:**

Personal Response

_____

_____

_____

_____

_____

_____

_____

DAILY SCRIPTURE
READINGS • WEEK 1

THE **AWE REVERENCE WONDER** AT THE **NEARNESS HOLINESS BEAUTY** OF GOD = THE BEGINNING OF **WISDOM**

(PROVERBS 1:7A)

	HEBREW SCRIPTURE	NEW TESTAMENT	PSALM	PROVERBS
Day 1	Genesis 1:1-2:25	Matthew 1:1-2:12	1:1-6	1:1-6
Day 2	Genesis 3:1-4:26	Matthew 2:13-3:6	2:1-12	1:7-9
Day 3	Genesis 5:1-7:24	Matthew 3:7-4:11	3:1-8	1:10-19
Day 4	Genesis 8:1-10:32	Matthew 4:12-25	4:1-8	1:20-23
Day 5	Genesis 11:1-13:4	Matthew 5:1-26	5:1-12	1:24-28
Day 6	Genesis 13:5-15:21	Matthew 5:27-48	6:1-10	1:29-33
Day 7	Genesis 16:1-18:19	Matthew 6:1-24	7:1-17	2:1-5

Personal Notes and Glimpses of Wisdom:

"I wonder where the shepherd is leading us next?"

PLEASE NOTE: Daily Scripture Readings are designed to take the reader through the Protestant Bible in one year. To find wisdom, it is necessary to search the Scripture. Readings can be done from any translation. For those who are already familiar with Scripture, it will be helpful to read from a translation which is less familiar – since we tend to "over-hear" the message. The New Revised Standard Version is used throughout The Wisdom Series (except for Psalm 23 in this Session).

Daily Scripture Readings are taken from *The One-Year Bible*, published by World Bible Publishers, Inc., Iowa Falls, Iowa, and also distributed by Tyndale House Publishers, Inc., Wheaton, Illinois.

WISDOM IS THE WAY GOD SHEPHERDS US TO SHALOM

The Lord is my Shepherd; • I shall not want. He maketh me to lie down in green pastures; • he leadeth me beside the still waters. • he restoreth my soul; he leadeth me in the paths of righteousness for his name's sake. • Yea, though I walk through the valley of the shadow of death, I will fear no evil; for thou art with me; • Thou preparest a table before me in the presence of mine enemies; thou anointest my head with oil, my cup runneth over. • Surely goodness and mercy shall follow me all the days of my life; and I will dwell in the house of the Lord forever. • The Lord is my Shepherd;

SESSION 2 • CREATION WISDOM

*T*he aim of this session
is to glimpse the wisdom of God in creation.

MATERIALS NEEDED

Hymnals
Accompaniment
Bibles (New Revised Standard Version)
Chalkboard and chalk, or newsprint and marker
Pencils
Completed Search Sheet 1
Completed Insights from Daily Scripture Readings For Week 1
Copies for each participant of:
  Illustration 2A
  Illustration 2B
  Illustration 2C
  Illustration 2D
  Search Sheet 2
  Daily Scripture Readings For Week 2

▨ ASSEMBLING

Begin on time! Allow time to prepare the room, pray for each participant and for God's guidance in the session.

▨ THE APPROACH TO GOD   (5 to 10 minutes)

❧ **Singing A Hymn:** Select a hymn which expresses praise to the God of all creation. "How Great Thou Art" is an all-time favorite. Check the hymnal's Topical Index under "Creation" or Scripture Index under "Genesis 1" or "Psalm 8" for other possibilities.

❧ **Prayer:** Offer a prayer which expresses awe and wonder at a Good Shepherd who is also a wise and wonderful Creator longing to lead people to new pastures of ever-deepening insight into the length and breadth, height and depth of God's love for all.

▨ ENCOUNTERING THE WORD   (40 to 45 minutes)

➪ Invite participants to refer to Search Sheet 1. Ask participants to share the responses they made on the bottom line. Commend each response (there are no wrong personal responses!). Option: You may wish to summarize and list the insights on chalkboard or newsprint.

➪ Refer to Daily Scripture Readings For Week 1, and ask participants to share insights they noted. Where did they see the Good Shepherd in these readings? Again, thank those who share.

⇨ Give "A Picture Of Creation" lecturette. Have copies of Illustration 2A and pencils on hand for distribution as called for in the lecturette.

When sketching is complete, invite participants to share their sketches and/or the ideas and insights gained during the lecturette. Commend them for their participation whether or not they choose to share.

⇨ *Distribute Illustration 2B.* This is a synthesis of other sketches (with special thanks to Dr. Thomas Boogaart, Professor of Old Testament at Western Theological Seminary, Holland, Michigan, who developed Creation story sketches in his classes).

> **Commentary:** Notice the **windows** on Day 2. The Hebrew people pictured "storehouses" of heaven with windows (or doors or gates) which God opened to send rain, blessings, etc. See Genesis 7:11, Deuteronomy 28:12, Jeremiah 10:13, Malachi 3:10. Genesis 7:11 also indicates fountains (or windows) of the deep.

⇨ *Distribute Illustration 2C.* Note the **windows, pillars** and **navel**.

> **Commentary:** The Hebrew world view also contained two **pillars**: The pillars of **justice** and **righteousness,** which are the foundation of God's throne. See Psalm 89:14, Psalm 97:2.
>
> Elsewhere in Scripture, we read of the **navel** or **center** of the earth. The Hebrew people pictured Mt. Zion (temple location) in Jerusalem as the center of the earth where people would come from all nations to learn about God, and from which the Word of God would come forth. See Isaiah 2:3, Jeremiah 3:17, Ezekiel 5:5, 38:12.
>
> Continuing with "navel theology," an umbilical cord contains three vessels: two **arteries** and one **vein.** The two **arteries** might be compared to the prophets and the sages (wise storytellers) who heard the Word of God and spoke it to the people. The **vein** might be compared to the priests who offered up the praises, thanksgiving, sacrifices and gifts, cries and requests of the people to God.

⇨ While wondering about the birth imagery of creation, it may be helpful to see the earth (God's precious baby) compared to a fetus in utero. Illustration 2D is offered as a comparison. (*Distribute Illustration 2D*). Allow participants to reflect on this illustration. Invite them to share their insights, observations, and comments.

⊞ GOING FORTH IN GOD'S NAME   (5 to 10 minutes)

❥ **Sing a hymn** of thanksgiving to God for creation.

❥ Offer a **closing prayer** expressing awe and wonder of creation.

❥ Distribute copies of:
   Search Sheet 2 (which needs to be completed for use in Session 3)
   Daily Scripture Readings For Week 2

■ "A PICTURE OF CREATION"

A LECTURETTE WITH GROUP SKETCHING

No one saw God create the galaxies of space, the earth with its intricate ecosystem, plants, animals, and people. So where did the creation story come from?

Alex Haley, author of *Roots*, (Doubleday & Company, Inc., Garden City, New York, 1976) says "Everyone goes back to a time when no writing existed (p. 574)." Through seven generations of **storytelling** (which Haley heard from his aunts on the porch of the family home in Henning, Tennessee), containing a few African words such as "Kin-tay," "Ko," and "Kamby Bolongo," Haley was eventually able to trace his roots to the Mandinka tongue spoken by the Mandingo people in Juffure, Gambia (population, 70), on the Gambia river in Africa. Here a "griot" (an oral historian who can recite genealogies and tell stories for three days straight without repetition) recited a series of "begats" (King James Version, Matthew 1 and elsewhere) which sounded much like Biblical narrative, eventually telling of one, Kunta Kinte, who "went away from his village to chop wood . . . and he was never seen again."

So in the Scriptures, there was some **great truth** about their relationship with God, some **practical wisdom** that the first parents wanted to preserve for their children. Since they did not read or write, they communicated that truth and wisdom by the **art of storytelling.** In the art of storytelling, a story is stripped of all unnecessary detail and told with a familiar **rhythm** or pattern of **repetition.** As it is told, the listener forms a **picture** of the unfolding drama and associates it with the familiar words and voice inflection so the story can be told and retold in exactly the same way.

I wonder what Genesis 1:1 - 2:3 would look like if we **listened** to it as if it were being told by a "griot" and **sketched it out** in seven little windows or one large picture. How might the storyteller have **pictured** it to tell it the same way over and over? *(Distribute Illustration 2A and pencils if needed.)* As I read the creation story (New Revised Standard Version), make seven quick sketches of how the storyteller may have pictured it or turn the page over and make one large sketch. (There are no wrong sketches, you don't have to show your sketches to anyone, and "stick people" are fine!)

Introduction:	"In the beginning when God created the heavens and the earth, the earth was a formless void and darkness covered the face of the deep, while a wind from God swept over the face of the waters.
Day 1:	"Then God said, *'Let there be light;'* and there was light. And God saw that the light was good; and God separated the light from the darkness. God called the light day, and the darkness he called night. And there was evening and there was morning, the first day. *(Pause)*
Day 2:	"And God said, *'Let there be a dome in the midst of the waters, and let it separate the waters from the waters.'* So God made the dome and separated the waters that were under the dome from the waters that were above the dome. And it was so. God called the dome sky. And there was evening and there was morning, the second day. *(Pause)*
Day 3:	"And God said, *'Let the waters under the sky be gathered together into one place, and let the dry land appear.'* And it was so. God called the dry land earth, and the waters that were gathered together he called seas. And God saw that it was good. Then God said, *'Let the earth put forth vegetation: plants yielding seed, and fruit trees of every kind on earth that bear fruit with the seed in it.'* And it was so. The earth brought forth vegeta-

tion: plants yielding seed of every kind, and trees of every kind bearing fruit with the seed in it. And God saw that it was good. And there was evening and there was morning, the third day. *(Pause)*

Day 4: "And God said, ***'Let there be lights in the dome of the sky to separate the day from the night; and let them be for signs and for seasons and for days and years, and let them be lights in the dome of the sky to give light upon the earth.'*** And it was so. God made the two great lights — the greater light to rule the day and the lesser light to rule the night — and the stars. God set them in the dome of the sky to give light upon the earth, to rule over the day and over the night, and to separate the light from the darkness. And God saw that it was good. And there was evening and there was morning, the fourth day. *(Pause)*

Day 5: "And God said, ***'Let the waters bring forth swarms of living creatures, and let birds fly above the earth across the dome of the sky.'*** So God created the great sea monsters and every living creature that moves, of every kind, with which the waters swarm, and every winged bird of every kind. And God saw that it was good. God blessed them, saying, ***'Be fruitful and multiply and fill the waters in the seas, and let birds multiply on the earth.'*** And there was evening and there was morning, the fifth day. *(Pause)*

Day 6: "And God said, ***'Let the earth bring forth living creatures of every kind: cattle and creeping things and wild animals of the earth of every kind.'*** And it was so. God made the wild animals of the earth of every kind, and the cattle of every kind, and everything that creeps upon the ground of every kind. And God saw that it was good. Then God said, ***'Let us make humankind in our image, according to our likeness; and let them have dominion over the fish of the sea, and over the birds of the air, and over the cattle, and over all the wild animals of the earth, and over every creeping thing that creeps upon the earth.'*** So God created humankind in his image, in the image of God he created them, male and female he created them. God blessed them, and God said to them, ***'Be fruitful and multiply, and fill the earth and subdue it; and have dominion over every living thing that moves upon the earth.'*** God said, ***'See, I have given you every plant yielding seed that is upon the face of all the earth, and every tree with seed in its fruit; you shall have them for food. And to every beast of the earth, and to every bird of the air, and to everything that creeps on the earth, everything that has the breath of life, I have given every green plant for food.'*** And it was so. God saw everything that he had made, and indeed, it was very good. And there was evening and there was morning, the sixth day. *(Pause)*

Day 7: "Thus the heavens and the earth were finished, and all their multitude. And on the seventh day God finished the work that he had done, and he **rested on the seventh day** from all the work that he had done. So God **blessed** the seventh day and hallowed it, because on it God rested from all the work that he had done in creation." (Invite participants to sketch ways they rest and enjoy the gifts of creation; or they may wish to make a completed sketch of all creation.)

1. **There are two creation stories in Genesis: Genesis 1:1-2:3, and Genesis 2:4-25. Name one way they differ in purpose.** _____

2. **Where was Jesus during creation?** (John 1:1-3, 15), Colossians 1:15-17, Hebrews 1:1-2) _____
   _____

3. **What was the role of wisdom in creation?** (Jeremiah 10:12, and Proverbs 8:22-31 where Lady Wisdom or Wisdom personified speaks) _____
   _____

4. **"In the beginning" God spoke a word, and a world came into being.** Read John 1:1-14. **What does it tell about the relationship of God and God's Word?** _____
   _____

5. **Is creation an event? Ongoing process? Both? Tell why you believe this is so.** _____
   _____
   _____

6. **Based on Genesis 1:28 and 2:15, what are the tasks of people in the world God created?** _____
   _____
   How do these tasks compare to agriculture, science, education, administration, ecology, etc.? _
   _____
   If God created everything good, is it possible for people to make it better? _____
   _____

7. Read Genesis 1:11-12, 20, 24 in the King James Version. **What similar or repeated words or phrases do you find?** _____
   Compare with Luke 2:7 in the King James Version: _____
   _____

8. **What distinguished Israel's God from the gods of other nations?** (I Chronicles 16:26)
   _____
   _____

9. **What was God's purpose for the seventh day of creation?** (Exodus 20:8-11) _____
   _____
   The length of time from the beginning of Israel's united kingdom until the fall of Jerusalem was nearly 490 years. The exile to Babylon was to last 70 years (Jeremiah 25:11), **one-seventh of 490 years. Why?** (II Chronicles 36:21)_____
   _____
   What does this tell us about the importance of Sabbath in the rhythm of daily life? _____
   _____

10. **There are various ideas of how closely God is connected to creation. Listed below are some of those ideas. Place an "X" beside those you feel Scripture supports: (see Deuteronomy 4:7, Job 34:14-15, and draw on insights from daily readings)**

___**AGNOSTICISM** (God is unknowable) ___**ATHEISM** (there is no God) ___**DEISM** (God created, but takes no interest in the world) ___**DUALISM** (spirit good, matter evil) ___**MONOTHEISM** (belief in one God) ___**PANENTHEISM** (God is in everything) ___**PANTHEISM** (everything is God - nature worship) ___**POLYTHEISM** (belief in many gods) ___**SECULAR HUMANISM** (belief that morality should be based on the well-being of people, not religious systems) ___**THEISM** (belief in Creator God revealed in creation)

1. **There are two creation stories in Genesis: Genesis 1:1-2:3, and Genesis 2:4-25. Name one way they differ in purpose.** *First is a seven-stage picture; second is creation of humans*

2. **Where was Jesus during creation?** (John 1:1-3, 15), Colossians 1:15-17, Hebrews 1:1-2) *With God before all things were created, before creation*

3. **What was the role of wisdom in creation?** (Jeremiah 10:12, and Proverbs 8:22-31 where Lady Wisdom or Wisdom personified speaks) *"established the world by his wisdom," created at beginning beside God as master worker, delighting in the human race*

4. **"In the beginning" God spoke a word, and a world came into being.** Read John 1:1-14. **What does it tell about the relationship of God and God's Word?** *Word was God, became flesh, dwelt among us*

5. **Is creation an event? Ongoing process? Both? Tell why you believe this is so.** *Both – we're designed to be ongoing co-creators with God, "being fruitful"*

6. **Based on Genesis 1:28 and 2:15, what are the tasks of people in the world God created?** *Be fruitful, multiply, fill, subdue, and have dominion over, till and keep.* **How do these tasks compare to agriculture, science, education, administration, ecology, etc.?** *Agriculture – fruitful, dress, till; science - fill and subdue; administration – dominion; ecology —keep* **If God created everything good, is it possible for people to make it better?** *No, our task is to maintain via obedience*

7. **Read Genesis 1:11-12, 20, 24 in the King James Version. What similar or repeated words or phrases do you find?** *Put forth, brought forth, bring forth* **Compare with Luke 2:7 in the King James Version:** *"And she 'brought forth' her firstborn son" (Jesus, the New Creation)*

8. **What distinguished Israel's God from the gods of other nations?** (I Chronicles 16:26) *"The Lord made the heavens"*

9. **What was God's purpose for the seventh day of creation?** (Exodus 20:8-11) *Rest, consecration* **The length of time from the beginning of Israel's *united kingdom* until the fall of Jerusalem was nearly 490 years. The exile to Babylon was to last 70 years** (Jeremiah 25:11), **one-seventh of 490 years. Why?** (II Chronicles 36:21) *To make up for all the missed Sabbaths* **What does this tell us about the importance of Sabbath in the rhythm of daily life?** *A natural law, to rest 1/7th of the time*

10. **There are various ideas of how closely God is connected to creation. Listed below are some of those ideas. Place an "X" beside those you feel Scripture supports:** (see Deuteronomy 4:7, Job 34:14-15, and draw on insights from daily readings)

___**AGNOSTICISM** (God is unknowable) ___**ATHEISM** (there is no God) ___**DEISM** (God created, but takes no interest in the world) ___**DUALISM** (spirit good, matter evil) _X_ **MONOTHEISM** (belief in one God) _X_ **PANENTHEISM** (God is in everything) ___**PANTHEISM** (everything is God – nature worship) ___**POLYTHEISM** (belief in many gods) ___**SECULAR HUMANISM** (belief that morality should be based on the well-being of people, not religious systems) _X_ **THEISM** (belief in Creator God revealed in creation)

DAILY SCRIPTURE
READINGS • WEEK 2

THE **AWE REVERENCE WONDER** AT THE **NEARNESS HOLINESS BEAUTY** OF GOD = THE BEGINNING OF **WISDOM**

(PROVERBS 1:7A)

	HEBREW SCRIPTURE	NEW TESTAMENT	PSALM	PROVERBS
Day 1	Genesis 18:20-19:38	Matthew 6:25-7:14	8:1-9	2:6-15
Day 2	Genesis 20:1-22:24	Matthew 7:15-29	9:1-12	2:16-22
Day 3	Genesis 23:1-24:51	Matthew 8:1-17	9:13-20	3:1-6
Day 4	Genesis 24:52-26:16	Matthew 8:18-34	10:1-15	3:7-8
Day 5	Genesis 26:17-27:46	Matthew 9:1-17	10:16-18	3:9-10
Day 6	Genesis 28:1-29:35	Matthew 9:18-38	11:1-7	3:11-12
Day 7	Genesis 30:1-31:16	Matthew 10:1-25	12:1-8	3:13-15

Personal Notes and Glimpses of Wisdom:

"I wonder how God made sheep and stars out of nothing..."

DAY 2
Dome of firmament
with windows

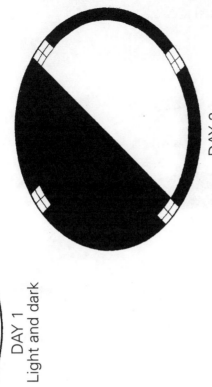

DAY 1
Light and dark

DAY 3
Sea, trees, and
vegetation

DAY 4 – Sun, moon, stars

DAY 7
Rest, worship

DAY 6
Animals, people

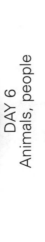

DAY 5
Birds and fish

CREATION
with navel and pillars

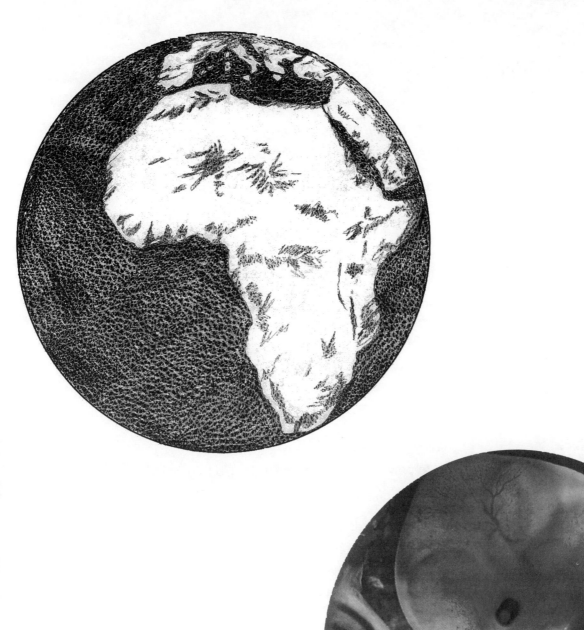

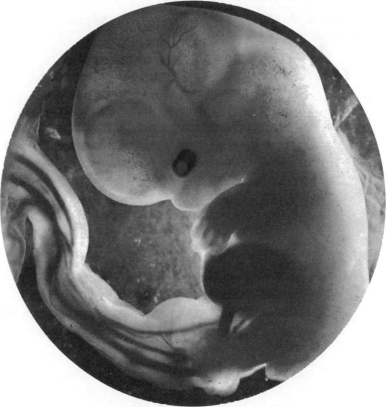

Session 3 • More Creation Wisdom

The aim of this session
is to look at some ways creation wisdom affects our daily lives.

MATERIALS NEEDED

Hymnals
Accompaniment
Bibles
Chalkboard and chalk, or newsprint and marker
Completed Search Sheet 2 (focus of the session)
Completed Insights from Daily Scripture Readings For Week 2
Illustration 2C for reference
Copies for each participant of:
    Search Sheet 3
    Daily Scripture Readings For Week 3

▨ ASSEMBLING

As before, prepare the room, leaving time to pray for each participant, for God's guidance in the session, and growth in wisdom.

▨ THE APPROACH TO GOD   (5 to 10 minutes)

❧ **Singing A Hymn:** Sing a hymn of praise to the God of all creation.

❧ **Prayer:** Create your own group prayer in the form of a litany. Give participants a few moments to scan the "Insights" from their Daily Scripture Readings, Week 2. Was there something that made them wonder about God in a new way? Something they read which seemed new or different? Humorous? Wise? . . . As each participant shares a sentence or two of insights, the group responds, **'We thank you, O God, for these insights of wisdom.'** (If no one seems ready to begin, be prepared to start by sharing a sentence or two of your own insights. Then lead them in the response phrase which may be printed on chalkboard or newsprint for convenience.)

▨ ENCOUNTERING THE WORD   (40 to 45 minutes)

⇨ Since an understanding of Creation is vital to understanding all Scripture, a second week is devoted to that endeavor. Use Search Sheet 2 as a framework for discussion, inviting participants to respond to the questions given. Use "Commentary On Search Sheet 2" to supplement the discussion.

⇨ Refer to Daily Scripture Readings For Week 2, and ask participants to share insights they noted. Where did they see the Good Shepherd in these readings? Again, thank those who share.

▦ GOING FORTH IN GOD'S NAME   (5 to 10 minutes)

❧   Invite participants to think of an aspect of creation they will continue to wonder about. (Be sure to think of one yourself!) Invite them to name their particular area of wonder in the silent moments of the prayer that follows: "We give thanks, O Lord, for your awesome and wise creation. We especially give thanks for that which we do not fully understand, things which are too wise and wonderful for us. We name them before you: . . . . Give us wisdom as we wonder and search the Scriptures and listen for you in our lives each day. Amen."

❧   Suggest that participants look for verses which speak to their particular area of wonder as they do the daily readings, making note of them in the "Insights" section.

❧   Distribute copies of:
    Search Sheet 3 (noting that completion of it is necessary preparation for Session 4)
    Daily Scripture Readings for Week 3

COMMENTARY ON SEARCH SHEET 2

1. Genesis 1:1- 2:3 is an **overall description** of Creation in seven days or stages. Genesis 2:4-25 is primarily concerned with the **creation of people,** male and female **in the image of God,** and their role in the created world.

2. Living in a complex world where it is necessary to label and compartmentalize for purposes of better understanding, there has been a tendency to compartmentalize our understanding of God as well. Specifically, we often separate the Christ of the Cross from the Christ of Creation. This question invites **"reuniting" Christ.**

3. Jeremiah 10:12 suggests wisdom is the way or method by which God creates. Proverbs 8:22-31 **personifies wisdom** as a woman (Sophia) created at the beginning, working beside God as a master builder, rejoicing as God spoke and the world came into being, delighting in the human race. Can you picture her rejoicing, delighting, cheering, dancing in Creation?

4. While we live and work with people whose **words** and **works** are often miles apart, in God there is **no separation** of word and deed. God speaks; a world comes into being.

   God spoke the word "Jesus;" the angel delivered the message to Mary. Within her womb God's Word became flesh, was born and lived among us, embodying the glory, grace, and truth of God.

   We, too, create **"worlds"** with our **words.** Think back to the last group or committee meeting you attended. What **words** were spoken? What **worlds** were created as a result of those **words**?

5. **An event?** Yes! Creation was a great happening remembered and celebrated throughout Scripture! **An ongoing process**? Yes! When we plant seeds, "create" children, teach children, "create" new formulas, new medicines, new buildings, draw or paint pictures, discover new and better ways to conserve earth's resources, we, as humans, are crowned co-creators with God in an ever-unfolding, wise and wonderful creative process.

6. These verses describe the **various, meaningful activities** God gave us all to do. Raising a family, agriculture, science, education, administration, ecology — all engage **human co-creativity with God.**

   It is important to note that **work** is a **blessing,** a **high honor** given to people as the crown of God's creation. Only later, after the created ones rebel against their Creator, is work frustrated and thus a curse.

   If God created all things **good,** can we make them **better**? The answer can make a great difference in one's approach to life. Some would point out how science and technology have made our lives better. Others would counter by asking what this has done to the environment — the ozone layer upon which we are all dependent for life. **Good, better, best**? Progress? And, at what price? From the beginning, as subsequent sessions will show, people have tried many ways **to "be wiser than God,"** to be able to live independent of God, to "play God." Subsequent sessions will also show the **tragedy** of such attempts.

   But if we cannot "make things better," then **what is the human role** in a wise and wonderful creation? After all, God did make humans the **crown of all creation**, made in the image of God, capable of discovering and mastering their environment. But "improving" on God's "good" — well, isn't that **arrogant**? So what would be **humility's perspective**?

   Is it possible for people to use their God-given creativity and intelligence in maintaining what God has created? Maintaining the pillars of **justice** and **righteousness** while exploring, discovering, and caring for all that God has created? More on this subject in future sessions.

7. "Put forth," "brought forth," "bring forth," . . . "And she **brought forth** her firstborn son." Christ is the **New Creation** and "If anyone is in Christ, there is a **new creation:** everything old has passed away; see, everything has become new!" (2 Corinthians 5:17) from this new perspective comes the Christian **ministry of reconciliation** — bringing new ways of thinking, feeling, and living into places of stagnation, pain and brokenness. It has been said that Christian ministry is one of **midwifery** — encouraging and assisting the birthing process.

8. The idols of other nations (self-made gods) just sat there. They were powerless, uncreative. But the God of the Hebrew people **made the heavens.** The **awesome power and creativity** of God distinguished the God of the Hebrew people from the Canaanite gods.

9. The **necessity of rest and worship one-seventh of the time** is borne out by God's rest following creation, the fourth commandment, and the length of the exile compared to the years of missed Sabbaths. Compare with the current phenomenon of "burn-out."

   Worship on the first day of the week (for many Christians) is for three reasons: 1) To rest and remember the gifts of **Creation** which began on the first day of the week, 2) To celebrate the **resurrection** which took place on the first day of the week, and 3) To give thanks for the gospel which is a message of **"new beginnings."**

10. Three are scriptural: **MONOTHEISM, PANENTHEISM,** and **THEISM.** *Notice how Creation is central to each choice.*

    A word about "New Age." Much discussion centers around whether "New Age" is **good** or **bad.** There are Christians who can see no evil in it; likewise, there are Christians who see nothing but evil in it. Take the discussion a step further. New Age of what? Voodoo or grace? Peace with justice or crystal power? Does it serve the purposes of the Creator for Creation and the created ones? Or is it an attempt of the created ones to usurp the power of the Creator? *Notice again how Creation becomes central in the decision-making process.*

"Glimpses Of Scripture's Garden-Like Places"

In Session 4, we will take a look at the beautiful garden of Eden and explore its meaning. To prepare for Session 4, this Search Sheet looks at some of Scripture's garden-like places — places filled with God's glory, centers of **SHALOM** (harmony, wholeness, justice).

1. The garden is a protected place in which God is seen as the _____ (Psalm 23:1, 28:8-9). _____(Psalm 91:11) **also protect those who** _____ (91:14), **and this is symbolized by** _____ **protecting the inner sanctuary or Holy of Holies of the Temple** (I Kings 6:23-28).

2. **Psalm 133:1 describes garden-like places as** _____ **and** _____, **places where people live together in** _____ **which results in** _____ (Psalm 133:3). **Psalm 144:15 describes those whose God is the Lord as** _____ **people.**

3. **When the people of God went out from Egypt in "The Exodus,"** _____ **became God's sanctuary/garden** (Psalm 114:1-2), **and for them God turned rock into** _____ (114:8). **Loving and obeying the law of God resulted in** _____ (Psalm 119:165).

4. **God chose a city,** _____ (2 Chronicles 6:6), **as a home. Solomon built the Temple there. What evidence of the Garden can be seen in the carvings in the Temple?** (1 Kings 6:18,29) _____. **It took** ___ **years to build the Temple** (I Kings 6:38). **With God at the center, Solomon received great** _____ (I Kings 4:29-34). **What were the blessings of the people who lived under Solomon's reign with God as its center?** (I Kings 4:20,24,25) _____

5. **When God's people strayed from God's way, Isaiah described them as a vineyard which yielded** _____(Isaiah 5:2) **symbolizing not justice but** _____ (5:7). **In the midst of human failure, prophets looked forward to a time when God would again teach from** _____ (Isaiah 2:3), **international Center for** _____ (2:4). _____**and** _____ **will be taskmasters there** (Isaiah 60:17). **The prophet Ezekiel describes a future city named** _____ (Ezekiel 48:35). **Habakkuk speaks of a future earth filled with the** _____ **of the Lord** (Habakkuk 2:14). **When God removes the people's sins, they will** _____ (Zechariah 3:10). **John describes a Holy City, the new** _____ (Revelation 21:2) **in which there is a** _____ (22:1) **flowing from the throne of God, with a** _____ (22:2) **on either side.**

6. **Psalm 92:12 describes the righteous as a** _____ **which is planted in the** _____ (92:13) **of the Lord. Much like a garden with many trees, Jesus describes heaven as a** _____**with many** _____ (John 14:2).

7. **When the Spirit of God enters people and they are filled with the awe and wonder, holiness and power of God, they live together in peace. Describe how this might look** (Acts 2:43-47): _____

8. In I Corinthians 3:5-9, the Apostle Paul describes the process of spiritual growth in gardening terms. Who plants? _____ Who waters? _____ Who gives growth? _____ Is the relationship between those who plant and those who water the field/garden one of (A) Competition or (B) Cooperation? _____

9. Those who are victorious in listening to the Spirit and faithfully living in God's love receive permission to "eat from the _____ in the _____ of God" (Revelation 2:7). Spend some time reflecting on the mysterious "Garden of Shalom," that place where God is the Center and all is peace. Where is that Garden for you?_____.

SEARCH SHEET 3
ANSWER GUIDE

"Glimpses Of Scripture's Garden-Like Places"

In Session 4, we will take a look at the beautiful garden of Eden and explore its meaning. To prepare for Session 4, this Search Sheet looks at some of Scripture's garden-like places — places filled with God's glory, centers of **SHALOM** (harmony, wholeness, justice).

1. **The garden is a protected place in which God is seen as the** _Shepherd_ (Psalm 23:1, 28:8-9). _Angels_ (Psalm 91:11) **also protect those who** _love (trust) God_ (91:14)**, and this is symbolized by** _cherubim (angels)_ **protecting the inner sanctuary or Holy of Holies of the Temple** (I Kings 6:23-28).

2. **Psalm 133:1 describes garden-like places as** _good_ **and** _pleasant_, **places where people live together in** _unity / harmony_ **which results in** _blessing / life_ (Psalm 133:3). **Psalm 144:15 describes those whose God is the Lord as** _happy_ **people.**

3. **When the people of God went out from Egypt in "The Exodus",** _Judah / Israel_ **became God's sanctuary/garden** (Psalm 114:1-2), **and for them God turned rock into** _a pool of water_ (114:8). **Loving and obeying the law of God resulted in** _great peace_ (Psalm 119:165).

4. **God chose a city,** _Jerusalem ("God's Peace")_ (2 Chronicles 6:6), **as a home. Solomon built the Temple there. What evidence of the Garden can be seen in the carvings in the Temple?** (1 Kings 6:18,29) _gourds, open flowers, cedar, cherubim, palm trees_. **It took** _7_ **years to build the Temple** (I Kings 6:38). **With God at the center, Solomon received great** _wisdom_ (I Kings 4:29-34). **What were the blessings of the people who lived under Solomon's reign with God as its center?** (I Kings 4;20, 24,25) _numerous, ate, drank, were happy, peace, safety, "vines and fig trees" = houses and gardens_

5. **When God's people strayed from God's way, Isaiah described them as a vineyard which yielded** _wild grapes_ (Isaiah 5:2) **symbolizing not justice but** _bloodshed_ (5:7). **In the midst of human failure, prophets looked forward to a time when God would again teach from** _Zion / Jerusalem_ (Isaiah 2:3), **international center for** _arbitration/peace_ (2:4). _Peace_ **and** _Righteousness_ **will be taskmasters there** (Isaiah 60:17). **The prophet Ezekiel describes a future city named** _"The Lord Is There"_ (Ezekiel 48:35). **Habakkuk speaks of a future earth filled with the** _glory_ **of the Lord** (Habakkuk 2:14). **When God removes the people's sins, they will** _invite each other (create community)_ (Zechariah 3:10). **John describes a Holy City, the new** _Jerusalem_ (Revelation 21:2) **in which there is a** _river of the water of life_ (22:1) **flowing from the throne of God, with a** _tree of life_ (22:2) **on either side.**

6. **Psalm 92:12 describes the righteous as a** _palm tree (or cedar of Lebanon)_ **which is planted in the** _house_ (92:13) **of the Lord. Much like a garden with many trees, Jesus describes heaven as a** _house_ **with many** _dwelling places_ (John 14:2).

7. **When the Spirit of God enters people and they are filled with the awe and wonder, holiness and power of God, they live together in peace. Describe how this might look** (Acts 2:43-47): _Awe, signs, wonders, sharing possessions, communion, (community), generosity, praise, goodwill, increase in number_

8. **In I Corinthians 3:5-9, the Apostle Paul describes the process of spiritual growth in gardening terms. Who plants?** _Paul_ **Who waters?** _Apollos_ **Who gives growth?** _God_ **Is the relationship between those who plant and those who water the field/garden one of (A) Competition or (B) Cooperation?** _B_

9. **Those who are victorious in listening to the Spirit and faithfully living in God's love receive permission to "eat from the _tree of life_ in the _paradise_ of God"** (Revelation 2:7). **Spend some time reflecting on the mysterious "Garden of Shalom," that place where God is the Center and all is peace. Where is that Garden for you?** _(This may be a quiet place in one's home, nature, memory, worship center, etc.)_

DAILY SCRIPTURE
READINGS • WEEK 3

THE **AWE REVERENCE WONDER** AT THE **NEARNESS HOLINESS BEAUTY** OF GOD = THE BEGINNING OF **WISDOM**

(PROVERBS 1:7A)

	HEBREW SCRIPTURE	NEW TESTAMENT	PSALM	PROVERBS
Day 1	Genesis 31:17-32:12	Matthew 10:26-11:6	13:1-6	3:16-18
Day 2	Genesis 32:13-34:31	Matthew 11:7-30	14:1-7	3:19-20
Day 3	Genesis 35:1-36:43	Matthew 12:1-21	15:1-5	3:21-26
Day 4	Genesis 37:1-38:30	Matthew 12:22-45	16:1-11	3:27-32
Day 5	Genesis 39:1-41:16	Matthew 12:46-13:23	17:1-15	3:33-35
Day 6	Genesis 4:17-42:17	Matthew 13:24-46	18:1-15	4:1-6
Day 7	Genesis 42:18-43:34	Matthew 13:47-14:12	18:16-36	4:7-10

Personal Notes and Glimpses of Wisdom:

"I wonder how a sheep can celebrate creation today..."

SESSION 4 • THE WISDOM OF THE GARDEN

The aim of this session
is to take a close look at "garden wisdom" and to consider the choices it presents.

MATERIALS NEEDED

Hymnals with "In the Garden"
Accompaniment
Bibles
Chalkboard or newsprint
Completed Search Sheet 3
Completed Insights from Daily Scripture Readings For Week 3
Copies for each participant of:
    Illustration 4A
    Search Sheet 4
    Daily Scripture Readings For Week 4

▓ ASSEMBLING

As you prepare the room, pray for each participant, for God's guidance in and through yourself and each participant, and for growth in wisdom.

▓ THE APPROACH TO GOD   (5 to 10 minutes)

❧ **Sharing Shalom Places:** Have participants take up Search Sheet 3, "Glimpses of Scripture's Garden-Like Places," and share their responses to the last question, "Where is that Garden for you?"

❧ **Singing A Hymn:** "In the Garden" is an expression of the wisdom of the Garden, an all-time favorite. Enjoy singing the hymn together!

❧ **Prayer:** Offer a prayer of thanksgiving for the hymn, the writer, and the wisdom so many have found in this hymn.

▓ ENCOUNTERING THE WORD   (40 to 45 minutes)

Invite participants to go on a **journey** with you to a beautiful garden. Let them close their eyes as you read Genesis 2:4b-25 [from the New Rivsed Standard Version (NRSV) or New International Verision (NIV)]. Read slowly, with expression and pauses, savoring each phrase, as if you are in the garden. Allow some moments of silence following the reading as they picture what they saw there.

⇨ Using chalkboard or newsprint, invite participants to name what they saw in the garden. *List their responses.*

⇨ Using "The Garden of Shalom" lecturette, gradually draw Illustration 4 on newsprint or chalkboard (or distribute copies of Illustration 4 and omit the drawing portion – if using chalkboard or newsprint, distribute Illustration 4 after drawing). Invite comments and questions as time permits. Discussion starter questions might include:

What keys to **Shalom** can you think of that Jesus gave? Answers might include The Golden Rule (Matthew 7:12), The Beatitudes (Matthew 5:3-12), The Lord's Prayer (Matthew 6:9-13), etc.

▨ GOING FORTH IN GOD'S NAME   (5 to 10 minutes)

❥ **Sing a hymn** such as "The Beautiful Garden of Prayer" which reflects upon the peaceful garden.

❥ **Offer a closing prayer** of praise for the Garden, with an opportunity for participants to join in naming new insights gained in this session.

❥ Distribute copies of:
Search Sheet 4
Daily Scripture Readings For Week 4

■ "THE GARDEN OF SHALOM"

The beautiful garden *(draw a large oval)*, planted by God, is a place of **Shalom** – wholeness and peace with justice – all that God intended for creation, a place of wisdom, beauty, right and joyous living. This **"Garden of Shalom"** has a **center** or **navel** *(draw a small circle in the center of oval)*, from which the word/lifebreath/glory of God (Hebrew word *ruach*) flows like a river (Genesis 2:10-14) to nourish the garden, dividing into branches *(draw the four branches from the center)* which nourishes the whole earth. God's **Shalom** is experienced in four ways:

Peace with God – *(label the first river)* God breathes the breath of life into humans (2:7), male and female, who reflect the very image of God (1:27). God walks and talks with them on a regular basis (3:8). God gives them meaningful activity, the sacred task of nurturing and caring for all that is created (1:28, 2:15) and the privilege of naming every living creature (2:19,20).

Peace Within – *(label the second river)* God gives humankind freedom to enjoy all that is created (3:16). The sacred tasks (1:28, 2:15) provide satisfaction and fulfillment without failure and frustration.

Social Peace – *(label the third river)* God created humankind, male and female (1:27) so they would not be lonely (2:18). Although caring for the animals provides some relief from loneliness, God gives a greater gift to humankind — the gift of human sexuality (1:28a), divinely united uniqueness, the joy of intimacy without shame (2:21-25). (For further reading, see *God and the Rhetoric of Sexuality*, by Phyllis Trible; Fortress Press, Philadelphia, 1978, pp.1-30).

Peace with Nature – *(label the fourth river)* God made plants and trees "pleasant to the sight and good for food" (2:9). God created humankind free to enjoy nature and to care for it (1:28-31, 2:15-20).

There were many trees in the garden. Of particular note are two trees (2:9). *(Draw trees)*. The **Tree Of Life** *(label one tree)* represents obedient, God-related, God-centered living. The **Tree Of Knowledge Of Good And Evil** *(label other tree)* represents going our own way without God, human attempts to play God or be wiser than God, usurping God's power.

Also, as in Creation Illustration 2C, the pillars of **Justice** and **Right Living** (Righteousness) are present in the garden *(draw and label the pillars)*, for the **key** to maintaining **Shalom** in the garden is given to humankind (2:17), "do not eat of the fruit of the tree of the knowledge of good and evil." Preserving **Shalom** now depends upon human **obedience** to God and God's design for all creation *(write **"Obedience"** inside key)*.

SEARCH SHEET 4
"CHOICES"

God gave great joy and freedom to the man and woman in the garden. In the midst of that freedom was a life-and-death choice between the "tree of _____" and the "tree of _____" (Genesis 2:9). Elsewhere Scripture presents important choices:

1.   Deuteronomy 29:18 – Choice between serving _____ or _____.

2.   Deuteronomy 30:15-20 – Choice of _____ to God with resultant _____ or _____ with resultant _____.

3.   Psalm 1 – The way of the w_____ or the way of the r_____.

4.   Psalm 119:101 – Holding back from _____ to keep _____.

5.   Proverbs 14:1 – Building or _____.

6.   Proverbs 15:2 – W_____ vs. f_____ tongue/mouth.

7.   Isaiah 2:17 – H_____ vs. h_____.

8.   Isaiah 5:7 – Justice vs. _____.

9.   Ezekiel 44:23 – Priestly duty to teach difference between h_____ and c_____, c_____ and u_____.

10. Habakkuk 2:4 – The spirit of the p_____ is not r_____ in them, but the r_____ live by their f_____.

11. John 3:18 – B_____ vs. not b_____.

12. John 6:38 – Doing _____ will vs. doing the will of _____.

13. Romans 6:16 – Slaves of _____ or slaves of _____.

14. Romans 7:6 – Not slaves of the old _____, but of new _____.

15. Romans 12:2 – Not conformed to the _____ but _____.

16. 1 Corinthians 3:1 – S_____ people vs. people of _____.

17. Ephesians 4:25 – Falsehood vs. _____.

18. 1 John 2:10-11 – Those who _____ each other walk in _____, while those who _____ each other walk in _____.

19. 3 John 1:11 – Doing _____ or doing _____.

God gave great joy and freedom to the man and woman in the garden. In the midst of that freedom was a life-and-death choice between the "tree of _life_" and the "tree of _knowledge of good / evil_" (Genesis 2:9). **Elsewhere Scripture presents important choices:**

1. **Deuteronomy 29:18 – Choice between serving** _the Lord_ or _the gods of other nations_.

2. **Deuteronomy 30:15-20 – Choice of** _obedience_ **to God with resultant** _life_ **or** _serving other gods (disobedience)_ **with resultant** _death_.

3. **Psalm 1 – The way of the** _wicked_ **or the way of the** _righteous_.

4. **Psalm 119:101 – Holding back from** _evil_ **to keep** _God's Word_.

5. **Proverbs 14:1 –** _Building_ **or** _tearing down_.

6. **Proverbs 15:2 –** _Wise_ **vs.** _foolish_ **tongue/mouth.**

7. **Isaiah 2:17 –** _Haughty_ **vs.** _humble_.

8. **Isaiah 5:7 –** _Justice_ **vs.** _bloodshed_.

9. **Ezekiel 44:23 – Priestly duty to teach difference between** _holy_ **and** _common_, _clean_ **and** _unclean_.

10. **Habakkuk 2:4 – The spirit of the** _proud_ **is not** _right_ **in them, but the** _righteous_ **live by their** _faith_.

11. **John 3:18 –** _Believing_ **vs. not** _believing_.

12. **John 6:38 – Doing** _my own_ **will vs. doing the will of** _God_.

13. **Romans 6:16 – Slaves of** _sin / death_ **or slaves of** _obedience / righteousness_.

14. **Romans 7:6 – Not slaves of the old** _law_, **but of new** _life of the Spirit_.

15. **Romans 12:2 – Not conformed to the** _world_ **but** _transformed by renewing of mind_.

16. **1 Corinthians 3:1 –** _Spiritual_ **people vs. people of** _the flesh_.

17. **Ephesians 4:25 –** _Falsehood_ **vs.** _truth_.

18. **1 John 2:10-11 – Those who** _love_ **each other walk in** _light_, **while those who** _hate_ **each other walk in** _darkness_.

19. **3 John 1:11 – Doing** _good_ **or doing** _evil_.

DAILY SCRIPTURE
READINGS • WEEK 4

THE **AWE REVERENCE WONDER** AT THE **NEARNESS HOLINESS BEAUTY** OF GOD = THE BEGINNING OF **WISDOM**

(PROVERBS 1:7A)

	HEBREW SCRIPTURE	NEW TESTAMENT	PSALM	PROVERBS
Day 1	Genesis 44:1-45:28	Matthew 14:13-36	18:37-50	4:11-13
Day 2	Genesis 46:1-47:31	Matthew 15:1-28	19:1-14	4:14-19
Day 3	Genesis 48:1-49:33	Matthew 15:29-16:12	20:1-9	4:20-27
Day 4	Genesis 50:1-Exodus 2:10	Matthew 16:13-17:9	21:1-13	5:1-6
Day 5	Exodus 2:11-3:22	Matthew 17:10-27	22:1-8	5:15-21
Day 6	Exodus 4:1-5:21	Matthew 18:1-22	22:19-31	5:15-21
Day 7	Exodus 5:22-7:24	Matthew 18:23-19:12	23:1-6	5:22-23

"I wonder if sheep can stay in this beautiful garden forever..."

Personal Notes and Glimpses of Wisdom:

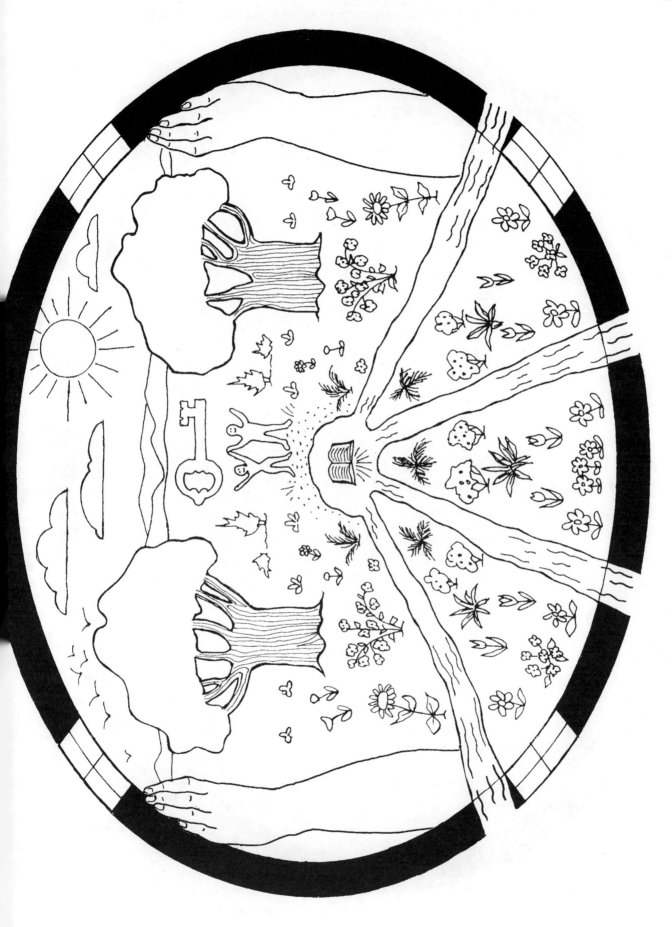

THE GARDEN OF SHALOM

4.8

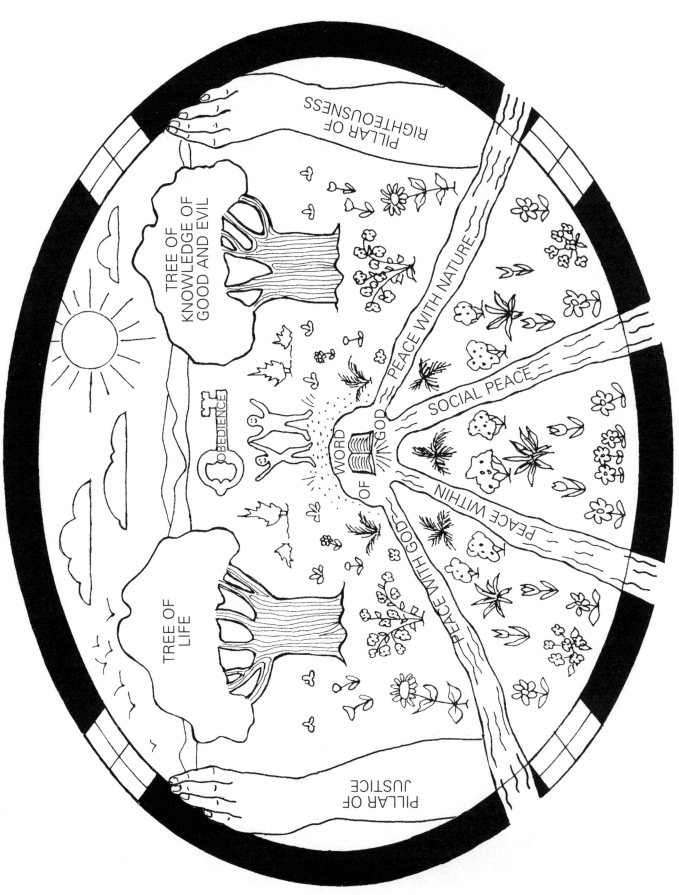

SESSION 5 • REBELLING AGAINST WISDOM

The aim of this session
is to explore the far-reaching consequences of rebelling against the Wisdom of God.

MATERIALS NEEDED

Hymnals
Accompaniment
Bibles
Chalkboard or Newsprint
Completed Search Sheet 4
Completed Insights from Daily Scripture Readings For Week 4
Copies for each participant of:
    Illustration 5A
    Search Sheet 5
    Daily Scripture Readings For Week 5

▨ ASSEMBLING

Session 5 conveys the far-reaching consequences of **sin**. Some participants may have preconceived ideas about what **sin** is – "missing the mark," "doing what's wrong," "not doing what is right," "separation from God," etc. Some may think of **sin** as an inherited quality. This session presents **sin** as a deliberate human choice which affects all that God created. Like an earthquake, **sin** ruptures the very foundation of **Shalom** which cannot be humanly repaired.

Since a conviction of **sin** is a necessary prelude to receiving God's grace, pray for the Spirit to lead you and each participant as you prepare and assemble for this session.

▨ THE APPROACH TO GOD   (5 to 10 minutes)

❧ **Singing A Hymn:** A familiar hymn which speaks of temptation, sins and griefs is "What A Friend We Have In Jesus." Invite reflection on these themes during singing.

❧ **Prayer:** Ask the Spirit to lead to a deeper understanding of temptation and sin, that we may grow in the grace God offers to us.

▨ ENCOUNTERING THE WORD   (40 to 45 minutes)

⇨ Search Sheet 4 illustrates how freedom of choice is understood throughout Scripture. Ask if there are any questions on Search Sheet 4, clarify if necessary, appeal to group wisdom where there is uncertainty, and make the transition to "The Choice."

⇨ Lead participants through "The Choice" as a story. (Because "The Fall" is a familiar story and may be "over-heard," it is presented here with emphasis on **the choice**).

▨ GOING FORTH IN GOD'S NAME   (5 to 10 minutes)

❥   **Sing a hymn** such as "I Need Thee Every Hour," noting especially the phrase, "temptations lose their power when Thou art nigh."

❥   **Offer a closing prayer** of thanks to God for a deeper understanding of human tragedy in the beautiful garden. Offer praise to God for not abandoning sinful people but instead reaching out again in lovingkindness and tender mercy.

❥   Distribute copies of:
        Search Sheet 5
        Daily Scripture Readings For Week 5

■ "THE CHOICE"

1. THE STORY (based on Genesis 3:1-7)

One day as the man and the woman were enjoying the Garden of Shalom, talking with the animals, fish, and birds while transplanting seedlings and arranging flowers, a wily character named **Serpentation** (note: In Eastern literature, the **serpent** often symbolized **temptation**) subtly slithered into the garden. Serpentation wriggled up to the woman and ever-so-innocently asked, "Excuse me, Ma'am, but was there anything God said you could **not** do in the Garden of Shalom?

The woman explained God's Word, "We are free to enjoy the Garden and do anything we please **except** eat from the Tree of Self-Centeredness – you know, putting ourselves in the Center which belongs to God only. If we put ourselves in the place where only God belongs, we will shatter the Shalom of the whole garden and bring misery, frustration and death upon ourselves and all that God has created."

"That's a commendable interpretation, Ma'am," said Serpentation. "But I assure you that you and all creation won't really die. The real reason God doesn't want you to fully taste your own potential is because if you did, you'd be **wiser than God!**"

The woman wondered . . . to be wiser than God – to have more wealth, more beauty, more intelligence, more power than God – to taste more freedom – Mmmmmmm!

The woman made her choice – **she reached for a taste!** She gave to the man who was with her. And he **chose to taste also.**

Then they looked at each other through the eyes of this new "freedom." They felt painfully vulnerable, self-conscious and ashamed of their nakedness. So instead of transplanting seedlings and talking to the animals, they spent their time taking leaves from the trees to cover themselves.

(Allow moments of silence for participants to absorb the story.
Then begin writing "The Steps To Temptation" below on newsprint or chalkboard.)

2. THE STEPS TO TEMPTATION

A. Doubt of God's Word (vs. 1)
B. Denial of God's Truth (vs. 4)
C. Suspicion of God's motive (vs. 5)
D. Desire for what God forbids (vs. 6)

Sin is a deliberate choice, a rebellion against the Wisdom of the Garden of Shalom, disobedience.

3. THE CONSEQUENCES OF SIN (Genesis 3:8-24)

Using Illustration 5 on chalkboard or newsprint or as handout, write **"disobedience"** in the broken key and **"distorted"** in the Center, the Word of God. One by one, ask the questions below and have participants read the Scripture.

A. What happened to **Peace with God**? (3:8-13, 22-24)

B. What happened to **Peace Within**? (3:8-13)

C. What happened to interpersonal or **Social Peace**? (3:12-13, 16-19) (**Note**: Do not misinterpret vs. 16 as authorization for male domination. It connotes loss of the fullness of joy which sexual intimacy was created to give.)

D. What happened to **Peace with Nature**? (3:17-19)

When the man and the woman broke the key of **obedience** which maintained **Shalom** in the Garden/Universe, everything in the Garden was ruptured by sin. The pillars of **Justice** and **Right Living** were bent *(label the pillars "bent justice" and "bent righteousness")*. Joyous and eternal God-centered life ended with the death penalty *(label one tree "limited life" and the other "death")*. Guilt, fear, and anxiety came between people and God, breaking **Peace with God** *(label rivers as they are named, "broken peace with God," etc.)*. Painful self-consciousness and self-centeredness fractured the **Inner Peace** of the man and the woman. Shame, rivalry, betrayal and distrust came between people shattering human intimacy and **Social Peace. Peace with Nature** was replaced with the thorns and thistles of labor frustrated by failure. These are the far-reaching consequences of human rebellion against Wisdom.

The tragedy of the Garden of Shalom in Genesis 3 is not simply a historical account of **sin.** Isaiah 53:6 describes the human predicament in a shepherd/sheep relationship: *(Have someone look up and read this verse)*. The Apostle Paul in his letter to the Romans describes the **human tragedy**. *(Have a group member read Romans 3:10-18)*.

The tragedy of the Garden of Shalom demonstrates that **individual actions produce universal consequences** *(write this statement on board or newsprint)*. Note the hole in the "dome" or "firmament" in Illustration 5. Compare with earth's ozone layer. What individual (and collective) actions have caused the alarming deterioration of earth's protective layer?

4. GOD'S RESPONSE TO HUMAN SIN

What comes after God's pronouncement of the consequences (cause and effect) of human rebellion against wisdom? God, in truth and holiness, **cannot** change The Law of Sin and Death. But God **can** make a New Law – a Promise of Mercy and Grace! Thanks be to God who does not abandon sinful people! Tenderly, God sews garments of skin, more permanent than those of leaves, and clothes the man and woman (3:21). And in the midst of human pain and struggle, God promises childbearing (3:16) and offspring through whom **ultimate victory over temptation and evil will come** (3:15).

1. The temptations of the man and woman in the garden are seen elsewhere in Scripture and in our lives. Complete the following for comparison:

	GARDEN	ISRAEL'S EXPERIENCE	JESUS	OUR POPULARITY CRITERIA
Body	Gen.3:6a	Num. 11:4-6	Mt. 4:3	Wealth
	_____	_____	_____	
	_____	_____	_____	
Mind	Gen. 3:6c	Ex. 7:1	Mt. 4:6	Intelligence
	_____	_____	_____	
	_____	_____	_____	
Spirit	Gen. 3:6b	Ex. 32:1-6	Mt. 4:8-9	Beauty
	_____	_____	_____	
	_____	_____	_____	

2. In 1 Corinthians 10:6-10, the Apostle Paul warns the Corinthian Christians of the temptations endured by their ancestors in the wilderness. Name them: _____

_____

Compare them with the above temptations.

Paul warns in Verse 12: _____

In Verse 13, he encourages: _____

3. Paul describes God as the One who will show the way out of temptation (1 Corinthians 10:13) - the picture of a Shepherd leading sheep who have all _____ (Isaiah 53:6, Romans 3:12). In Ephesians 6:10-20, Paul teaches the Ephesian Christians about the reality of temptation and evil; and thus the necessity of spiritual warfare. List the weapons of spiritual warfare (Ephesians 6:14-17):

The **belt** of _____   The **shield** of _____

The **breastplate** of _____   The **helmet** of _____

The **shoes** of _____   The **sword** of _____

a. Which of the above weapons did Jesus use against temptation? _____

b. Was this weapon available to Jesus only because he is divine? (See Deuteronomy 6:13,16, 8:3 to explain your answer) _____

c. Why was it necessary for Jesus to be tempted? (Hebrews 2:17-18) _____

d. Why can we trust Jesus to be our High Priest? (Hebrews 4:15) _____

e. How do we trust Jesus? (Hebrews 4:14) _____

1. The temptations of the man and woman in the garden are seen elsewhere in Scripture and in our lives. Complete the following for comparison:

	GARDEN	ISRAEL'S EXPERIENCE	JESUS	OUR POPULARITY CRITERIA
Body	Gen.3:6a _good for food_	Num. 11:4-6 _dissatisfied, longing for better food_	Mt. 4:3 _turned stones into bread_	Wealth
Mind	Gen. 3:6c _desired to "make wise"_	Ex. 7:1 _Moses "like God to Pharaoh"_	Mt. 4:6 _prove divinity, angels rescue_	Intelligence
Spirit	Gen. 3:6b _delight to the eyes_	Ex. 32:1-6 _golden calf / gods of own making_	Mt. 4:8-9 _kingdoms for worshipping evil one_	Beauty

2. In 1 Corinthians 10:6-10, the Apostle Paul warns the Corinthian Christians of the temptations endured by their ancestors in the wilderness. Name them: _idolatry, immorality, putting Christ to test, complaining_.

   Compare them with the above temptations. _(Note similarities)_

   Paul warns in Verse 12: _"If you think you're standing, watch out..._

   In Verse 13, he encourages: _Testing is common, God is faithful, offers a way out._

3. Paul describes God as the One who will show the way out of temptation (1 Corinthians 10:13) - the picture of a Shepherd leading sheep who have all _gone astray, their own way_ (Isaiah 53:6, Romans 3:12). In Ephesians 6:10-20, Paul teaches the Ephesian Christians about the reality of temptation and evil; and thus the necessity of spiritual warfare. List the weapons of spiritual warfare (Ephesians 6:14-17):

   The **belt** of _TRUTH_   The **shield** of _FAITH_

   The **breastplate** of _RIGHTEOUSNESS_   The **helmet** of _SALVATION_

   The **shoes** of _PEACE_   The **sword** of _THE SPIRIT (GOD'S WORD)_

   a. Which of the above weapons did Jesus use against temptation? _Sword of the Spirit_

   b. Was this weapon available to Jesus only because he is divine? (See Deuteronomy 6:13,16, 8:3 to explain your answer) _No, Moses taught these words before Christ's birth_

   c. Why was it necessary for Jesus to be tempted? (Hebrews 2:17-18) _To understand us_

   d. Why can we trust Jesus to be our High Priest? (Hebrews 4:15) _Was tested, but didn't sin_

   e. How do we trust Jesus? (Hebrews 4:14) _By holding fast (living) our statement of faith_

DAILY SCRIPTURE
READINGS • WEEK 5

THE **AWE REVERENCE WONDER** AT THE **NEARNESS HOLINESS BEAUTY** OF GOD = THE BEGINNING OF **WISDOM**

(PROVERBS 1:7A)

	HEBREW SCRIPTURE	NEW TESTAMENT	PSALM	PROVERBS
Day 1	Exodus 7:25-9:35	Matthew 19:13-30	24:1-10	6:1-5
Day 2	Exodus 10:1-12:13	Matthew 20:1-28	25:1-15	6:6-11
Day 3	Exodus 12:14-13:16	Matthew 20:29-21:22	25:16-22	6:12-15
Day 4	Exodus 13:17-15:18	Matthew 21:23-46	26:1-12	6:16-19
Day 5	Exodus 15:19-17:7	Matthew 22:1-33	27:1-6	6:20-26
Day 6	Exodus 17:8-19:15	Matthew 22:34-23:12	27:7-14	6:27-35
Day 7	Exodus 19:16-21:21	Matthew 23:13-39	28:1-9	7:1-5

Personal Notes and Glimpses of Wisdom:

"I wonder if sheep will ever see the beautiful garden again..."

📖 5.8

THE SHATTERED GARDEN OF SHALOM

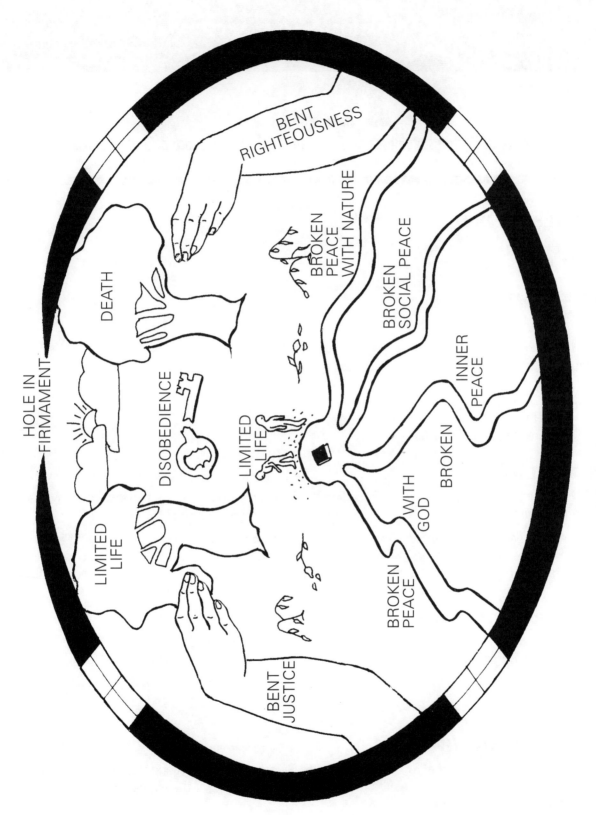

THE SHATTERED GARDEN OF SHALOM

SESSION 6 • WISDOM'S CLEANSING WATERS

The aim of this session
is to see the extent of human sinfulness and the need, wisdom, and grace of God's cleansing waters.

MATERIALS NEEDED

Hymnals
Accompaniment
Bibles
Newsprint or chalkboard
Pitcher of water
Bowl
Completed Search Sheet 5
Completed Insights from Daily Scripture Readings For Week 5
Copies for each participant of:
    "Questions On The Ark"
    Search Sheet 6
    Daily Scripture Readings For Week 6

▣ ASSEMBLING

After the Holy Spirit's convicting of **sin** in "Rebelling Against Wisdom" (Session 5), Session 6 invites a look at the extent of human sinfulness – How degenerated can humans become?

When we see the depth of human sin, God in wisdom offers **grace** and "new beginnings." Pray that God will lead you and each participant to new depths of understanding of the undeserved favor (**grace**) God offers in the midst of the chaotic (**flooded**) lives of people who chose their own way without God.

▣ THE APPROACH TO GOD   (5 to 10 minutes)

❧ **Singing A Hymn:** Briefly introduce Session 6 as a time of considering God's grace in the midst of human sinfulness. Sing a hymn such as "Just As I Am" or a hymn which speaks specifically of Noah or The Flood.

❧ **Prayer:** Ask the Spirit's leading into new depths of wisdom and understanding of God's mercy and grace to sinful people.

▣ ENCOUNTERING THE WORD   (35 to 40 minutes)

⇨ Refer to the "popularity criteria" on Search Sheet 5. Give participants an opportunity for brief questions or clarifications. Call attention to results of unchecked temptation and evil. Make a transition to "The Noah Family."

⇨ Read "The Noah Family." Invite participants to imagine themselves as members of the Noah family on the three-story houseboat with the animals and birds for over a year.

⇨ *Distribute copies of "Questions On The Ark."* Invite participants to work as a group or in teams to record answers. Divide the list as needed for the time frame. After 20 minutes, bring the group together to share answers and insights as you record them on newsprint or chalkboard.

Note: The word *"nave"* (from the Latin word "navis" meaning "ship") means the main body or sanctuary of a church. In what way is the ark like a **sanctuary** (or the sanctuary like the ark)?

▦ GOING FORTH IN GOD'S NAME   (10 to 15 minutes)

The **waters of the flood** washing evil, wickedness and degeneration from the face of the earth provide the symbolism for the sacrament of **holy baptism**. In baptism, we **repent** from the evil inclination of our human hearts (Genesis 8:21), **reject sin** and **make a U-turn in our lives**, turning **from** sin **to** Christ as the Source and Center of all life and blessing. "So if anyone is **in Christ**, there is a **New Creation**: Everything old has passed away; see, **everything has become new**!" (2 Corinthians 5:17)

Baptism recalls the imagery of **God creating** the heavens and the earth out of the dark and shapeless waters of chaos. It recalls the imagery of the **flood** and the new covenantal creation, the Israelite **exodus** from slavery to freedom through the Red Sea and Jordan River, the water of the **womb** in which Jesus, the New Creation, was nurtured and from which he was brought forth. It recalls **Jesus' baptism** by John The Baptist (John 1:29-34), the **"born again" conversation** of Nicodemus and Jesus regarding baptism by water and the Spirit (John 3:1-22), Jesus' baptism by **suffering and death** (Mark 10:38-39, Romans 6:4, Colossians 2:12) followed by his glorious **resurrection** and **ascension** through which we are **cleansed, healed,** and **saved** (1 Peter 3:21) to live no longer by human desires but **by God's will** (1 Peter 4:2).

❧ *(Pour water from pitcher into bowl without speaking. Listen; then touch the water in a washing motion, "baptizing" one hand with the other or dipping a finger in the water and making the sign of the cross on your forehead. Invite participants to touch the water for washing, sprinkling or signing).*

❧ **Prayer** – Offer a prayer of thanksgiving to God for grace and mercy in new beginnings and new creation within and among all people.

❧ Distribute copies of:
    Search Sheet 6
    Daily Scripture Readings For Week 6

■ "THE NOAH FAMILY"

Many, many years after **Shalom** was broken by people who went their own way without God, playing God with their own possessions, beauty, and intelligence, a child was born to Methuselah's son Lamech. They named him **"Noah"** meaning **"relief"** from the hard and frustrating work of farming which God declared as the consequence of human revolt.

When Noah was over 500 years old, he and Mrs. Noah became the parents of three sons, Shem, Ham, and Japheth. A population explosion was taking place all around them, and most people thought they didn't need God anymore. Human self-centeredness, greed, lust, and violence were so rampant that even the soil and the animals were hurt. The pillars of **Justice** and **Right Living** were so shattered that they couldn't hold up the dome between heaven and earth anymore. The heart of God was deeply grieved. The whole earth would be destroyed unless God acted. God had a plan to save the earth and showed the way to someone who would listen.

Noah was a God-centered person who listened to God and did what God said. One day God said to Noah, "The whole earth is nearly ruined by human sin! It needs a great **cleansing to heal** it. If people do not turn away from their greed and lust and violence, I will send a great **flood** and wash away all that is evil. So get ready! Build a three-story houseboat with many rooms for you and your family and the animals and birds."

Noah did what God said. It took many years to build the boat. Then Mr. and Mrs. Noah and family took a pair of each kind of animal and bird into the houseboat, along with enough food for them all. When Noah was 600 years old, he and his wife and three sons and three daughters-in-law entered the houseboat as God had said.

Soon God opened the windows of heaven and pulled the stoppers on the fountains of the deep, and **the whole earth was flooded with God's cleansing waters**, washing away the evil and sinfulness which threatened life as God had created it to be. And all the people and animals who were not in the houseboat died. Then God closed the windows of heaven and replaced the stoppers in the fountains of the deep and blew the earth dry with a wind. The Noah family and birds and animals were in the houseboat for over a year before the waters receded. The **dove** they had sent out returned with an **olive branch**, and all those on board stepped into **a new creation**.

??? QUESTIONS ON THE ARK ???

1. Make a list of the things you wondered about during the many years you worked to build the boat:

2. Now that you are aboard the Ark, what tasks need to be done?

3. How do you decide who will do these tasks?

4. How do you deal with the following:

   a. Rationing food supply?

   b. Births?

   c. Motion sickness?

   d. Other illnesses?

   e. "Cabin Fever"?

   f. Quarrels?

   g. Waste management?

5. Where, when, and how do you worship?

6. How do you feel about God's way of saving you and your family now that the dove has returned with the olive branch?

7. How will you maintain the pillars of **Justice** and **Right Living** (righteousness) now that God has cleansed the earth of injustice and unrighteousness and made a new beginning?

8. After the years of building and the year of living on the Ark, do you feel that receiving **God's grace** is **(A)** An active experience, or **(B)** A passive experience? ____ Why?

SEARCH SHEET 6

Through the waters of the flood, God brought forth a new creation and renewed God-centered world order. Look up the following **Creation** and **Re-Creation** verses and compare the following themes:

	CREATION	RE-CREATION
The wind of God	Gen. 1:2	Gen. 8:1
Fruitfulness	Gen. 1:28b	Gen. 9:7
The blessing	Gen. 1:28a	Gen. 9:1a
Curse - blessing	Gen. 3:17	Gen. 8:21
God-given human dominion	Gen. 1:28b-30	Gen. 9:1-3
Peace with God, nature, social and inner peace	Gen. 1:26-2:25	Gen. 8:15-9:17

From Creation to The Flood, God walked and talked with ordinary people who listened for God the way sheep listen for the voice of their shepherd. From each family, God chose one who would listen and **follow the way of wisdom**. List the names in the succession from Adam to Noah, recorded in Genesis 5:

Adam _____ _____ _____ _____ _____

_____ _____ _____ _____ Noah

While Noah's complete family are listed in Genesis 10, it is his son Shem (thus, "Semites") whose line extends to the patriarch Abram and Sarai his wife (changed to Abraham and Sarah in Genesis 17:5 and 15 in an eternal covenantal blessing). List the succession from Noah's son Shem to Abram, recorded in Genesis 11:11-27.

Shem _____ _____ _____ _____ _____

_____ _____ _____ _____ Abram

SEARCH SHEET 6
ANSWER GUIDE

Through the waters of the flood, God brought forth a new creation and renewed God-centered world order. Look up the following **Creation** and **Re-Creation** verses and compare the following themes:

	CREATION	RE-CREATION
The wind of God	Gen. 1:2 *Swept over waters*	Gen. 8:1 *Wind blew, water subsided*
Fruitfulness	Gen. 1:28b *Be fruitful & multiply*	Gen. 9:7 *Be fruitful & multiply*
The blessing	Gen. 1:28a *God blessed them*	Gen. 9:1a *God blessed Noah*
Curse - blessing	Gen. 3:17 *Ground is cursed*	Gen. 8:21 *Never again curse ground*
God-given human dominion	Gen. 1:28b-30 *over plants, beasts, etc.*	Gen. 9:1-3 *over everything*
Peace with God, nature, social and inner peace	Gen. 1:26-2:25 *beauty of garden (nature)*	Gen. 8:15-9:17 *rainbow, garden (nature)*

From Creation to The Flood, God walked and talked with ordinary people who listened for God the way sheep listen for the voice of their shepherd. From each family, God chose one who would listen and **follow the way of wisdom**. List the names in the succession from Adam to Noah, recorded in Genesis 5:

Adam	Seth	Enosh	Kenan	Mahalel
Jared	Enoch	Methuselah	Lamech	Noah

While Noah's complete family are listed in Genesis 10, it is his son Shem (thus, "Semites") whose line extends to the patriarch Abram and Sarai his wife (changed to Abraham and Sarah in Genesis 17:5 and 15 in an eternal covenantal blessing). List the succession from Noah's son Shem to Abram, recorded in Genesis 11:11-27.

Shem	Arpachshad	Shelah	Eber	Peleg
Reu	Serug	Nahor	Terah	Abram

DAILY SCRIPTURE
READINGS • WEEK 6

THE **AWE REVERENCE WONDER** AT THE **NEARNESS HOLINESS BEAUTY** OF GOD = THE BEGINNING OF **WISDOM**

(PROVERBS 1:7A)

	HEBREW SCRIPTURE	NEW TESTAMENT	PSALM	PROVERBS
Day 1	Exodus 21:22-23:13	Matthew 24:1-28	29:1-11	7:6-23
Day 2	Exodus 23:14-25:40	Matthew 24:29-51	30:1-12	7:24-27
Day 3	Exodus 26:1-27:21	Matthew 25:1-1:30	31:1-8	8:1-11
Day 4	Exodus 28:1-43	Matthew 25:31-26:13	31:9-18	8:12-13
Day 5	Exodus 29:1-30:10	Matthew 26:14-46	31:19-24	8:14-26
Day 6	Exodus 30:11-31:18	Matthew 26:47-68	32:1-11	8:27-32
Day 7	Exodus 32:1-33:23	Matthew 26:69-27:14	33:1-11	8:33-36

Personal Notes and Glimpses of Wisdom:

"I wonder if a rainbow could fit inside a sheep..."

SESSION 7 • COVENANTAL WISDOM

*T*he aim of this session is to glimpse the wisdom of God in designing a "Kingdom (kin-dom) of priests" (all the people of God) through an eternal covenant of promises, purpose and prophecy.

MATERIALS NEEDED

Hymnals
Accompaniment
Bibles
Newsprint or chalkboard
Three small tables or one table large enough for three stations
Utensils and ingredients for baking bread (listed below)
Completed Search Sheet 6
Completed Insights from Daily Scripture Readings For Week 6
Copies for each participant of:
    Search Sheet 7 (two pages)
    Daily Scripture Readings For Week 7

Utensils And Ingredients For Baking Bread

Station 1	Four-cup glass measure	1/3 cup warm water
	Fork, Tablespoon	1 Tablespoon sugar
	1/3-cup measure	1 Tablespoon dry yeast
Station 2	Large mixing bowl	2 Tablespoons sugar
	Large mixing fork	2 teaspoons salt
		1/4 cup oil or melted oleo
		2 cups warm milk
		6 cups flour (wheat, spelt, barley, rye, buckwheat - variety can represent ethnic inclusiveness)
Station 3	3 greased loaf pans or one	oil for greasing pans
	9" x 13" pan for rolls	one batch of dough pre-mixed and rising, ready for shaping
For the Going-Forth Meal	Small plates	Loaf of warm bread (or toast)
	Napkins	Butter or margarine
	Knives	Juice
	Juice glasses	(sliced bread)
	(Toaster)	

▩ ASSEMBLING

This session seeks to provide continuity between God's covenant with the faithful Noah family and the family of Abram and Sarai. The covenant is an important key to understanding all Scripture. Allow plenty of time for preparation, assembling, set-up (you may delegate!), and personal prayer before the session.

▩ THE APPROACH TO GOD   (5 to 10 minutes)

❥ **Singing A Hymn:** A hymn such as "One Bread, One Body" or a hymn which expresses God's covenantal relationship with us may be sung.

❥ **Prayer:** Thank God for the covenantal grace and wisdom offered to Noah, Abram and Sarai and to us. Ask that each participant experience grace and wisdom in a new way in this session.

▩ ENCOUNTERING THE WORD   (40 to 45 minutes)

➪ Briefly review Search Sheet 6, highlighting the similarities between Creation and Re-Creation after the flood. Then ask if anyone would like to pronounce the names of the genealogies . . . Whether or not anyone offers, simply note that each person is known to God who **calls each of us by name** into a holy covenantal relationship.

➪ Lead participants in "A Covenantal Experience" as outlined on those pages.

▩ GOING FORTH IN GOD'S NAME   (10 to 15 minutes)

❥ Gather the group around a table where napkins, plates, knives, a loaf of warm bread (or slices of toast), butter and small glasses of juice have been placed. Give thanks to God for the bread and the covenant. Share the food and enjoy the fellowship, inviting participants to share what was most meaningful for them in the experience.

❥ Close with the Aaronic (priestly) benediction: "The Lord bless you and keep you; the Lord make his face to shine upon you, and be gracious to you; the Lord lift up his countenance upon you, and give you peace." (Numbers 6:24-26)

❥ Distribute copies of:
    Search Sheet 7 (two pages)
    Daily Scripture Readings For Week 7

■ "A CONVENANTAL EXPERIENCE"

➤ INTRODUCING THE EXPERIENCE: Read (or paraphrase) the following to the group.

Through faithful Noah and family, God offered **cleansing and grace** to sinful humanity and the birds and animals and earth damaged by human sin. Through the line of Noah's son Shem, God led people in paths of wisdom and grace until faithful Abram and Sarai became recipients of an eternal covenant which contains a *PROMISE, PURPOSE,* and *PROPHECY.*

This **covenant** is a key to understanding the Scriptures, for it runs throughout the Bible, binding God to people and people to God. In Jesus, a new dimension to this sacred covenant is given which flows out of the Scriptures and into our lives. This is celebrated in the sacraments of Baptism and The Eucharist or Holy Communion. God continues to call people into that covenantal relationship and shape them into a "Kingdom (Kin-dom) of Priests" or the whole people of God – people who listen for a wisdom greater than their own and do the will of the One True God who calls and leads.

When people asked Jesus what this "Kingdom (Kin-dom)" was like, he answered in parables like the one in Matthew 13:33 (or Luke 13:20,21) where he said the covenantal people were like yeast mixed with flour until all of it was leavened. We will now experience the Covenantal Wisdom of Genesis 12:1-3 through the art of making bread.

AT STATION 1 *(Write **PROMISE** on chalkboard or newsprint)*

➤ *(Ask a participant to put ¹⁄₃ cup warm water in the 4-cup glass measure, stir 1 Tablespoon of sugar into the water using the fork, and then slowly stir in the 1 Tablespoon of yeast. Read the following during the mixing and growing of the yeast plants.)*

"I will bless you" – This is the **PROMISE** God made to Abram and Sarai when they were called to leave their homeland and family to go to a land God would show them (Gen. 12:1) – a land they had never seen. This **PROMISE OF BLESSING** included the promise of so many descendants (like the little grains of yeast) that they would form a great nation (Gen. 15:5). The **PROMISE** included land, a special place within boundaries (like this glass measure), to call their own (Gen. 12:1,7). God repeats the **PROMISE** of many descendants (Gen. 17:6, 22:17, 28:14), and of land (Gen. 13:15, 15:7,18, 17:8, 26:2-3, 28:4, 35:12, 48:4, 50:24).

While the Kingdom (Kin-dom) or Nation was in its infancy, just beginning to live, it needed to be protected from other peoples who could absorb it into extinction or destroy it militarily. Likewise, the yeast needs to be incubated (kept separate at a special temperature in a container free from drafts) while it is beginning to grow. God called Abram and Sarai and their descendants not to marry non-Israelites (Gen. 24:1-4, 28:1-5), lest they be **tempted** to worship other gods and forget the **SACRED PROMISE**. God gave the covenant-bearers land where they would be separated from people who worshipped other gods (Gen. 47:6). Here in Goshen, their own "shepherd section" of Egypt during the famine in Canaan, the descendants of Abram and Sarai increased in strength and number like the yeast growing in the measuring cup.

- I wonder what the yeast would accomplish if it were kept in the measuring cup forever?

- I wonder what would happen if the covenant-bearers were kept isolated forever?

AT STATION 2 *(Write **PURPOSE** on chalkboard or newsprint).*

➤ *(Invite participants to mix the yeast with the other liquid ingredients and then add the dry ingredients, mixing and kneading until dough is smooth but not stiff, ready to be placed in a covered greased pan for rising. While they work, read the following.)*

"I will bless you . . . **so that you may be a blessing**," God said. The covenant was a **PROMISE** with a **PURPOSE** like yeast which must be mixed (or hidden) with other ingredients to grow, causing them to rise.

As at Creation, God spoke, called a world into existence, and pronounced it good. So now God speaks and calls a "holy" people into existence (Ex. 19:56, Lev. 20:26, Deut. 7:6), and gives them a **blessing and a promise**. And like the first people created, God calls the covenant-bearers to fruitfulness (Gen. 17:6), their **PURPOSE**. The yeast has a **PURPOSE**, retaining the properties of yeast while **uniting** with other ingredients and causing them to grow. Likewise, the covenantal people of God are called to retain their unique identity while "bearing fruit" and "making disciples." (Mt. 28:19)

- I wonder how the yeast can be united with all the other ingredients and still retain its "yeastly purpose?"
- I wonder how the covenant-bearers can be united with other people and still retain their "priestly purpose?"

AT STATION 3 *(Write **PROPHECY** on chalkboard or newsprint)*

❧ *(Invite participants to take some of the bread which has risen and shape it into loaves or rolls, placing it in the greased pans. While they are working, read the following.)*

The dough is now ready to be shaped into loaves (or rolls) and placed in pans in an oven. Here it will rise again before baking. Here the yeast fulfills its **PROPHECY** of bringing all the ingredients to completion just as the **PROPHECY** of the covenant is that "**ALL** the families of the earth shall be blessed" through the covenantal people (Genesis 12:3, Acts 3:25).

Just 1 Tablespoon of yeast has been **incubated** or **nurtured** *(write "incubated" or "nurtured" beside* **PROMISE** *on chalkboard or newsprint)*, united *(write **"united"** beside* **PURPOSE** *on chalkboard or newsprint)*, with 6 cups of flour, 2 cups of liquid, and approximately 1 cup of other ingredients. This forms an equation of 1:144 (9 cups x 16 Tablespoons-per-cup = 144). In Revelation 7:4 and 14:1 and 3, the 144,000 (12,000 from each of the 12 tribes) symbolize **all faithful believers** who have survived the tribulation and sing the song of the redeemed. This is the **PROPHECY** of the covenant – **blessing and peace for all (Shalom)** - *(write **"completed"** beside* **PROPHECY** *on chalkboard or newsprint)*.

- I wonder what all the people of the earth will look like after they are **nurtured, united,** and **completed**?
- I wonder how I may help bring about that completion, blessing and peace for all?

(**NOTE** – In preparing for the "Going Forth" meal, if it is inconvenient or impossible to bake the bread in the classroom, a toaster may be used to experience the aroma and warmth of bread).

Melchizedek is a mysterious kingly priest, without ancestors or descendants, with whom Abram has a brief encounter. Complete the crossword search using the New Revised Standard Version of the Bible. Then write your observations and insights on the lines provided beneath the crossword. These insights will be needed for sharing in next week's session on the wisdom of the patriarchs.

1. **In Genesis 14:18-20, Abram is blessed by the mysterious Melchizedek who is King of _____.**

2. **In Psalm 76:2, the _____ of the God of Israel is the place named in Number 1.**

3. **According to Hebrews 7:2, the name of this place means _____.**

4. **Hebrews 7:2 says mysterious Melchizedek's name also means "King of _____."**

5. **Genesis 14:20 and Hebrews 7:2 say Abram gave mysterious Melchizedek one _____ of all his possessions.**

6. **Like mysterious Melchizedek, Abraham's descendants were called by God to be a _____ nation.** (Exodus 19:6)

7. **And they were called to be a _____ kingdom.** (Exodus 19:6)

8. **To be** (No. 6) **and** (No. 7)**, the covenant bearers' task was to _____ God's voice.** (Exodus 19:5)

9. **Their task was to _____ their promise to God.** (Exodus 19:5)

10. **(Across) The prophet Ezekiel tells why it was important for the people in this city to obey – they "live at the _____ of the earth."** (Ezekiel 38:12)

11. **Mysterious Melchizedek must have been greater than Abraham because the one who gives the blessing is _____ to the one who receives it.** (Hebrews 7:7)

12. **Jesus is compared to Mysterious Melchizedek because they both hold their priesthoods _____.** (Hebrews 7:24)

13. **(10 Down) Jesus is high priest of a new _____.** (Hebrews 8:8)

14. **Christ, like Aaron and Mysterious Melchizedek, became high priest by being divinely _____.** (Hebrews 5:5)

15. **Instead of sacrifices, Christ as high priest offered up _____.** (Hebrews 5:7)

16. **These** (No. 15) **were accompanied with _____.** (Hebrews 5:7)

17. **Jesus'** (No. 15) **were heard by God because of his reverent _____.** (Hebrews 5:7)

18. **Even though Jesus as high priest was God's Son, "he learned obedience through what he _____.** (Hebrews 5:8)

19. **Having been made perfect in this way** (No. 18)**, Jesus became the _____ of salvation for all who obey.** (Hebrews 5:9)

20. **Under the new covenant, God's laws are written in the minds and hearts of people** (Hebrews 8:10)**. This is done so "they shall all _____ me."** (Hebrews 8:11)

21. **"If you belong to _____, then you are Abraham's offspring, heirs according to the promise."** (Galatians 3:29)

22. Peter calls all believers to be living stones in a spiritual house, "to be a holy _____." (1 Peter 2:5)

23. Before the throne of God in John's vision, the elders and creatures sing a new song to the Lamb for taking people from every tribe, language, people and nation (Revelation 5:6-9) **and making them into "a kingdom and _____ serving God and reigning on earth."** (Revelation 5:10)

24. The covenantal kingly priesthood of Mysterious Melchizedek into which God calls us through Abraham and Jesus is one of people who say with Jesus, "Your _____ come," (Matthew 6:10) **and**

25. "Your _____ be done." (Matthew 6:10)

From your research on Mysterious Melchizedek, describe what the covenantal priestly kingdom (kin-dom) or the whole people of God were meant to be: _____

_____

_____

_____

"MYSTERIOUS MELCHIZEDEK"

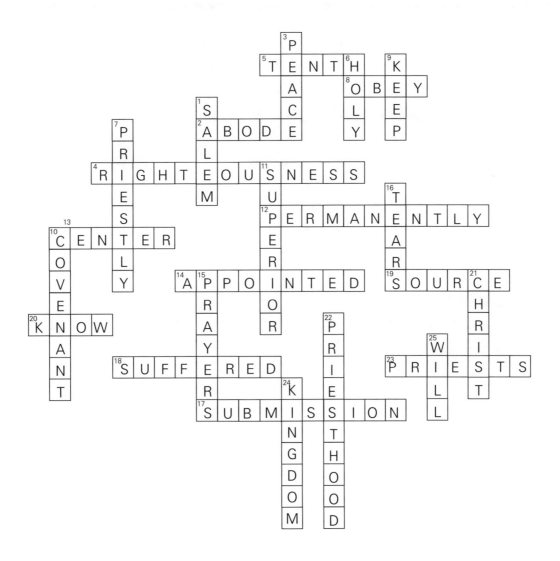

From your research on Mysterious Melchizedek, describe what the covenantal priestly kingdom (kin-dom) or the whole people of God were meant to be: _____

_____

_____

_____

DAILY SCRIPTURE
READINGS • WEEK 7

THE ⬤AWE REVERENCE WONDER AT THE ⬤NEARNESS HOLINESS BEAUTY OF GOD = THE BEGINNING OF ⬤WISDOM

(PROVERBS 1:7A)

	HEBREW SCRIPTURE	NEW TESTAMENT	PSALM	PROVERBS
Day 1	Exodus 34:1-35:9	Matthew 27:15-31	33:12-22	9:1-6
Day 2	Exodus 35:10-36:38	Matthew 27:32-66	34:1-10	9:7-8
Day 3	Exodus 37:1-38:31	Matthew 28:1-20	34:11-22	9:9-10
Day 4	Exodus 39:1-40:38	Mark 1:1-28	35:1-16	9:11-12
Day 5	Leviticus 1:1-3:17	Mark 1:29-2:12	35:17-28	9:13-18
Day 6	Leviticus 4:1-5:19	Mark 2:13-3:6	36:1-12	10:1-2
Day 7	Leviticus 6:1-7:27	Mark 3:7-30	37:1-11	10:3-4

Personal Notes and Glimpses of Wisdom:

"I wonder how many sheep there can be in Mysterious Melchizedek's flock..."

SESSION 8 • PATRIARCHAL WISDOM

*The aim of this session
is to experience covenantal wisdom from a patriarchal perspective.*

MATERIALS NEEDED

Hymnals
Accompaniment
Bibles
Candle, fire-safe container, matches, glass container for used matches
Newsprint or chalkboard
Completed Search Sheet 7
Completed Insights from Daily Scripture Readings For Week 7
Copies (in proportion to number of participants) of:
    "Abram and Sarai"
    "Isaac and Rebekah"
    "Jacob, Leah and Rachel"
    "Joseph"
    "Judah"
Copies for each participant of:
    Search Sheet 8
    Daily Scripture Readings For Week 8

▧ ASSEMBLING

Continuing on the covenantal theme, this session facilitates a look at the covenant through the eyes of its first recipients, the patriarchal families. Pray that participants may sense the awe and wonder of Holy God entering into a sacred and binding contract with sin-prone people.

▧ THE APPROACH TO GOD   (about 5 minutes)

❧ **Lighting a Candle:** With the group seated in a circle, place a candle (taking precautions for fire safety) on the floor or a table in the center of the group. Slowly and silently light it, placing the used match in a glass container. Say, "To light a candle is to become aware of mystery - the mystery of Holy God entering into a contract or covenant with people. Let us enjoy the mystery during a few moments of silence."

❧ **Giving and Receiving the Covenant:** Introduce the experience like this: In this session, we will experience the sacred covenant through the eyes of the patriarchal families. The world is run by promises, contracts and covenants. But that Holy God would enter into a sacred and binding contract with sin-prone people – that God would offer an ***eternal promise*** – that is reason for ***awe and wonder***!

The covenant God made with Abram and Sarai consisted of a ***PROMISE***, with a ***PURPOSE*** and a ***PROPHECY***. It was given to be shared with all people through Abram and Sarai and their descendants. To experience that sharing of the covenant with succeeding generations, I will stand and put my hands on the hands of the person on my left and repeat the covenant to him or her, and she or he will pass it to the left until everyone has received it: ***"I will bless you, that you may be a blessing, and through you all people will be blessed."***

▨ ENCOUNTERING THE WORD   (45 to 50 minutes)

Refer to Search Sheet 7, "Mysterious Melchizedek," and ask participants to describe what covenantal priestly/kingly people are meant to be. *List their responses on chalkboard or newsprint.* Leave the list visible as participants work on patriarchal wisdom.

Assign the patriarchal sheets (listed under "Materials") to individuals if the group is small, or to pairs or small groups as needed. After looking up the Scripture references and answering the questions, each individual or group will **write a summary of the covenantal experience** of the patriarchal family or individual. These will be shared with the whole group at the conclusion of the session. Make extra paper available. Allow 30 minutes for research and writing. Then bring the group together to share their summaries in chronological order.

▨ GOING FORTH IN GOD'S NAME   (about 5 minutes)

❥   **Sing a hymn** such as "O God Our Help In Ages Past" or "God of the Ages" (formerly "God of our Fathers"), using the hymn as a **prayer** celebrating the covenantal connection which unites past, present, and future believers.

❥   **Carefully extinguish the candle.**

❥   Distribute copies of:
        Search Sheet 8
        Daily Scripture Readings For Week 8

■ "ABRAM AND SARAI"

Answer the following questions, looking up the Scripture references (all from Genesis except as noted). Use your answers to give a summary of the covenantal experience from the viewpoint of Abram and Sarai. Share your story with the group at the end of this session.

1. Tell your experiences of receiving the covenant:

12:1-3, 7	15:1-7, 13-21
13:14-17	17:1-8, 15-16

2. How was the covenant made real to you?

12:7	17:10-11, 23-27
15:8-21	17:21
17:5, 15-16	21:1-5

3. How did you respond to God's covenant with you?
Genesis 15:6
Romans 4:11
Hebrews 11:8-10

4. In what ways were you "Mysterious Melchizedek" (kingly/priestly) people?

13:5-9	18:1-8
14:13-16	18:19
14:20b	18:23-33
14:21-24	21:25-32
17:3a, 17a	23:1-20

5. Describe the times you doubted God's promise:

12:10-20	18:12, 15
15:2-3	20:1-18
16:1-4a	21:8-14
17:17	

6. Tell how God tested your family's faith and loyalty to God and the covenantal promise:
22:1-19

7. How did you pass the sacred covenant on to Ishmael ("God hears") and Isaac ("he laughs")?

17:12, 18	22:7-19
25:12-18	24:3-4, 62-67

■ "ISAAC AND REBEKAH"

Answer the following questions, looking up the Scripture references (all from the Book of Genesis). Use your answers to give a first-person narrative of the covenantal experience from the viewpoint of Isaac and Rebekah. Share your story with the group at the end of this session.

1. **Tell how you received the covenant and how it was made real to you:**
   17:19, 21   24:1-67
   21:4, 8, 12   25:9-11
   22:1-19   26:1-6, 12-25

2. **In what ways were you "Mysterious Melchizedek" (kingly/priestly) people?**
   25:21-23   27:4, 27-29
   26:17-33   28:1-5

3. **Describe the times you doubted God's promise:**
   22:9   27:5-10
   26:7-11

4. **What difficulties did you encounter as you struggled to be faithful covenant bearers?**
   26:1a   27:33-38
   26:14b-21   27:41
   26:34-35

5. **How did you pass the covenant on to Esau and Jacob?**
   27:28-29   28:1-8
   27:39-40

■ "JACOB AND LEAH AND RACHEL"

Answer the following questions, looking up the Scripture references (all from the Book of Genesis). Use your answers to give a first-person narrative of the covenantal experience from the perspective of Jacob and Leah and Rachel. Share your story with the group at the end of this session.

1. **Tell your experiences of receiving the covenant:**

   25:19-34   29:9-30
   27:1-29   31:3, 10-13
   27:41 – 28:5   32:1-2, 24-32
   28:10-22   35:1-15

2. **In what ways were you "Mysterious Melchizedek" (kingly/priestly) people?**

   28:18-22   33:10
   30:27b-30a   35:2-5
   32:24-32   35:29

3. **Throughout your lives, there were many twists and turns of irony and deception. Describe them:**

   25:23, 26-28   30:14-21
   25:29-34   30:27-43
   27:19, 35   31:5-9
   29:23-25   32:9-12
   29:31   33:3-4, 10
   30:1-4, 9   48:13-19

4. **What difficulty did God use to test your family's faithfulness?**

   37:2b-4, 18, 28, 31-35

5. **How did God shepherd your family so that this difficulty became a blessing which preserved an emerging nation?**

   41:38-49, 57
   42:1-2, 43:1
   45:1-7, 25-28, 46:29-30
   46:31-47:12, 27
   50:15-21

6. **How did you pass the sacred covenant on to your descendants?**

   47:29-31
   48:1-49:27

■ **"JOSEPH"**

Answer the following questions, looking up the Scripture references (all from the Book of Genesis, except as noted). Use your answers to give a summary of the covenantal experience from the viewpoint of Joseph or Judah. Share your story with the group at the end of this session.

1. **Tell of your experiences of receiving the covenant:**

37:3	41:50-52
37:5-9	48:3-6, 15-16, 21-22
39:2-6, 21-23	49:22-26
41:25-36	

2. **How were you a "Mysterious Melchizedek" (kingly/priestly) person, a faithful covenant-bearer?**

37:13	40:8, 12-19
39:2-6	41:16, 25-45, 47
39:7-10	50:1-14
39:22-23	50:15-21

3. **How did you pass the sacred covenant on to your family and descendants?**

41:57	48:1, 8-20
45:7	50:24-25
46:31-34	Hebrews 11:22

■ **"JUDAH"**

1. **Tell how you received the covenant:**

29:35	49:8-12

2. **Tell of a time in your life when you did not live as a faithful covenant-bearer:**
   38:11-26

3. **In what ways were you a "Mysterious Melchizedek" (kingly/priestly) person?**

37:26-27	43:1-9
38:26	44:16-34

4. **How was the sacred covenant passed on through you?**
   Zechariah 10:3-6
   Hebrews 7:14
   Hebrews 8:8
   Revelation 5:5

■   **"ABRAM AND SARAI" (Answer Guide)**

Answer the following questions, looking up the Scripture references (all from the Book of Genesis except as noted). Use your answers to give a summary of the covenantal experience from the viewpoint of Abram and Sarai. Share your story with the group at the end of this session.

1. **Tell your experiences of receiving the covenant:**
   12:1-3, 7 *Leave home for new land*
   13:14-17 *See, walk through new land*

   15:1-7, 13-21 *Believe promise of heir*
   17:1-8, 15-16 *God appears, name changed*

2. **How was the covenant made real to you?**
   12:7 *Lord appeared; built altar*
   15:8-21 *Torch divides sacrifice*
   17:5, 15-16 *Names changed; new life*

   17:10-11, 23-27 *Circumcision, sign of covenant*
   17:21 *Birth of Isaac promised*
   21:1-5 *Isaac born*

3. **How did you respond to God's covenant with you?**
   Genesis 15:6 *Believed and was counted righteous*
   Romans 4:11 *Circumcision, a seal of righteousness by faith*
   Hebrews 11:8-10 *Obeyed and went even though we had not seen*

4. **In what ways were you "Mysterious Melchizedek" (kingly/priestly) people?**
   13:5-9 *Peacemaking with Lot*
   14:13-16 *Organized army to protect*
   14:20b *Tithed to Melchizedek*
   14:21-24 *Accepted nothing from Sodom*
   17:3a, 17a *Fell face down toward God*

   18:1-8 *Hospitality to three men*
   18:19 *Directed household Lord's way*
   18:23-33 *Pleaded to save Sodom*
   21:25-32 *Treaty with Abimelech*
   23:1-20 *Bought burial plot in land God gave*

5. **Describe the times you doubted God's promise:**
   12:10-20 *Distrusted God in Egypt*
   15:2-3 *In many childless years*
   16:1-4a *Used Hagar to get heir*
   17:17 *Laughed at elderly parenthood*

   18:12, 15 *Laughing, lying at promise*
   20:1-18 *Lying*
   21:8-14 *Ishmael mocked; family divided*

6. **Tell how God tested your family's faith and loyalty to God and the covenantal promise:**
   22:1-19 *In asking to sacrifice Isaac*

7. **How did you pass the sacred covenant on to Ishmael ("God hears") and Isaac ("he laughs")?**
   17:12, 18 *Circumcision, prayer*
   25:12-18 *Ishmael's sons, 12 tribes*

   22:7-19 *Worshipped together on mountain*
   24:3-4, 62-67 *Chose Isaac's wife from kin*

■ **"ISAAC AND REBEKAH"** (Answer Guide)

Answer the following questions, looking up the Scripture references (all from the Book of Genesis). Use your answers to give a first-person narrative of the covenantal experience from the viewpoint of Isaac and Rebekah. Share your story with the group at the end of this session.

1. **Tell how you received the covenant and how it was made real to you:**

   17:19, 21 *Promise of birth*   24:1-67 *Married kin*

   21:4, 8, 12 *Circumcision, weaning feast*   25:9-11 *Burying father in promised land*

   22:1-19 *Almost sacrificed on mountain*   26:1-6, 12-25 *Blessed in midst of famine*

2. **In what ways were you "Mysterious Melchizedek" (kingly/priestly) people?**

   25:21-23 *Prayed about barrenness*   27:4, 27-29 *Passed covenant to son Jacob*

   26:17-33 *Peacemaking with Abimelech*   28:1-5 *Commanded Jacob to marry kin*

3. **Describe the times you doubted God's promise:**

   22:9 *When bound on altar*   27:5-10 *During deception in family*

   26:7-11 *Lying, fearing Philistines*

4. **What difficulties did you encounter as you struggled to be faithful covenant bearers?**

   26:1a *Famine*   27:33-38 *Grief after deception/division*

   26:14b-21 *Envied, feared by others*   27:41 *Hatred, grudge between sons*

   26:34-35 *Son Esau married Canaanite*

5. **How did you pass the covenant on to Esau and Jacob?**

   27:28-29 *Blessing of Jacob*   28:1-8 *Instructions not to marry Canaanites*

   27:39-40 *Blessing of Esau*

...

8.9

■ "JACOB AND LEAH AND RACHEL" (Answer Guide)

Answer the following questions, looking up the Scripture references (all from the Book of Genesis). Use your answers to give a first-person narrative of the covenantal experience from the perspective of Jacob and Leah and Rachel. Share your story with the group at the end of this session.

1. **Tell your experiences of receiving the covenant:**
   - 25:19-34 *Esau sells birthright*
   - 27:1-29 *Deceived father to get blessing*
   - 27:41 – 28:5 *Fled home to marry kin*
   - 28:10-22 *Dream at Bethel; vow, tithe*
   - 29:9-30 *Marriage within kin*
   - 31:3, 10-13 *Leaving Laban as God said*
   - 32:1-2, 24-32 *Wrestled with God*
   - 35:1-15 *Blessed, name change at Bethel*

2. **In what ways were you "Mysterious Melchizedek" (kingly/priestly) people?**
   - 28:18-22 *Worship, encounter, oath, tithe*
   - 30:27b-30a *Laban blessed because of us*
   - 32:24-32 *Struggled with God*
   - 33:10 *Peacemaking gifts to Esau*
   - 35:2-5 *Getting rid of foreign gods*
   - 35:29 *Buried father in promised land*

3. **Throughout your lives, there were many twists and turns of irony and deception. Describe them:**
   - 25:23, 26-28 *Two nations in womb*
   - 25:29-34 *Traded stew for birthright*
   - 27:19, 35 *Deception of father Isaac*
   - 29:23-25 *Laban switches Leah/Rachel*
   - 29:31 *Unloved/fertile; loved/barren*
   - 30:1-4, 9 *Maids increase productivity*
   - 30:14-21 *Wives compete for husband*
   - 30:27-43 *Genetic engineering*
   - 31:5-9 *Laban cheats; Jacob profits*
   - 32:9-12 *Fear of Esau; trust in God*
   - 33:3-4, 10 *Reconciliation with brother*
   - 48:13-19 *Blessed grandsons, hands crossed*

4. **What difficulty did God use to test your family's faithfulness?**
   - 37:2b-4, 18, 28, 31-35 *Favoritism of Joseph; jealousy; Joseph sold, thought dead*

5. **How did God shepherd your family so that this difficulty became a blessing which preserved an emerging nation?**
   - 41:38-49, 57 *God's Spirit seen in Joseph, causes him to rise to prominence in Egypt*
   - 42:1-2, 43:1 *Famine sends brothers to Egypt to buy grain*
   - 45:1-7, 25-28, 46:29-30 *Famine reunites family*
   - 46:31 – 47:12, 27 *Joseph settles the family in fertile Goshen*
   - 50:15-21 *Forgiveness, reconciliation; God meant events for good*

6. **How did you pass the sacred covenant on to your descendants?**
   - 47:29-31 *By requesting burial in the promised land*
   - 48:1 – 49:27 *By blessing each son individually*

■ "JOSEPH" (Answer Guide)

Answer the following questions, looking up the Scripture references (all from the Book of Genesis, except as noted). Use your answers to give a summary of the covenantal experience from the viewpoint of Joseph or Judah. Share your story with the group at the end of this session.

1. **Tell of your experiences of receiving the covenant:**

   37:3 *Received special robe from father*

   37:5-9 *Through dreams of leadership*

   39:2-6, 21-23 *Leadership recognized*

   41:25-36 *Ability to interpret dreams*

   41:50-52 *Sons named for covenantal exper.*

   48:3-6, 15-16, 21-22 *Sons blessed by father*

   49:22-26 *Blessed by Jacob; double portion*

2. **How were you a "Mysterious Melchizedek" (kingly/priestly) person, a faithful covenant-bearer?**

   37:13 *"Here I Am" attitude*

   39:2-6 *Good overseer for Potiphar*

   39:7-10 *Resisted immorality*

   39:22-23 *Good overseer in jail*

   40:8, 12-19 *Honestly interpreted dreams*

   41:16, 25-45, 47 *Acknowledging God*

   50:1-14 *Buried father in homeland*

   50:15-21 *Humility, forgiving brothers*

3. **How did you pass the sacred covenant on to your family and descendants?**

   41:57 *All world came to buy grain*

   45:7 *Preserved a remnant*

   46:31-34 *Got family assigned to Goshen*

   48:1, 8-20 *Had father bless sons*

   50:24-25 *Requested burial in promised land*

   Hebrews 11:22 *Foretold exodus*

■ "JUDAH" (Answer Guide)

1. **Tell how you received the covenant:**

   29:35 *Name = "Praise the Lord"*

   49:8-12 *Blessed by Jacob; scepter*

2. **Tell of a time in your life when you did not live as a faithful covenant-bearer:**

   38:11-26 *Unfaithful to daughter-in-law who tricks and exposes unfaithfulness*

3. **In what ways were you a "Mysterious Melchizedek" (kingly/priestly) person?**

   37:26-27 *"Sell not kill" Joseph*

   38:26 *"She is more right than I"*

   43:1-9 *Offers to be surety for Benjamin*

   44:16-34 *Offers self in Benjamin's place*

4. **How was the sacred covenant passed on through you?**

   Zechariah 10:3-6 *"Out of Judah shall come the cornerstone"*

   Hebrews 7:14 *Jesus descended from Judah*

   Hebrews 8:8 *"New covenant with the house of Judah"*

   Revelation 5:5 *Christ = Lion of the tribe of Judah*

SEARCH SHEET 8

The stories of the patriarchs show that the wisdom of God is made known to people who are **faithful – not perfect**. God chose leaders in each family, not always by birth order as was tradition, but by their **sensitivity to the Way of Wisdom** – the willingness to hear and do God's will. The Hebrew Scriptures give only glimpses of individuals, showing the main direction of their lives – toward self-interest or toward God's will, as given in the covenant. The Scriptures also show us human "side-trips," doubts in faith and weaknesses in character.

In preparation for a session on the shaping of leadership, look up the following verses on the patriarchs (from Genesis) and give each a **"Wisdom Rating"** of **A, B, C, D, or E**, with **"A"** for the greatest sensitivity in knowing and doing God's will, and **"E"** for the least.

_____ **Abraham** 13:8-9, 14-18 14:18-24 17:23 22:1-19	_____ **Lot** 13:10-13 19:4-8 19:15-20 19:30-38
_____ **Isaac** 17:19-21 21:1-6 24:1-6, 62-67 26:12-16 28:1-5	_____ **Ishmael** 16:11-12 17:18-20, 25-26 21:15-21 25:12-18
_____ **Jacob** 25:22-26 25:29-34 27:5-29 28:1-5, 29:21-30 32:9-12 48:1-49:33	_____ **Esau** 25:22-26 25:29-34 27:30-41 26:34-35, 28:6-9 33:4, 11, 15-16
_____ **Joseph** 37:13 37:5-9 39:2-6,7-12,21-23 40:8, 41:16 41:38-39 44:4, 50:20-21	_____ **Joseph's Brothers** 37:2, 4, 18-32 42:6b, 43:28b, 44:14 42:8 42:21 43:33 50:15-21
_____ **Judah** 37:26-27 38:11-26 43:8-9 44:32-34 49:8-12	_____ **Reuben (eldest)** 35:22 37:21-22, 29-30 42:22 42:37 49:3-4

SEARCH SHEET 8
ANSWER GUIDE

The stories of the patriarchs show that the wisdom of God is made known to people who are **faithful – not perfect**. God chose leaders in each family, not always by birth order as was tradition, but by their **sensitivity to the Way of Wisdom** – the willingness to hear and do God's will. The Hebrew Scriptures give only glimpses of individuals, showing the main direction of their lives – toward self-interest or toward God's will, as given in the covenant. The Scriptures also show us human "side-trips," doubts in faith and weaknesses in character.

In preparation for a session on the shaping of leadership, look up the following verses on the patriarchs (from Genesis) and give each a **"Wisdom Rating"** of **A, B, C, D, or E**, with **"A"** for the **greatest sensitivity** in knowing and doing God's will, and **"E"** for the **least**.

_____ **Abraham**
13:8-9, 14-18 *Makes peace with Lot*
14:18-24 *Blessed, tithes, 0 for self*
17:23 *Circumcised all as God said*
22:1-19 *Offers Isaac as God said*

_____ **Lot**
13:10-13 *Takes best for self*
19:4-8 *Offers daughters to rapists*
19:15-20 *Lingered in Sodom*
19:30-38 *Incest while drunk*

_____ **Isaac**
17:19-21 *Given everlasting covenant*
21:1-6 *Fulfills Sarah's laughter*
24:1-6, 62-67 *Wife from kin; comfort*
26:12-16 *Blessed; powerful; peace oaths*
28:1-5 *Tells Jacob to get wife from kin*

_____ **Ishmael**
16:11-12 *At odds with kin*
17:18-20, 25-26 *Blessed/circumcised*
21:15-21 *God hears – Great nation*
25:12-18 *Twelve tribes*

_____ **Jacob**
25:22-26 *Elder to serve younger*
25:29-34 *Gives stew for birthright*
27:5-29 *Deceives to get blessing*
28:1-5, 29:21-30 *Wives from kin*
32:9-12 *Prays for mercy, deliverance*
48:1 – 49:33 *Deathbed blessings*

_____ **Esau**
25:22-26 *Elder to serve younger*
25:29-34 *Gives birthright for stew*
27:30-41 *Wronged; begs; hates*
26:34-35, 28:6-9 *Married non-kin*
33:4, 11, 15-16 *Reconciled w/ Jacob*

_____ **Joseph**
37:13 *" Here I Am" attitude*
37:5-9 *Dream of sheaves, stars bowing*
39:2-6,7-12,21-23 *Successful; faithful*
40:8, 41:16 *Acknowledges Source*
41:38-39 *Spirit of Wisdom seen by Pharaoh*
44:4, 50:20-21 *God uses evil for good*

_____ **Joseph's Brothers**
37:2, 4, 18-32 *Hated; kidnapped/sold*
42:6b, 43:28b, 44:14 *Bow to Joseph*
42:8 *Did not recognize Joseph*
42:21 *Guilt at treatment of Joseph*
43:33 *Amazed at birth order seating*
50:15-21 *Fear; reconciliation*

_____ **Judah**
37:26-27 *"Sell rather than kill" Joseph*
38:11-26 *Wrongs, then preserves Tamar*
43:8-9 *"I will be surety for Benjamin"*
44:32-34 *Begs substitution for Benjamin*
49:8-12 *Blessing of plenty, scepter*

_____ **Reuben (eldest)**
35:22 *Slept with father's concubine*
37:21-22, 29-30 *Wants to help Jos.*
42:22 *Reminds of wanting to help*
42:37 *Offers sons as surety*
49:3-4 *Blessing though unstable*

DAILY SCRIPTURE
READINGS • WEEK 8

THE **AWE REVERENCE WONDER** AT THE **NEARNESS HOLINESS BEAUTY** OF GOD = THE BEGINNING OF **WISDOM**

(PROVERBS 1:7A)

	HEBREW SCRIPTURE	NEW TESTAMENT	PSALM	PROVERBS
Day 1	Leviticus 7:28-9:6	Mark 3:31-4:25	37:12-29	10:5
Day 2	Leviticus 9:7-10:20	Mark 4:26-5:20	37:30-40	10:6-7
Day 3	Leviticus 11:1-12:8	Mark 5:21-43	38:1-22	10:8-9
Day 4	Leviticus 13:1-59	Mark 6:1-29	39:1-13	10:10
Day 5	Leviticus 14:1-57	Mark 6:30-56	40:1-10	10:11-12
Day 6	Leviticus 15:1-16:28	Mark 7:1-23	40:11-17	10:13-14
Day 7	Leviticus 16:29-18:30	Mark 7:24-8:10	41:1-13	10:5-16

Personal Notes and Glimpses of Wisdom:

"I wonder how a covenant can be like yeast..."

SESSION 9 • SHAPING A WISE LEADER

The aim of this session
is to explore the ways God shaped Moses, wise leader of Israel.

MATERIALS NEEDED

Hymnals
Accompaniment
Bibles
Newsprint or chalkboard
Clay, Play-Doh, or other modeling compound (enough for seven lumps per participant)
Completed Search Sheet 8
Completed Insights from Daily Scripture Readings For Week 8
Copies for each participant of:
    Search Sheet 9
    Daily Scripture Readings For Week 9

⊞ ASSEMBLING

As you wait for group members to arrive, read Psalm 90, a prayer of Moses, and let it be your prayer as a leader. Note especially the key to a "wise heart" (verses 11-12) given by one who walked and talked so closely with God that he was called the "friend of God."

⊞ THE APPROACH TO GOD   (5 to 10 minutes)

❥ **Read** Psalm 90 responsively or sing a hymn which expresses its theme (see Scripture Reference section of hymnal). The hymn, "God of Grace and God of Glory" is a possibility.

❥ **Offer a prayer** which paraphrases Psalm 90:11-12.

⊞ ENCOUNTERING THE WORD   (40 to 45 minutes)

Refer to Search Sheet 8. Using newsprint or chalkboard, list the nine individuals and one group. Invite (and record) participants' comments on their willingness to hear and do God's will. Then lead participants through "The Shaping" experience.

⊞ GOING FORTH IN GOD'S NAME   (5 to 10 minutes)

❥ **Sing** "Have Thine Own Way, Lord" as a prayer for the shaping of leaders.

❥ Distribute copies of:
    Search Sheet 9
    Daily Scripture Readings For Week 9

■ "THE SHAPING"

One of the most important instruments in fashioning a people who hear and do God's will is a wise leader. This "shaping" session will take a look at how God shaped the wise leader, Moses. It will look at seven eras of Moses' life, inviting expression of that shaping with lumps of clay. *(Distribute seven lumps of clay to each participant).* There will be time for reflection and shaping following each era.

(Note: Participants may wish to listen with eyes closed to feel the clay taking shape from within themselves as the stories are read.)

THE FIRST ERA – (Exodus 1 and 2) Over four centuries elapsed since the time Joseph preserved his family in Egypt. The Hebrew people were fruitful and multiplied until the Pharaoh saw them as a potential threat to Egypt. The Pharaoh set taskmasters over them and made them do hard physical labor. When this did not check the growth of God's people, the Pharaoh commanded Hebrew midwives Shiphrah and Puah to kill all boy babies at birth. But before his birth, baby Moses was **protected by the wit and wisdom of women who heard and did God's will**, even when it conflicted with the Pharaoh's.

Shiphrah and Puah did not do as the Pharaoh commanded them, because they knew killing babies was against God's plan for their emerging nation to "be fruitful." When reprimanded by the Pharaoh, they had an answer: The Hebrew women are more vigorous than the Egyptian women; they give birth **before** the midwife can get to them! (1:19) How could a king argue with that wisdom? So the Pharaoh commanded that all Hebrew baby boys be thrown into the Nile River.

Once again, baby Moses was **protected by the wit and wisdom of women who knew and did God's will.** The son of Amram and Jochebed of the tribe of Levi, Moses was first protected in the **womb** of Jochebed. When he was born and she saw what a fine baby he was, Jochebed hid him at home for three months. Then she thought of a way to be obedient to God **and** Pharaoh; she put him in the Nile River – in a papyrus basket plastered with pitch so it would float! She placed the basket among the reeds along the bank of the river and appointed Moses' sister Miriam to watch from a distance.

An Egyptian woman, Pharaoh's daughter, came to bathe at the river, found a crying baby in a basket, and **felt compassion** for him. Just then, Sister Miriam sprang into action; she offered to get a Hebrew nurse to raise the child. She ran to get Jochebed. Pharaoh's daughter offered Jochebed wages to raise the child. And so a contract between two women, brought about by a young girl, preserved the early life of God's chosen leader.

Feel the protection of your family before your birth, in your infancy and early childhood. Feel the political forces, laws, church and community that shaped you during your early years. Feel God's shaping through the special or unique difficulties which affected you during your childhood. Feel the moments of compassion which shaped you then. Feel the wit and wisdom of special people who guided you as you grew.

(Allow time for shaping. When shaping is completed, invite participants to place completed shape aside. As each takes a new lump, proceed with the Second Era.)

THE SECOND ERA – (Exodus 2:11 – 4:32) Moses grew up in Pharaoh's palace, but one day when he saw an Egyptian beating a Hebrew, he identified with the oppressed Hebrews and killed the Egyptian. This angered Pharaoh. So Moses ran for his life and settled in the land of Midian. He helped some women draw water for their flock. He was welcomed into their home and married a shepherdess, Zipporah, daughter of a Midianite shepherd/priest. They had a son, Gershom.

Meanwhile, a new king came to power in Egypt, and he oppressed the Hebrew people even more, so that they cried out to God for liberation and deliverance. God heard. In Midian, where Moses was keeping his father-in-law's flock, the angel of the Lord appeared to him in a flame of fire, a burning bush which was not consumed by the fire. God called him by name, "Moses, Moses!" And Moses said, "Here I am." Then God said, "Take off your sandals; you are standing on holy ground. I am the God who made the covenant with Abraham, Isaac, and Jacob. My people are suffering terribly in Egypt, and I want you to go before Pharaoh and lead the people to freedom."

Moses felt inadequate. **"Who am I to do a job like this?"** And God said, "I will be with you."

But Moses said, "If I tell the Israelites the God of their ancestors sent me and they ask me your name, what shall I say?" God said, **"I AM WHO I AM,** Yahweh, the God of the covenant."

Moses said, **"What if** they don't believe when I say You sent me?" God gave Moses power to turn his staff into a snake and back into a rod again, power to put his hand inside his cloak and become leprous, power to put it back in again and have it healed. And God said if they still don't believe, take water from the Nile, pour it on the ground, and it will become blood.

But Moses said, "I'm not an eloquent speaker; I'm a slow thinker with a thick tongue. Please send someone else!" And God became angry and said, "Now go! I will be with your mouth and teach you what you are to say. And your eloquent brother Aaron will go with you also."

Feel the back-and-forth pulling of the identity struggle of youth. Feel the shape of an enormous task being assigned to you and your lack of ability and training for the task. Feel yourself being stretched by God to do this task.

(Allow time for shaping)

THE THIRD ERA – (Exodus 5 – 15) Moses **listened** closely to God, and **went** before the Pharaoh **again and again** and told him, "God says 'Let my people go!'" Each time, Pharaoh **refused**. The cries of the people, the voice of God with specific instructions, the awful plagues on Egyptians but not on nearby Hebrews, and the anger of Pharaoh kept Moses and Aaron in a **constant cycle**. Finally, God set the date. A week of preparation began. Each family ate unleavened bread, selected a lamb without blemish and slaughtered it on the fourteenth day, put blood on the doorposts, roasted the lamb, ate standing up, staying inside the house until morning — an event they would celebrate every year to remember God's deliverance and teach it to their children.

The Passover had come – the night the Lord struck down all the firstborn of Egypt, even the cattle. There was wailing that dark night in Egypt. Pharaoh finally said, "Go!" So Moses led two million people (600,000 men plus women and children) out of Egypt, along with their cattle and hurriedly-packed possessions, plus gold and silver and clothing they plundered from the Egyptians. God told Moses just where to camp and told him the Egyptians would pursue them. The Hebrew people **cried out** in fear. Moses told the people to **stand firm and see the deliverance of God**. Then Moses **cried out** to God. God told him to stretch out his staff over the Red Sea. God blew an east wind over the waters all night, shaping two walls of water with dry ground between.

Feel God's insistent call, the painful cries of oppressed people, the thundering of powerful political forces resisting liberation of oppressed people, and the roar of deep waters ahead – pulling you away from all that is familiar, pressing you toward God's promised (but unseen) deliverance and freedom.

(Allow time for shaping.)

THE FOURTH ERA – (Exodus 15:22 – 17:13) After trusting and obeying and leading the people to experience God's powerful deliverance, Moses **mediated the covenant** between God and the priestly people. When the only water at Marah was bitter and the people complained, Moses took the matter to God in prayer. God instructed Moses; Moses threw a piece of wood into the water to heal it, and it became sweet. When the people complained of hunger, Moses and Aaron took it to God in prayer. God provided a flaky substance as fine as frost, white like coriander seed, tasting like wafers made with honey. They called it **manna** and discovered many ways to prepare it. God gave specific instructions for collecting it so none would be hoarded or wasted and there would always be enough – one day at a time.

When the people complained of having no meat in their diet, Moses and Aaron took it to God in prayer. God said, "Tell the people to come near to God, for God has heard your complaining." The glory of the Lord appeared in a cloud, and in the evening quails covered the camp!

Again at Rephidim, when the people complained of thirst, Moses took it to God in prayer. God told him to strike the rock. And when he did, water flowed out of the rock. He called the place Massah and Meribah because the Israelites tested God's presence among them there.

Feel yourself being shaped as a mediator between the cries of two million needy, frightened people – and the voice of the God who miraculously delivers, leads, and feeds them.

(Allow time for shaping.)

THE FIFTH ERA – (Exodus 19 – 24) God told Moses to **consecrate** the people, to get them ready for a great happening at the holy mountain where **God would speak to them**. They washed their clothing, and on the third day they waited at the foot of the mountain for God to tell them how to live as holy priestly people among the nations. There was thunder and lightning, and the people trembled at God's voice rumbling from the holy mountain; so Moses alone went up to listen and talk with God, receiving the keys to the wisdom of the covenant – the Ten Commandments written by the finger of God on tablets of stone – laws protecting people, laws dealing with property, laws regarding social and worship rites, laws regarding annual celebrations, laws in which justice extended to helping one's enemy, and laws for instituting and maintaining the priestly order.

Feel the presence of God very near, shaping you to lead by giving you the secrets to wise and peaceful living.

(Allow time for shaping.)

THE SIXTH ERA – (Exodus 18) With the newly-received secrets to wise covenantal living, Moses worked long days **listening** to the people's disputes and **interpreting** God's covenant with them. One day his father-in-law, Jethro along with his wife, Zipporah and sons Gershom and Eliezer visited him. When Jethro saw how much of Moses' time was given to discerning God's will for the people and how this was wearing Moses out, he offered him timely advice in **shared leadership**.

"Select from among the people leaders who live wisely and obey God. Teach them the secrets to the wisdom of the covenant that God gave you, and appoint them over tens, fifties, hundreds, and thousands. By reorganizing administrative tasks, others can discern God's will in routine matters while you, Moses, handle only those cases without legal precedent. By **sharing** the burden of leadership, you will be able to **endure**, and there will be **peace** among the people." (Exodus 18:21-23, paraphrased)

Feel God shaping your leadership abilities through the wise counsel of a more experienced leader. Feel the freedom that results from shared leadership.

(Allow time for shaping.)

THE SEVENTH ERA – (Exodus 35-40) Moses continued to *lay the spiritual foundations* of the people of God by organizing them to build the tabernacle according to the instructions God gave. He appointed Bezalel and Oholiab who had received divine spirit with ability, intelligence, and knowledge in every kind of craft needed in the construction of the sanctuary. Then, the people brought supplies to the artisans – so much that Moses had to ask them to stop bringing gifts!

When all parts of the tabernacle were completed as God had instructed, Moses assembled them. He laid the foundation, set up the frames, and raised the pillars. He placed the tablets of covenantal wisdom inside the ark, set the mercy seat above the ark, and put the ark in the tabernacle. Then the ***glory of the Lord filled the tabernacle*** and the cloudy pillar which had led them since Egypt was on the tabernacle each day, becoming a pillar of fire by night.

Feel the glory of God surrounding you in blessed peace and unity — the results of pure worship of God in which each person shares the unique gifts God has given, living out the wise terms of God's covenant.

(Allow time for shaping.)

Reflecting On The Word:

- Invite participants to arrange their clay shapes into a circle, grouped by era. Then go around the circle enjoying the shapes.

- Invite participants to share which shape was most meaningful to them and why.

- Read Deuteronomy 34:10-12. How did Moses receive the prophetic wisdom needed for unequaled leadership? (vs. 10)

- How is the Spirit of Wisdom for leadership transferred? (Deuteronomy 34:9)

- How can you and I receive wisdom for the tasks God gives to us? (James 1:5-8)

- What is the "shape" of the wisdom which comes from God? (James 3:13-18)

SEARCH SHEET 9

Moses, the great leader **shaped by God**, received the keys to wisdom through conversations with God. He faithfully used the wisdom of God to shape the spiritual foundation of the priestly/kingly people of God. **How did this wisdom extend beyond his lifetime?** Look up the following verses, taking notes on each. Then write a summary at the bottom of this sheet.

Exodus 40:15b _____

Numbers 25:10-13 _____

2 Chronicles 1:3 _____

2 Chronicles 30:16a, 35:6 _____

Nehemiah 8:1-3, 18, 10:29 _____

Psalm 103:7, 145:13 _____

Isaiah 24:5, 55:3 _____

Isaiah 63:10-14 _____

Jeremiah 31:1-3, 32:40 _____

Mark 1:44, 12:26 _____

Luke 16:31 _____

Luke 24:27 _____

John 1:17, 45, 5:46 _____

Acts 7:17-45 _____

Romans 10:5 _____

2 Corinthians 3:7-18 _____

Hebrews 3:1-5, 9:18-22 _____

Hebrews 11:23-29 _____

Revelation 15:3-4 _____

Write your summary of how a leader's wisdom extends beyond his/her lifetime: _____

_____

_____

_____

_____

_____

_____

_____

_____

_____

SEARCH SHEET 9
ANSWER GUIDE

Moses, the great leader shaped by God, received the keys to wisdom through conversations with God. He faithfully used the wisdom of God to shape the spiritual foundation of the priestly/kingly people of God. How did this wisdom extend beyond his lifetime? Look up the following verses, taking notes on each. Then write a summary at the bottom of this sheet.

Exodus 40:15b *Anointing was for a perpetual priesthood*

Numbers 25:10-13 *Covenant of peace to Phinehas, covenant of perpetual priesthood*

2 Chronicles 1:3 *For over 400 years people worship at tabernacle made in Moses' time*

2 Chronicles 30:16a, 35:6 *Priests perform as per law of Moses, keep Passover*

Nehemiah 8:1-3, 18, 10:29 *While reading book of Moses, people renew vows to obey*

Psalm 103:7, 145:13 *God's ways made known to Moses, foundation for eternal kingdom*

Isaiah 24:5, 55:3 *Earth polluted by broken law/covenant; call to live by covenant*

Isaiah 63:10-14 *Recalls days of Moses when God put Holy Spirit within and led*

Jeremiah 31:1-3, 32:40 *God loves with an everlasting love/covenant*

Mark 1:44, 12:26 *Jesus quotes from and heals/advises from book of Moses*

Luke 16:31 *If people didn't listen to Moses, they won't listen to someone who rises*

Luke 24:27 *Emmaus – Jesus reveals Scriptures about himself, beginning with Moses*

John 1:17, 45, 5:46 *Law/Moses, Grace/Christ, "Moses wrote about me"*

Acts 7:17-45 *Stephen's wisdom sermon refers much to Moses*

Romans 10:5 *Moses wrote regarding righteousness from law*

2 Corinthians 3:7-18 *Law lesser / Spirit greater; all transform*

Hebrews 3:1-5, 9:18-22 *Moses faithful servant; first, second covenants begun by blood*

Hebrews 11:23-29 By faith, *Moses hidden, joined people, suffered, kept Passover*

Revelation 15:3-4 *Song of Moses, servant of God, and Song of Lamb*

Write your summary of how a leader's wisdom extends beyond his/her lifetime:

These verses show the everlasting nature of the covenant of grace/peace God gave to Moses. They show Jesus upholding covenantal law, Stephen referring to it as a point of reference in Israel's history and in early Christianity. Moses' suffering abuse for Christ before Jesus' birth refers to the pre-existent Christ who empowered Moses. In the end, the Song of Moses is used side by side with the Song of the Lamb. When one is part of God's eternal covenant, his/her work/leadership has an eternal quality.

DAILY SCRIPTURE
READINGS • WEEK 9

 THE **AWE REVERENCE WONDER** AT THE **NEARNESS HOLINESS BEAUTY** OF GOD = THE BEGINNING OF **WISDOM**

(PROVERBS 1:7A)

	HEBREW SCRIPTURE	NEW TESTAMENT	PSALM	PROVERBS
Day 1	Leviticus 19:1-20:21	Mark 8:11-38	42:1-11	10:17
Day 2	Leviticus 20:22-22:16	Mark 9:1-29	43:1-5	10:18
Day 3	Leviticus 22:17-23:44	Mark 9:30-10:12	44:1-8	10:19
Day 4	Leviticus 24:1-25:46	Mark 10:13-31	44:9-26	10:20-21
Day 5	Leviticus 25:47-27:13	Mark 10:32-52	45:1-17	10:22
Day 6	Leviticus 27:14-Numbers 1:54	Mark 11:1-26	46:1-11	10:23
Day 7	Numbers 2:1-3:51	Mark 11:27-12:17	47:1-9	10:24-25

Personal Notes and Glimpses of Wisdom:

SESSION 10 • GOD'S SAVING WISDOM

The aim of this session
is to glimpse the wisdom of God's saving grace.

MATERIALS NEEDED

Hymnals
Accompaniment
Bibles
Newsprint or chalkboard
Completed Search Sheet 9
Completed Insights from Daily Scripture Readings For Week 9
Copies for each participant of:
    "God's Saving Grace"
    Search Sheet 10
    Daily Scripture Readings For Week 10

▣ ASSEMBLING

This session looks at God's saving grace as Moses leads the people of God **from** slavery and oppression in Egypt, **through** the walls of water of the Red Sea, **to** freedom and purpose on the other side. This event looks forward to God's saving grace given in the life, death, resurrection and ascension of Jesus. As you prepare to lead, reflect on the wisdom of God in shepherding people through dangerous places and delivering them safely to the other side.

▣ THE APPROACH TO GOD   (5 to 10 minutes)

❧ **Sing a hymn** centering on God's saving grace. "Amazing Grace" is a favorite. "I Sought The Lord And Afterward I Knew" is another possibility. Check the Topical Index of your hymnal for others.

❧ **Offer a prayer** focusing on the grace of God in providing a way through oppression and darkness to new life on the other side.

▣ ENCOUNTERING THE WORD   (40 to 45 minutes)

Using Search Sheet 9, share your summary of the covenantal wisdom of Moses which extended beyond his lifetime. Invite participants to share their summaries. Limit the sharing to about 10 minutes.

Give the "Lecturette" with Timeline Illustration, Old Covenant/New Covenant Comparison, and "From - To" Ceremony.

▣ GOING FORTH IN GOD'S NAME   (5 to 10 minutes)

❧ **Sing** "The Horse and Rider" (using both verses).

❥ **Close with a prayer** of thanksgiving paraphrasing Exodus 15:1-2, 13.

❥ Distribute copies of:
    Search Sheet 10
    Daily Scripture Readings For Week 10

■ "LECTURETTE"

Timeline Illustration: We've seen the wisdom of God in Moses extend beyond his lifetime. Now we'll go back to Abram and Sarai and take a brief look at a time line to see the covenantal wisdom of God being fulfilled. *(Draw a horizontal line on chalkboard or newsprint, with 2091 BC at the left, 1446 BC at the right; 1876 BC one-third of the way between.)* It was the year 2091 BC when Abram and Sarai heard the call of the God of the Covenant to move to Canaan. It was 1876 BC (215 years later) when their grandson Jacob and family went to Egypt during a famine and Joseph used his position to preserve the covenantal family in Goshen. It was exactly 430 years (Exodus 12:40-41) from the time they came that Moses took the bones of Joseph (Exodus 13:19) and led the people out of Egypt's slavery and oppression in 1446 BC. It had been 645 years since God made the covenant with Abram and Sarai. In the 430 years in Egypt, the covenantal family had grown from 66 (Genesis 46:26) to 600,000 men (Exodus 12:37), who, with women and children would total about 2 million people!

The exodus from Egypt through the Red Sea is **God's great act of deliverance** for the covenantal people in the Hebrew Scriptures. God's deliverance in the exodus so completely **unites the people of God** that it is celebrated annually and taught to children. This great act of God's deliverance extends to the time Jesus comes to inaugurate the New Covenant, which extends until **all the people of God** are gathered to be with Christ.

Old Covenant / New Covenant Comparison: *(Distribute copies of "God's Saving Grace" and assign the Scripture references.)* Compare God's great act of deliverance in the Hebrew Scriptures (Old Testament/Covenant) with God's deliverance in Jesus Christ (New Testament/Covenant).

Invite participants to share from the Scripture references while you summarize and list their responses on chalkboard or newsprint under the headings of OLD COVENANT and NEW COVENANT.

From - To Ceremony: Allow time for participants to complete the "From . . . To . . ." portion of "God's Saving Grace." While they are writing, set up a barrier such as a row of chairs to represent the Red Sea. Make a way for the barrier to be "interrupted" to allow "crossing." Invite sharing of FROM - TO responses, stating the "FROM" portion on one side and the "TO" portion on the other side of the barrier. If the chancel area is available for use, light the candles. The "FROM" portion could be stated below and the "TO" portion from the altar. Close by stating, "**God has called us FROM darkness INTO marvelous light.**"

"GOD'S SAVING GRACE"

	Old Covenant	New Covenant
Ways of getting ready for God's deliverance	Exodus 12:3,7, 13:12, 19:14-15 _____ _____ _____ _____ _____	Matthew 3:2,3,6,8 Mark 1:4, I Peter 2:1 _____ _____ _____
Responsibilities of recipients of God's Covenantal grace	Exodus 12:24, 19:5, 24:7, _____ Jeremiah 11:4 _____ _____ _____	John 15:10, Hebrews 5:9 _____ _____
The Sacrifice	Exodus 12:3-11 _____ _____ _____	John 1:29, 1 Peter 1:19 _____ _____ _____
The Blood	Exodus 12:7,13, 24:6-8 Leviticus 17:11 _____ _____ _____ _____	Mat. 26:28, Eph. 1:7, Col. 1:20, Rev. 1:5 _____ _____ _____
God's Act (Not Ours)	Exodus 13:18b, 14:14 _____ _____ _____	Ephesians 2:8-9 _____ _____ _____
Delivered From . To .	Exodus 19:4,6 _____ _____ _____	1 Peter 2:9b, 10 _____ _____ _____

God acts. God delivers each person from the slavery of sin. This is an act none of us can do for ourselves. But God does not deliver us so that we can do as we please. God delivers us **TO** a new purpose or task. Name something God has delivered you **FROM**. Then name the **purpose or task** God calls you **TO**.

FROM	**TO**
_____	_____
_____	_____
_____	_____
_____	_____
_____	_____

"GOD'S SAVING GRACE" (Answer Guide)

	Old Covenant	New Covenant
Ways of getting ready for God's deliverance	Exodus 12:3,7, 13:12, 19:14-15 _Select lamb, put blood on doorposts, dedicate firstborn, wash clothes, sexual abstinence_	Matthew 3:2,3,6,8 Mark 1:4, I Peter 2:1 _Repent, straighten paths, baptism, bear fruit of repentance & forgiveness, rid selves of sin_
Responsibilities of recipients of God's Covenantal grace	Exodus 12:24, 19:5, 24:7, Jeremiah 11:4 _Celebrate Passover annually, hear and obey law/covenant_	John 15:10, Hebrews 5:9 _Keep commandments, abide in Christ's love, obey Christ_
The Sacrifice	Exodus 12:3-11 _a year-old male lamb without blemish_	John 1:29, 1 Peter 1:19 _Christ is the Lamb without blemish_
The Blood	Exodus 12:7,13, 24:6-8 Leviticus 17:11 _blood as sign, blood of covenant sprinkled on people; life is in the blood_	Mat. 26:28, Eph. 1:7, Col. 1:20, Rev. 1:5 _Forgiveness, redemption through Christ's blood; reconciliation, peace_
God's Act (Not Ours)	Exodus 13:18b, 14:14 _God led (people prepared for battle); Lord will fight for you; keep still_	Ephesians 2:8-9 _Saved by grace, God's gift, not by works - no boasting_
Delivered From . To .	Exodus 19:4,6 _From slavery in Egypt to be a kingdom of priests (holy distributors of God's love)_	1 Peter 2:9b, 10 _From darkness into marvelous light; from being without distinction to people of God; mercy_

God acts. God delivers each person from the slavery of sin. This is an act none of us can do for ourselves. But God does not deliver us so that we can do as we please. God delivers us **TO** a new purpose or task. Name something God has delivered you **FROM**. Then name the **purpose or task** God calls you **TO**.

FROM	TO
Being a "pewsitter"	_Accepting leadership responsibility_
A life of futility	_A life of meaning and purpose in Christ_
Sin	_Salvation and service_
Organizing life around others' approval	_Organizing life around will of God_

SEARCH SHEET 10

While God fought for the covenantal people and accomplished deliverance for them (Exodus 14:13-14), God's saving grace was not just a passive experience! There was much to see and hear, taste and feel and do to get ready for God's saving and healing grace, to receive it, explore its meaning, and respond faithfully to it. Use the following verses (all from the Book of Exodus) to go on the journey with them, recording what you see, hear, taste and do. Then, on the lines below, describe how you felt while taking the journey.

TASTES
12:8 _____

15:22-26 _____

16:12-13 _____

16:14-15, 31, 35_____

17:1-7_____

SOUNDS
19:9_____

19:16-19_____

20:19 _____

24:7_____

SIGHTS
7:8-13_____

7:19 - 11:5_____

13:21-22 _____

14:19-20 _____

14:21-31 _____

16:10 _____

17:8-13 _____

20:18-21 _____

24:15-17 _____

31:18 _____

ACTIONS
12:15 _____

12:21-28_____

12:34-36_____

12:39 _____

13:1-2 _____

14:22, 29 _____

15:20 _____

19:7-8 _____

24:3_____

Describe what the journey was like for you: _____

_____

_____

_____

_____

_____

_____

_____

_____

_____

_____

_____

While God fought for the covenantal people and accomplished deliverance for them (Exodus 14:13-14), God's saving grace was not just a passive experience! There was much to see and hear, taste and feel and do to get ready for God's saving and healing grace, to receive it, explore its meaning, and respond faithfully to it. Use the following verses (all from the Book of Exodus) to go on the journey with them, recording what you see, hear, taste and do. Then, on the lines below, describe how you felt while taking the journey.

TASTES

12:8 *Bread, mutton, bitter herbs*

15:22-26 *Bitter water / sweet water*

16:12-13 *Fresh roasted quail*

16:14-15, 31, 35 *Manna (wafers & honey)*

17:1-7 *Thirst; water from rock*

SOUNDS

19:9 *Thundering voice of God from cloud*

19:16-19 *Thunder, voice of trumpet*

20:19 *Voice of the people (fear, awe)*

24:7 *Book of Covenant read; promise /obey*

SIGHTS

7:8-13 *Rod becomes snake*

7:19 - 11:5 *Ten Plagues*

13:21-22 *Cloud pillar; fire pillar*

14:19-20 *Angel of God / pillar of cloud*

14:21-31 *Red Sea parting, walls of water*

16:10 *Glory of God in the cloud*

17:8-13 *Moses' hands raised in victory*

20:18-21 *Lightning, smoking mountain*

24:15-17 *God's glory, cloud, Mt. Sinai*

31:18 *Tablets of stone written by God*

ACTIONS

12:15 *Get rid of yeast; bake bread without*

12:21-28 *Prepare the lamb*

12:34-36 *Pack dough, get jewelry, clothing*

12:39 *Baking bread*

13:1-2 *Consecrate the firstborn*

14:22, 29 *Walk between Red Sea walls*

15:20 *Dance and sing with Miriam*

19:7-8 *Say "I Do" to Covenant with God*

24:3 *Obey Covenant with God*

Describe what the journey was like for you: *It was exciting and frightening to leave all that was familiar and follow God into a strange wilderness. There were so many things to learn - 365 ways to prepare manna, following the cloud and pillar, even through the walls of water, the new songs Miriam taught us on the other side, the special way God called us to live - even wrote it on tablets of stone! My favorite part was the cloudy pillar by day and the pillar of fire at night. Any time of day, one could sit and wonder how powerful and mysterious the Living God of the Covenant must be! And then there were the special times when God showed glory and blessed us. There never was better tasting water than the water from the rock in the wilderness. I will sing of the mercies of the Lord forever!*

DAILY SCRIPTURE
READINGS • WEEK 10

AWE
THE **REVERENCE** AT THE   **NEARNESS** OF GOD = THE BEGINNING OF   **WISDOM**
WONDER   **HOLINESS**
BEAUTY

(PROVERBS 1:7A)

	HEBREW SCRIPTURE	NEW TESTAMENT	PSALM	PROVERBS
Day 1	Numbers 4:1-5:31	Mark 12:18-37	48:1-14	10:26
Day 2	Numbers 6:1-7:89	Mark 12:38-13:13	49:1-20	10:27-28
Day 3	Numbers 8:1-9:23	Mark 13:14-37	50:1-23	10:29-30
Day 4	Numbers 10:1-11:23	Mark 14:1-21	51:1-19	10:31-32
Day 5	Numbers 11:24-13:33	Mark 14:22-52	52:1-9	11:1-3
Day 6	Numbers 14:1-15:16	Mark 14:53-72	53:1-6	11:4
Day 7	Numbers 15:17-16:40	Mark 15:1-47	54:1-7	11:5-6

Personal Notes and Glimpses of Wisdom:

"I wonder what it's like on the other side of the river..."

SESSION 11 • THE LAW – WISDOM'S SECRETS

The aim of this session is to discover the secrets of convenantal wisdom in the law given to Moses.

MATERIALS NEEDED

Hymnals
Accompaniment
Bibles
Newsprint or chalkboard
Completed Search Sheet 2 (for completion of "Secrets" Part 2)
Completed Search Sheet 10
Completed Insights from Daily Scripture Readings For Week 10
Copies for each participant of:
    "Secrets of the Covenant"
    Search Sheet 11
    Daily Scripture Readings For Week 11

▨ ASSEMBLING

Take a moment to pray for each participant's needs and growth in faith. How might the wisdom of the law speak to those needs or challenge their growth? Thank God for needs which have been met and for growth which has taken place. Ask God's guidance in this ongoing process.

▨ THE APPROACH TO GOD   (5 to 10 minutes)

With completed Search Sheet 10 in hand, ask each participant to share a part of the journey which was particularly meaningful for them. After all have shared, gather in a circle, standing, with hands joined and held up high. **Sing** "The Doxology."

▨ ENCOUNTERING THE WORD   (45 to 50 minutes)

Setting the Stage – You are scribes among the covenantal people of God who have just come through the waters of the Red Sea. You have celebrated and sung a song of praise to the God who delivered you. Now the time has come to consider what God has called you **TO**. How do newly-delivered covenantal people live out their praise and thanksgiving to God in their daily lives? The wilderness is such a strange place compared to the familiar farmlands of Goshen. Will there be enough to eat and drink? Is there a way to make sure everyone will get enough and no one will be greedy? How will life and property be protected? What needs to be done to keep God at the center of covenantal living? How will the sick, elderly, widowed and orphaned in your midst be treated?

There are so many ways to go. You join with Moses in asking God to show you how to be the people of God in a strange new situation. God speaks from a thundering mountain which is so frightening that you and all the people ask Moses to talk alone with God and tell you what God says. Later, Moses comes down from the mountain with tablets of written law. His face is aglow from being in God's presence, but his voice is weak. He needs your help to read a portion of the law to the people and to help them understand it. Study a particular portion of the law, and prepare to present it, sharing its secrets of wisdom.

(Assign the four pages of "Secrets of the Covenant" to individuals, teams, or small groups. Give them 20 to 25 minutes to read the Scripture and prepare presentations. Then bring them back into a circle to share their portion of the Law and the secrets of wisdom discovered in it. Provide newsprint or chalkboard for their presentations. Allow 20 to 25 minutes for sharing, comments, and questions.)

▣ GOING FORTH IN GOD'S NAME   (5 to 10 minutes)

❥ **Print** the words of acceptance of covenantal responsibility from Exodus 24:3 on newsprint or chalkboard and invite participants to say them together: "All the words that the Lord has spoken we will do."

❥ **Close** the "Secrets of the Covenant" experience by reading Psalm 119:97-104 responsively and/or singing a hymn based on this Scripture.

❥ Distribute copies of:
Search Sheet 11
Daily Scripture Readings For Week 11

SECRETS OF THE COVENANT – PART 1

■ "A SUMMARY – THE TEN COMMANDMENTS"

1. The Ten Commandments are a summary of God's covenantal agreement with the people. Read them in Exodus 20:1-21 or Deuteronomy 5:1-21. The other laws expand on this summary.

2. The Ten Commandments were summarized into a shorter statement which was memorized by the Hebrew people. This can be found in Deuteronomy 6:4-9. It is known as the "Shema" (pronounced "shah-mah") meaning "hear." Compare Deuteronomy 6:4-5 with Mark 12:29-30 (also Matthew 22:37-40 and Luke 10:25-28). What two major parts are identified in these summaries? _____

3. Look up the following verses. What do they reveal about the intent, spirit, unity and timelessness of the Law?
   Leviticus 19:17-18 _____
   Matthew 19:17c _____
   Romans 13:8-10 _____
   Galatians 5:13-14 _____
   James 2:8 _____

4. How do the Ten Commandments apply the "law of love" to:
   People's relationship to God? _____
   Family relationships _____
   Regard for human life? _____
   Sexuality? _____
   Property? _____
   Speech? _____
   Thought? _____

5. Covenants were a way of life in Eastern culture. They typically contained five parts as listed below. Using Exodus 20:1-21, identify these parts in the Ten Commandments:
   • Statement of author (vs. 2a) _____
   • Statement of history of relationship between covenanting parties prior to offering the covenant – specifically stating the grace and mercy given by the author (2b) _____
   _____
   • Responsibilities of recipients (3-17) _____
   _____
   • Curses for breaking (5, 7b) _____
   • Blessings for keeping (6, 12b) _____

Prepare a brief presentation to share these secrets with the other "scribes." Use chalkboard or newsprint if desired.

SECRETS OF THE COVENANT – PART 2

■ "THE CENTRALITY OF WORSHIP"

To be a "Kingdom (kin-dom) of Priests" – a "Mysterious Melchizedek" people – there needed to be a Source of strength and wisdom. There needed to be a way to stay in touch with that Source.

1. Read Exodus 19:4-6. Why was it important for the people to do what God said ? _____
   _____
   _____

2. What preparations were needed before worship? (Exodus 19:10-15) _____
   _____
   _____

3. What do you think was the purpose of these preparations? (Jeremiah 4:14) _____
   _____
   _____

4. How was stewardship of the land related to worship and Sabbath? (Exodus 23:10-13) _____
   _____
   _____

5. Refer to Search Sheet 2, Question 9. Summarize the wisdom of Sabbath found there: _____
   _____
   _____

6. Read Exodus 23:20-23. Make a list of the warnings and the reasons for them: _____
   _____
   _____

7. Make a list of the blessings which result from listening and obeying: _____
   _____
   _____

8. Read Deuteronomy 4:5-8. How would Israel's fulfillment of covenantal responsibilities help her be a "Mysterious Melchizedek" people to other people and nations? _____
   _____
   _____

Prepare a brief presentation to share these secrets with the other "scribes." Use chalkboard or newsprint if desired.

SECRETS OF THE COVENANT – PART 3

■ "THE WISDOM OF CIVIL LAW"

1. In the nations around Israel, a slave was regarded as property. Read Exodus 21:1-11. Do Hebrew slaves seem to be considered as people or as property in this passage? _____

    Why do you think so? _____

    _____

    Read Jeremiah 34:8-22, especially vs. 17. Why do you think this law is so important to God?

    _____

2. Human life was of great importance in covenantal law. To preserve and protect life, the covenant included one punishment per crime. Read Exodus 21:12-32. Do you think the punishments fit the crimes? _____ Why or why not? _____

    _____

    Note vss. 23-25. Compare with Matthew 5:38-42. Are these laws more about fairness and retaliation OR about peace with justice? _____ Why do you think so? _____

    _____

3. Protection of property was also an important part of the covenant. Read Exodus 21:33 - 22:15. Note especially vss. 5, 7, 9. What do they say about the nature of restitution? _____

    _____

4. Read Exodus 22:16-31. Note especially vss. 22-27. What do they tell us about God's concern for the weak or vulnerable people in society? _____

    Compare with Matthew 25:31-45: _____

5. Read Exodus 23:1-9. Note vss. 4-5. How does the covenant teach people to treat those who are hostile to them? _____

    Is this a matter of fairness OR justice and mercy? _____

    Compare with Jesus' teaching in Matthew 5:44_____

    _____

6. Israel's covenantal civil law was given 1500 years before Jesus' earthly ministry. Now, nearly 3500 years since it was given, how does its wisdom compare with the laws of your country? _____

    _____

    Would you agree with Psalm 119:144, 152, and 160? _____

7. What part does the law play in the Shepherding relationship of God with people? (Psalm 119:176)

    _____

    According to Psalm 119:165, where was the covenantal law designed to lead? _____

    _____

Prepare a brief presentation to share these secrets with the other "scribes." Chalkboard or newsprint may be used if desired.

SECRETS OF THE COVENANT – PART 4

■ "THREE FEASTS TO REMEMBER"

1. The *first* feast is the **Feast of Unleavened Bread**, celebrated for seven days, usually during mid-March to mid-April. Read Exodus 23:15 and 12:17. What event was this feast designed to help Israel remember?

   _____

   Describe the way this feast was to be celebrated: (Exodus 12:14-20 _____

   _____

   Throughout history, cakes baked of grain were a dietary mainstay. But it was the ancient Egyptians who first milled flour and made and ate bread with yeast. They also used the leavened bread as money, "paying the laborers who built the pyramids three loaves of bread" each day *(Betty Crocker's New Picture Cookbook,* McGraw Hill Book Co., Inc., 1961, p. 97). While the Hebrew people learned this art from the Egyptians, the suddenness of the exodus did not allow time for baking yeast bread. What other reasons might there be for remembering God's deliverance in the exodus with unleavened bread? _____

   _____

   What did yeast later symbolize? (Luke 12:1, 1 Corinthians 5:8) _____

   _____

2. The *second* feast was the **Feast Of Harvest** (Exodus 23:16a) celebrating the firstfruits of crops. This was also called the **"Feast Of Weeks"** because it was held seven weeks after the Feast of Unleavened Bread. This usually came sometime between mid-May and mid-June. Later, this feast was used to remember the giving of the covenantal law at Mt. Sinai. Later still, this feast was called P_____ (Acts 2:1, 20:16) meaning "fifty" for the number of days from the Feast of Unleavened Bread. Describe how to celebrate the **Feast of Harvest/Firstfruits/Weeks**: (Leviticus 23:15-21) _____

   _____

   _____

3. The *third* feast was the **Feast Of Ingathering**, also called the **"Feast Of Tabernacles (or Booths)."** It was celebrated for a week usually falling around mid-September to mid-October. Read Leviticus 23:33-43. What was its purpose? _____

   _____

   Describe how it was celebrated: _____

   _____

   What promise did God give for keeping the feasts? (Exodus 34:24) _____

   _____

   What is the significance of eating and drinking together in Genesis 26:30 and 31:53-54? _____

   _____

   In 1 Corinthians 11:25-26? _____

   _____

Prepare a brief presentation to share these secrets with the other "scribes." Use chalkboard or newsprint if desired.

■ "A SUMMARY – THE TEN COMMANDMENTS"

1. The Ten Commandments are a summary of God's covenantal agreement with the people. Read them in Exodus 20:1-21 or Deuteronomy 5:1-21. The other laws expand on this summary.

2. The Ten Commandments were summarized into a shorter statement which was memorized by the Hebrew people. This can be found in Deuteronomy 6:4-9. It is known as the "Shema" (pronounced "shah-mah") meaning "hear." Compare Deuteronomy 6:4-5 with Mark 12:29-30 (also Matthew 22:37-40 and Luke 10:25-28). What two major parts are identified in these summaries? *Love God; Love others/neighbors*

3. Look up the following verses. What do they reveal about the intent, spirit, unity and timelessness of the Law?
   Leviticus 19:17-18 *No hate in heart, rebuke frankly, no revenge*
   Matthew 19:17c *If you want to enter life, obey commandments*
   Romans 13:8-10 *Love is the summary and fulfillment of the law*
   Galatians 5:13-14 *Serve one another in love; love neighbor as self*
   James 2:8 *Royal law = love neighbor as self, without favoritism*

4. How do the Ten Commandments apply the "law of love" to:
   People's relationship to God? *Love and trust God, no idols or misuse of God's name*
   Family relationships *Holiness, Sabbath rest, honor father and mother*
   Regard for human life? *No murder (physical, emotional or spiritual)*
   Sexuality? *No adultery or misuse of gift of human sexuality*
   Property? *No stealing or coveting*
   Speech? *No false testimony, lying*
   Thought? *No wanting what we do not have*

5. Covenants were a way of life in Eastern culture. They typically contained five parts as listed below. Using Exodus 20:1-21, identify these parts in the Ten Commandments:
   - Statement of author (vs. 2a) *I am the Lord your God*
   - Statement of history of relationship between covenanting parties prior to offering the covenant - specifically stating the grace and mercy given by the author (2b) *God brought the people out of slavery in Egypt*
   - Responsibilities of recipients (3-17) *Love God; Love neighbor*
   - Curses for breaking (5, 7b) *Punishment for idolatry, hatred, misuse of God's name*
   - Blessings for keeping (6, 12b) *God's love for keeping; long life for honoring parents*

Prepare a brief presentation to share these secrets with the other "scribes." Use chalkboard or newsprint if desired.

■ "THE CENTRALITY OF WORSHIP"

To be a "Kingdom (kin-dom) of Priests" - a "Mysterious Melchizedek" people - there needed to be a Source of strength and wisdom. There needed to be a way to stay in touch with that Source.

1. Read Exodus 19:4-6. Why was it important for the people to do what God said ? _God is jealous (watchful, holy), punishing sin, loving and blessing devotion and obedience_

2. What preparations were needed before worship? (Exodus 19:10-15) _Wash clothes, be ready, set limits, ram's horn blast, abstinence from sexual relations_

3. What do you think was the purpose of these preparations? (Jeremiah 4:14) _They symbolize washing evil from the heart and wicked thoughts from the mind_

4. How was stewardship of the land related to worship and Sabbath? (Exodus 23:10-13) _Letting the land rest each seventh year was like resting each seventh day_

5. Refer to Search Sheet 2, Question 9. Summarize the wisdom of Sabbath found there: _490 years of unkept Sabbaths result in 70 years of exile, one-seventh_

6. Read Exodus 23:20-23. Make a list of the warnings and the reasons for them: _Do not rebel; no forgiveness. Do not worship Canaanite gods or make covenant with other people or gods; they'll cause you to sin_

7. Make a list of the blessings which result from listening and obeying: _Listen and do; protection from enemies. Worship God; God will bless with food and water, take away sickness, barrenness, give full life span, destroy enemies gradually so land does not become desolate_

8. Read Deuteronomy 4:5-8. How would Israel's fulfillment of covenantal responsibilities help her be a "Mysterious Melchizedek" people to other people and nations? _Obedience to God and the law will show wisdom and understanding to other nations, showing God is near in righteous (and advanced) laws_

Prepare a brief presentation to share these secrets with the other "scribes." Use chalkboard or newsprint if desired.

SECRETS OF THE COVENANT – PART 3
ANSWER GUIDE

■ "THE WISDOM OF CIVIL LAW"

1. In the nations around Israel, a slave was regarded as property. Read Exodus 21:1-11. Do Hebrew slaves seem to be considered as people or as property in this passage? _People_
Why do you think so? _They have rights, spouses stay together, freedom in the seventh year, no selling to foreigners, freedom if neglected_
Read Jeremiah 34:8-22, especially vs. 17. Why do you think this law is so important to God? _As you do to others, so God will do to you under terms of covenant_

2. Human life was of great importance in covenantal law. To preserve and protect life, the covenant included one punishment per crime. Read Exodus 21:12-32. Do you think the punishments fit the crimes? _Yes_ Why or why not? _There are allowances for first crimes, more severe punishment for repeat crimes_
Note vss. 23-25. Compare with Matthew 5:38-42. Are these laws more about fairness and retaliation OR about peace with justice? _Peace with justice_ Why do you think so? _Avoids court costs, deals effectively with root of problem, fits crime to law of love_

3. Protection of property was also an important part of the covenant. Read Exodus 21:33-22:15. Note especially vss. 5, 7, 9. What do they say about the nature of restitution? _Offender must restore from "the best" or "double;" restitution is a serious matter!_

4. Read Exodus 22:16-31. Note especially vss. 22-27. What do they tell us about God's concern for the weak or vulnerable people in society? _Compassionate God's primary concern_ Compare with Matthew 25:31-45: _Care of vulnerable is separation criteria_

5. Read Exodus 23:1-9. Note vss. 4-5. How does the covenant teach people to treat those who are hostile to them? _Help enemy; return enemy's ox or donkey if you find_
Is this a matter of fairness OR justice and mercy? _Justice and mercy_
Compare with Jesus' teaching in Matthew 5:44 _Love your enemies; pray for those who persecute you_

6. Israel's covenantal civil law was given 1500 years before Jesus' earthly ministry. Now, nearly 3500 years since it was given, how does its wisdom compare with the laws of your country? _It is the basis for many of our laws_
Would you agree with Psalm 119:144, 152, and 160? _Eternally right – yes!_

7. What part does the law play in the Shepherding relationship of God with people? (Psalm 119:176) _We stray; God seeks, recalls commandments, restores_
According to Psalm 119:165, where was the covenantal law designed to lead? _Great peace_

Prepare a brief presentation to share these secrets with the other "scribes." Chalkboard or newsprint may be used if desired.

■ **"THREE FEASTS TO REMEMBER"**

1. The **first** feast is the **Feast of Unleavened Bread**, celebrated for seven days, usually during mid-March to mid-April. Read Exodus 23:15 and 12:17. What event was this feast designed to help Israel remember? *The day God brought Israel out of Egypt*

   Describe the way this feast was to be celebrated: (Exodus 12:14-20 *Eat bread without yeast 7 days; rid house of yeast; Assemblies 1st and 7th days; no work on these days*

   Throughout history, cakes baked of grain were a dietary mainstay. But it was the ancient Egyptians who first milled flour and made and ate bread with yeast. They also used the leavened bread as money, "paying the laborers who built the pyramids three loaves of bread" each day *(Betty Crocker's New Picture Cookbook,* McGraw Hill Book Co., Inc., 1961, p. 97*)*. While the Hebrew people learned this art from the Egyptians, the suddenness of the exodus did not allow time for baking yeast bread. What other reasons might there be for remembering God's deliverance in the exodus with unleavened bread? *Separating nationality with Egypt, establishing a new nation*
   What did yeast later symbolize? (Luke 12:1, 1 Corinthians 5:8) *hypocrisy, malice and wickedness vs. sincerity and truth*

2. The **second** feast was the **Feast Of Harvest** (Exodus 23:16a) celebrating the firstfruits of crops. This was also called the **"Feast Of Weeks"** because it was held seven weeks after the Feast of Unleavened Bread. This usually came sometime between mid-May and mid-June. Later, this feast was used to remember the giving of the covenantal law at Mt. Sinai. Later still, this feast was called *Pentecost* (Acts 2:1, 20:16) meaning "fifty" for the number of days from the Feast of Unleavened Bread. Describe how to celebrate the **Feast of Harvest/Firstfruits/Weeks:** (Leviticus 23:15-21) *Offering: new grain, 2 loaves of yeast bread, 7 male lambs, one bull, 2 rams as burnt offering, assembly, no work*

3. The **third** feast was the **Feast Of Ingathering**, also called the **"Feast Of Tabernacles (or Booths)."** It was celebrated for a week usually falling around mid-September to mid-October. Read Leviticus 23:33-43. What was its purpose? *To remember living in tents during exodus*
   Describe how it was celebrated: *1st and 8th day Sacred Assembly, no work, 7 days of offerings, choice fruit on 1st day, rejoice before Lord, live in booths*

   What promise did God give for keeping the feasts? (Exodus 34:24) *God will drive out enemies, and no one will covet Israel's land*
   What is the significance of eating and drinking together in Genesis 26:30 and 31:53-54? *Oath of peace-making, to secure an oath*
   In 1 Corinthians 11:25-26? *Remember New Covenant, Christ's body/blood; proclaim it*

Prepare a brief presentation to share these secrets with the other "scribes." Use chalkboard or newsprint if desired.

SEARCH SHEET 11

This Search Sheet offers an opportunity to review what has been studied in the first eleven sessions. Use the word list below to write a summary of what you have learned in the previous sessions:

SHEPHERD	COVENANT	MOSES
SHEEP	MYSTERIOUS	OPPRESSION
CREATION	MELCHIZEDEK	RED SEA
GARDEN	HOLY	DELIVERANCE
REBELLED	PRIESTLY	LAW
FLOOD	PATRIARCHS	OBEY
CLEANSING	JOSEPH	LIFE
ARK	EGYPT	PEACE

_____

_____

_____

_____

_____

_____

_____

_____

_____

_____

_____

_____

_____

_____

_____

_____

_____

_____

_____

_____

_____

SEARCH SHEET 11
ANSWER GUIDE

This Search Sheet offers an opportunity to review what has been studied in the first eleven sessions. Use the word list below to write a summary of what you have learned in the previous sessions:

SHEPHERD	COVENANT	MOSES
SHEEP	MYSTERIOUS	OPPRESSION
CREATION	MELCHIZEDEK	RED SEA
GARDEN	HOLY	DELIVERANCE
REBELLED	PRIESTLY	LAW
FLOOD	PATRIARCHS	OBEY
CLEANSING	JOSEPH	LIFE
ARK	EGYPT	PEACE

*The Wisdom Series began by glimpsing the relational wisdom of God as **SHEPHERD** and people as **SHEEP**. Beginning at the beginning of the Scriptures, Sessions 2 and 3 explored the wisdom of God in **CREATION**. God prepared a beautiful place for people to live and work; this was pictured as a **GARDEN** in Session 4. The peace and balance of this beautiful place was shattered when people **REBELLED** against the wisdom of God which preserved its beauty.*

*Through the waters of the **FLOOD**, God provided **CLEANSING** of the earth, preserving the faithful Noah family in the **ARK** they had built. Ten generations later, God offered an everlasting **COVENANT** to childless Abram and Sarai, promising to make of them a great nation. This special promise with blessing was God's "rod and staff" to fulfill this nation's purpose of becoming **MYSTERIOUS MELCHIZEDEK** people: **HOLY** and **PRIESTLY** people to other nations. This promise with purpose and prophecy went forward through the **PATRIARCHS**. Faithful **JOSEPH** was in a position to feed 66 covenantal family members (and the whole world) in **EGYPT** during a famine. They settled in the fertile farmland of Goshen. There they grew in numbers to 2 million, causing the threatened Egyptians to enslave them.*

*God shaped a leader named **MOSES** to lead the people out from this **OPPRESSION**, through the waters of the **RED SEA**. Here they experienced God's mighty hand and outstretched arm of **DELIVERANCE**. In the desert, they experienced God's miraculous provision for them and heard the terms of their covenant of grace in the **LAW** given from thundering Mt. Sinai. They accepted the responsibilities, promising to **OBEY**, shepherding other nations in ways of **LIFE** and **PEACE**.*

DAILY SCRIPTURE
READINGS • WEEK 11

THE **AWE REVERENCE WONDER** AT THE **NEARNESS HOLINESS BEAUTY** OF GOD = THE BEGINNING OF **WISDOM**

(PROVERBS 1:7A)

	HEBREW SCRIPTURE	NEW TESTAMENT	PSALM	PROVERBS
Day 1	Numbers 16:41-18:32	Mark 16:1-20	55:1-23	11:7
Day 2	Numbers 19:1-20:29	Luke 1:1-25	56:1-13	11:8
Day 3	Numbers 21:1-22:20	Luke 1:26-56	57:1-11	11:9-11
Day 4	Numbers 22:21-23:30	Luke 1:57-80	58:1-11	11:12-13
Day 5	Numbers 24:1-25:18	Luke 2:1-35	59:1-17	11:14
Day 6	Numbers 26:1-51	Luke 2:36-52	60:1-12	11:15
Day 7	Numbers 26:52-28:15	Luke 3:1-22	61:1-8	11:16-17

Personal Notes and Glimpses of Wisdom:

"I wonder what would happen if every sheep knew the secrets of wisdom..."

SESSION 12 • A CENTER FOR WISDOM AND GLORY

The aim of this session
is to discover individual and corporate centers for God's wisdom and glory.

MATERIALS NEEDED

Hymnals
Accompaniment
Bibles
Newsprint or chalkboard
Crayons
Sheets of plain paper for each participant
Completed Search Sheet 11
Completed Insights from Daily Scripture Readings For Week 11
Copies for each participant of:
  "Lecturette With Questions"
  Search Sheet 12
  Daily Scripture Readings For Week 12

▓ ASSEMBLING

This session considers the tabernacle, the temple, and the temple within as centers of God's wisdom and glory. Allow quiet time for yourself as you prepare to lead this session. Listen for the wisdom and glory of God in your "center."

▓ THE APPROACH TO GOD   (5 to 10 minutes)

❥   With completed Search Sheet 11 in hand, invite participants to share their paragraph written from the Word Search list. After sharing, *sing a hymn* of praise and thanksgiving to God for the gifts of The Wisdom Series thus far.

▓ ENCOUNTERING THE WORD   (40 to 45 minutes)

⇨ *Distribute copies of the "Lecturette With Questions."* Assign questions to individuals or teams (allow 15 to 20 minutes). Then read through the lecturette, calling for answers to questions as indicated (15 to 20 minutes).

⇨ *Reflecting On The Temple Within:* Ask, "What shapes and colors might there be in the temple within?" Distribute plain paper and crayons and invite participants to make a design of the beauty of that inner temple. (Optional sharing may follow.)

▦ GOING FORTH IN GOD'S NAME (5 to 10 minutes)

❥ *Use Psalm 27 as a closing prayer* - in the form of a responsive reading or hymn.

❥ Distribute copies of:
      Search Sheet 12
      Daily Scripture Readings For Week 12

■ "LECTURETTE WITH QUESTIONS"

The Hebrew people's first experience in worshipping God together was at the thundering, smoking Mt. Sinai. In order for them to be "Mysterious Melchizedek" people, **showing the nations the way to peace on earth**, it was necessary for them to be **united in worshipping God**. So, while Moses was meeting with God to receive the terms of the covenant, God also told Moses to make a sanctuary, a **tabernacle** (dwelling place for God) with special furnishings. Below is a diagram of the tabernacle:

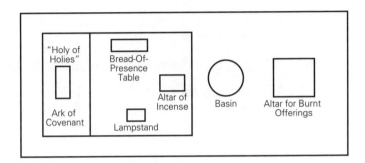

1. It began with a grass roots movement. The Israelites were to bring an offering of items needed – whatever their hearts prompted them to give. But how would they know exactly how to put the pieces together? (Exodus 25:9)

2. Why was it so important that the tabernacle be put together exactly as directed? (Hebrews 8:5)

3. The tabernacle furnishings were **symbols of God's redemptive covenant** with Israel. Consider each furnishing:
*   What did the ark symbolize? (2 Samuel 6:2)
*   What did the ark contain? (Exodus 25:16, 31:18, 1 Kings 8:9)
*   What was placed on the table? (Exodus 25:29-30, Leviticus 24:5-9)
*   What was the purpose of the lampstand? (Exodus 25:37, 27:20-21)
*   What did its light symbolize? (Exodus 29:43)
*   What does the fragrance from the altar of incense symbolize? (Building instructions, Exodus 30:34-38; see also Exodus 30:1-10, Psalm 141:2, Revelation 5:8)
*   What was the purpose of the altar of burnt offering? (Building instructions, Exodus 27:1-8; see also Leviticus 4:13-21)

4. How did nomadic shepherd people get the skills and craft abilities to make the tabernacle and furnishings? (Exodus 31:1-11)

5. When all the work on the tabernacle was completed and Moses inspected it, what did he find? (Exodus 39:42)

6. What did he do then? (Exodus 39:43)

7. How did Moses assemble the tabernacle? (Exodus 40:16,19,23,25,27,29,32)

8. How did God respond to this obedience? (Exodus 40:34-38)

9. The tabernacle was built around 1445-1440 BC. For over five centuries, it served as Israel's center of the wisdom and glory of God. After the battles led by the judges and the wars fought skillfully by King David and the Israelite army, Israel's borders were secured. The Israelites were no longer a wandering people; they settled into their promised homeland. Instead of living in tents, they built houses of stone.

Soon they desired a more permanent dwelling place for God. David purchased the land for the temple (1 Chronicles 21:18-30) and assembled skilled workers and materials for the task. But David was not allowed to build the temple. Why? (1 Chronicles 22:7-8)

10. Why was Solomon selected? (1 Chronicles 22:9-10)

11. King David gave the plans for the building of the temple and the organization of worship to his son Solomon. But where did David get the plans? (1 Chronicles 28:11-12, 19, Revelation 11:19)

12. David then called for workers to consecrate themselves for this enormous task. He led by example. What is the attitude demonstrated by David? (1 Chronicles 28:9, 29:2-3)

13. Next, the leaders gave, also leading by example. What is their response? (1 Chronicles 29:6-9)

14. Read David's prayer of praise in 1 Chronicles 29:10-19, noting especially vss. 16-17. Note the response of the people in vs. 20.

15. Read also 1 Chronicles 29:21-22. What was the mood here?

16. How is this mood related to the actions of all Israel in vs. 23, and the actions of the officers and powerful persons in vs. 24?

17. When the temple was completed and the furnishings placed inside, what happened? (1 Kings 8:10-11, 2 Chronicles 7:1-3)

18. What did Solomon do? (1 Kings 8:14, 55)

19. Note the condition for blessing in 1 Kings 8:61.

20. Note the warning and results of disobedience in 2 Chronicles 7:19-22.

The **temple** in Jerusalem, like the less permanent **tabernacle** constructed in the wilderness, was the **center** for the presence of God's wisdom and glory. (Refer to Illustration 2C for the concept of the earth's navel or center.) The Hebrew people believed Mt. Zion in Jerusalem, on which the temple was built, was **earth's navel or center**. (See Judges 9:37, Isaiah 2:3, Jeremiah 3:17, Ezekiel 5:5, 38:12.) The "Mysterious Melchizedek" people, particularly their Levitical priesthood, were specially **_blessed_ and _called_ to maintain this touchpoint** of earth with heaven, of human with divine.

This temple in Jerusalem lasted for nearly 400 years before it was destroyed by the Babylonian army in the exile. It was rebuilt some 70 years later by returning exiles. It was destroyed again and rebuilt by Herod the Great, beginning in 20 BC. The Herodian temple was the one in which Jesus learned, read Scripture, and encountered moneychangers.

21. Although Jesus worshipped at this temple, he identified the center of God's wisdom and glory elsewhere. Where? (John 2:21)

22. Where does the Apostle Paul say the temple is? (1 Corinthians 3:16, 6:19, 2 Corinthians 6:16, Ephesians 2:21)

23. In John's vision of the Holy City, the New Jerusalem coming down out of heaven, where is the temple? (Revelation 21:22)

■ "LECTURETTE WITH QUESTIONS" (Answer Guide)

1. *As God told Moses.*

2. *It was a copy of the heavenly sanctuary.*

3. • *The throne of God*
   • *Stone tablets of covenantal law*
   • *Plates for incense, bowls for drink offerings, and bread of the Presence*
   • *To give light continually*
   • *The glory of God*
   • *Prayers of the people/saints*
   • *Sacrifice of animals as atonement for sins and receiving God's forgiveness*

4. *God gives skills, fills people with divine spirit to do tasks.*

5. *People had done work just as God had commanded Moses.*

6. *Moses blessed the people.*

7. *"Just as God had commanded."*

8. *The glory of God filled the tabernacle.*

9. *David had shed too much blood in his great wars.*

10. *Solomon was a man of peace.*

11. *David received through God's direction - a copy of heaven's temple.*

12. *Single-mindedness, willing heart, giving his own treasures to God with great devotion.*

13. *Freewill offerings, willingly and joyfully given with great rejoicing.*

14. *Gifts "come from your own hand and is all your own," from upright hearts; people blessed the Lord, bowed heads, prostrated themselves.*

15. *Sacrificing with great joy!*

16. *All obeyed; officers pledge allegiance to king.*

17. *Fire from heaven consumed offering; glory of God filled temple; people bowed, gave thanks.*

18. *Solomon blessed the assembly while they stood.*

19. *Condition for blessing is complete devotion to God; obedience.*

20. *If people worship other gods, they will be plucked up and the temple will be cast out of God's sight.*

21. *Christ's body.*

22. *Within our bodies – we are the temple of the living God, joined by Christ to grow into holiness.*

23. *The Temple is the Lord God the Almighty and the Lamb.*

SEARCH SHEET 12

1. The front of the tabernacle, where the Holy of Holies was located, faced which direction? (Exodus 27:13) _____
Camping on this side was a favored location. Who camped there? (Numbers 3:38)
_____

   Which way did the temple face? (Ezekiel 44:1, 46:1, 47:1) _____ Where was its inner court located? (Ezekiel 40:32) _____ At which gate did the prince enter to bring an offering? (Ezekiel 46:12) _____

   What significance is attached to this direction in the following verses:

   • Genesis 3:24 _____

   • Exodus 27:13 _____

   • Exodus 14:21 _____

2. Interestingly, the birth of Jesus is announced to the Magi by a _____ (Matthew 2:2). Jesus spoke of his coming again as _____
(Matthew 24:27). And in John's vision, the angel with the seal of the living God comes from the_____ (Revelation 7:2).

3. Returning to tabernacle/temple imagery, look at the diagram of the tabernacle above. Its dimensions were 100 cubits long and 50 cubits wide (1 cubit = 18 inches). How large was the entrance to the court-yard? (Exodus 27:16) _____

   Imagine God sitting on the throne (the Holy of Holies) in the tabernacle, with the courtyard walls repre-senting the arms of God. What gesture does this suggest God is making to the people via the taber-nacle? _____
Try this gesture with your arms. To complete this symbolism, look up the following verses:

   • Exodus 6:6-7 _____

   • Deuteronomy 4:34 _____

   • Deuteronomy 5:15 _____

   • Deuteronomy 7:19 _____

   • Deuteronomy 11:2 _____

   • Deuteronomy 33:27 (use King James Version) _____

   • Psalm 77:15 _____

   • Isaiah 40:11 _____

   • Isaiah 59:15b-16 _____

   • Luke 1:51-55 _____

   • John 12:38 _____

   • Acts 13:17 _____

SEARCH SHEET 12
ANSWER GUIDE

1. The front of the tabernacle, where the Holy of Holies was located, faced which direction? (Exodus 27:13) *East* Camping on this side was a favored location. Who camped there? (Numbers 3:38) *Moses, Aaron and Aaron's sons*

   Which way did the temple face? (Ezekiel 44:1, 46:1, 47:1) *East* Where was its inner court located? (Ezekiel 40:32) *East side* At which gate did the prince enter to bring an offering? (Ezekiel 46:12) *Gate facing east*

   What significance is attached to this direction in the following verses:

   - Genesis 3:24 *Angel guards tree of life at east end of Eden*

   - Exodus 27:13 *Location of the court on the front*

   - Exodus 14:21 *Lord drove Red Sea back by a strong east wind*

2. Interestingly, the birth of Jesus is announced to the Magi by a *star in the east* (Matthew 2:2). Jesus spoke of his coming again as *lightning coming from the east* (Matthew 24:27). And in John's vision, the angel with the seal of the living God comes from the *east* (Revelation 7:2).

   Returning to tabernacle/temple imagery, look at the diagram of the tabernacle above. Its dimensions were 100 cubits long and 50 cubits wide (1 cubit = 18 inches). How large was the entrance to the court-yard? (Exodus 27:16) *20 cubits*

3. Imagine God sitting on the throne (the Holy of Holies) in the tabernacle, with the courtyard walls repre-senting the arms of God. What gesture does this suggest God is making to the people via the taber-nacle? *"Come unto me" – offering a hug*
   Try this gesture with your arms. To complete this symbolism, look up the following verses:

   - Exodus 6:6-7 *"I will redeem you with an outstretched arm"*

   - Deuteronomy 4:34 *God taking nation with mighty hand and outstretched arm*

   - Deuteronomy 5:15 *God delivered Israel with mighty hand and outstretched arm*

   - Deuteronomy 7:19 *When afraid, remember God's mighty hand and outstretched arm*

   - Deuteronomy 11:2 *Acknowledge the Lord's mighty hand and outstretched arm*

   - Deuteronomy 33:27 (use King James Version) *Underneath are the everlasting arms*

   - Psalm 77:15 *Redeemed people with strong arm*

   - Isaiah 40:11 *Like a shepherd, God will gather lambs in arms*

   - Isaiah 59:15b-16 *God's arm brought victory/justice where there was none*

   - Luke 1:51-55 *Mary's Magnificat – strength of God's arm brought justice and mercy*

   - John 12:38 *To whom has the arm of the Lord been revealed?*

   - Acts 13:17 *God led people out of Egypt with uplifted arm*

DAILY SCRIPTURE
READINGS • WEEK 12

THE **AWE REVERENCE WONDER** AT THE **NEARNESS HOLINESS BEAUTY** OF GOD = THE BEGINNING OF **WISDOM**

(PROVERBS 1:7A)

	HEBREW SCRIPTURE	NEW TESTAMENT	PSALM	PROVERBS
Day 1	Numbers 28:16-29:40	Luke 3:23-38	62:1-12	11:18-19
Day 2	Numbers 30:1-31:54	Luke 4:1-30	63:1-11	11:20-21
Day 3	Numbers 32:1-33:39	Luke 4:31-5:11	64:1-10	11:22
Day 4	Numbers 33:40-35:34	Luke 5:12-28	65:1-13	11:23
Day 5	Num. 36:1-Deut. 1:46	Luke 5:29-6:11	66:1-20	11:24-26
Day 6	Deut. 2:1-3:29	Luke 6:12-38	67:1-7	11:27
Day 7	Deut. 4:1-49	Luke 6:39-7:10	68:1-18	11:28

Personal Notes and Glimpses of Wisdom:

"I wonder where my center really is..."

_____

_____

_____

_____

_____

_____

_____

_____

_____

SESSION 13 • THE WISDOM OF GOD'S FORGIVENESS

The aim of this session is to look at the way Holy God provided for forgiveness and restored community when people sinned and turned away from the covenant.

MATERIALS NEEDED

Hymnals
Accompaniment
Bibles
Newsprint or chalkboard
Materials for **Stations of Sacrifice**
1. Pieces of stew meat, tealight candle in fire-safe container, matches, tongs
2. Saltines, tealight candle in fire-safe container, matches, tongs, small bottle of juice, small cups or glasses
3. Pieces of stew meat and saltines, tealight candle in fire-safe container, matches, tongs
4. Same as number 3 above, with flour in metal container instead of saltines
5. Same as number 1 above

Instruction cards for each station (copied and cut)
Backpack
Plain paper, pencils or pens
"Questions For Reflection" printed on chalkboard or newsprint
Completed Search Sheet 12
Completed Insights from Daily Scripture Readings For Week 12
Copies for each participant of:
    Search Sheet 13
    Daily Scripture Readings For Week 13

▨ ASSEMBLING

The sacrificial system is difficult for post-Easter people to understand. Yet it is essential to explore its meaning to the people who first received it. Pray that all may experience the holiness of God, come to a new appreciation of the mercy of God, and feel the forgiveness of God in this session.

(If space permits, set up Stations of Sacrifice before the session begins, placing materials and cards at each of the five stations.)

▨ THE APPROACH TO GOD   (5 to 10 minutes)

❥ *Introduce the session* as "exploring the ancient sacrificial system." One of the keys to understanding this system is **the blood**. Look for the wisdom of God as you sing *"Nothing But The Blood"* or *"There Is A Fountain Filled With Blood"* (or another hymn regarding the significance of the blood).

❥ *Offer a prayer* that the power of Christ's **blood** and of God's **forgiveness** be felt in your life and the lives of participants.

▩ ENCOUNTERING THE WORD   (40 to 45 minutes)

⇨ Briefly review Search Sheet 12, inviting questions and comments.

⇨ Make a transition to *"The Sacrificial System,"* and lead participants through the Sacrificial Stations, Day of Atonement, and Questions for Reflection.

▩ GOING FORTH IN GOD'S NAME   (5 to 10 minutes)

❥ Close with David's prayer of forgiveness, Psalm 51, as a responsive reading or a hymn based on this Scripture. Note especially verse 17. Allow moments of silence.

❥ Distribute copies of:
    Search Sheet 13
    Daily Scripture Readings For Week 13

■ "THE SACRIFICIAL SYSTEM"

Sacrificial Stations: (about 15 minutes)

*(Place the **materials** and **cards** at each station, if this was not done at the beginning of the session. Introduce the Stations as follows.)*

The Book of Leviticus with its sacrificial laws seems violent and repulsive at first. But if we look beyond the gore, it gives a deeper understanding of the death of Jesus Christ.

Israel's God was different than the idols of other nations. God is a *living* God – one who wants to walk and talk with people, one who wants people to live in wholeness, peace and unity. God is a *holy* God. God hates sin – it destroys life, communion with God and God-centered community.

God gave people freedom of choice. All people chose their own way, breaking communion and community. God refused to give up. Like a Shepherd, God provided a way to restore lost sheep – sinful people. But the way was costly. The punishment for sin was *death* – a life for a life. God in mercy offered *substitution*. Ritual sacrifice was God's way of accepting the life of an animal, a bird, or a plant *as a substitute* for the life of the sinner. (Note that an animal had to be without defect or blemish!) The person bringing the offering would lay a hand on the head of the animal acknowledging that it was a *substitute* for his/her life.

(Invite participants to rotate through the stations. The stations do not need to be experienced in numerical order.)

Day Of Atonement: (about 10 minutes)

(Introduce this experience as follows.)

While sacrifices were made at the tabernacle throughout the year, there was one special day, the tenth day of the seventh month, for atonement of the sins of the whole Israelite community. This was called the *Day Of Atonement*. (Leviticus 16)

Only the high priest could do this. It was a very special day – the day the high priest entered the Holy of Holies (or Most Holy Place) where the Ark of the Covenant was kept. This was the innermost place where God met Israel's special intercessor. It was not something to be taken lightly.

The high priest began with ritual bathing. Then he put on special sacred garments, offered a young bull as a burnt offering for his sins and the sins of his household *(note that Israel's priesthood was not a celibate priesthood).*

Then the high priest took two goats and cast lots to decide which would be for *sacrifice* and which would be the *scapegoat*. The *sacrificial goat* was slaughtered ceremonially; the priests, in reverence for all life as God's gift, slaughtered in a way which was painless to the animal. The goat's *blood* was sprinkled on the atonement cover of the Most Holy Place, thus making atonement for the people's **uncleanness, wickedness, and rebellion.**

The high priest then laid both hands on the head of the *scapegoat* and confessed over it all the *wickedness and rebellion of the community*. Then an appointed person led the *scapegoat*, laden with the sins of the people, to a solitary place in the desert - a practical and picturesque way of demonstrating transfer and removal of sins.

*(Distribute plain paper and pencils or pens. Invite each participant to write on the paper the ways the group sins and rebels against God. Ask for a volunteer to be the **scapegoat** or offer to do so yourself. Put the backpack on the **scapegoat**. All other participants put their hands on the **scapegoat's** head, name their corporate sins, crumple their papers and stuff them in the backpack. Then ask another participant to lead the scapegoat away from the group where he or she deposits the stuffed backpack.)*

(Announce:) With their sin and shame cleansed, ***lifeblood*** shed for their sins, and their sins transferred and removed, the people experience ***AT-ONE-MENT*** with God, each other, and the earth, as in the beginning.

Questions For Reflection: (15 to 20 minutes)

1. How did it feel to have your sins transferred and removed?

   (Note: The remaining questions may be written on chalkboard or newsprint and assigned to individuals or teams, followed by group sharing.)

2. Why was the shedding of **blood** necessary? (Leviticus 17:11, Hebrews 9:22)

3. What is the relationship between repentance (turning away from sin and back toward God), forgiveness, and healing? (2 Chronicles 7:14)

4. God required high standards for the Levitical priests who led the "Mysterious Melchizedek" people. Read Ezekiel 44:23 and tell why you think this is so.

5. Of what importance were the **attitude** and **actions** of those seeking forgiveness through sacrifice? (Leviticus 5:5, Numbers 5:5-7, 1 Samuel 15:22-23, Psalm 51:17, Isaiah 1:11-17, Jeremiah 7:22-23, Matthew 5:23-24)

■ "INSTRUCTION CARDS FOR STATIONS OF SACRIFICE"

1. Burnt Offering   (Leviticus 1, 6:8-13)

- Place your finger on a piece of meat (representing a bull, ram, or male bird). Remember that an animal's life has been given for yours (the priests have sprinkled its blood).
- Worship God by asking forgiveness for unintended sin in general. Express your dedication, renewed commitment, and total surrender to God in your life.
- Using tongs, pick up the piece of meat you touched and burn it over the candle. The aroma symbolizes your prayer rising to God.
- Leave the "burnt" meat at the altar (put it back on plate).

2. Grain Offering   (Leviticus 2, 6:14-23)

- The saltine is a "wafer" made without yeast or honey (like other nations used in fermented products which they used to excess), seasoned with salt (symbol of the covenant and source of healing).
- Worship God by giving thanks for all the good things God provides. Express your devotion to God.
- Using tongs, toast a saltine over the candle. The aroma is your thanksgiving ascending to God. (Do not eat the saltine; place it back on the plate, leaving the rest for the priest.)
- Pour a small amount of juice into the glass. Lift the glass, thereby dedicating all the drink offering to God. (Be priestly; drink the juice.)

3. Peace or Fellowship Offering   (Leviticus 3, 7:11-34)

- Choose a piece of meat OR a saltine (grain). Lay your finger on it symbolizing its substitution for your life. Wave your offering before the Lord.
- Give thanks for the restoration of a right relationship with God (fellowship). Or express gratitude to God for delivering you from illness, injury, trouble, or death.
- Using tongs, roast the meat or toast the saltine over the candle flame. The aroma represents your prayer of thanksgiving rising to God. (Place the roasted meat or toasted saltine back on the plate - it is for the priests to eat.)

4. Sin Offering   (Leviticus 4:1-5:13, 6:24-30)

- Choose a piece of meat OR flour, and put it in a metal container. Place your hand on it to show it is a substitute for your life.
  The sin offering is made when a priest or leader sins unintentionally and thus brings sin on all the people. It is also made by people who sin unintentionally, when they become aware of their sins. *(Note: There is no sacrifice to atone for defiant intentional sin – Numbers 15:27-31)*
- Name an unintentional sin you have become aware of. Take tongs and roast the meat or toast the flour until the aroma rises to God with your confession. (Place the offering back on the plate. It is for the use of the priests.)

5. Guilt or Repayment Offering   (Leviticus 5:14-6:7, 7:1-6)

- Place your hand on a piece of meat to indicate the substitution of an animal's life for yours.
- Confess to God an unintentional sin which you have just become aware of, which has resulted in some kind of loss to someone else.
- Using tongs, roast the meat over the candle. The aroma represents your confession rising to God who hears and forgives.
- Place the roasted meat back on the plate. It must be given to the priests. With a guilt offering, an additional gift worth 20% of the cost of the animal is given as restitution.

1. In preparation for God's mighty act of deliverance from slavery in Egypt, the Hebrew people put **blood** on their doorposts. In meeting with God at their center, the tabernacle, the priests sprinkled blood on the altar. The people were forbidden to eat the blood (Leviticus 7:26) because "_____ is in the blood." (Leviticus 17:11) God was teaching the people the **sacredness of life,** how **sin** against one another and against God **kills life**, and how in *love* and *mercy* God **forgives** and renews life through sacrificial **substitution**.

2. God's absolute **holiness** was not something to be trifled with. What happened when priests were disobedient? (Leviticus 10:1-3) _____
What was the task of the priesthood (and the priestly people) which Nadab and Abihu's disobedience had ignored? (10:10-11) _____
_____

3. Worship with sacrificing was common in eastern religious cults. In the midst of other cults, God called Israel to be uniquely different:

COMMON	**HOLY**
• Worshipping many gods	Deuteronomy 6:4 _____
• Human sacrifice	Genesis 22:12-13, Leviticus 1:4, 18:21 _____
	_____
• Use of yeast and honey (fermentation) and wine to excess	Leviticus 2:11-13 _____
	_____
	_____
• "Fertility rites," orgies, and temple prostitution	Exodus 19:15 _____
	_____
• Magic and sorcery	Leviticus 19:31 _____
• Unrestricted sexuality	Leviticus 18:1-5, 24-30 _____

4. Scan-read Leviticus 11 through 15. What wisdom found there parallels modern prevention and medicine?_____
_____

   How might these laws bring about God's promise in Exodus 23:25-26? _____
_____

5. At the heart of the book of Leviticus (19:2) is God's call to the "Mysterious Melchizedek" people: Record it: _____

   How does this compare with Peter's call to Christians in 1 Peter 1:15-16 _____
_____

1. In preparation for God's mighty act of deliverance from slavery in Egypt, the Hebrew people put **blood** on their doorposts. In meeting with God at their center, the tabernacle, the priests sprinkled blood on the altar. The people were forbidden to eat the blood (Leviticus 7:26) because "_Life_ is in the blood." (Leviticus 17:11) God was teaching the people the **sacredness of life**, how **sin** against one another and against God **kills life**, and how in _love and mercy_ God **forgives** and renews life through sacrificial **substitution.**

2. God's absolute **holiness** was not something to be trifled with. What happened when priests were disobedient? (Leviticus 10:1-3) _Fire from God's presence consumed them, and they died_

   What was the task of the priesthood (and the priestly people) which Nadab and Abihu's disobedience had ignored? (10:10-11) _Distinguishing between **holy** and **common**, clean and unclean_

3. Worship with sacrificing was common in eastern religious cults. In the midst of other cults, God called Israel to be uniquely different:

COMMON	HOLY
• Worshipping many gods	Deuteronomy 6:4 _The Lord alone is God_
• Human sacrifice	Genesis 22:12-13, Leviticus 1:4, 18:21 _Animals as substitutes for sacrificing_
• Use of yeast and honey (fermentation) and wine to excess	Leviticus 2:11-13 _No grain offering with yeast; no leaven and honey offered by fire; salt symbolizes the covenant in offerings_
• "Fertility rites," orgies, and temple prostitution	Exodus 19:15 _Sexual abstinence before holy convocation_
• Magic and sorcery Unrestricted sexuality	Leviticus 19:31 _Sorcery defiles pure worship_ Leviticus 18:1-5, 24-30 _Sexual perversion defiles land – makes land vomit_

3. Scan-read Leviticus 11 through 15. What wisdom found there parallels modern prevention and medicine? _Diet and hygiene are common-sense methods of prevention and treatment of diseases_

   How might these laws bring about God's promise in Exodus 23:25-26? _Obedience to God's laws brings blessing, full life span, removal of sickness and barrenness_

2. At the heart of the book of Leviticus (19:2) is God's call to the "Mysterious Melchizedek" people: Record it: _Be holy because I the Lord your God am holy_

   How does this compare with Peter's call to Christians in 1 Peter 1:15-16 _Be holy as God who called you is holy_

DAILY SCRIPTURE
READINGS • WEEK 13

THE **AWE REVERENCE WONDER** AT THE **NEARNESS HOLINESS BEAUTY** OF GOD = THE BEGINNING OF **WISDOM**

(PROVERBS 1:7A)

	HEBREW SCRIPTURE	NEW TESTAMENT	PSALM	PROVERBS
Day 1	Deut. 5:1-6:25	Luke 7:11-35	68:19-35	11:29-31
Day 2	Deut. 7:1-8:20	Luke 7:36-8:3	69:1-18	12:1
Day 3	Deut 9:1-10:22	Luke 8:4-21	69:19-36	12:2-3
Day 4	Deut. 11:1-12:32	Luke 8:22-39	70:1-5	12:4
Day 5	Deut. 13:1-15:23	Luke 8:40-9:6	71:1-24	12:5-7
Day 6	Deut. 16:1-17:20	Luke 9:7-27	72:1-20	12:8-9
Day 7	Deut 18:1-20:20	Luke 9:28-50	73:1-28	12:10

Personal Notes and Glimpses of Wisdom:

"I wonder how high I can skip when I'm forgiven..."

SESSION 14 • WILDERNESS WISDOM

The aim of this session is to
search for the wisdom of God in Israel's wilderness journey.

MATERIALS NEEDED

Hymnals
Accompaniment
Bibles
Newsprint or chalkboard
"Wilderness Journey" Gameboard (colored and laminated if desired – clear Con-Tact paper works well)
Assorted coins and/or buttons
Question Cards (cut and laminated if desired)
Completed Search Sheet 13
Completed Insights from Daily Scripture Readings For Week 13
Copies for each participant of:
 Search Sheet 14
 Daily Scripture Readings For Week 14

⊞ ASSEMBLING

This session invites participants to view the whole sweep of God shepherding Israel, the "Mysterious Melchizedek" people, through the wilderness years. It offers an opportunity to review Sessions 9-13 and to demonstrate knowledge gained from Daily Scripture Readings. Enjoy the journey!

⊞ THE APPROACH TO GOD (5 to 10 minutes)

❧ **Sing a hymn** which expresses the pilgrim nature of the people of God. *"All The Way My Savior Leads Me"* is a possibility. Search the index of the hymnal for others. Follow with a ***prayer*** for insight into God's leading and guiding through this session and in daily life.

⊞ ENCOUNTERING THE WORD (40 to 45 minutes)

Search Sheet 13 illustrates the priestly task of teaching the difference between the common and the holy. Ask if there are comments or questions . . . Search Sheet 13 also prepares for some of the questions on the **"Wilderness Journey"** game.

⇨ Introduce the **"Wilderness Journey"** game. Rules are as follows:

1. You have just left the only home you have ever known, Egypt, to travel through the unfamiliar desert terrain to worship God, who has promised to lead you to a new homeland. You stand on the west bank of the Red Sea, while the Egyptian army thunders toward you. Select a coin or button as your gamepiece. Take turns drawing cards (one card per player), and proceed through the Red Sea as indicated in Rule 2.

2. Unless otherwise stated, move forward **three spaces** for each correct answer you give, **two spaces** for each correct answer you receive from comrades on the journey, and **one space** for each answer you or your comrades need to look up in the Bible. If the answer is received from the leader with answer sheet, stay where you are.

3. The first one to arrive at the Gateway to the Promised Land is the "Most Mysterious Melchizedek" person who then assists comrades until all arrive at the Gateway.

⇨ Playing proceeds until all arrive at the Gateway. Use cards in numerical order. Start through a second time if needed.

⇨ When all players arrive at the Gateway to the Promised Land, use chalkboard or newsprint to list their responses to the following:

1. What was the most difficult part of the journey for you?

2. How do you see God's leading through the wilderness experience?

GOING FORTH IN GOD'S NAME   (5 to 10 minutes)

❧ *Sing a hymn* such as *"Where He Leads Me, I Will Follow,"* or *"He Leadeth Me,"* (pardoning the lack of inclusive language – or substituting "God" for "He").

❧ *Close with a prayer of thanksgiving* for God's leading. Incorporate into the prayer the "difficult parts" of the journey named by participants.

❧ Distribute copies of:
    Search Sheet 14
    Daily Scripture Readings For Week 14

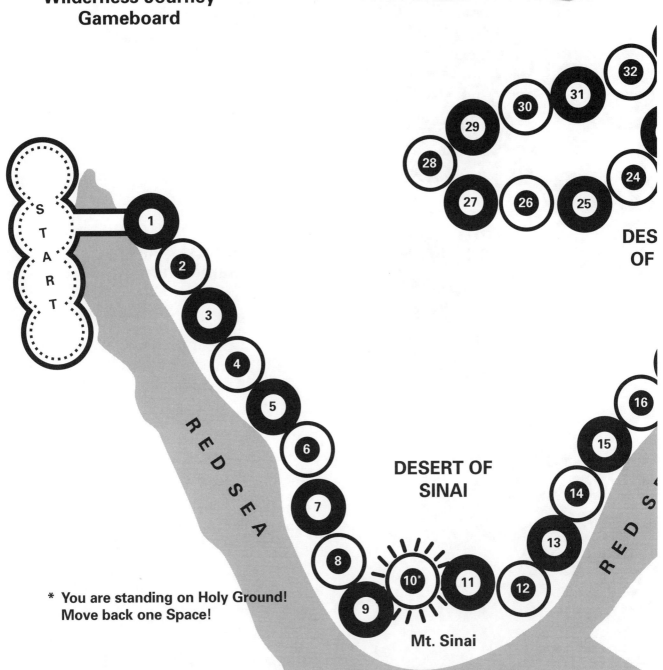

Wilderness Journey Gameboard

MEDITERRANEAN SEA

RED SEA

DESERT OF SINAI

Mt. Sinai

DESERT OF

RED SEA

* You are standing on Holy Ground!
Move back one Space!

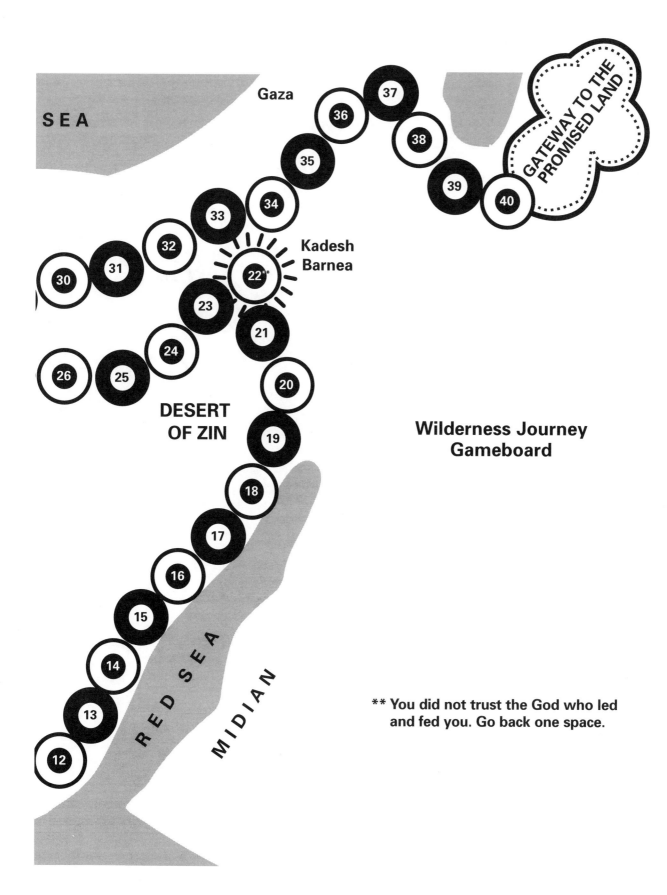

SEA

Gaza

Kadesh
Barnea

GATEWAY TO THE
PROMISED LAND

DESERT
OF ZIN

RED SEA

MIDIAN

**Wilderness Journey
Gameboard**

** You did not trust the God who led
and fed you. Go back one space.

■ "QUESTION CARDS"

1. What did the people of God remove from their houses for seven days before they left slavery in Egypt? (Exodus 12:15-20, 13:3-7)

2. What was put on the top and sides of doorframes the night before God's people left Egypt? (Exodus 12:7, 21-23)

3. What was the last of the ten plagues God brought on stubborn Pharaoh and Egypt? (Exodus 11:4-8, 12:29-30)

4. Whose bones did Moses take with him out of Egypt? (Exodus 13:19)

5. Why did God lead the people on the "long route" into the desert, toward the Red Sea? (Exodus 13:17-18) ADVANCE 2 EXTRA SPACES

6. God drove back the Red Sea waters with a strong wind from which direction? (Exodus 14:21)

7. The prophetess _____ led the people in singing and dancing with joy for God's salvation at the Red Sea. (Exodus 15:20-21)

8. When the waters at Marah proved bitter, what way did God show Moses to make them sweet? (Exodus 15:23-25)

9. In what visible way did God go ahead of the people to show them the way by day and by night? (Exodus 13:21-22)

10. For 40 years, God rained a mysterious bread each morning except Sabbath. What was it called? (Exodus 16:31)

11. What happened when the people tried to keep the "bread" overnight? (Exodus 16:20)

16. What wisdom did Moses' father-in-law, Jethro give Moses when he visited? (Exodus 18:17-23)

12. When the people were hungry for meat, how did God satisfy them? (Exodus 16:13)

17. Before giving them the terms of the covenant, God called the people to be a "kingdom (kin-dom) of _____" (Exodus 19:6)

13. Manna was given to teach that "man does not live by bread alone but by __ _____" (Deuteronomy 8:3) ADVANCE 2 EXTRA SPACES

18. What did the people do to get ready to listen to God at the mountain? (Exodus 19:10, 14-15)

14. When there was no water at Rephidim, how did God provide? (Exodus 17:6)

19. With what two "laws" did Jesus summarize the Ten Commandments? (Matthew 22:37-39)

15. When Moses sent Joshua to fight the Amalekites, how did God help through Moses? (Exodus 17:8-15)

20. On what were the Ten Commandments written? (Exodus 31:18)

21. What did Aaron and the people build while Moses was with God on the mountain? (Exodus 32:2-4)

22. What did Moses do with the tablets when he came down from the mountain and saw the people running wild? (Exodus 32:19)

23. After Moses read the Book of the Covenant and people promised to obey, what did Moses do as a sign of the Covenant? (Exodus 24:8)

24. Name the three annual festivals the people were to celebrate: (Exodus 23:14-16)
ADVANCE 2 EXTRA SPACES

25. What were the people to do with their land every seventh year? (Leviticus 25:1-7)

26. What happened every fiftieth year – the Year of Jubilee? (Leviticus 25:10-12)

27. God gave Moses a pattern for constructing a _____, a place where God would live among them. (Exodus 25:8-9)

28. What happened when Moses, Bezalel and Oholiab asked for freewill offerings for the tabernacle? (Exodus 36:5-7)

29. What was kept inside the Ark of the Covenant? (Deuteronomy 10:5, 1 Kings 8:9)

30. After Moses saw that the tabernacle was completed just as God said, he _____ the people. (Exodus 39:43)

31. After Moses set up the tabernacle just as God instructed, the _____ __ ___ ____ filled it. (Exodus 40:34-35)

32. Which tribe was chosen for care of the tabernacle, sacrificial service and priestly duties? (Numbers 3:5-13)

33. What happened to Aaron's sons Nadab and Abihu when they offered unholy fire to the Lord? (Leviticus 10:1-3)

34. God showed the people an orderly way to camp and march. Where were the Levites and the tabernacle? (Numbers 2:17)

35. Aaron's priestly blessing began, "The Lord bless you" and ended, "and give you _____." (Numbers 6:22-26)

36. What happened to Miriam when she and Aaron challenged Moses' prophetic gift and authority? (Numbers 12:10)

37. Of the 12 spies who explored the promised land, which two trusted God to help defeat the powerful people there? (Numbers 14:6)

38. What was the penalty for all Israelites over twenty who did not trust God enough to go into Canaan? (Numbers 14:32-34)

39. What were the names of the three men who opposed Moses' and Aaron's God-given authority? (Numbers 16:1, 23)

40. How did God punish the three rebels and their households? (Numbers 16:31-33)

41. What did God do to Aaron's staff to reaffirm him as high priest after the rebellion? (Numbers 17:5, 8)

42. How did Moses disobey God and lose his right to lead the people into the promised land? (Numbers 20:7-12)

43. What plague did God send upon the people when they grumbled about the manna and water God provided? (Numbers 21:4-6)

44. How did God heal the people from this plague? (Numbers 21:8-9)

45. How did God provide shoes and clothes for the people during their 40 years in the wilderness? (Deuteronomy 29:5)

46. How did the Psalmist describe the way God brought the people from Egypt to the promised land? (Psalm 78:52)

■ "QUESTION CARDS" (Answer Guide)

1. Yeast
2. The blood of the lamb
3. Death of the firstborn
4. Joseph's
5. To avoid war
6. East
7. Miriam
8. Throw in a piece of wood
9. Pillar of cloud/fire
10. Manna
11. Bred worms, became foul
12. Quails
13. Every word that comes from God
14. Water from a rock
15. Moses held up his hands
16. Organize; delegate judging
17. Priests
18. Wash clothes; abstinence
19. Love God; love neighbor
20. Tablets of stone
21. Golden calf
22. Threw and broke them
23. Dashed blood on people
24. Unleavened Bread; Harvest (Weeks); Ingathering (Tabernacles or Booths)
25. Let land rest; Sabbath year
26. Liberty for all; rest
27. Tabernacle
28. People gave too much
29. Tablets of the law
30. Blessed
31. Glory of the Lord
32. Levi
33. God's fire consumed them
34. In the center of the camp
35. Peace
36. She became leprous
37. Joshua and Caleb
38. They'd die in the wilderness
39. Korah, Dathan, Abiram
40. Earth opened and swallowed them
41. Bore almond buds and fruit
42. Struck rock (not spoke)
43. Poisonous biting snakes
44. Bronze serpent on a pole
45. Clothes, shoes didn't wear out
46. Led people like sheep

SEARCH SHEET 14

Israel's "wilderness journey" describes an emerging nation's relationship with God from the time of their liberation from Egypt and throughout 40 years of camping in the desert. Psalm 105 is a hymn of praise to God for signs and wonders during those years. What do vss. 8-11 and 42 tell about the promises of God?

_____

_____

There were many times when the people did not feel God close to them. Where do you think God was during those times? (1 Corinthians 10:1-4) _____

_____

Write a few paragraphs describing your "wilderness journey" – your relationship to God throughout your life. Was there a time when you were fearful of leaving all behind? What deep waters has God led you through? At what times or places did you encounter God's nearness? God's awesome holiness? Times you felt far from God? How did you grumble or rebel or go your own way? Where is God leading you now? How do you envision God leading you in the future?

_____

_____

_____

_____

_____

_____

_____

_____

_____

_____

_____

_____

_____

_____

_____

_____

_____

_____

_____

Israel's "wilderness journey" describes an emerging nation's relationship with God from the time of their liberation from Egypt and throughout 40 years of camping in the desert. Psalm 105 is a hymn of praise to God for signs and wonders during those years. What do vss. 8-11 and 42 tell about the promises of God? *God is mindful of the everlasting covenant. God keeps promises.*

There were many times when the people did not feel God close to them. Where do you think God was during those times? (1 Corinthians 10:1-4) *The rock they drank from in the wilderness was Christ.*

Write a few paragraphs describing your "wilderness journey" – your relationship to God throughout your life. Was there a time when you were fearful of leaving all behind? What deep waters has God led you through? At what times or places did you encounter God's nearness? God's awesome holiness? Times you felt far from God? How did you grumble or rebel or go your own way? Where is God leading you now? How do you envision God leading you in the future?

_____

_____

_____

_____

_____

_____

_____

_____

_____

_____

_____

_____

_____

_____

_____

_____

_____

_____

_____

_____

_____

DAILY SCRIPTURE
READINGS • WEEK 14

THE **AWE REVERENCE WONDER** AT THE **NEARNESS HOLINESS BEAUTY** OF GOD = THE BEGINNING OF **WISDOM**

(PROVERBS 1:7A)

	HEBREW SCRIPTURE	NEW TESTAMENT	PSALM	PROVERBS
Day 1	Deut. 21:1-22:30	Luke 9:51-10:12	74:1-23	12:1
Day 2	Deut. 23:1-25:19	Luke 10:13-37	75:1-10	12:12-14
Day 3	Deut. 26:1-27:26	Luke 10:38-11:13	76:1-12	12:15-17
Day 4	Deut. 28:1-68	Luke 11:14-36	77:1-20	12:18
Day 5	Deut. 29:1-30:20	Luke 11:37-12:7	78:1-31	12:19-20
Day 6	Deut. 31:1-32:27	Luke 12:8-34	78:32-55	12:21-23
Day 7	Deut. 32:28-52	Luke 12:35-59	78:56-74	12:24

Personal Notes and Glimpses of Wisdom:

"I wonder how I'll make it through this big scary wilderness..."

_____
_____
_____
_____
_____
_____
_____
_____
_____
_____

SESSION 15 • WISDOM'S JOURNEY

The aim of this session is to
view the various stages of Wisdom's journey – a journey of faith.

MATERIALS NEEDED

Hymnals
Accompaniment
Bibles
Newsprint or chalkboard
Illustration 1A from Session 1
Completed Search Sheet 14
Completed Insights from Daily Scripture Readings For Week 14
Copies for each participant of:
    "Journey Of Faith"
    Search Sheet 15
    Daily Scripture Readings For Week 15

▨ ASSEMBLING

This session invites participants to look at their lives, the life of the Hebrew people, and the corporate life of the church as a *journey of various stages of growth in wisdom.*

<u>A</u>lways <u>B</u>e <u>C</u>autious – when working with "stages." People are too precious and complex to fit neatly into categories. Each person is involved in more than one identifiable stage at any given moment; however, one or more may predominate.

The greatest *benefit* of viewing the "stages" may be an increased ability to name and focus upon a particular area of growth and *see new possibilities for growth.*

The greatest *pitfall* would be for participants *to label or stereotype* one another for purposes of domination and control, thus stifling growth. Pray for the Counselor's wisdom and guidance in this session.

▨ THE APPROACH TO GOD   (5 to 10 minutes)

❧ *Sing a hymn* which reflects the "pilgrim perspective" of life's journey – such as *"Savior, Like A Shepherd Lead Us."*

❧ *Offer a prayer* for God's guidance on this journey.

▨ ENCOUNTERING THE WORD   (40 to 45 minutes)

⇨ Using Completed Search Sheet 14, invite participants to share portions of their "Wilderness Journeys." If there is no eager volunteer, lead by example, sharing a portion of your own journey. After everyone has shared, distribute copies of "Journey Of Faith." Go through the "Lecturette with Times for Sharing."

▦ GOING FORTH IN GOD'S NAME (5 to 10 minutes)

❧ *Close with a hymn* which is also a much-loved prayer of the church for wisdom on the journey, "God Of Grace And God Of Glory."

❧ Distribute copies of:
   Search Sheet 15
   Daily Scripture Readings For Week 15

■ "LECTURETTE WITH TIMES FOR SHARING"

(Before reading through the "Journey," invite participants to roll the page so the arrows line up - like kids do with their Sunday School papers.) Explain: "Stages" may not follow each other in a straight line. Most likely they will appear in cycles as below *(illustrate on chalkboard or newsprint):*

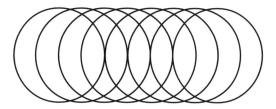 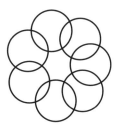

For example, a young child may learn to **trust** God as a Shepherd like he or she trusts Mom and Dad to provide regular meals, clothing, and other basic needs. This child may go on to **imitating, joining**, and other stages. However, if the child experiences injury or illness, the loss of someone close, or if his or her trust is betrayed by abuse or neglect, he or she will need to re-work this basic **trust** stage.

Each person can be in several identifiable stages at any given time. Perhaps there will be one that will seem to stand out among the rest, or one that begs to be explored further. Human beings are marvelously complex. While the "stages" are not meant to be rigidly applied, they are a **means of naming places where we have been** (or where we may be again), and of **giving us vision** where we may yet go on our journey of faith.

The **first column**, "Psalm 23," identifies **seven parts** of the Psalm. These are pictured in a circle on Illustration 1 from Session 1.

Column 2, "Annual Shepherding Cycle," is a summary of the story heard in Session 1. These "stages," like an annual church lectionary, may be experienced each year (although not necessarily in sequence).

Take a look at the **third column**, "Theological Corollary" (of the annual shepherding cycle). What does it mean to my journey of faith that "The Lord is my shepherd?" It means that I'm no longer a stray sheep going my own way; God has called me to follow in the way of Shalom (peace and wholeness) and I've said "Yes." I **belong** to God now. I've begun the journey of faith.

(Invite participants to silently read through the remaining theological corollaries and identify one or two which best describe their journey at this time. Give each one an opportunity to share. Share your own insights.)

Column 4 is a list of faith stages identified by James W. Fowler in his book *Stages of Faith*, Harper and Row, San Francisco, 1981. While Fowler identifies stages which are primarily found in certain age groups, once again, a person may be (or need to be) working on any of the other stages. Some may identify themselves as being between certain stages. A church (like television) may program its adult curriculum to the **"Adolescence And Beyond"** issues of **responsibility** and **integration**. Critical self-awareness may be discouraged because it makes people uncomfortable. This makes it difficult for people to grow toward the **universalizing, self-giving love** of a Mother Theresa. You may wish to read more about these stages in the above book or in *Weaving The New Creation, (Stages of Faith and the Public Church)*, also by James W. Fowler, Harper Collins, San Francisco, 1991).

*(Invite participants to read through **Fowler's Faith Stages** column and identify and share the stage they feel their local church is in. Optional: Identify and share the stage the church universal is in.)*

Erikson's General Stages column (from *Childhood and Society,* by E. Erikson, Norton, 1964) show that there is a **positive** and **negative** aspect to the stages. Each person or group balances the two while working through the particular stage. Care should be taken not to interpret the negative aspect as "unhealthy." In the *"Trust vs. Mistrust"* stage, mistrust of someone who encourages touching a hot stove burner or running out into a busy street is **healthy mistrust**. Likewise, in the *"Intimacy vs. Isolation"* stage, solitude may be misinterpreted as unhealthy "isolation" when it is actually a time of **intimacy with God**, meditation, and healthy growth in faith.

*(Invite participants to read through the **Erikson's General Stages** column, identify and share the stage they most identified with during the past week.)*

The **Theological Themes** column again names some areas most pilgrims will encounter on their journey toward *"Awareness of the Holy."*

*(Allow some time for participants to read through these themes. Then invite their response to: "Where have you encountered **"the Holy"** this past week?")*

The **Vice/Virtue** column places a negative connotation on the vices. Once again, these cannot be rigidly interpreted as "good" or "bad." **Anger**, listed as a vice, is an energy which can be virtuously channeled: anger combined with courage can bring about needed changes – reformation. **Pride**, listed as a vice, does not mean good self-esteem. And "ownership pride" in the appearance of personal property or church property is not "bad." But pride which tramples others to put self first is not a virtue!

*(The **virtue of "wisdom"** is a goal of the journey of faith. Invite each participant to picture someone who has "journeyed" for many years in faith, and share what that **"wisdom"** looks like in this person.)*

JOURNEY OF FAITH

	Psalm 23	Annual Shepherding Cycle	Theological Corollary	Fowler's Faith Stages	Erickson's General Stages	Theological Themes	Virtue/ Vice
1.	The Lord is my shepherd	Ownership Branding Bonding	Choosing God's way vs. my way	INFANCY Basic trust	Trust vs. Mistrust	Providence	Hope/ Gluttony
2.	No want Green Pastures	Leading sheep from ranch HQ up greening slopes in spring	Trust in God's nourishing and nurturing; freedom from self-striving	EARLY CHILDHOOD Imagination Imitation Intuition	Autonomy vs. Shame/Doubt	Grace or Gratefulness	Will/ Anger
3.	Still Waters	Leading to oasis of still clean waters to satisfy thirst	Restlessness satisfied by taking in God's Living Truth	CHILDHOOD AND BEYOND Logic, joining, belonging	Initiative vs. Guilt	Repentance	Purpose/ Greed
4.	Restores soul; Right Paths	Shearing off old wool; helping fallen sheep to new paths	Set free from self-will; Holy Spirit leads to new growth	ADOLESCENCE AND BEYOND Responsibility, integration	Industry vs. Inferiority	Vocation	Competence/ Envy
5.	Valley of shadow; Rod & staff	Rugged passageways where rod & staff guide and correct	Accepting adversity as movement to new growth. Correction, comfort	YOUNG ADULT-AND BEYOND Critical self-awareness	Identity vs. Role Confusion	Faith	Fidelity/ Pride
6.	Table/ enemies; Anointing oil Cup overflows	Grassy mesas of summer where predators loom. Healing balms.	Communion with God; protection from oppressors. Salvation, healing.	EARLY MID-LIFE AND BEYOND Accept paradox, embrace polarities.	Intimacy vs. Isolation Generativity vs. Stagnation	Communion Vocation	Love/Lust Care/ Indifference
7.	Goodness and mercy, Now and forever.	Safe arrival at ranch HQ for winter completes cycle	Enjoying wholeness unity, love justice, peace. SHALOM!	MID-LIFE AND BEYOND Universalizing, self-giving love	Integrity vs. Despair	Awareness of the Holy	Wisdom/ Melancholy

SEARCH SHEET 15

This is a time of transition of leadership as the people move into the land God promised them nearly 700 years previously through Abraham and Sarah. Israel's wilderness journey under the leadership of Moses has ended, but the people's **covenantal relationship with God continues** under the leadership of Joshua. Summarize the ways **Joshua** was prepared for **leadership** in the following passages:

Exodus 17:8-16 _____

_____

Exodus 24:12-14 _____

Exodus 32:15-20 _____

Exodus 33:11 _____

Numbers 13:16 _____

Note: *The name* **Joshua** *was the Hebrew form of* **Jesus** *meaning* **"God saves"** *or* **"God heals."**

Numbers 14:6-10 _____

_____

Numbers 14:30, 38 _____

Numbers 27:15-23 _____

Numbers 32:12 _____

Deuteronomy 1:38 _____

Deuteronomy 31:7-8 _____

Deuteronomy 31:14-15, 23 _____

Deuteronomy 34:9 _____

Joshua 5:13-15 _____

_____

The Book of Deuteronomy is **Moses' farewell message** in which the **terms of the covenant** are read and interpreted before the transition in leadership and before entering the Promised Land. **Worship of God** is **central** to the life of the "Mysterious Melchizedek" people. Deuteronomy 30:15-20 summarizes Moses' message. He sets before the people a **choice** of two ways to go in life, much like the choice between the two trees in the Garden of Eden. Read the summary. Then think of how you might say it if you were a Baccalaureate or Commencement speaker (be brief!) and write it below: (Option: you may wish to put it in poetic form).

_____

_____

_____

_____

_____

_____

This is a time of transition of leadership as the people move into the land God promised them nearly 700 years previously through Abraham and Sarah. Israel's wilderness journey under the leadership of Moses has ended, but the people's **covenantal relationship with God continues** under the leadership of Joshua. Summarize the ways **Joshua** was prepared for **leadership** in the following passages:

Exodus 17:8-16 *He was a military leader under Moses, fought Amalekites, experienced special power of God in battle as Moses held hands up to God*

Exodus 24:12-14 *Went up mountain with Moses to receive the tablets of the law*

Exodus 32:15-20 *Was with Moses when Moses came down and saw golden calf*

Exodus 33:11 *Served in tent while Moses talked face to face with God*

Numbers 13:16 *Name changed from Hoshea (salvation) to Joshua (God saves)*

Note: The name **Joshua** was the Hebrew form of **Jesus** meaning **"God saves"** or **"God heals."**

Numbers 14:6-10 *Was one of two spies (with Caleb) who believed God was stronger than people of Canaan, urged obedience on entering land, not rebellion*

Numbers 14:30, 38 *Other 10 spies die of plague; Joshua & Caleb enter land*

Numbers 27:15-23 *Appointed by God to succeed Moses, commissioned by priest*

Numbers 32:12 *Unreservedly followed God - thus can enter Canaan*

Deuteronomy 1:38 *Moses is commanded to encourage his assistant Joshua*

Deuteronomy 31:7-8 *Moses' blessing and commanding Joshua "God goes before you"*

Deuteronomy 31:14-15, 23 *Cloud pillar appears at Joshua's commissioning*

Deuteronomy 34:9 *"Full of spirit of wisdom" because Moses laid hands on him*

Joshua 5:13-15 *Joshua meets mysterious commander of Lord's army and removes sandals – holy ground (parallel to Moses' burning bush experience)*

The Book of Deuteronomy is **Moses' farewell message** in which the **terms of the covenant** are read and interpreted before the transition in leadership and before entering the Promised Land. Worship of God is central to the life of the "Mysterious Melchizedek" people. Deuteronomy 30:15-20 summarizes Moses' message. He sets before the people a **choice** of two ways to go in life, much like the choice between the two trees in the Garden of Eden. Read the summary. Then think of how you might say it if you were a Baccalaureate or Commencement speaker (be brief!) and write it below: (option: you may wish to put it in poetic form).

Life and prosperity	*vs.*	*Death and adversity*
Obey and live	*vs*	*Heart that turns away*
Become numerous	*vs*	*Led astray by other gods*
Blessed in land	*vs*	*Perish*

THEREFORE,

Choose life; love and obey God

and realize the fulfillment of God's promise!

DAILY SCRIPTURE
READINGS • WEEK 15

THE **AWE REVERENCE WONDER** AT THE **NEARNESS HOLINESS BEAUTY** OF GOD = THE BEGINNING OF **WISDOM**

(PROVERBS 1:7A)

	HEBREW SCRIPTURE	NEW TESTAMENT	PSALM	PROVERBS
Day 1	Deut. 33:1-29	Luke 13:1-21	78:65-72	12:25
Day 2	Deut 34:1-Josh.2:24	Luke 13:22-14:6	79:1-13	12:26
Day 3	Joshua 3:1-4:24	Luke 14:7-35	80:1-19	12:27-28
Day 4	Joshua 5:1-7:15	Luke 15:1-32	81:1-16	13:1
Day 5	Joshua 7:16-9:2	Luke 16:1-18	82:1-8	13:2-3
Day 6	Joshua 9:3-10:43	Luke 16:19-17:10	83:1-18	13:4
Day 7	Joshua 11:1-12:24	Luke 17:11-37	84:1-12	13:5-6

Personal Notes and Glimpses of Wisdom:

"I wonder what my next stage will be like..."

SESSION 16 • WISDOM'S CONQUEST

T he aim of this session is to see the relationship of obedience and victorious living as Joshua leads the "Mysterious Melchizedek" people in conquering the land God gave them.

MATERIALS NEEDED

Hymnals
Accompaniment
Bibles
Reporter's journal and pen (for leader)
Completed Search Sheet 15
Completed Insights from Daily Scripture Readings For Week 15
Copies for each participant of:
    "Questions For Joshua" (two pages)
    Map
    Search Sheet 16
    Daily Scripture Readings For Week 16

▓ ASSEMBLING

This session covers the Book of Joshua which begins the Prophetic Historical section of the Bible – Israel's **history** as they move into the land promised to Abraham, interpreted from a **prophetic perspective.** If participants have kept up with Daily Scripture Readings, they will have read most of the Book of Joshua in the week prior to this session.

The **violence** used in the conquest may be difficult to understand. One of the questions deals with this issue; a **"Commentary On The Questions"** is included for the leader's use in facilitating discussion.

In this session, participants are cast as "Joshua" while you as leader/reporter ask questions. Enjoy!

▓ THE APPROACH TO GOD   (5 to 10 minutes)

❧ **Sing a hymn** the spiritual, *"Joshua Fit The Battle Of Jericho,"* or *"Onward Christian Soldiers,"* or a song of courage in the face of challenge.

❧ **Offer a prayer** petitioning God for guidance in discovering the wisdom of the conquest for living our faith today.

▓ ENCOUNTERING THE WORD   (40 to 45 minutes)

⇨ With reporter's journal and pen in hand, inform participants that for the next 40 – 45 minutes they are **"Joshua"** and you are a reporter. Ask them to look at their completed Search Sheet 15 and answer some initial questions: *(remember to take notes . . .)*

A. "Leading millions of people with all their possessions into a new homeland is a difficult task. What background experience do you have to qualify you for a job like this?"

B. "The people you are leading have been called a "Mysterious Melchizedek" people – a people who are supposed to bring about a world order of peace and justice. Your predecessor, Moses, gave you and your people some pertinent advice to accomplish that goal. Please give a summary of that advice:"

C. "Joshua, your predecessor Moses had many encounters with the Living God of your people – one of them at a bush which was on fire but didn't burn up, a place which was so holy he had to take off his sandals. I hear you had a similar encounter. Can you tell us about that?"

D. "I have some other questions about your experiences of leading the "Mysterious Melchizedek" people. I'll give you a copy and be back in 20 minutes to complete this interview."

➪ *(Distribute copies of **"Questions For Joshua"** and the **Map**. Resume questioning in 20 minutes, journal in hand, taking notes and supplementing discussion from the **"Commentary Page."**)*

▓ GOING FORTH IN GOD'S NAME (5 to 10 minutes)

❧ *Sing a hymn*, *"Trust And Obey,"* in closing. It is through trust and obedience that God's people conquer and inherit the territory given to them.

❧ *Offer a prayer* of thanksgiving (or petition) to God for wise leaders who trust God and obey God's voice.

❧ Distribute copies of:
Search Sheet 16
Daily Scripture Readings For Week 16

■ "QUESTIONS FOR JOSHUA"

1. There were two tribes and one half-tribe who received inherited land east of the Jordan. Name them: (Joshua 1:12)
   What was the condition for granting this inheritance? (Joshua 1:14 – 15)

2. You secretly sent two spies ahead to Jericho, and they made a deal with a prostitute there. Tell us what that deal was: (Joshua 2:14, 17 – 21)
   Did you honor that deal? (Joshua 6:17, 22 – 25)
   Did taking in a prostitute bring reproach upon you and your people? (Joshua 2:11b, Matthew 1:5, Hebrews 11:31, James 2:25)

3. Forty years earlier, when Moses led your people out of Egypt, God performed a mighty miracle at the Red Sea. Something like that happened under your leadership. Tell us about it: (Joshua 3:14 – 17)
   How did the people feel about God's leadership through you after this experience? (Joshua 3:7, 10, 4:14)
   How did you remember God's mighty power working in you and the "Mysterious Melchizedek" people? (Deuteronomy 27:1 – 8, Joshua 4:1 – 9, 19 – 24)

4. Obedience to God's command of circumcision (Joshua 5:2) was important to you. Why? (Joshua 5:4 – 9)

5. God's promise and command regarding your people's possessing the land indicates that it wouldn't happen all at once. Why is that? (Exodus 23:29 – 30)
   Exodus 23:31 – 33 also indicates that while God does the initial conquering, you and your people are expected to do something. What did God ask of you?

6. The conquest shows evidence of military strategy. There appear to be three stages. Please point them out on the map:
   A. Joshua 6:1 - 8:35
   B. Joshua 9:1 - 10:43
   C. Joshua 11:1 - 23

7. You won a spectacular victory at Jericho! What was the curse you pronounced on Jericho? (Joshua 6:26)
   Do you think it was ever carried out? (1 Kings 16:34)

8. After the victory at Jericho, confidence was at a high. Then your troops were beaten at little Ai. What happened there? (Joshua 6:18 - 19, 7:1 - 5)
   What do you think God was teaching you and your people about the relationship of a nation's moral strength to its physical strength? (Joshua 7:11 - 13)
   What do you think God was teaching you and your people about the relationship between individual sin and national consequences? (Joshua 7:11 - 13, 15, 25 - 26)

9. Joshua, some of us have difficulty understanding the violence of a "holy war" by a people who were supposed to bring about peace and justice. How would you explain that to us? (Exodus 23:33, Deuteronomy 20:10 - 18, Joshua 3:5, 4:24, 5:15)

10. After the Gibeonites deceived you and became your slaves, you defended them from an attack by five powerful kings. There were two mysterious acts of God on your behalf that day. Would you tell us about them? (Joshua 10:11, 12 – 14)

11. After the battles were over, what equitable way did you use to divide the land among the 12 tribes?

(Numbers 26:52 - 56, 34:16 - 17, Joshua 14:2, Proverbs 16:33)
Joshua, we know that yours was a patriarchal society. What rights were there for women in this society? Could they own and inherit land? (Numbers 36)

12. Joshua, as a descendant of Joseph through his son Ephraim, what ancient request was honored by your people? (Joshua 24:32)

13. Joshua, you followed God obediently and saw the fulfillment of a promise made hundreds of years before your lifetime. This seems to be the theme of your life's work. Would you tell us about it? (Joshua 21:43 - 45)

14. What parting advice did you give (and illustrate) to the "Mysterious Melchizedek" people to maintain peace and justice? (Joshua 24:14 - 27)

■ "QUESTIONS FOR JOSHUA" (Answer Guide)

1. (Joshua 1:12) *Reuben, Gad and Manasseh* (Joshua 1:14 – 15) *Their warriors had to cross Jordan and help "take possession."*

2. (Joshua 2:14, 17 - 21) *"Our life for yours" – her household was saved for saving the spies' lives – a crimson cord identified her household.* (Joshua 6:17, 22 – 25) *Yes!*
    (Joshua 2:11b, Matthew 1:5, Hebrews 11:31, James 2:25) *No. She acknowledged the God of heaven and earth, is ancestress of David and Jesus, remembered for her faith and good works.*

3. (Joshua 3:14 - 17) *Flooded waters heaped up, leaving dry ground for people to cross the Jordan River.* (Joshua 3:7, 10, 4:14) *Exalted in sight of Israel like Moses, "living God is among you," awed like Moses.* (Deuteronomy 27:1 - 8, Joshua 4:1 - 9, 19 - 24) *By setting up 12 stones from the river bed as a memorial.*

4. (Joshua 5:2, 4 - 9) *To "roll away the disgrace" of the fearful who wanted to return to Egypt rather than fight for God to inherit the land 40 years earlier — rededication, recognition of God's holiness.*

5. (Exodus 23:29 - 30) *Land would become desolate and wild animals would multiply against people. God gives gradual increase.* (Exodus 23:31 – 33) *"I will hand them over – you shall drive them out, make no covenant with them or their gods lest they cause you to sin against God."*

6. (Joshua 6:1 - 8:35) *Central Region,* (9:1 - 10:43) *Southern Region,* (11:1 - 23) *Northern Region.*

7. (Joshua 6:26) *Curse for rebuilding: firstborn dies when foundation laid; youngest when gates set up.* (1 Kings 16:34) *Hiel of Bethel rebuilt; his oldest son, Abiram, died when the foundation was laid; his youngest, Sebug, when setting up gates.*

8. (Joshua 6:18 - 19, 7:1 - 5) *Booty was "devoted," but Achan took some and hid it in his tent. 36 Israelis were killed in battle; others retreat.* (Joshua 7:11 - 13) *Sin is the cause of national military defeat.* (Joshua 7:11 - 13, 15, 25 - 26) *Individual sin brings trouble on the whole nation.*

9. (Exodus 23:33, Deuteronomy 20:10 - 18, Joshua 3:5, 4:24, 5:15) *Idolatry must be completely rooted out so that Holy God reigns through holy people.*

10. (Joshua 10:11, 12 - 14) *Hailstones from heaven kill more than sword. Sun stood still until Israel defeated enemies. God fought for people and listened to human (Joshua's) voice.*

11. (Numbers 26:52 - 56, 34:16 - 17, Joshua 14:2, Proverbs 16:33) *By lot and size of tribe, by Joshua and Eleazar and one leader per tribe, by lot/ God's decision.* (Numbers 36) *Yes, but they must marry within tribe to keep land within tribe.*

12. (Joshua 24:32) *Burying bones of Joseph at Shechem, a town of his son Ephraim's half-tribe.*

13. (Joshua 21:43 - 45) *God fulfilled promise to ancestors in my lifetime, through my leadership, gave peace from enemies. Not one of God's promises failed!*

14. (Joshua 24:14 - 27)) *Worship God; no other gods. Choose! Upon people's pledge of obedience to God, I renewed covenant, wrote it in book of law, set stone as witness.*

■ COMMENTARY PAGE (For The Reporter)

1. The descendants of the tribe of Levi were not included in the census for land division because they were not to inherit land (Numbers 1:47-53). They were **devoted** to caring for the tabernacle and priestly duties. To keep the number of tribes at the original number of 12, Joseph's descendants are listed under the names of his two sons, Ephraim and Manasseh (1:32-33). This honored Joseph with the **"double portion"** of ranking heir (Genesis 49:22-26). Though treated badly by his family and others, Joseph persevered faithfully so that he was in a position to save his family and all Egypt from famine.

2. God does not limit salvation and blessings to the Hebrew people. Rahab is **saved by her act of faith in God**. A New Testament parallel is the story of Jesus (a Jew) and the Samaritan (despised "half-breed") woman at the well (John 4:1-26, 39-42). Blessed is she who **believes** in the Lord!

3. Here, stones are a **memorial** of God's power and faithfulness. Can stones really hear and speak? Later, (Joshua 24:27) Joshua sets up a stone as a witness of covenant renewal. Upon Jesus' triumphal entry into Jerusalem, when his disciples proclaimed him as Messiah and Pharisees tried to silence them, Jesus said, "If they keep quiet, the stones will cry out." (Luke 19:40)

4. (No commentary needed)

5. Like the Hebrew people conquering and inheriting the land "little by little," our growth in faith usually does not come all at once but in **stages** (refer to Session 15's *"Journey of Faith"*).

6. (No commentary needed)

7. Be careful what you say! Blessings and curses are not to be taken lightly!

8. God, through the person of Joshua, teaches the difference between the **common** and the **holy.** Booty from Jericho was **"devoted"** – thus the seriousness of Achan's sin, taking the **holy** as if it were **common.** Awe for the **holy** and **obedience** to God were necessary for the people of God to bring about **righteousness and justice.**

9. What happens to a gallon of water if just a few E coli bacteria are allowed to remain in it? . . . The Canaanite people worshipped gods who could not see or speak. They engaged in temple prostitution and other perversions, including human sacrifice. Could the people of God remain a **holy people** and bring about peace and justice if "just a little evil" were allowed to remain?

   While non-violent tactics may seem preferable to us, it is important to note that God ordered and led in the destruction. Also, **God can transform** violent destruction (and other situations we do not understand) **into saving grace** for many as in the case of Joseph (see Genesis 50:20).

10. (No commentary needed)

11. The **Urim** and **Thummim** (Exodus 28:30, Numbers 27:21) were **sacred lots, a means of discerning God's will** in an important situation.

12. (No commentary needed)

13. The theme of the Book of Joshua is that **God is faithful and keeps promises.**

14. As in the Garden (Illustration 4), so now in the Promised Land, continued peace depends upon **obedience** to serving God – maintaining the pillars of **justice** and **right living.**

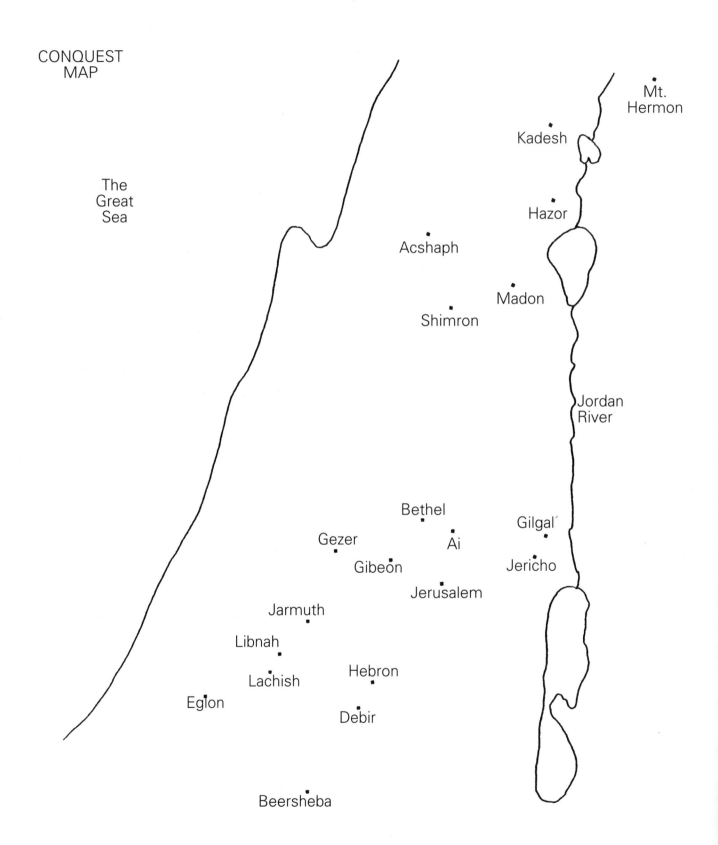

CONQUEST
MAP

The
Great
Sea

Mt.
Hermon

Kadesh

Hazor

Acshaph

Madon

Shimron

Jordan
River

Bethel

Gilgal

Gezer

Ai

Gibeon

Jericho

Jerusalem

Jarmuth

Libnah

Hebron

Lachish

Eglon

Debir

Beersheba

Through Joshua, God continues the **prophetic leadership** of Moses which led the people **from** slavery **to** a greatness feared by surrounding peoples. Although Joshua continues God-centered leadership, there are some changes. Like a parent who places increasing responsibility upon children and young people, so God requires greater responsibility from the "Mysterious Melchizedek" people:

What benefit did God withdraw as the people entered their promised land? (Joshua 5:11-12) _____
_____

What increased responsibility do you think this would require of the people? _____
_____

As Joshua prepares to die, he summarizes their relationship with their God (Joshua 24:1-13). Then he challenges them with their responsibility of choosing. What is this choice? (Joshua 24:15) _____
_____

How did the people respond? (24:16-18) _____

What was Joshua's further concern? (24:19-20) _____
_____

The people's response? (24:24) _____

What did Joshua do to renew the covenant of God with the people? (24:25-27) _____
_____
_____

How long was this effective? (24:31) _____
_____

After the death of the **"Joshua Generation,"** what happened to Israel's understanding of their covenantal relationship with God? (Judges 2:10) _____
_____

When Joshua died, he did not appoint one single successor as Moses had. To whom does he address his farewell message? (Joshua 24:1) _____

What does the wisdom writer say of a nation in such a situation? (Proverbs 28:2) _____
_____

A dysfunctional pattern develops (and repeats) in Israel after Joshua's death. Describe it:

1. Judges 2:10-13 _____

2. Judges 2:14-15 _____

3. Judges 2:18 (2nd half) _____

4. Judges 2:16, 18 (1st half) _____

5. Judges 2:19 _____

Through Joshua, God continues the **prophetic leadership** of Moses which led the people **from** slavery **to** a greatness feared by surrounding peoples. Although Joshua continues God-centered leadership, there are some changes. Like a parent who places increasing responsibility upon children and young people, so God requires greater responsibility from the "Mysterious Melchizedek" people:

What benefit did God withdraw as the people entered their promised land? (Joshua 5:11-12) _Manna stopped the day after eating produce from the land_
What increased responsibility do you think this would require of the people? _They'd have to grow their own food (agriculture)_

As Joshua prepares to die, he summarizes their relationship with their God (Joshua 24:1-13). Then he challenges them with their responsibility of choosing. What is this choice? (Joshua 24:15) _Choose between serving God or serving other gods_
How did the people respond? (24:16-18) _We will serve the Lord our God_
What was Joshua's further concern? (24:19-20) _You are unable to serve a holy God; your rebellion against God will bring disaster upon you_
The people's response? (24:24) _We will serve and obey God_
What did Joshua do to renew the covenant of God with the people? (24:25-27) _Recorded these things in the Book of the Law of God, then set up a large stone as witness and memorial_
How long was this effective? (24:31) _People served God throughout lifetime of Joshua and the elders who outlived him and had seen God's mighty acts_

After the death of the **"Joshua Generation,"** what happened to Israel's understanding of their covenantal relationship with God? (Judges 2:10) _The new generation did not know God or what God had done for Israel_
When Joshua died, he did not appoint one single successor as Moses had. To whom does he address his farewell message? (Joshua 24:1) _Elders, leaders, judges, and officials of Israel_
What does the wisdom writer say of a nation in such a situation? (Proverbs 28:2) _When a country is rebellious, it has many rulers, but a man (or woman) of understanding and knowledge maintains order_

A dysfunctional pattern develops (and repeats) in Israel after Joshua's death. Describe it:

1. Judges 2:10-13 _People forsook God, did evil, worshipped other gods_

2. Judges 2:14-15 _God allowed enemies to oppress them_

3. Judges 2:18 (2nd half) _People cried to God; God had compassion on them_

4. Judges 2:16, 18 (1st half) _God raised up a judge to save them from their enemies_

5. Judges 2:19 _People followed God until the judge died, then again did evil_

DAILY SCRIPTURE
READINGS • WEEK 16

THE **AWE REVERENCE WONDER** AT THE **NEARNESS HOLINESS BEAUTY** OF GOD = THE BEGINNING OF **WISDOM**

(PROVERBS 1:7A)

	HEBREW SCRIPTURE	NEW TESTAMENT	PSALM	PROVERBS
Day 1	Joshua 13:1-14:15	Luke 18:1-7	85:1-13	13:7-8
Day 2	Joshua 15:1-63	Luke 18:18-43	86:1-17	13:9-10
Day 3	Joshua 16:1-18:28	Luke 19:1-27	87:1-7	13:11
Day 4	Joshua 19:1-20:9	Luke 19:28-48	88:1-18	13:12-14
Day 5	Joshua 21:1-22:20	Luke 20:1-26	89:1-13	13:15-16
Day 6	Joshua 22:21-23:16	Luke 20:27-47	89:14-37	13:17-19
Day 7	Joshua 24:1-33	Luke 21:1-28	89:38-52	13:20-23

Personal Notes and Glimpses of Wisdom:

"I wonder how happy sheep can be when they obey their Shepherd's voice..."

_____

_____

_____

_____

_____

_____

_____

_____

_____

_____

_____

SESSION 17 • WISDOM THROUGH THE JUDGES

The aim of this session is to see the covenantal wisdom of God applied in Israel by "The Judges."

MATERIALS NEEDED

Hymnals
Accompaniment
Bibles
Six "Judge Scripts," copied and cut
Podium/lectern/pulpit for reading scripts
Newsprint or chalkboard
Completed Search Sheet 16
Completed Insights from Daily Scripture Readings For Week 16
Copies for each participant of:
    Search Sheet 17
    Daily Scripture Readings For Week 17

▨ ASSEMBLING

This session covers the Book of Judges. The judges are not only **legal counselors** but also **deliverers from oppression**. They are ordinary people who are empowered by the Spirit of God to lead Israel **from** repeated wandering to wise, faithful and peaceful living.

This session's dramatic format follows the repeated pattern of the Book of Judges: Israel **deserts** God, **suffers** from enemies, **cries** to God for help, **receives** help from God through a judge/deliverer, and **follows** God until the judge's death.

You as leader become narrator (seated) while participants act as "The Judges." As they are introduced by the narration, invite them to go to a podium/lectern/pulpit (place of leadership) and read their scripts.

▨ THE APPROACH TO GOD   (5 to 10 minutes)

❧ *Sing a hymn* –Choose a hymn which reflects the grace and mercy of God reaching to sinful humanity. An "oldie but goodie" is *"The Mercies Of God."*

❧ *Offer a prayer* of thanksgiving to the Good Shepherd who faithfully offers love and grace to those who have gone astray. ("The Judges" could represent the Shepherd's rod and staff of correction and restored direction.)

▨ ENCOUNTERING THE WORD   (40 to 45 minutes)

⇨ Refer to Search Sheet 16 and ask participants to identify the five stages of Israel's dysfunctional pattern following the death of Joshua. Condense each to a word or phrase and *write them on newsprint or chalkboard.*

⇨ *Distribute the six "Judge Scripts"* to participants who are willing to read them as part of the drama of the era of Israel's judges. Invite each reader to stand at a podium, lectern, or pulpit, the place of leadership – because "God **raised up** judges" – as their judge is introduced by the narrator. Enjoy the drama together!

▣ GOING FORTH IN GOD'S NAME (5 to 10 minutes)

❥ *Sing a hymn* such as "Still, Still With Thee," or another hymn which reflects people (prone to straying) still following because of divine faithfulness.

❥ *Offer a prayer* of thanksgiving to the One who comes to us when we have strayed and draws us back to the everlasting arms.

❥ Distribute copies of:
Search Sheet 17
Daily Scripture Readings For Week 17

■ "THE DRAMA OF THE JUDGES" (Narrator's Script)

After the death of Joshua and the high priest Phinehas and the elders who had seen God's mighty acts, there was **no central leader** in Israel. The 12 tribes worked territorially (individually and cooperatively) to complete the conquest of Canaan. But as they began to enjoy the fruit of the land, they grew weary of the struggle and adopted a "live and let live" attitude. They forgot God and began compromising their covenantal relationship with the Living God by worshipping the Baals, the gods of the Canaanites.

Then God allowed the Edomites to oppress Israel for eight years. The Israelites cried to God, and God **raised up** a deliverer and judge, **Othniel.**

Othniel Script Is Read

The country had peace for 40 years. After the death of Othniel, the Israelites again did evil in God's sight, turning away from worshipping the Living God by worshipping the Canaanite gods. Then God allowed Eglon, King of Moab, to march upon Israel and capture the City of Palm Trees, making the Israelites slaves of Moab for 18 years. Then the Israelites cried out to God, and God **raised up** a deliverer and judge, **Ehud.**

Ehud Script Is Read

The country had peace for 80 years. After Ehud, a deliverer named **Shamgar** routed 600 Philistines with an ox-goad. But after the death of Ehud, the Israelites again did evil in God's sight, turning away from the eternal God and enjoying the sensual but temporary pleasures of Baal worship. Then God allowed Jabin, King of Canaan (who had 900 iron chariots) and his military general Sisera to oppress the Israelites for 20 years. The Israelites cried to God for deliverance, and God **raised up** a prophetess named **Deborah** to judge Israel.

Deborah Script Is Read

The country had peace for 40 years. After Deborah and Barak, the Israelites again did evil in God's sight, turning away from the Living God who made a covenant with them. So God allowed the Midianites to move in and take all Israel's crops, leaving them nothing to live on for seven years. Then the Israelites cried out to God. This time God sent a prophet who said, "This is what God says, 'I brought you out of slavery in Egypt; I gave you this country. I am your God, the God of the Covenant; under the terms of the covenant you promised to worship only me. But you have broken the covenant; you are worshipping other gods; you have not listened to my voice.'"

After the prophet, God **raised up** a judge named **Gideon.**

Gideon Script Is Read

The country had peace for 40 years. After Gideon's death, the people of Israel prostituted themselves to the Baals, forgetting the God of the Covenant. Gideon had 70 sons. One of them, **Abimelech,** became king at Shechem after killing 68 of his brothers. He ruled for three years. Then God sent a spirit of discord which led to civil war. Abimelech was finally killed by a woman who dropped a millstone on his head and by his armor-bearer who put a sword through him so history would not record that a woman killed him.

After Abimelech, **Tola** from the tribe of Issachar judged Israel for 23 years. After him, **Jair** of Gilead judged for 22 years. He had 30 sons who rode 30 young donkeys and owned 30 towns.

After Jair, the Israelites wandered away from the God of the Covenant again, worshipping idols. So God allowed the Philistines and Ammonites to oppress them for 18 years. Then the people cried out to God for help. This time God told them to "go cry to the gods you have chosen." But the people repented and put away their foreign gods and worshipped the God of the Covenant who had delivered them in the past. Then they drafted *Jephthah* to lead them.

Jephthah Script Is Read

After Jephthah, **Ibzan** of Bethlehem judged Israel for seven years. Following Ibzan, **Elon** of Zebulun judged for 10 years. And **Abdon** of Ephraim judged for eight years.

Then the people of Israel stubbornly returned to their corruption and did not follow the way of the God of the Covenant. God allowed the Philistines to oppress them for 40 years. Then the angel of God appeared to Manoah and his wife, a childless couple, and promised them a son who would rescue Israel from the Philistines. His name was *Samson.*

Samson Script Is Read

After the death of Samson, morality in Israel deteriorated. Idol worship and violent crime were rampant, leading to civil war with 11 tribes against Benjamin, the worst offender. The drama ends with this tragic description of a nation without leadership: ***"In those days there was no king in Israel, and everyone did as he(or she) saw fit."*** (Judges 21:25)

Othniel Script

I am Othniel, nephew of Caleb the brave spy who stood with Joshua, ready to go into the land, fully trusting God to give victory over the giants in the land. Courage seems to run in our family. Once when Uncle Caleb was working with Joshua to conquer the land, he offered his beautiful daughter Achsah in marriage to the man who attacked and conquered the Canaanite city of Debir. So I scouted the city, drew up a battle plan, and led a successful attack. After Achsah and I were married, Uncle Caleb gave us our inheritance of land; but there was no water on it, so Achsah asked Uncle Caleb for springs of water also. And he gave us the upper and lower springs.

We were very happy in our new life in the promised land. Life was good and sweet, the way it was meant to be. But many of Israel's people grew weary of fighting the Canaanites and soon accepted life as is. They compromised their faith in the One True God and worshipped the Baals, gods of the Canaanites. Then God allowed the Edomites to oppress my people. After eight years of oppression, we people cried out to God and began looking for someone who still worshipped the Living God of the Covenant - someone who had military skills and courage to fight the Edomites.

One day I felt the Spirit of the Lord come upon me in a very powerful way, and I knew God was calling me to lead the people in battle against the Edomites. I listened closely to God's leading, and the battle went well. The Edomites were quickly and easily defeated. I reminded the people that a nation's physical strength depends upon its moral strength - that peace is the result of worshipping only the Living God of the Covenant. And there was peace in the land as long as I judged Israel.

Ehud Script

I am Ehud, a Benjamite. Like many of the Benjamites, I am left-handed or ambidextrous. Our tribe is famous for its left-handed slingers. And some of us could shoot arrows or sling stones equally well with our left or right hand. Anyway, after my people had forgotten their God again and the Moabites had enslaved them, my people selected me to be their representative to take the annual payment personally to Eglon, fat king of Moab. I began to wonder . . . With God's help and our wits, we could use this time to defeat the Moabites . . .

Before I left for Moab, I asked all volunteer warriors to gather in the hill country of Ephraim and wait for my signal. Then I strapped a double-edged sword about 18 inches long to my right thigh under my clothing, where no one would suspect it to be. I made a formal presentation to King Eglon, dismissed those who had come with me, and started for home. Then I turned and went back to King Eglon and said, "I have a secret message for you, O King." He dismissed all his attendants, and we went into his inner chambers. I said, "I have a secret message from God for you." As he rose to receive it, I reached with my left hand, drew the sword from my right thigh, and plunged it into his fat belly. He was so fat that the handle sank in after the blade, which came out his back. Believe me, I didn't stay to pull it out; I just watched as the fat closed in over it. Then I quietly closed and locked the doors and left. His attendants waited a long time, thinking he was using the chamber pot and wanted privacy. When they went in and found him dead, mass chaos broke out.

When I arrived in the hill country of Ephraim, I blew the trumpet, and the Israeli warriors blocked the fords of the Jordan so none of the Moabite warriors could escape. We killed 10,000 Moabites that day; not one escaped. Then the Moabites became our slaves. My country worshipped the Living God of the Covenant who had delivered them once again. And God gave us peace.

Deborah Script

I am Deborah, prophetess from the tribe of Ephraim. For many years, I had been holding court under the Palm of Deborah between Ramah and Bethel in the hill country of Ephraim. Lately, I had been hearing many complaints about Canaanites in the north oppressing my people. Their king, Jabin, had iron swords, shields and chariots. My people had no iron weapons. One day the Word of the Living God of the Covenant came to me, and I knew it was time for us to act. I summoned Barak, our military general, and told him to take 10,000 men to Mt. Tabor while I lured Jabin's general Sisera to the Kishon River. But Barak did not trust his ability to listen to the voice of God; he insisted that I go with him. I agreed but rebuked his lack of faith and prophesied that the honor of victory would go to a woman.

Heber the Kenite, a metalworker, warned Sisera of an approaching attack, and Sisera prepared his 900 iron chariots for war. As Sisera's army came near Mt. Tabor, I told Barak, "Go! God goes before you to give Sisera into your hands." Barak led the army down Mt. Tabor to attack. Just then, God fought from above with thunder and lightning, and a flash flood bogged Sisera's chariots in the mire. Barak's army pursued on foot, destroying all Sisera's men.

Sisera took refuge in Heber the Kenite's tent. "Please give me some water," he begged, "And guard the doorway." Heber's wife Jael gave him goat's milk; and when he slept, she picked up a tent peg and hammer and drove the peg through his temple into the ground, and he died. When Barak came looking for Sisera, Jael went out to meet him and said, "Come, I'll show you the man you're looking for!" She took Barak to her tent and showed him the dead Sisera. And so God used a woman with domestic implements to undo a military general with 900 iron chariots! Our nation sang and praised God who sent the flash flood and delivered us. And God gave us peace.

Gideon Script

I am Gideon from the tribe of Manasseh. I never planned to be a leader. I was just doing what I had to do to survive. The Midianite and Amalekite camel-riders were going through our land and taking our food as fast as we could produce it. So we hid it in caves and threshed our grain in our winepresses. One day while I was threshing, an angel from the Lord came and said, "The Lord is with you and tells you to 'Go in the strength you have and save Israel from Midian.'" I protested, "I'm the least in the family of the weakest clan in Manasseh." God said, "I will be with you." God told me to tear down my father's altar to Baal and build an altar to the Living God of the Covenant. I was afraid, so I did it at night. But the Midianites and Amalekites found out and joined forces for war.

Then the Spirit of the Lord came upon me in a powerful way, and I blew a trumpet calling my people to prepare for war. I still didn't feel very confident of my leadership ability, so I asked God for a sign - wet fleece on a dry threshing floor. And another sign – dry fleece on a wet ground. And both times, God answered as I had asked. Then God said, "I want to make it perfectly clear that Israel is not being saved by her own strength, but mine." So I told those who felt fearful to leave. 22,000 left, leaving 10,000. But God said, "That's still too many." So I sorted them by the way they drank water – kept the "lappers," sent the "kneelers" home. This left just 300 men. I still didn't feel very confident about this, so God told me to go to the Midianite camp at night and listen. I heard a man telling of a dream that a barley loaf tumbled into the Midianite camp with such force it collapsed the tent. And his friend interpreted: "This means God has given the Midianites into Gideon's hands." Then I worshipped God and I knew God was with me. I divided the 300 men into three companies. On signal, we blew our trumpets, smashed empty jars and shouted. The Midianites began killing each other. We kept on until they were destroyed. And God gave us peace.

Jephthah Script

I am Jephthah of Gilead, known as a mighty warrior. My mother was a prostitute who gave birth to many sons, and when they were grown, they drove me away from home. But when the Ammonites made war on them, they came to me and asked me to lead them in battle. I agreed, as long as they promised to respect my authority as their leader. Together we made a vow before the Lord at Mizpah.

I began by attempting to negotiate with the Ammonite king. However, my message was ignored. Then the Spirit of the Lord came upon me powerfully, and I led our army against them. As I left for battle, I made a vow to God to offer as a sacrifice whatever came out of the door of my house to meet me upon my triumphant return. My army devastated 20 towns and finally subdued Ammon. And when I returned from victory, my daughter, my only child, came singing and dancing to meet me. I cried and tore my clothes! Human sacrifice is a pagan practice! But my daughter said, "My father, you have given your word to the Lord. Do to me as you promised, now that God has avenged you of your enemies. Only let me have two months with my friends to roam the hills and weep because I will never marry." I granted her that request. Then I kept my vow to God. And from then on, every year the young women of Israel go out for four days to remember my daughter.

The men of Ephraim threatened to burn my house because I didn't ask them to fight the Ammonites with us Gileadites. They called us renegades! So we fought them and captured the fords of the Jordan. When they wanted to cross over, we asked, "Are you an Ephraimite?" And if they said "No," we asked them to pronounce "Shibboleth." If they lisped and said "Sibboleth," we knew they were lying because Ephraimites lisp, so we killed them - 42,000 of them. I guess I was one of the most brash and ruthless of the judges. Still, God called me, empowered me, and led me as I led Israel to victory over the Ammonites. And God gave us peace.

Samson Script

I am Samson of Dan, the last of the judges. I was set apart to God before my birth, a lifetime Nazirite who could drink no fermented drinks, never have my hair cut, and never go near a dead body (human or animal). God gave me special strength to begin Israel's deliverance from their most difficult enemy, the Philistines. My parents were careful to do and teach me all that God commanded. So they did not understand when I fell in love with a young Philistine woman. Shortly before our wedding, the Spirit of the Lord came upon me and I killed an attacking lion with my bare hands and later ate honey from a beehive in its carcass. I used this experience as a riddle to entertain our wedding guests. But my wife nagged until I told her, and then she betrayed my confidence causing me to lose my wager. The Spirit of the Lord came upon me powerfully, and I killed and looted in Ashkelon to pay my bet. I left my new wife and went back home. When her father gave her to the best man, I tied 150 pair of foxes together by their tails with a torch for each pair. I turned them loose in the Philistine grain fields, vineyards and olive groves. When they tried to get revenge, the Spirit of God came upon me again, and I killed 1000 men with the jawbone of a donkey. Afterwards, when I was very thirsty, God caused a spring to bubble up near me so I could drink and revive.

Once when the Philistines thought they had me cornered in Gaza where they planned to kill me, I carried the city gates and doorposts on my shoulders to the top of a hill. I suppose it's difficult for you to understand that a strong man like me could be undone by a whining, nagging Philistine woman; but that is exactly what happened. I fell in love with Delilah, and after evading her questions several times, I finally weakened and told her the secret of my strength, my special dedication to God. She betrayed me. The Philistines cut my hair, gouged out my eyes, made me a slave, and made sport of me. But God empowered me one last time to pull out the pillars of a crowded pagan temple to kill thousands of Philistines as I also died.

How mysterious is the covenantal wisdom of God in choosing and using unlikely people to lead Israel as the young nation learns how closely its physical strength depends on its moral strength! Below is an opportunity to match the judge with his/her personality style as portrayed in "The Drama Of The Judges."

Othniel　　　Ehud　　　Deborah　　　Gideon　　　Jephthah　　　Samson

_____ Assassin who outwits and betrays

_____ Overly cautious organizer

_____ Faithful visionary with a visionless general

_____ Selfish, sensual and irresponsible rogue

_____ Ruthless, brash member of a dysfunctional family

_____ Courageous, romantic warrior

Besides the unusual personalities God chose to work through in the saga of the Judges, the unusual faithfulness of God emerges in sharp contrast to the repeated faithlessness of the people of the nation of Israel. Look up the references below (all from the Book of Judges) to compare the number of years of **oppression** with the number of years of peace of God which follows obedience.

Reference	Years of Oppression	Judge	Years of Peace	Reference
3:8	_____	Othniel	_____	3:11
3:14	_____	Ehud	_____	3:30
4:3	_____	Deborah	_____	5:31
6:1	_____	Gideon	_____	8:28

Read Psalm 25. Then summarize it below **in your own words** as a prayer a leader in Israel might have offered during the time of the Judges.

_____

_____

_____

_____

_____

_____

_____

How mysterious is the covenantal wisdom of God in choosing and using unlikely people to lead Israel as the young nation learns how closely its physical strength depends on its moral strength! Below is an opportunity to match the judge with his/her personality style as portrayed in "The Drama Of The Judges."

Othniel   **Ehud**   **Deborah**   **Gideon**   **Jephthah**   **Samson**

Ehud	Assassin who outwits and betrays
Gideon	Overly cautious organizer
Deborah	Faithful visionary with a visionless general
Samson	Selfish, sensual and irresponsible rogue
Jephthah	Ruthless, brash member of a dysfunctional family
Othniel	Courageous, romantic warrior

Besides the unusual personalities God chose to work through in the saga of the Judges, the unusual faithfulness of God emerges in sharp contrast to the repeated faithlessness of the people of the nation of Israel. Look up the references below (all from the Book of Judges) to compare the number of years of oppression with the number of years of peace of God which follows obedience.

Reference	Years of Oppression	Judge	Years of Peace	Reference
3:8	_8_	Othniel	_40_	3:11
3:14	_14_	Ehud	_80_	3:30
4:3	_20_	Deborah	_40_	5:31
6:1	_7_	Gideon	_40_	8:28

Read Psalm 25. Then summarize it below **in your own words** as a prayer a leader in Israel might have offered during the time of the Judges.

I trust only in you, O God; show me your way out of this oppression so your people will not be the laughingstock of the nations. I ask this not because we've been faithful but because You are merciful and because of the covenantal relationship You gave to us. While we have not kept our part of the covenant, You are good and faithful and will keep Your Word. Help us to be humble, teachable, leadable - so that your integrity may live in us. Redeem us, O Lord!

DAILY SCRIPTURE
READINGS • WEEK 17

THE **AWE REVERENCE WONDER** AT THE **NEARNESS HOLINESS BEAUTY** OF GOD = THE BEGINNING OF **WISDOM**

(PROVERBS 1:7A)

	HEBREW SCRIPTURE	NEW TESTAMENT	PSALM	PROVERBS
Day 1	Judges 1:1-2:9	Luke 21:29-22:13	90:1-91:16	13:24-25
Day 2	Judges 2:10-3:31	Luke 22:14-34	92:1-93:5	14:1-2
Day 3	Judges 4:1-5:31	Luke 22:35-53	94:1-23	14:3-4
Day 4	Judges 6:1-40	Luke 22:54-23:12	95:1-96:13	14:5-6
Day 5	Judges 7:1-8:17	Luke 23:13-43	97:1-98:9	14:7-8
Day 6	Judges 8:18-9:21	Luke 23:44-24:12	99:1-9	14:9-10
Day 7	Judges 9:22-10:18	Luke 24:13-53	100:1-5	14:11-12

Personal Notes and Glimpses of Wisdom:

"I wonder if there were any sheep judges..."

SESSION 18 • WISDOM IN CRISIS

The aim of this session is to look at Israel's wisdom crisis and to see the impact of their response.

MATERIALS NEEDED

Hymnals
Accompaniment
Bibles
Newsprint or chalkboard
Completed Search Sheet 17
Completed Insights from Daily Scripture Readings For Week 17
Copies for each participant of:
    "Agenda For Elders' Meeting"
    Search Sheet 18
    Daily Scripture Readings For Week 18

▦ ASSEMBLING

This session covers the life of Samuel, a prophet, priest, and judge who led Israel following the period covered in the Book of Judges. During Samuel's leadership, the nation of Israel faced a crisis in its relationship with God. In this session, participants become a part of that crisis and its solution.

▦ THE APPROACH TO GOD   (5 to 10 minutes)

❥ *Background for Scripture:* In the hill country of Ephraim, Elkanah lived with two wives, Peninnah (with children), and Hannah (barren). One year when they went to Shiloh to worship, Hannah vowed that if God would give her a son, she would dedicate him for lifetime service to God. God answered and gave Hannah a little son named Samuel, "because I asked the Lord for him." When Samuel was weaned, Hannah and Elkanah took him to Shiloh to work in the tabernacle with Eli the priest. God had vowed Eli's greedy and immoral sons would die young, and God would call a faithful priest.

❥ *Scripture:* 1 Samuel 3:1-21
❥ *Hymn:* "Here I Am, Lord"

▦ ENCOUNTERING THE WORD   (40 to 45 minutes)

⇨ Using the "Dilemma Guide," lead participants through Israel's wisdom crisis.

▦ GOING FORTH IN GOD'S NAME   (5 to 10 minutes)

❥ *Sing* "Lead On, O King Eternal."
❥ Distribute copies of:
    Search Sheet 18
    Daily Scripture Readings For Week 18

■ "DILEMMA GUIDE"

Samuel and Eli: *(Leader assumes the role of Samuel; participants assume role of Eli)* I am Samuel; you are Eli. Using Search Sheet 17, remind me of the varied personalities and **leadership styles** of the judges who preceded you and me . . . Then remind me of the **mercies of God** to our nation . . . How many years of **oppression** did we receive before the judgeship of Othniel? Ehud? Deborah? Gideon? . . . And how many years of **peace** did God give us after the leadership of each? . . . From what you learned about the wisdom of God through the judges, what would be your **prayer** for Israel?

Samuel and Elders: *(Leader remains in role of Samuel; participants' roles change to that of the Elders)* I am Samuel; you are The Elders of Israel. We have a **serious crisis** in our nation, and we need to have a meeting to **decide how our nation should respond**. This is a description of the crisis and the advice I need from you. *(Distribute copies of "Agenda For Elders' Meeting" to each participant. If group is larger than six, form two groups. Leader/Samuel does not participate in discussion but goes to the tabernacle to pray. . . Allow 15-20 minutes for the Elders' Meeting/s. Then use the following questions - an option would be to write the questions on 3 x 5 cards and distribute them among participants - to see how the crisis appeared from the **Philistine, Israeli** and **prophetic** viewpoints.)*

From The Philistine Viewpoint:

1. How did the Philistines view the Ark of the Covenant before the battle? (1 Samuel 4:5-9)

2. How did the Philistines view the Ark of the Covenant after they captured it and placed it in Dagon's temple (and Dagon toppled and bubonic plague broke out)? (1 Samuel 5:7)

3. What did Philistine priests advise about the Ark? (1 Samuel 6:1-3)

4. What unbiased method of discernment did they use? (1 Samuel 6:7-9)

From The Israeli Elders' Viewpoint:

1. When they lost the first battle at Ebenezer, what did the elders of Israel conclude? (1 Samuel 4:3-5)

2. How did Phinehas' dying wife describe the significance of the capture of the Ark of God? (1 Samuel 4:22)

3. When Samuel was old, what did the elders of Israel ask for as a symbol of national power and unity? (1 Samuel 8:4-5, 19-20)

From The Prophetic Wisdom Viewpoint:

1. How did God interpret the request for a king to Samuel? (1 Samuel 8:6-9)

2. What prophecy was made about Israel's desire for a king? (1 Samuel 8:18)

3. How and when was this prophecy fulfilled? (1 Kings 12:4, Jeremiah 22:13-17)

Conclusions:

_____ True or false? God is with those who possess a symbol of God's presence.

_____ True or false? God is with those who know and do God's will.

■ "DILEMMA GUIDE" (Answer Guide)

From The Philistine Viewpoint:

1. They were afraid and fought hard.
2. Get it out of here!
3. Return it with guilt offering and you will be healed.
4. Put the Ark on a cart pulled by two never-yoked cows that have just calved, and let it go its way.

From The Israeli Elders' Viewpoint:

1. They believed the presence of the Ark of the Covenant would bring certain victory.
2. She named her newborn son "Ichabod," meaning, "The glory has departed from Israel."
3. A king (monarchy).

From The Prophetic Wisdom Viewpoint:

1. God interpreted the request as rejection of God (not Samuel) as leader/king.
2. When the king's taxes are oppressive, people will cry to God, but God will not hear.
3. People cried to Solomon's son Rehoboam for relief from the heavy yoke, harsh labor, but Rehoboam increased taxes and labor. Jeremiah taught that a good king does not build by oppressing workers but by defending the poor and needy.

Conclusions:

False

True

■ "AGENDA FOR ELDERS' MEETING"

Devotions: Deuteronomy 31:3-6, 15-21   Prophecy of Moses
Joshua 3:3-4   Sacred Power of Ark
Judges 8:22-23   God's Kingship

Purpose of Special Meeting:

Elders of Israel, I have called you together at our tabernacle in Shiloh because of a **crisis** in our nation. Yesterday our nation was **defeated** by the Philistine army (they control all the iron and have better weapons) at Ebenezer, killing 4000 of our soldiers. You elders of Israel called for the Ark of the Covenant, and Hophni and Phinehas (sons of Eli the priest) brought it to Ebenezer. But 30,000 soldiers were killed, Hophni and Phinehas were killed, and **our sacred Ark of the Covenant was captured** by the Philistines. When Eli heard this, he fell backwards off his chair and died. His daughter-in-law went into labor, named her son Ichabod ("the glory has departed from Israel"), and then she died.

You can be sure the **Philistines will be back**, for they want our rich farmland. Today they came very close to getting it. Our nation with its sacred covenant has been **humiliated** for all to see. It is obvious that we're not doing something right. We need to make some **changes.** What changes do you feel need to be made?

Possible Solutions:

1. The problem is **political/military.** The nation which defeated us has a central government with a king who levies taxes. Philistia thus has a defense budget large enough to develop the best iron weapons - swords, shields, fast chariots. We need a **king, a defense budget,** and **iron weapons.**

2. The problem is **spiritual.** There is corruption in the priesthood; Eli's sons took bribes, grabbed sacrifices before the givers could offer them, and slept with women who served at the entrance to the Tabernacle (1 Samuel 2:12-17, 22-25). The people have Baal and Ashtoreth idols and have been worshipping them. Our nation needs a time of corporate **confession, repentance, sacrifice and rededication to the God of the Covenant.** When our spiritual strength is **renewed,** physical strength will return.

3. Other: _____
   _____
   _____

Discuss possible solutions, and **be ready to present your advice to Samuel** when he returns.

1. Israel's crisis at Ebenezer invites consideration of the relationships of God, people, and earthly governments. Read and summarize the following passages:

   Romans 13:1-7 _____

   _____

   _____

   1 Timothy 2:1-4 _____

   _____

   _____

   1 Peter 2:13-17 _____

   _____

   _____

2. What were Samuel's (and God's) reasons for opposing a king/monarchy? (1 Samuel 8:7-9, 17-18, 10:17-19, 12:12, 17-19) _____

   _____

   _____

   _____

3. After God told Samuel to anoint a king, how did Samuel instruct the people on the relationship of God, king and people? (1 Samuel 12:13-15) _____

   _____

   _____

4. When the laws of a king/government conflict with the laws of God, which takes priority? (Exodus 1:17, Acts 4:19, 5:29) _____

   _____

   _____

5. When we make wrong or less-than-ideal decisions, does God abandon us to forever suffer the consequences? Explain your answer. (1 Samuel 12:20-25) _____

   _____

   _____

   _____

SEARCH SHEET 18
ANSWER GUIDE

1. Israel's crisis at Ebenezer invites consideration of the relationships of God, people, and earthly governments. Read and summarize the following passages:

    Romans 13:1-7 _Submit to governmental authorities because they are God's servants; they receive their authority from God._

    1 Timothy 2:1-4 _Pray for all those in authority. This will result in peaceful quiet lives, holy living which will bring all people to a saving knowledge of God's truth._

    1 Peter 2:13-17 _Doing good silences gossip. Live in freedom as God's servants, not using freedom as a cover for evil. Respect everyone; love the church universal, worship God, honor the king (governmental authority)._

2. What were Samuel's (and God's) reasons for opposing a king/monarchy? (1 Samuel 8:7-9, 17-18, 10:17-19, 12:12, 17-19) _Monarchy (earthly king) represented rejection of God as leader, compromise with evil. A monarchy would oppress the people with taxation and add to other sins of rebellion by the people._

3. After God told Samuel to anoint a king, how did Samuel instruct the people on the relationship of God, king and people? (1 Samuel 12:13-15) _The king and the people are to obey and follow God._

4. When the laws of a king/government conflict with the laws of God, which takes priority? (Exodus 1:17, Acts 4:19, 5:29) _The laws of God, sometimes by direct means, other times using indirect ways._

5. When we make wrong or less-than-ideal decisions, does God abandon us to forever suffer the consequences? Explain your answer. (1 Samuel 12:20-25) _No – God calls and chooses people, makes a covenant with people; and God keeps the covenant faithfully even when the people don't. God is merciful and gracious!_

DAILY SCRIPTURE
READINGS • WEEK 18

THE **AWE REVERENCE WONDER** AT THE **NEARNESS HOLINESS BEAUTY** OF GOD = THE BEGINNING OF **WISDOM**

(PROVERBS 1:7A)

	HEBREW SCRIPTURE	NEW TESTAMENT	PSALM	PROVERBS
Day 1	Judges 11:1-12:15	John 1:1-28	101:1-8	14:13-14
Day 2	Judges 13:1-14:20	John 1:29-51	102:1-28	14:15-16
Day 3	Judges 15:1-16:31	John 2:1-25	103:1-22	14:17-19
Day 4	Judges 17:1-18:31	John 3:1-21	104:1-23	14:20-21
Day 5	Judges 19:1-20:48	John 3:22-4:3	104:24-35	14:22-24
Day 6	Judges 21:1-Ruth 1:22	John 4:4-42	105:1-15	14:25
Day 7	Ruth 2:1-4:22	John 4:43-54	105:16-36	14:26-27

Personal Notes and Glimpses of Wisdom:

"I wonder which way to go now...

SESSION 19 • WISDOM IN A UNITED MONARCHY

The aim of this session is to glean insights into just and peaceful living by exploring Israel's zenith era, the united monarchy.

MATERIALS NEEDED

Hymnals
Accompaniment
Bibles
Newsprint or chalkboard
Completed Search Sheet 18
Completed Insights from Daily Scripture Readings For Week 18
Copies for each participant of:
    "United Monarchy References"
    "Peace and Justice Perspectives"
    Search Sheet 19
    Daily Scripture Readings For Week 19

▧ ASSEMBLING

Although a monarchy was not God's ideal for Israel (theocracy - rule by God - was the ideal), God blessed Israel greatly during the reigns of Saul, David and Solomon. Through these kings, God delivered the people from Philistine oppression, united them with Jerusalem as their capital, led them in construction of a beautiful Temple, and gave them many years of peaceful living with justice for all. Pray for wisdom as you lead participants to discover what makes for **peaceful and just living.**

▧ THE APPROACH TO GOD   (5 to 10 minutes)

❧ *Sing a hymn* such as *"Praise To The Lord, The Almighty, The King of Creation,"* or *"The King Of Love My Shepherd Is."* (Note: For a variation from singing, a hymn can be read by participants and leader responsively as a prayer.)

❧ *Offer a prayer* for insight and guidance in this session as participants and leader search together for keys to peaceful and just living.

▧ ENCOUNTERING THE WORD   (40 to 45 minutes)

⇨ Briefly review Search Sheet 18 on the relationships of God, government, and people. Invite participants' responses to the last question. Then proceed with the following transition to this session:

A monarchy was seen by God and Samuel as a departure from God's kingly shepherding of the Hebrew people. God retains kingship by choosing the king. Samuel reaffirms God's kingship by rededicating the newly-anointed king and people to serving God as a kingdom (kin-dom) of priests, their covenantal calling. This session shows God blessing the people richly during the time of their united monarchy. One of the greatest gifts the nation of Israel experienced during this 120-year era was **peace with justice**. The hand-out, "United Monarchy References," lists Scripture from the United Monarchy era and related passages which shows ways of **building** or **destroying peace.**

⇨ (Invite participants to divide the passages among themselves, look them up, summarizing each with a phrase or two. Allow up to 20 minutes for looking up the references.)

⇨ (Then bring the group together. Distribute copies of "Peace and Justice Perspectives." Make two columns on chalkboard or newsprint: **Ways That Build Peace** and **Ways That Destroy Peace**. Using the summarized "United Monarchy References" and drawing on the knowledge and experience of participants, create a group list of **"Peace and Justice Perspectives."** Allow about 20 minutes for this exercise.)

▩ GOING FORTH IN GOD'S NAME   (5 to 10 minutes)

❧ *Sing* *"Let There Be Peace On Earth"* as a closing **prayer.**

❧ Distribute copies of:
  Search Sheet 19
  Daily Scripture Readings For Week 19

■ "UNITED MONARCHY REFERENCES"

Summarize each passage in a phrase or two. What is happening in the passage that **builds** or **destroys** *peace and justice?*

KING SAUL

1 Samuel 9:21 _____

1 Samuel 10:6, 9-11 _____

1 Samuel 10:25 _____

1 Samuel 10:26 _____

1 Samuel 11:6 _____

1 Samuel 12:14-15, 24-25, 13:13 _____

1 Samuel 15:22-23 _____

KING DAVID

1 Samuel 16:7 _____

1 Samuel 17:37, 47 _____

1 Samuel 18:14-16 _____

1 Samuel 22:2 _____

1 Samuel 24:1-8, 12-22, 26:9, 23-24 _____

1 Samuel 30:23-25 _____

2 Samuel 1:11-12, 17-27 _____

2 Samuel 5:1-3 _____

2 Samuel 5:6-10 _____

2 Samuel 5:12 _____

2 Samuel 5:19, 22-25 _____

2 Samuel 6:1-5, 17-19 _____

2 Samuel 8:15 _____

2 Samuel 9:1-13, 21:7 _____

2 Samuel 12:7-12 (fulfilled in Chapters 13-21) _____

2 Samuel 23:2-4 _____

Proverbs 24:17, Luke 6:27-35 _____

KING SOLOMON

1 Kings 2:2-4, 3:3 _____

1 Kings 3:5-15, 5:12 _____

1 Kings 3:16-28 _____

1 Kings 4:20, 25 _____

1 Kings 4:29-34 _____

1 Kings 6:11-13 _____

1 Kings 8:10-11, 20-21, 54-56 _____

1 Kings 9:3-9 _____

1 Kings 10:23-24 _____

1 Kings 11:1-13 _____

■ "UNITED MONARCHY REFERENCES" Answer Guide

Summarize each passage in a phrase or two. What is happening in the passage that *builds* or *destroys* *peace and justice?*

KING SAUL

1 Samuel 9:21 *King anointed from least clan, smallest tribe (humility)*
1 Samuel 10:6, 9-11 *King empowered and changed by the Spirit of God*
1 Samuel 10:25 *Regulations of kingship were communicated clearly*
1 Samuel 10:26 *King's associates are "of valor," with hearts touched by God*
1 Samuel 11:6 *Spirit of God gives King anger, with compassion for oppressed*
1 Samuel 12:14-15, 24-25, 13:13 *Obey = enjoy goodness; disobey = oppression*
1 Samuel 15:22-23 *God delights in obedience; rebellion , stubbornness are idolatry*

KING DAVID

1 Samuel 16:7 *Man looks on outward appearance; God looks at heart*
1 Samuel 17:37, 47 *David's trust is in God alone; God gives victory*
1 Samuel 18:14-16 *David successful because God is with him; people love & respect*
1 Samuel 22:2 *David organizes those in distress, debt, discontent*
1 Samuel 24:1-8, 12-22, 26:9, 23-24 *David spares King Saul's life*
1 Samuel 30:23-25 *Equality among the troops; all share alike*
2 Samuel 1:11-12, 17-27 *David mourns, writes lament for Saul upon his death*
2 Samuel 5:1-3 *Unites 12 tribes by covenant at Hebron*
2 Samuel 5:6-10 *Conquers Jerusalem, makes it a Center for God*
2 Samuel 5:12 *Recognizes God's hand in establishing his kingship*
2 Samuel 5:19, 22-25 *Inquires of God before battle*
2 Samuel 6:1-5, 17-19 *Brings Ark of Covenant to Jerusalem, celebrates, blesses*
2 Samuel 8:15 *David did what is just and right*
2 Samuel 9:1-13, 21:7 *Shows kindness to Saul's grandson Mephibosheth*
2 Samuel 12:7-12 (fulfilled in Chapters 13-21) *Sin results in family disintegration*
2 Samuel 23:2-4 *Spirit of God speaks through those who rule justly*
Proverbs 24:17, Luke 6:27-35 *Don't gloat; love enemies*

KING SOLOMON

1 Kings 2:2-4, 3:3 *Receives advice from father David and follows it*
1 Kings 3:5-15, 5:12 *Asks God for wisdom; God gives wisdom and peace*
1 Kings 3:16-28 *Judges wisely between disputing mothers*
1 Kings 4:20, 25 *People have plenty of food, housing, are happy, celebrate*
1 Kings 4:29-34 *Solomon is a lover of arts, student of biology, science and nature*
1 Kings 6:11-13 *God promises blessing for obedience in building Temple*
1 Kings 8:10-11, 20-21, 54-56 *God's glory fills well-built Temple; blesses people*
1 Kings 9:3-9 *God promises blessing for obedience, curse for disobedience*
1 Kings 10:23-24 *Whole world seeks to hear Solomon's wisdom*
1 Kings 11:1-13 *Solomon's many foreign marriages bring God's judgment*

■ PEACE AND JUSTICE PERSPECTIVES

Ways That Build Peace   Ways That Destroy Peace

_____   _____
_____   _____
_____   _____
_____   _____
_____   _____
_____   _____
_____   _____
_____   _____
_____   _____
_____   _____
_____   _____
_____   _____
_____   _____
_____   _____
_____   _____
_____   _____
_____   _____
_____   _____
_____   _____
_____   _____
_____   _____
_____   _____
_____   _____
_____   _____
_____   _____
_____   _____
_____   _____
_____   _____

The **peace, justice** and **unity** of Israel's united monarchy was so great that in the years to come people longed for the return of such an era – particularly King David's reign. Look up and summarize the following references. Then, on the lines below, write a brief paragraph describing what the Hebrew people expected their Messiah to be like.

2 Samuel 7:16 _____

1 Kings 8:25-26 _____

2 Chronicles 11:17_____

Nehemiah 12:24, 45 _____

Psalm 132:11-18 _____

Isaiah 9:7_____

Jeremiah 23:5-6 _____

Matthew 12:22-23_____

Mark 11:9 _____

Luke 2:4, 11 _____

John 7:40-42_____

Acts 1:6_____

The Hebrew people expected their Messiah to be_____

_____

_____

_____

_____

_____

_____

_____

_____

_____

_____

_____

_____

The **peace, justice** and **unity** of Israel's united monarchy was so great that in the years to come people longed for the return of such an era – particularly King David's reign. Look up and summarize the following references. Then, on the lines below, write a brief paragraph describing what the Hebrew people expected their Messiah to be like.

2 Samuel 7:16 _God promises David the kingdom and throne forever_

1 Kings 8:25-26 _Solomon petitions God to fulfill the promise to David_

2 Chronicles 11:17 _Strengthened Judah by walking in the ways of David and Solomon_

Nehemiah 12:24, 45 _Praise, purification, singing done as commanded by David_

Psalm 132:11-18 _Promise of blessing, "sprout" from David because of obedience_

Isaiah 9:7 _Messiah will establish throne of David via peace, justice, righteousness_

Jeremiah 23:5-6 _Righteous, just and wise "Branch" raised up for David_

Matthew 12:22-23 _After healing, "Can this be the Son of David?"_

Mark 11:9 _Blessed is kingdom of our father David - Hosanna!_

Luke 2:4, 11 _Jesus is born in Bethlehem, the "City of David"_

John 7:40-42 _Messiah to be descended from David, coming from Bethlehem_

Acts 1:6 _Lord, will you at this time restore the kingdom to Israel?_

The Hebrew people expected their Messiah to be _a descendant of David, born in Bethlehem, the City of David, one who would rule with peace, justice, and righteousness. Their Messiah would be filled with an extraordinary measure of God's Spirit, a prophet who could heal the sick. But most of all, their Messiah would be a military leader, like David, who would free Israel from foreign rule._

DAILY SCRIPTURE
READINGS • WEEK 19

THE **AWE REVERENCE WONDER** AT THE **NEARNESS HOLINESS BEAUTY** OF GOD = THE BEGINNING OF **WISDOM**

(PROVERBS 1:7A)

	HEBREW SCRIPTURE	NEW TESTAMENT	PSALM	PROVERBS
Day 1	1 Samuel 1:1-2:21	John 5:1-23	105:37-45	14:28-29
Day 2	1 Samuel 2:22-4:22	John 5:24-47	106:1-12	14:30-31
Day 3	1 Samuel 5:1-7:17	John 6:1-21	106:13-31	14:32-33
Day 4	1 Samuel 8:1-9:27	John 6:22-42	106:32-48	14:34-35
Day 5	1 Samuel 10:1-11:15	John 6:43-71	107:1-43	15:1-3
Day 6	1 Samuel 12:1-13:22	John 7:1-29	108:1-13	15:4
Day 7	1 Samuel 13:23-14:52	John 7:30-53	109:1-31	15:5-7

Personal Notes and Glimpses of Wisdom:

"I wonder if this is the path to peace and justice...

_____

_____

_____

_____

_____

_____

_____

_____

_____

_____

SESSION 20 • WISDOM IN A DIVIDED MONARCHY

The aim of this session is to view the kings of Israel and Judah through the eyes of God and to reflect on their wisdom.

MATERIALS NEEDED

Hymnals
Accompaniment
Bibles
Chalkboard or newsprint
75" long x 20" wide newsprint-covered wall area, dated as on "The Divided Monarchy"
Tape or push pins
Gummed stars (or colored markers to make stars)
Lectern/podium
"Drama Of The Kings" copied and cut for assigning to participants
Completed Search Sheet 19
Completed Insights from Daily Scripture Readings For Week 19
Copies for each participant of:
    "The Divided Monarchy"
    Entire "Drama Of The Kings" (optional)
    Search Sheet 20
    Daily Scripture Readings For Week 20

▩ ASSEMBLING

The drama of the kings of Israel and Judah provides leader and participants with an opportunity to view earthly governments through God's eyes via prophetic wisdom writers. It is the story of people searching for a **peace** they know is possible, yet so difficult to attain. Both branches of the divided kingdom (**"Israel" = northern** 10 tribes; **"Judah"** = tribes of Judah and Benjamin, or **southern** tribes) end in tragic failure on the part of the people of God. There is hope, however, that the triumphs and failures of the people led by the kings may lead to greater discernment of the **cause and effect** of **peace.**

▩ THE APPROACH TO GOD　(5 to 10 minutes)

❥ *Sing a hymn* – Begin with a hymn/prayer which petitions God's leadership.

▩ ENCOUNTERING THE WORD　(40 to 45 minutes)

➪ With Search Sheet 19 in hand, invite participants to name the qualities the people of God looked for in their promised Messiah. *Option: List them on chalkboard or newsprint.*

➪ Then *make the transition* to the "Drama of the Kings" saying: The people's expectation of their Messiah helps us see how they viewed their leaders, the kings of Israel and Judah. The books of 1 and 2 Kings and 1 and 2 Chronicles tell how the kings of the divided monarchy were seen **in the eyes of God.** The prophetic writers indicate other volumes which record all the acts of these kings. But in Biblical writings only the most essential details are included: ancestry from David, the naming (and thus importance) of the king's mother, the direction of the king's heart, whether they led and upheld pure worship of God (or idolatry), consistency in following the law of God given through Moses, military victories (and defeats) and how they are affected by pure worship (or idolatry), and what kind of burial the king received.

⇨ ***Distribute copies*** *of "The Divided Monarchy" and scripts of the kings among participants. Inform them they're going to present the "Drama Of The Kings" by taking turns reading first-person narratives of the kings. Following the reading,* **tape or pin** *the script on the 75" long x 20" wide newsprint-covered wall area – with dates written in center during a "trial run" – first going through the kings of* **Israel** *in order, then of* **Judah** *as on "The Divided Monarchy." Next,* **choose a color** *(gummed foil star or marker to make a star) to represent* **"good"** *and another color to represent* **"evil."** *Place the appropriate star next to the king's (or queen's) name. Also select another color to represent* **"dynasty change."** *Place a star of this color beside the king's name whenever he was not related to the king who preceded him.* **Let the drama begin – (and remember to save the set-up for next session!)**

Questions For Reflection Following Drama:

1. How many **dynasty changes** were there in Israel? Judah?

2. What were some **repeated themes or phrases** in the drama?

3. What was the status of national security when the king led the people in **pure worship** and followed God's laws? What happened to national security when the king allowed or led the nation in **idolatry?**

4. What is the **relationship** between pure worship of God and national security in your country?

5. What criteria does God use to measure the **wisdom** of leaders?

▨ GOING FORTH IN GOD'S NAME (5 to 10 minutes)

❧ ***Sing a hymn*** which reflects or petitions the wisdom of God-centered leaders. *"I Need Thee Every Hour"* is a possibility.

❧ Distribute copies of:
Entire "Drama Of The Kings" (optional)
Search Sheet 20
Daily Scripture Readings For Week 20

■ "THE DIVIDED MONARCHY"

Northern (Israel)	Year (BCE**) Reign Began	Southern (Judah)
Jeroboam I	< 930 >	Rehoboam
	913 >	Abijam
	910 >	Asa*
Nadab	< 909	
Baasha	< 908	
Elah	< 886	
Zimri	< 885	
Omri	< 885	
Ahab	< 874	
	872 >	Jehoshaphat*
Ahaziah	< 853	
Joram (Jehoram)	< 852	
	848 >	Jehoram*
Jehu	< 841	
	841 >	Ahaziah
	841 >	Athaliah
	835 >	Joash
Jehoahaz	< 814	
Jehoash	< 798	
	796 >	Amaziah*
Jeroboam II	< 793	
	792 >	Azariah (Uzziah)*
Zechariah	< 753	
Shallum	< 752	
Menahem	< 752	
	750 >	Jotham*
Pekahiah	< 742	
Pekah*	< 740	
	735>	Ahaz
Hoshea	< 732	
Israel Falls to Assyria	< 722	
	715 >	Hezekiah*
	686 >	Manasseh*
	642 >	Amon
	640 >	Josiah
	609 >	Jehoahaz
	609 >	Jehoiakim
	598 >	Jehoiachin
	587 >	Zedekiah
	586 >	Judah Falls To Babylon
	THE EXILE	
	538	
	THE RESTORATION	
	432	
	THE INTER-TESTAMENTAL YEARS	

* Denotes overlapping reigns or co-regencies which cause discrepancies in number of years reigned. Discrepancies also occur when the year the king ascended the throne is counted or not counted.

** BCE = Before The Common Era – current archaeological interpretation

■ "DRAMA OF THE KINGS"

JEROBOAM I
Northern (Israel) 930-909 BCE
(1 Kings 11:26-40, 12:1-24, 14:21-31)

I, Jeroboam I, was chief foreman for King Solomon's labor force when the prophet Ahijah came to me and told me God was going to **divide** the kingdom because of Solomon's breach of the most basic terms of the covenant; he joined his foreign wives in **worshipping idols**, and his **heart turned away** from God. Solomon tried to kill me, but I fled to Egypt and stayed there until he died.

When Solomon's son Rehoboam refused to lighten the taxes, ten of the twelve tribes of Israel drafted me as their king. I am an Ephraimite, so I built forts in the hill country of Ephraim. Then I got worried that the people might give allegiance to King Rehoboam when they went to Jerusalem to offer sacrifices. So I made two **golden calves** (symbols of virility, upon which Canaanite gods rode) and put one at Dan in the north and the other at Bethel in the south. I led the people in offering sacrifices at these shrines. God warned me of this sin of **idolatry** through prophets; but I did not listen. I did so much evil in the eyes of the Lord that God vowed to cut off my entire family. I reigned over the ten tribes for 22 years and was buried with my fathers. My son Nadab succeeded me as king.

NADAB
Northern (Israel) 909-908 BCE
(1 Kings 15:25-31)

I, Nadab, am the son of Jeroboam. I reigned for two years and followed in the steps of my father, doing evil in the eyes of the Lord. I was murdered by Baasha, son of Ahijah of the tribe of Issachar.

BAASHA
Northern (Israel) 908-886 BCE
(1 Kings 15:27 - 16:6)

I, Baasha, of the tribe of Issachar, **murdered** Jeroboam's son Nadab and became king of the ten tribes. I **killed** all of Jeroboam's family as the prophet Ahijah had predicted because of their sinfulness in leading the people of Israel into **idolatry**. However, as the prophetic writer records, I did not do much better. I followed in the ways of Jeroboam and Nadab and **did evil** in the eyes of the Lord. I led Israel in civil war against King Asa of Judah throughout the 24 years of my reign. The prophet Jehu, son of Hanani, pronounced God's judgment on my family because of my wickedness. I died and was buried with my fathers, and my son Elah succeeded me as king.

ELAH
Northern (Israel) 886-885 BCE
(1 Kings 16:8-14)

I, Elah, son of Baasha, reigned over the ten tribes for two years. I followed in the ways of my father and led Israel in the **worship of idols**. One night, one of my officials, Zimri, plotted against me. While I was at the home of Arza, the man in charge of the palace at Tirzah, I got **drunk.** Zimri came in, struck me down, and killed me so he could be king.

ZIMRI
Northern (Israel) 885 BCE
(1 Kings 16:9-20)

I, Zimri, an official of King Elah, became king of the ten tribes by killing Elah while he was drunk. I promptly **killed** all of Elah's (and his father Baasha's) family in the seven days of my reign as prophesied by the prophet Jehu because of their sins of idolatry. I did nothing to stop the idolatry but **continued idol worship** the way Jeroboam began it. I was not accepted as king by the Israelites in Tirzah because I **killed the king**. They proclaimed Army Commander Omri as King instead. Omri besieged Tirzah. When I saw that the city was taken, I went into the citadel of the royal palace and **set the palace on fire** around me. The prophetic writer records my death as the result of my sins, **rebellion** against King Elah, and **idolatry** – doing **evil** in the eyes of the Lord.

OMRI
Northern (Israel) 885-874 BCE
(1 Kings 16:16-28)

I, Omri, overcame division and became one of the most **politically powerful** kings of Israel. The Assyrians referred to Israel as the "land of Omri." I bought a hill and built the city of Samaria on it. I made a **marriage alliance** with King Ethbaal of Tyre and Sidon by uniting his daughter Jezebel with my son Ahab. This gave **Baalism** a strong foothold in a land whose covenant clearly prohibited worship of anyone but the God who led and delivered a holy priestly people as a good shepherd leads sheep. The prophetic writer says I **sinned more** in the eyes of the Lord during the 12 years of my reign than all the kings before me, walking in the **idolatrous ways** of King Jeroboam.

AHAB
Northern (Israel) 874-853 BCE
(1 Kings 16:29 - 22:40)

I, Ahab, son of Omri, reigned over the ten tribes for 22 years. My wife, Queen Jezebel, was an **active queen** who **murdered** the Lord's priests and prophets in order to spread Baalism throughout the land. I helped her by building a temple to Baal in Samaria and erecting Asherah poles, wooden representations of the fertility goddess, throughout the land.

Since Baal was a **weather god**, the prophet Elijah proclaimed God's sovereignty over the weather by announcing there would be no rain for three years. After the three years of drought, he challenged the prophets of Baal to a showdown at Mt. Carmel. They lost, and Elijah slaughtered the prophets of Baal. Then God sent rain.

In spite of **God's miracle of rain**, Jezebel and I continued to sin and tried to kill Elijah. We **shed the innocent blood** of Naboth because he refused to sell me his beautiful vineyard. I did more **evil** in the eyes of the Lord than any of the kings before me. But because I **humbled myself** God's prophecy of destruction of my royal family was delayed. I was killed in battle by a random arrow and buried in Samaria.

AHAZIAH
Northern (Israel) 853-852 BCE
(1 Kings 22:51 - 2 Kings 1:18)

I, Ahaziah, son of Ahab and Jezebel, ruled over the ten tribes for two years. Like Jeroboam and my parents, I did **evil** in the eyes of the Lord, serving and worshipping Baal and Asherah. Once, when I was ill, I **sinned by consulting a foreign prophet** of a Philistine god. As he had rebuked my parents, so Elijah rebuked me for this, saying, "Is it because there is no God in Israel for you to consult that you have consulted with Baal-Zebub?" And as Elijah predicted, I never recovered from my illness. Because I had no son, my younger brother Joram succeeded me as king.

JORAM
Northern (Israel) 852-841 BCE
(2 Kings 1:17, 3:1 - 9:26)

I, Joram, younger son of Ahab and Jezebel, ruled Israel for 12 years. I continued the **idol worship** begun by Jeroboam and my parents, but I got rid of the sacred Baal stone they made. When Moab rebelled against paying the 100,000 lambs they owed from an agreement with my father, I got King Jehoshaphat of Judah to help me fight them. When we ran out of water and things looked bad for us, Jehoshaphat asked for a prophet to interpret the word of the Lord for us. Elisha wouldn't speak to me because I worshipped Baal; but as a harpist played, he prophesied victory against Moab. His word came true. God provided water which looked red like blood to the Moabites. They became over-confident, and we defeated them. When the defeated King of Moab sacrificed his firstborn son, the Moabite army retreated.

After I was **wounded in a battle** with the Arameans and was recovering at Jezreel, I saw a chariot charging toward us and went to meet it. It was fast-driving Jehu! "Do you come in **peace**?" I asked. "How can there be peace as long as the idolatry and witchcraft of your mother Jezebel abound?" he replied. Jehu shot me between the shoulders with an arrow which pierced my heart. Then, to fulfill the prophecy of the Lord through Elisha, he **threw my body in Naboth's vineyard**.

JEHU
Northern (Israel) 841-814 BCE
(2 Kings 9 and 10)

I, Jehu, was anointed by one of Elisha's company of prophets to be king over the ten tribes. My task was to **fulfill the judgment of the Lord** on the house of Ahab. I drove a fast chariot and killed King Joram in a surprise attack. I had Jezebel thrown from the palace window to her death below where horses trampled her. I had Ahab and Jezebel's 70 grandsons beheaded. In Samaria, I killed all who were related to Ahab and Jezebel. I pretended I was going to make a great sacrifice to Baal and invited all the Baal priests and prophets, provided robes for them, ambushed and killed them in their temple. Because of my **faithfulness in destroying Baal worship**, God promised that my descendants would sit on the throne of Israel to the fourth generation. While I destroyed Baal worship in Israel, I **allowed the golden calves to remain** at Bethel and Dan; and I was not **careful to keep the laws of the Lord with all my heart**. I reigned in Samaria 28 years and was buried there with my fathers.

JEHOAHAZ
Northern (Israel) 814-798 BCE
(2 Kings 10:35, 13:1-9)

I, Jehoahaz, am the son of Jehu who ruled Israel as king for 17 years. Although I did not restore the Baal worship my father Jehu had so vigorously destroyed, I **allowed worship of the golden calves to continue** in Bethel and Dan. And I allowed the Asherah pole to remain standing in Samaria. In anger, God allowed the Syrian kings to oppress us. When I prayed, God listened and delivered us. But we still **did not turn away from idolatry**. I died and was buried with my fathers in Samaria.

JEHOASH
Northern (Israel) 798-782 BCE
(2 Kings 13:10-25, 14:8-16)

I, Jehoash, am the son of Jehoahaz and grandson of Jehu. During my reign, King Amaziah of Judah made war on me, so I fought and won, taking hostages and temple treasures to Samaria. Syria remained a threat to Israel, so I consulted with Elisha. As he prophesied, we defeated Syria three times. I led Israel in **continuing to worship the golden calves** at Dan and Bethel, and the prophetic writers record that I did evil in the eyes of the Lord because I **did not turn away from the sins** of Jeroboam son of Nebat. When I died, I was buried in Samaria with the kings of Israel.

JEROBOAM II
Northern (Israel) 793-753 BCE
(2 Kings 14:23-29)

I, Jeroboam II, son of Jehoash, great-grandson of Jehu, ruled Israel for 41 years, part of that time as a co-regent with my father Jehoash. I was a ***politically strong leader*** and ***regained territory*** previously lost to Syria. This had been predicted by the prophet Jonah. However, there was ***internal corruption*** during my reign. Prophets Hosea and Amos record extremes of wealth and poverty, with oppression of the poor by the wealthy. For this ***lack of justice*** and for ***not turning from the sins of Jeroboam***, the prophetic writers record me as a king who did evil in the eyes of the Lord. I died and was buried with the kings of Israel.

ZECHARIAH
Northern (Israel) 753-752 BCE
(2 Kings 15:8-12)

I, Zechariah, am the son of Jeroboam II, ***fourth generation king descending from Jehu***. As God had said to my great-great-grandfather Jehu, his dynasty would end in the fourth generation. It ended in the sixth month of my reign when I was assassinated by Shallum. I did ***evil*** in the eyes of the Lord and ***did not turn away from the sins*** of Jeroboam I.

SHALLUM
Northern (Israel) 752 BCE
(2 Kings 15:10-15)

I, Shallum, son of Jabesh, ***killed*** King Zechariah and ***usurped*** the throne of Israel. But I reigned only one month and was assassinated by Menahem who succeeded me.

MENAHEM
Northern (Israel) 752-742 BCE
(2 Kings 15:14-22)

I, Menahem, son of Gadi, ***usurped*** the throne of Israel by killing Shallum. I spent most of my 10 years as king at war with Assyria. Once I attacked a town and ripped open all the pregnant women. But Assyria prevailed, and Israel became a vassal to Assyria and had to pay tribute. I obtained the tribute money by taking it from the wealthy people in Israel. My reign is recorded as ***evil in the eyes of the Lord*** because I ***did not turn away from the idolatry*** introduced by Jeroboam, son of Nebat.

PEKAHIAH
Northern (Israel) 742-740 BCE
(2 Kings 15:23-26)

I, Pekahiah, son of Menahem, ruled Israel for two years before being assassinated by chief officer Pekah. My reign is recorded as ***evil in the eyes of the Lord*** because I ***did not turn away from the sins*** of Jeroboam, son of Nebat.

PEKAH
Northern (Israel) 740-732 BCE
(2 Kings 15:25-31)

I, Pekah, chief officer of Pekahiah, ***assassinated*** Pekahiah and ruled for 20 years, 12 years as co-regent with Menahem. During my reign the King of Assyria took much land and deported many people. I ***did evil*** in the eyes of the Lord because I ***did not turn away from the idolatry*** of Jeroboam. I ***was assassinated*** by Hoshea.

HOSHEA

Northern (Israel) 732-723 BCE
(2 Kings 17)

I, Hoshea, am the **last king** of Israel, **usurping** the throne by **murdering** Pekah. I stopped paying tribute to the King of Assyria and **sought help from Egypt rather than from the Lord.** Assyria besieged Samaria for three years and deported many people. The Israelites rejected the covenant God made with their fathers and the warnings through the prophets. They continued to worship idols, practice divination and sorcery, sold themselves to do evil, and sacrificed their sons and daughters to idols. Even while they were worshipping the Lord, they were serving their idols. I **did evil** in the eyes of the Lord but not like the kings who preceded me. Even so, because of **persistent idolatry** and **turning away from the covenant**, God allowed Samaria to fall to Assyria, and the northern kingdom (Israel) ended.

Southern (Judah) 930-913 BCE   ## REHOBOAM
(1 Kings 12:1-24, 14:21-31, 2 Chronicles 12:1-12)

I, Rehoboam, son of Solomon and Naamah (an Ammonite), ruled Judah for 17 years. When I refused to reduce the taxes my father Solomon had levied, ten northern tribes revolted, led by Jeroboam I. The **kingdom was thus divided**, as God had said, **because of my father's idolatry**. There was **civil war** with Jeroboam I throughout my reign. The people of Judah **worshipped idols**, building sacred stones in high places and making Asherah poles. There were male shrine prostitutes and other detestable practices. I lost the temple treasures to King Shishak of Egypt. When I died, I was buried in the City of David with my fathers.

Southern (Judah) 913-910 BCE   ## ABIJAM
(1 Kings 15:1-8, 2 Chronicles 13)

I, Abijam, son of Rehoboam and Maacah, reigned over Judah for three years. **Civil war** with the ten tribes of Israel continued. Although Judah had only 400,000 fighting men compared to Israel's 800,000, **our little nation prevailed because we were the covenant-bearers of the Davidic dynasty** who had the **Levitical priesthood** while Israel had golden calves and their own non-Levitical priests. God delivered us, and we inflicted heavy casualties on Israel. Although we worshipped the God of our fathers, we **continued in the sins** of my father; and my **heart was not fully devoted** to God like my great-grandfather David's had been. The history of my reign was written by the prophet Iddo. Upon my death, I received a royal burial.

Southern (Judah) 910-869 BCE   ## ASA
(1 Kings 15:8-24, 2 Chronicles 15 & 16)

I, Asa, son of Abijam and Maacah, reigned in Judah for 41 years. I **repaired the altar** of the Lord, expelled the male prostitutes, got rid of my father's idols, and even deposed my mother Maacah because she made an Asherah pole. **My heart was fully committed to the Lord all my life**. There was civil war with Baasha of Israel, and I enlisted the help of the King of Syria, giving him the temple treasures and brutally oppressing some people. When I developed a severe foot disease in my old age, I sought help from physicians only and not from the Lord. When I died, I was buried with my fathers in the City of David.

Southern (Judah) 872-848 BCE   ## JEHOSHAPHAT
(1 Kings 22:41-50, 2 Chronicles 17:1 - 21:1)

I, Jehoshaphat, son of Asa and Azubah, reigned 25 years. I **did what was right in the eyes of the Lord**, like my father. I got rid of the prostitutes and shrines. During my reign, Judah was **at peace** with Israel. I fortified cities and stationed troops to keep peace. I sent out priests and officials to teach the ways of the Lord throughout Judah. This **religious education program** caused other nations to be in awe of the Lord our God so they did not make war on us. I appointed judges to turn the people back to the Lord by showing them **justice without partiality or bribery**. When there was war with the Moabites and Ammonites, I pleaded with God for deliverance. **While Jahaziel led the people in worship, the Lord ambushed the enemy**. We gave thanks and praise to God, and it took three days to collect the plunder! In spite of all I did, the prophet Jehu records that the hearts of the people were not set on God. When I died, I was buried in the City of David.

JEHORAM
Southern (Judah) 848-841 BCE
(2 Kings 8:16-24, 2 Chronicles 21:1-20)

I, Jehoram, son of Jehoshaphat, ruled Judah for eight years. I **killed my brothers** to establish the kingdom. I married Athaliah, daughter of Ahab and Jezebel of Israel, and walked in their **evil ways**. Because **I forsook God**, God allowed **enemy countries to attack**. The prophet Elijah sent me a letter saying God would bring a horrible bowel disease upon me as judgment for my **idolatry and murder**. No one mourned my death. I was **not buried with the kings**.

AHAZIAH
Southern (Judah) 841 BCE
(2 Kings 8:25-29, 9:21-29, 2 Chronicles 22:1-9)

I, Ahaziah, son of Jehoram and Athaliah, reigned one year in Judah. Encouraged by my mother, I **did evil** in the eyes of the Lord. My father's advisers turned against me. While King Joram of Israel and I were fighting King Hazael, Jehu killed me. Because my grandfather Jehoshaphat obeyed God, I was buried with my fathers in the City of David.

ATHALIAH
Southern (Judah) 841-835 BCE
(2 Kings 11:1-21, 2 Chronicles 22:10 - 23:21)

I, Queen Athaliah, wife of Jehoram, daughter of Ahab and Jezebel of Israel, saw that my son Ahaziah was dead. I **destroyed the whole royal family**, including **killing all my grandchildren**. I **led the people in the worship of Baal**, the god of my mother Jezebel the Sidonian. My daughter Jehoshabeath was married to Jehoiada the high priest of the God of the Covenant. She and Jehoiada managed to smuggle little grandson Joash away, keeping him safe in the Lord's temple, a place I never went. When he was seven, Jehoiada organized guards at the temple and crowned Joash king. When I went to see what all the fuss was about, the guards dragged me to the horse stables on the palace grounds and killed me there.

JOASH
Southern (Judah) 835-796 BCE
(2 Kings 12, 2 Chronicles 24)

I, Joash, son of Ahaziah and Zibiah, was crowned king when I was seven. Uncle Jehoiada, the high priest, and Aunt Jehoshabeath who rescued me from my wicked grandma Athaliah, **guided me to do what was right** in the eyes of the Lord. Together, we restored the temple and the Levitical priesthood. When Jehoiada died, he was **buried with the kings**. After his death, we **abandoned the Lord's temple** and worshipped the Asherah poles. We didn't listen to the Lord's prophets. When my cousin Zechariah, son of Uncle Jehoiada, prophesied doom because of our disobedience, I had him stoned. Then my officials killed me for murdering Zechariah. I was buried in the City of David, but **not with the kings**.

AMAZIAH

Southern (Judah) 796-767 BCE
(2 Kings 14:1-22, 2 Chronicles 25:1-17)

I, Amaziah, son of Joash and Jehoaddin, reigned in Judah 29 years. I ***did right*** in the eyes of the Lord but not like David, for I ***did not remove the high places***. I executed the officials who murdered my father but not their sons as the Law required. I defeated the Edomites, but I provoked the attack of Jehoash of Israel who defeated us because we worshipped the gods of the Edomites. Jehoash took the temple treasures and hostages. When I learned of a conspiracy against me in Jerusalem, I fled to Lachish, but they followed and ***killed me*** there. I was ***buried with my fathers*** in the City of David.

AZARIAH

Southern (Judah) 792-740 BCE
(2 Kings 14:21-22, 15:1-7, 2 Chronicles 26:1-23)

I, Azariah (also known as Uzziah), son of Amaziah and Jecoliah, ruled Judah for 52 years. I rebuilt the southern city of Elath and ***did right*** in the eyes of the Lord. ***As long as I sought the Lord, I enjoyed success*** against enemies such as the Philistines and Ammonites. I built towers in Jerusalem and in the desert. I ***loved the soil***! I had a well-trained army, but after becoming powerful, ***pride became my downfall***. *Although I was not a priest, I had a censer in my hand to burn incense in the Lord's temple.* When the priests told me to leave, I became angry and God struck me with leprosy. So I had to live in a separate house while my son Jotham governed the people. I was ***buried near*** my fathers on land which belonged to the kings, ***but not in the kings' tombs because I had leprosy.***

JOTHAM

Southern (Judah) 750-732 BCE
(2 Kings 15:32-38, 2 Chronicles 27:1-9)

I, Jotham, son of Azariah (Uzziah) and Jerusha, reigned 16 years in Jerusalem. I made war on the Ammonites, conquered them, and made them pay tribute. I rebuilt the Upper Gate of the temple. I ***grew powerful because I walked steadfastly before the Lord*** and did right in the eyes of the Lord like my father. When I died, I was buried with my fathers in the City of David.

AHAZ

Southern (Judah) 750-735 BCE
(2 Kings 16:1-20, 2 Chronicles 28)

I, Ahaz, son of Jotham, ruled Judah for 16 years. I ***worshipped the Baals***, burned sacrifices to them and even ***sacrificed my sons***! Therefore, God handed me over to the Syrians. I made a ***military alliance*** with Assyria for help against Syria. To please the Assyrian king, I ***changed the altar in the temple*** of the Lord to his liking, not God's. I ***did evil*** in the eyes of the Lord, unlike David. When I died, I was buried in Jerusalem, but ***not with the kings.***

HEZEKIAH

Southern (Judah) 715-686 BCE
*(2 Kings 18:1 - 20:21, 2 Chronicles 29:1 - 32:33
Isaiah 36 - 39)*

I, Hezekiah, son of Ahaz and Abijah, ruled Judah for 29 years. I removed the high places, cut down Asherah poles, broke the bronze snake which the people burned incense to, stood against the Assyrian king, and defeated the Philistines. When Sennacherib besieged Jerusalem, I consulted Isaiah and went to the temple in sackcloth to pray. The angel of the Lord defeated the Assyrians. When I was ill with boils, I called for Isaiah who told me to prepare to die. Then he returned and said God would give me ***15 extra years***. God gave a sign of this ***healing grace:*** the ***sundial went back 10 steps***. In my extra years, I made a water tunnel into the city of Jerusalem to reduce its vulnerability during siege. I **did what was right in the eyes of the Lord**, trusted in the Lord, held fast, and did not cease to keep the commands God gave. I led in temple purification, restoration of the Levitical priesthood, Passover celebration with rededication ceremony, and joyful tithing. Upon my death, I was **honored and buried with my fathers.**

MANASSEH
Southern (Judah) 697-642 BCE
(2 Kings 21:1-18, 2 Chronicles 33:1-20)

I, Manasseh, son of Hezekiah and Hephzibah, reigned 55 years in Judah. I **did evil** in the eyes of the Lord, rebuilt high places and Asherah poles, worshipped the starry host, built altars to them in the courts of the Lord, **sacrificed my sons**, practiced sorcery, put an idol in the temple and **shed innocent blood**. God allowed the Assyrians to take me prisoner. They put me in shackles and put a ring in my nose. There I prayed and humbled myself. **God restored me; I restored true worship**. When I died, I was **buried in the palace garden.**

AMON
Southern (Judah) 642-640 BCE
(2 Kings 21:19-26, 2 Chronicles 33:21-24)

I, Amon, son of Manasseh and Meshullemeth, reigned two years in Judah. Like my father, I **worshipped idols**. Unlike my father, I **did not humble myself**. I was **assassinated** by my own palace officials. The people of the land killed the assassins and made my son Josiah king. I was **buried with the kings**.

JOSIAH
Southern (Judah) 640-609 BCE
(2 Kings 22:1 - 23:30, 2 Chronicles 34:1 - 36:1)

I, Josiah, son of Amon and Jedidah, reigned 31 years in Judah. I began repair of the temple. Then Hilkiah the priest found the Book of the Law. I consulted the prophetess Huldah whose interpretation was that God was going to bring disaster on us because we have not obeyed God. This disaster would not come in my lifetime because of my faithfulness. I **began a great reformation movement**. I did away with idol worship and sorcery, renewed the covenant with the people, and read the Law to them. Then we celebrated the Passover. I **did right in the eyes of the Lord, not turning to the right or to the left**. I was killed by Pharaoh Neco at Megiddo in a battle I shouldn't have been in. I was buried with my fathers, and the prophet **Jeremiah composed laments** to mourn my death.

JEHOAHAZ
Southern (Judah) 609 BCE
(2 Kings 23:31-33, 2 Chronicles 36:2-4)

I, Jehoahaz, son of Josiah and Hamutal, reigned three months in Judah. I **levied high taxes** on the people and **did evil** in the eyes of the Lord. I was dethroned by the King of Egypt, Pharaoh Neco, and I **died in chains** in Egypt.

JEHOIAKIM
Southern (Judah) 609-598 BCE
(2 Kings 23:34 - 24:7, 2 Chronicles 36:4-8)

I, Jehoiakim (named Eliakim by my parents Josiah and Zebidah), had my name changed by the king of Egypt. I reigned 11 years and **did evil** in the eyes of the Lord. I had to pay Pharaoh Neco the tax levied on my brother Jehoahaz. Under my rule, Judah became a **vassal** of Nebuchadnezzar of Babylon. After three years of this, I rebelled, but the Lord sent raiders against us because of the sins of Manasseh and the shedding of innocent blood. I was buried with my fathers.

Southern (Judah) 598-597 BCE
(2 Kings 24:8-17, 25:27-30, 2 Chronicles 36:8-10)

JEHOIACHIN

I, Jehoiachin, son of Jehoiakim and Nehushta, reigned for three months in Judah. I **did evil** in the eyes of the Lord. At that time ten officers of Nebuchadnezzar of Babylon besieged Jerusalem. I **surrendered**, and my mother, my officials and I were taken as **prisoners** to Babylon as the Lord had declared. Nebuchadnezzar also took treasures from the temple and 10,000 people from Judah into exile. In the 37th year of my captivity, a new king took me from prison, **treated me kindly**, gave me an allowance, and fed me at his table until I died.

Southern (Judah) 597-586 BCE
(2 Kings 24:17 - 25:26, 2 Chronicles 36:10-23)

ZEDEKIAH

I, Zedekiah, son of Josiah and Hamutal, am the **last king of Judah**. I reigned for 11 years and **did evil** in the eyes of the Lord. I **did not humble myself** before Jeremiah when he spoke the word of the Lord. I **rebelled** against the Lord and against King Nebuchadnezzar of Babylon. So the Babylonians came and burned our beautiful temple and palaces. They killed my sons before my eyes and then **put my eyes out**, put me in **shackles** and led me to Babylon. Thus **Judah went into exile** and the land enjoyed its Sabbath rests for 70 years (one-seventh of the 490 years of united and divided monarchy when the people of God did not faithfully observe their Sabbaths and pure worship of God).

Note: *Do not dismantle the display of the kings. It will be needed for the next session.*

SEARCH SHEET 20

Throughout the leadership of the kings of Israel and Judah, there were three other kinds of leaders: **Levitical priests** (of a people called to be priests among the nations), **sages** (who told stories, and spoke and wrote wise sayings known as proverbs), and **prophets**.

The *prophets* **centered** their hearts on God, **listened** to God, and **spoke** the Word of God into the circumstances of Israel's and Judah's life stories. Prophets received little respect; their words were often unwelcome. They were **frequently ridiculed** because their messages seemed "out of sync" with the events surrounding them. Also, it was difficult for people to discern **true** from **false** prophets – because the ultimate test of a prophecy was whether it came true, and this often occurred after the prophet's death.

The *prophets* spoke many different kinds of messages, ranging from **doom and warning** to **hope and encouragement**. God gave them many ways to get their messages across. Sometimes they used **drama**. Listed below are some passages which illustrate the dramatic ways God used the prophets to speak to the people. Look up the passages. Then briefly **record the message God was speaking through the drama:**

Elijah and the showdown at Mt. Carmel (1 Kings 18:16-46) _____

_____

Elisha and the bow and arrow (2 Kings 13:14-19) _____

_____

Isaiah, nude and barefoot (Isaiah 20:1-6) _____

_____

Jeremiah and the linen loincloth (Jeremiah 13:1-11) _____

_____

Jeremiah and the clay pot (Jeremiah 19:1-15) _____

_____

Ezekiel's shaved head (Ezekiel 5:1-12 _____

_____

Hosea's unfaithful wife (Hosea 1:2) _____

_____

Throughout the leadership of the kings of Israel and Judah, there were three other kinds of leaders: **Levitical priests** (of a people called to be priests among the nations), **sages** (who told stories, and spoke and wrote wise saying known as proverbs), and **prophets**.

The *prophets* **centered** their hearts on God, **listened** to God, and **spoke** the Word of God into the circumstances of Israel's and Judah's life story. Prophets received little respect; their words were often unwelcome. They were **frequently ridiculed** because their messages seemed "out of sync" with the events surrounding them. Also, it was difficult for people to discern **true** from **false** prophets – because the ultimate test of a prophecy was whether it came true, and this often occurred after the prophet's death.

The *prophets* spoke many different kinds of messages, ranging from **doom and warning** to **hope and encouragement**. God gave them many ways to get their messages across. Sometimes they used **drama**. Listed below are some passages which illustrate the dramatic ways God used the prophets to speak to the people. Look up the passages. Then briefly **record the message God was speaking through the drama:**

Elijah and the showdown at Mt. Carmel (1 Kings 18:16-46) *God is God, Supreme over the weather - not the "weather god," Baal*

Elisha and the bow and arrow (2 Kings 13:14-19) *Shooting and striking arrows denotes Joash's victory over Aram three times*

Isaiah, nude and barefoot (Isaiah 20:1-6) *Symbolizes Assyria leading Egyptian army away, stripped and barefoot - a warning against alliance with Egypt*

Jeremiah and the linen loincloth (Jeremiah 13:1-11) *God's nearness to the people is ultimately rendered useless by Judah's apostasy - like used and buried underwear*

Jeremiah and the clay pot (Jeremiah 19:1-15) *Broken pot symbolizes an idolatrous nation which will be irreparably broken*

Ezekiel's shaved head (Ezekiel 5:1-12 *The "thirds" of Ezekiel's shaved hair represent "thirds" of Judah 1) dying by famine, 2) dying by sword, 3) and scattered*

Hosea's unfaithful wife (Hosea 1:2) *As Gomer broke the marriage covenant by adultery, so God's people have broken their sacred covenant, forsaking God*

DAILY SCRIPTURE
READINGS • WEEK 20

THE **AWE REVERENCE WONDER** AT THE **NEARNESS HOLINESS BEAUTY** OF GOD = THE BEGINNING OF **WISDOM**

(PROVERBS 1:7A)

	HEBREW SCRIPTURE	NEW TESTAMENT	PSALM	PROVERBS
Day 1	1 Samuel 15:1-16:23	John 8:1-20	110:1-7	15:8-10
Day 2	1 Samuel 17:1-18:4	John 8:21-30	111:1-10	15:11
Day 3	1 Samuel 18:5-19:24	John 8:31-59	112:1-10	15:12-14
Day 4	1 Samuel 20:1-21:15	John 9:1-41	113:1-114:8	15:15-17
Day 5	1 Samuel 22:1-23:29	John 10:1-21	115:1-18	15:18-19
Day 6	1 Samuel 24:1-25:44	John 10:22-42	116:1-19	15:20-21
Day 7	1 Samuel 26:1-28:25	John 11:1-53	117:1-2	15:22-23

Personal Notes and Glimpses of Wisdom:

"I wonder what would happen if I followed some other shepherd..."

SESSION 21 • PROPHETIC WISDOM

*T*he aim of this session is to listen to the wisdom of the prophets announced to the people of God.

MATERIALS NEEDED

Hymnals
Accompaniment
Bibles
Newsprint, chalkboard or bulletin board "Drama Of The Kings" from Session 20
Colored Markers
"Stories Of The Prophets," copied and cut
Completed Search Sheet 20
Completed Insights from Daily Scripture Readings For Week 20
Copies for each participant of:
    Entire "Stories Of The Prophets" (optional)
    Extra copies of "The Divided Monarchy" from Session 20 (optional)
    Search Sheet 21
    Daily Scripture Readings For Week 21

▨ ASSEMBLING

The **prophets** are special channels of God's Word to the "Mysterious Melchizedek" (priestly) people. Their messages are sometimes difficult to understand. This session places them in their historical perspective with the kings of Israel and Judah so that the wisdom of their difficult task may be more readily discerned.

▨ THE APPROACH TO GOD   (5 to 10 minutes)

❧ *Sing a hymn* – Sing a hymn which speaks of the prophet's call or task, such as *"O Young And Fearless Prophet"* or *"Here I Am, Lord,"* or *"Lord, Speak To Me That I May Speak,"* etc.

❧ *Lifting Hearts To God* – Offer a prayer of a prophet – those peculiar people who lift their hearts to God, listen for God's words of wisdom, and do or say what God asks.

▨ ENCOUNTERING THE WORD   (40 to 45 minutes)

⇨ Take a look at Search Sheet 20. Ask participants to share their favorite illustration and the prophetic message it conveys.

⇨ Use the Lecturette to introduce the "Stories Of The Prophets." After the readings, invite participants' responses to the "Questions For Reflection Following the Stories."

▨ GOING FORTH IN GOD'S NAME   (5 to 10 minutes)

❧   *Sing a hymn* of willingness to hear and speak the word of God such as "I'll Go Where You Want Me To Go," or one of the hymns suggested (but not used) in THE APPROACH TO GOD.

❧   Distribute copies of:
     Entire "Stories Of The Prophets" (optional)
     Search Sheet 21
     Daily Scripture Readings For Week 21

■ "LECTURETTE"

There were always **prophets** among God's people – Miriam, Deborah, Nathan, Gad, Iddo, Oded, Huldah, Micaiah, Shemaiah – who were **faithful** to God. And there were also some **false** prophets like Hananiah. This session will look at **Elijah** and **Elisha,** whose stories and prophecies are in the books of 1 and 2 Kings, and those whose prophecies are included among the books of the Bible. Isaiah, Jeremiah, Ezekiel and Daniel are called **"Major Prophets"** because the books devoted to their prophecies are larger than the 12 **"Minor Prophets:"** Hosea, Joel, Amos, Obadiah, Jonah, Micah, Nahum, Habbakuk, Zephaniah, Haggai, Zechariah and Malachi.

These **prophets** prophesied mostly during the 400-year era (from 800-400 BCE) of the Divided Kingdom, the Exile, and the Restoration. They were special people who knew God well, listened to God daily, were rooted in the history of the people of God, critically reflected on their present relationship with God in the life-and-death decisions of daily life, and remained open to God's plan for the future. God **"called"** these prophets, took them into the heavenly council, and compelled them to announce special messages – **judgment** for faithless living, **teachings** for faithful living, **encouragement** for the faithful who were enduring oppression, and **hope** for a covenantally faithful future, which included God's promised Messiah. Let's listen to their stories.

Distribute "prophet-reading assignments" from copies of the "Stories Of The Prophets." Have participants read them in order of Biblical arrangement by books (as given). After each reading, ask participants to write in the prophet's name on the "Drama Of The Kings" display from Session 20. **Write** *the prophet's name on the* **Northern** *or* **Southern** *side, depending on where he prophesied; and draw lines to the dates, if known, of his ministry.* **Distribute** *an extra copy of "The Divided Monarchy," from Session 20, if needed, to each participant, and invite them to write in the names of the prophets as on the display.*

Questions For Reflection Following The Stories Of The Prophets:

1. What **prophetic message** do you feel God is speaking to people today in your group, church, community, nation, and world?

2. Who in your group, church, community, nation, or world might be a **prophet**?

Stories Of The Prophets

ELIJAH
Northern (Israel) 875-848 BCE
(1 Kings 16:29 - 2 Kings 2:12)

I am Elijah ("the Lord is my God") the Tishbite from Gilead. God called me to **speak out against Baalism** during the time of King Ahab and Queen Jezebel's reign. Queen Jezebel was the daughter of Ethbaal, King of Sidon, Israel's northern neighbor. Through her influence, the people of Israel began worshipping Baal who they believed was lord of the rain clouds and Asherah the goddess of fertility. The people of Israel offered sacrifices to Baal and worshipped Asherah with pagan fertility rites (prostitution and orgies) which violated our covenant with God who led us out of slavery through the Red Sea and wilderness to this great land.

God told me to **announce three years of drought** in Israel because of the people's **idolatry and faithlessness**. During this time, Jezebel tried to kill me, so I hid by the brook Cherith where ravens fed me. When the brook dried up, I left Israel and went to Sidon where I showed a widow and her son God's providential care. Their jar of meal and oil never ran out. When the widow's son died, I prayed and God raised him.

The three-year drought did not convince the people of Israel that God, not Baal, is Lord of sun and rain, so I challenged the Baal prophets to a **showdown at Mt. Carmel**. Here God showed mighty power and Lordship of fire, wind and rain. I slaughtered all the Baal prophets and then had to run for my life from Ahab and Jezebel. I was so tired and discouraged I wanted to die. Angels fed and encouraged me. Then God told me to anoint Elisha to succeed me as prophet. Elisha stood by me while **God took me to heaven in a fiery chariot**.

ELISHA
Northern (Israel) 848-797 BCE
(1 Kings 19:15-21, 2 Kings 2:1 - 13:21)

I am Elisha ("God heals") son of Shaphat from Abel Meholah. I was plowing with twelve yoke of oxen when Elijah threw his cloak around me, making me his successor as a great prophet of God. After I watched Elijah go to heaven in a chariot of fire, I took his cloak and **struck the water of the Jordan River, and it divided**. With the Spirit of God upon me, I **healed bad water** with salt so that the land became productive and the people healthy. When young people mocked me saying, "Go away, baldhead!" I called down a **curse** on them in the name of the Lord and two she-bears came out of the woods and mauled them. As president of a seminary (school for prophets), I helped a student's widow keep from losing her sons to slavery. By God's **miraculous provision**, her jar of oil never ran dry. She filled empty jars and sold them to pay her debts. When a childless couple from Shunem built a special room for me, I **prayed and God gave them a son**. When this son suffered sunstroke, I prayed and **God healed** him. By God's power, I **healed poisonous stew** at seminary by throwing flour in it. Upon recommendation of a young slave girl from Israel, Syrian commander Naaman came to me for **healing of leprosy**, and God healed him. When we had only 20 loaves to feed 100 people, **God provided miraculously** so that there was plenty – and some left over. When a borrowed ax head fell into the water, I threw in a stick and **God made the iron float**. When Israel's king asked me for military advice during a Syrian siege, I prayed and **God struck the enemy with blindness**. Even after my death from illness and old age, when some Israelites hastily buried a man in my tomb during a Moabite raid, **God healed and raised** the man when his bones touched mine!

ISAIAH
Southern (Judah) 742-687 BCE
2 Kings 19:2 - 20:19, 2 Chronicles 26:22, 30:20-32, Book of Isaiah

I am Isaiah ("God is salvation") son of Amoz. I prophesied in Judah during the reign of Kings Azariah (Uzziah), Jotham, Ahaz and Hezekiah. The Northern (Israel) Kingdom had come under Assyrian rule, and the Southern (Judah) Kingdom was considering a military alliance with Egypt to protect them from Assyrian threat. Then God called me by a life-changing **vision** of the Almighty God, the Holy One of Israel, seated on a throne while the temple and the whole earth were **filled with God's glory**. I suddenly felt sinful and unclean. When I cried out, an angel touched my lips with a hot coal and said, "Your guilt is taken away and your sin atoned for." Then God said, "Whom shall I send? And who shall go for us (the heavenly council)?" And I said, **"Here am I. Send me!"**

The message God gave me was to **announce** Judah's consideration of a **military alliance with Egypt as rejection of Almighty God** who has always led and fed and delivered the people of the covenant. This rejection of God (and their sins of idolatry, blindness and apathy to God's way) would bring God's judgment unless they repented. I urged **quiet and confident faith in God** for salvation rather than desperate military alliances. King Hezekiah did repent, and God did not judge during his lifetime. I prophesied, however, that the **people would be exiled to Babylon**. Still, this would not be the end. I pointed ahead to the day God in compassion would **restore the people** to their land and **send the Messiah, a suffering servant** who would be a **Light** in their darkness, leading the people into the **day of God's rule of all people** and a **restored earth.** It was from the scroll of my prophecy that **Jesus read and quoted most** in the temple and in his teachings.

JEREMIAH
Southern (Judah) 626-585 BCE
Book of Jeremiah (and most likely Lamentations)

I am Jeremiah of Anathoth, born into a **priestly family.** I prophesied during the reigns of Kings Josiah, Jehoahaz, Jehoiakim, Jehoiachin and Zedekiah. Although I **felt inadequate** for the **difficult task** God gave me, God assured me that I had been **chosen before birth** to be a prophet. **God gave me the strength and courage I needed.** It was my painful duty to **warn** the people of Judah of their **sins** of idolatry and trust in military might rather than God. I had to tell them God was going to bring an awful **judgment** upon them if they did not repent. I was **mocked and ridiculed** for speaking only sad words from God. Because of the impending judgment, God told me not to marry and raise a family.

My ministry was **anguishing** because I could see judgment coming; but even though I did everything God told me to do, I could not prevent it. When the Babylonians besieged Jerusalem, God told me to **tell the people not to resist** – for this would keep our beautiful temple from being destroyed. But they called me a traitor, and I could only watch in horror as the Babylonians came into Jerusalem and destroyed and burned our beautiful temple, leaving the City of God in rubble and ruin. I preached of **God's promise to redeem and restore** the covenantal people after enduring the severe discipline of the exile. I reminded the people of their **duty and privilege of crying out to God** in their distress, and I composed many laments expressing the struggles of my heart. This earned me the title of **"weeping prophet."** But I also preached **hope** for a renewed covenantal relationship with God after the cleansing and purification of the judgment. As an object lesson of my belief in God's restoration, I purchased land and registered the deed before I was taken to Egypt to avoid Babylonian conquest.

EZEKIEL
Southern (Judah) 593-571 BCE
Book of Ezekiel

I am Ezekiel, like Jeremiah, a man of **priestly background**. But God called me also to be a prophet – to **warn** the people of Judah to turn from their wickedness because judgment was near. I felt *angry and bitter* about this task, but the strong hand of the Lord was upon me, and **the Spirit of God empowered me to go**. The warnings went unheeded, and the Babylonians destroyed Jerusalem and the temple. As a **living lesson** to the people of Judah, God told me my lovely wife would soon die and that I was not to mourn openly for her, just as they were not to mourn openly over the loss of their beautiful temple. Then I was taken with the captives to Babylon. Here I lived in a house of my own like many of the captives. I **ministered as a priest-prophet** to people who were cut off from the temple of the Lord with all its symbolism, sacrifices and rituals. I taught individual responsibility to God. And I assured the people of God's mercy and plan to restore them. I shared with them my visions of a just and holy God in a new temple in the midst of a cleansed people. But perhaps I'm most remembered for my **vision of the valley of dry bones** in which God told me to prophesy to the bones. The bones began to rattle and take on flesh and tendons. The Spirit of God breathed new life into them, and they received **new life** from God - God's promise of **resurrection and restoration!**

DANIEL
Babylonian Exile, 605-530 BCE
Book of Daniel

I, Daniel of Judah, was among those **taken captive** to Babylon. Like Joseph, I was God's representative in a foreign land in a time of crisis. My three friends and I refused to eat the king's rich food, which had been offered to idols. We went through training on a **vegetarian diet, worshipping our God.** We graduated at the top of the class! My three friends were thrown into a **fiery furnace** for refusing to worship an idol, and God miraculously delivered them. **My task was to faithfully serve God in the midst of intense opposition.** This **encouraged** others in exile to remain **faithful to God**. I was given the ability to interpret **dreams** and a mysterious handwriting on the wall. Once some leaders were jealous of my success as I followed only God. They tricked King Darius into making a law that anyone who didn't worship the king would be thrown into a **lion's den**. Still, I worshipped God, for God is sovereign over all earth's kingdoms and rulers. I was thrown into the lion's den, but God closed the lions' mouths and I was not harmed. I had many **visions** which showed that **those who are wise and consistently obey God will shine like bright stars on a dark night**. The visions showed that in the end **all evil will be done away with and God will reign forever!**

HOSEA
Northern (Israel), 750-715 BCE
Book of Hosea

I, Hosea, was a prophet in the Northern Kingdom while **Isaiah** was prophet in the Southern Kingdom. The Northern Kingdom was in a **great decline** after the reign of King Jeroboam II. For 40 years **I called the people to come back to the God who loved them** rather than worship idols and live immorally. To illustrate God's message of redeeming love to the people, God told me to **marry the prostitute** Gomer. We had three children and named each of them as a message from God: Jezreel = **"God scatters,"** Lo-Ruhamah = **"not love,"** Lo-Ammi = **"not my people"** - **warning** the people of God's impending **judgment** for their **apostasy.** When Gomer left me, breaking our marriage covenant, my task was to **describe to the people God's pain** at their breaking of the covenantal relationship with God through **idolatry** and **trusting in mil-**

itary might. When Gomer became the slave of another man, God called me to buy her back – the way God would go on **reaching to redeem the people and bring them back** into a **just** and **holy** relationship with their God.

JOEL
? place and time
Book of Joel, Acts 2:16

I, Joel, lived during a **locust plague** and **severe drought** which devastated Judah. I saw this plague as a warning of the "great and dreadful day of the Lord" when **God would punish Israel and Judah** for their **sins of idolatry**. I called for a national day of prayer, mourning and repentance. But I also looked **beyond God's severe discipline** of unfaithful people – to a time of **restoration and blessing after repentance** – a time when **God's Spirit would be poured out on everyone** like the cleansing rain of God's **forgiveness** after the drought of human **sin**.

AMOS
Northern (Israel), 760-750 BCE
Book of Amos

I am Amos, a **shepherd** and sycamore fig **farmer** from Tekoa, a small town about six miles south of Bethlehem. God sent me from my work in Tekoa of the Southern Kingdom into the Northern Kingdom to **announce God's coming judgment**. You see, both kingdoms were enjoying prosperity and had become smug in the idea that they could enjoy political peace and military security while worshipping idols, engaging in immoral conduct, living luxuriously and oppressing the poor. There were dishonest scales and judges who could be easily bribed. **Materialism increased the injustice**. The people **forgot** God's past punishment for unfaithfulness.

Into this scene, I preached a **call for return to true piety and social justice**. I denounced their **worship of God while doing as they pleased**. I reminded the people of their covenantal **task to be priests** among the nations, showing all people the way to **God's peace**. Using a **plumbline** as an illustration, I showed the people how far out of plumb they were. God also showed me a vision of a **ripe basket of fruit** – people ready to be plucked in **judgment**. I invited a look **beyond God's judgment** – to **repentance** which brings **God's forgiving love** and **restoration**. Of course, I was **treated as a traitor** for my message. So I reminded Israel that I was a Judean herdsman and fig picker specially **called by God**, not a formally trained prophet.

OBADIAH
Southern (Judah), ? 855-840 or 605-586 BCE
Book of Obadiah

I am Obadiah, prophet of few words. My message concerned **Edom** (descendants of Esau) and its **gloating at the downfall** of Israel and Judah (descendants of Jacob). Because they are related, they **should have assisted** Israel and Judah against their enemies. Since they perpetuated a 1000-year family feud between brothers who had reconciled, the **Edomites would surely be destroyed**. I pointed to the day when Israel and Judah would **return to possess a greatly extended land** including former Edomite territory, and the **Lord would reign supreme over all the nations, centered in Jerusalem**.

JONAH
Northern (Israel), 785-775 BCE
Book of Jonah

I am Jonah, son of Ammittai, from Gath Hepher in Zebulun. I was a **reluctant prophet**, for God gave me a **difficult task**! After Israel was finally safe from Assyrian attacks, God told me to go to its capital city, Nineveh, and **warn its people to repent** of their wickedness or be destroyed in 40 days. I **ran in the opposite direction**, boarding a ship for Tarshish. When a violent storm threatened shipwreck, the captain asked everyone to pray; but I was sleeping. The sailors cast lots and determined I was responsible for the storm because I was running away from the God who made the sea. They threw me overboard and the storm ceased! A **great fish swallowed me**, and I **cried out** to God to **save** me. And God did! The fish spit me out on dry land. Then I **obeyed God** and warned Nineveh to repent. They listened and fasted and prayed. God had compassion on them and did not bring the destruction I had prophesied. When I was **angry about losing face as a prophet,** God grew a vine for me to **pout** under. When a worm destroyed the vine, I was **angry at its loss**. Then God said, "If you're concerned about one vine, why shouldn't I have compassion on the 120,000 people of Nineveh?" **And in the midst of my anger, I learned that God's salvation and mercy extend beyond any covenant!**

MICAH
Northern (Israel) and Southern (Judah), 750-686 BCE
Book of Micah

I am Micah from the town of Moresheth in southern Judah. I prophesied during the reigns of Kings Jotham, Ahaz and Hezekiah. I **predicted the destruction of Samaria** in the Northern Kingdom and lived to see this **prophecy fulfilled**. My special concern was the **social injustice** I saw even in the small towns around my hometown. There were money-grabbing rulers, self-serving priests and prophets, wealthy people who exploited the poor and helpless. There was much **dishonesty** in business dealings and **insincere worship**. I was horrified as I saw the **corruption in government** spread to decay relationships among my friends and relatives. Families crumbled. I cried out against this corruption, warning that the time of God's **judgment was near**. While I preached impending doom, I also **pointed ahead** to the time a divine Deliverer would come to rule over ALL GOD'S PEOPLE in **righteousness and justice**. I am most remembered for asking, *"What does the Lord require of you but to do justice, and to love kindness, and to walk humbly with your God?"* (6:8)

NAHUM
Southern (Judah), 663-612 BCE
Book of Nahum

I am Nahum ("comfort"). I prophesied the **fall of proud, defiant Nineveh**, capital of Assyria, whose power was feared from Mesopotamia to the Mediterranean for centuries. Idolatry, brutality, pride and gloating combined to bring this empire to an end as Babylon conquered Assyria in 612 BCE. The fall of Assyria as a world power was **comforting** to Jerusalem. It **reaffirmed** God's **sovereignty** over the nations and God's **goodness** to those who are faithful. It also reminded Judah of God's **holiness** which cannot leave the guilty unpunished.

HABBAKUK
Southern (Judah), c. 605 BCE
Book of Habbakuk

I am Habbakuk, a prophet who had a dialogue with God which went like this:

Habbakuk: "Why do you let wickedness go unpunished in Judah, negating justice and the law?"

God: "I'm sending the Babylonians to punish Judah."

Habbakuk: "Why let such a sinful nation punish a nation more righteous than itself?"

God: "Babylon will be punished; faith will be rewarded."

From my struggle with God, I learned that *those who are faithful to God will endure* but those who are unfaithful will eventually be destroyed. I pronounced five woes against nations who plunder people, gain by violence, shed innocent blood, degrade their neighbors, and trust in idols. I learned to *rest* in God's appointments and to *await* God's working in a *spirit of worship*.

ZEPHANIAH
Southern (Judah), 640-609 BCE
Book of Zephaniah

I am Zephaniah, great-great-grandson of King Hezekiah. I was a prophet in Judah before King Josiah's great reform. I *warned of God's coming judgment* to Judah for religious perversion and social corruption. A *humble seeking of righteousness* could lessen God's wrath against Judah. While I warned of judgment and pleaded for repentance and righteousness, I also *taught of God's faithfulness and mercy* which would bring *redemption* and *restoration*. There is comfort and consolation for those who *patiently and faithfully wait on the Lord.*

HAGGAI
Southern (Judah), Restoration, 520 BCE
Book of Haggai

I am Haggai, a prophet in Judah *after the exile* to Babylon. I had seen the beautiful temple destroyed in 586 BCE. There followed some dark years in the lives of the people of God. Then in 538 BCE, Cyrus of Persia conquered Babylon and allowed 50,000 Jews to return to Jerusalem. Led by Zerubbabel, they worked *to rebuild the temple and restore pure worship*. But neighboring nations feared the rise of a Jewish state and halted the work until Darius became King of Persia in 522 BCE. I saw my Jewish brothers and sisters as more to blame than their enemies for the lack of progress in rebuilding. They all had nicely finished homes while the temple of God was unfinished. I *called the people from their lame excuses and lethargy, encouraging them with the Word of God and teaching that God withholds harvest blessings when people withhold praise and worship*. My *vision* of a temple filled with *glory* spurred them on. As Zerubbabel led, King Darius gave support, God strengthened the workers; and in 516 BCE the temple was *completed and dedicated*. God again gave harvest *blessings*!

ZECHARIAH
Southern (Judah) Restoration, 520-480 BCE
Book of Zechariah

I am Zechariah, prophet and priest, who *ministered to the returned exiles* during the same time as Haggai. I saw that the returning people were making one of the *same mistakes* that brought about the exile – *lack of pure worship*. I urged them to make pure worship and the rebuilding of the temple a priority. God gave me eight night visions picturing God's *loving concern, cleansing, guiding* Presence, *judgment* upon Babylon, and *plan for peace on earth*. I used these visions to *encourage the people in obedient, faithful, and just living* and to give them *hope* for their future as the people of God. I *pointed ahead* to a time when the Good Shepherd would come to be *smitten* for the entire flock and then *rule* over *all the peoples of the earth* from Jerusalem.

MALACHI
Southern (Judah) Restoration, 460-430 BCE
Book of Malachi

I am Malachi, the last of the 12 "Minor Prophets." I came on the scene *80 years after* Haggai and Zechariah encouraged the rebuilding of the temple and restoration of pure worship and lifestyle. I saw that *disillusionment had set in*. The land was still a small province of Persia, the blessings of God's glory in the temple and of prosperity in the land had not been realized. *Worship was a lukewarm exercise*; no one tithed or obeyed the law. I *spoke out against this indifference to God* and *lack of caring for one another* – marrying unbelievers, older men cruelly discarding aging wives for attractive young foreigners, and deteriorating family life. I *challenged* the people to put away foreign wives and to care for each other as God requires. I *encouraged* them to put God to the test by tithing – and seeing if God would then pour out blessings – for *when we hold back* in self-interest, *we deprive ourselves of the blessings* God longs to give. I urged them to keep the Sabbath holy and to rid the priesthood of corruption. *I pointed ahead* to a new age when the Messiah (Christ) will reconcile the world to God and the wicked will be trampled while the righteous rejoice.

■ "THE DIVIDED MONARCHY"

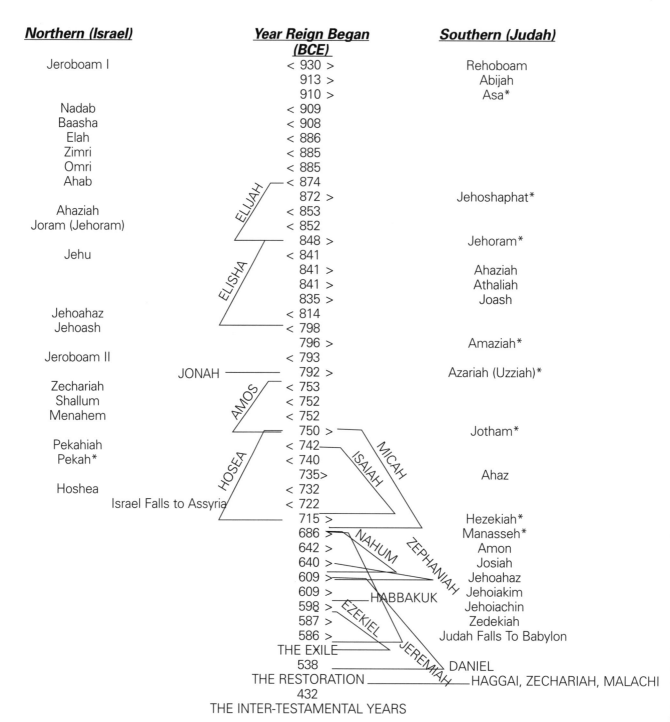

Northern (Israel)	Year Reign Began (BCE)	Southern (Judah)
Jeroboam I	< 930 >	Rehoboam
	913 >	Abijah
	910 >	Asa*
Nadab	< 909	
Baasha	< 908	
Elah	< 886	
Zimri	< 885	
Omri	< 885	
Ahab	< 874	
	872 >	Jehoshaphat*
Ahaziah	< 853	
Joram (Jehoram)	< 852	
	848 >	Jehoram*
Jehu	< 841	
	841 >	Ahaziah
	841 >	Athaliah
	835 >	Joash
Jehoahaz	< 814	
Jehoash	< 798	
	796 >	Amaziah*
Jeroboam II	< 793	
JONAH	792 >	Azariah (Uzziah)*
Zechariah	< 753	
Shallum	< 752	
Menahem	< 752	
	750 >	Jotham*
Pekahiah	< 742	
Pekah*	< 740	
	735>	Ahaz
Hoshea	< 732	
Israel Falls to Assyria	< 722	
	715 >	Hezekiah*
	686 >	Manasseh*
	642 >	Amon
	640 >	Josiah
	609 >	Jehoahaz
	609 >	Jehoiakim
	598 >	Jehoiachin
	587 >	Zedekiah
	586 >	Judah Falls To Babylon
THE EXILE		DANIEL
	538	HAGGAI, ZECHARIAH, MALACHI
THE RESTORATION		
	432	
THE INTER-TESTAMENTAL YEARS		

Prophets shown along the timeline: ELIJAH, ELISHA, AMOS, HOSEA, ISAIAH, MICAH, ZEPHANIAH, NAHUM, HABBAKUK, EZEKIEL, JEREMIAH

*   *Denotes overlapping reigns or co-regencies which cause discrepancies in number of years reigned. Discrepancies also occur when the year the king ascended the throne is counted or not counted.*

The period of the **exile** to Babylon was an especially **dark chapter** in the lives of God's people. Imagine yourself in their place – forced to leave your house and all your possessions, watching horrified as soldiers loot and destroy your hometown and burn the temple, then being forced to march hundreds of miles away to a strange land, while some of your friends and family became sick and died along the way. Then you are forced to work in other people's houses and gardens and fields.

How would you feel about your **circumstances**? How would you feel **about God** who had always provided for you and delivered you? How would you **worship God** so far away from the temple with its priests and choirs, altar and lamps, Bread of the Presence, Holy of Holies, Ark of the Covenant with tablets of the Law, and Guardian Angels?

Psalms 42, 84, and 137 give a glimpse of the **depth of feelings** during the **exile experience.** Read them. Then **write your own psalm** below, pouring out your heart to God. (Suggestion: Imagine such an experience in your country!)

_____

_____

_____

_____

_____

_____

_____

_____

_____

_____

_____

DAILY SCRIPTURE
READINGS • WEEK 21

THE **AWE REVERENCE WONDER** AT THE **NEARNESS HOLINESS BEAUTY** OF GOD = THE BEGINNING OF **WISDOM**

(PROVERBS 1:7A)

	HEBREW SCRIPTURE	NEW TESTAMENT	PSALM	PROVERBS
Day 1	1 Samuel 29:1-31:13	John 11:54-12:19	118:1-18	15:24-26
Day 2	2 Samuel 1:1-2:11	John 12:20-50	118:19-29	15:27-28
Day 3	2 Samuel 1:12-3:39	John 13:1-30	119:1-16	15:29-30
Day 4	2 Samuel 4:1-6:23	John 13:31-14:14	119:17-32	15:31-32
Day 5	2 Samuel 7:1-8:18	John 14:15-31	119:33-48	15:33
Day 6	2 Samuel 9:1-11:27	John 15:1-27	119:49-64	16:1-3
Day 7	2 Samuel 12:1-31	John 16:1-33	119:65-80	16:4-5

Personal Notes and Glimpses of Wisdom:

"I wonder if sheep can hear God speaking like the prophets did..."

SESSION 22 • THE WISDOM OF THE EXILE

The aim of this session is to glimpse the wisdom of God's judgment during the covenantal people's exile.

MATERIALS NEEDED

Hymnals
Accompaniment
Bibles
Chalkboard or newsprint (chalk or markers)
Completed Search Sheet 21
Completed Insights from Daily Scripture Readings, Week 21
Copies for each participant of:
    Illustration 22A
    Illustration 22B
    Exile Map
    Search Sheet 22
    Daily Scripture Readings For Week 22

▨ ASSEMBLING

From the **drama of the kings** and the **stories of the prophets**, this session moves into that most difficult time of the covenantal people's history – **The Exile**. While the ten Northern tribes (Israel) were taken to Assyria in 722 BCE, the Southern Kingdom (Judah) continued until 586 BCE when it was conquered by the Babylonians who had previously conquered Assyria. Jerusalem and the beautiful temple were looted, burned and left in ruins, while thousands of the people were marched to a far-away place, Babylon. It was a **dark** and **difficult** time.

▨ THE APPROACH TO GOD   (5 to 10 minutes)

❧ *Singing a hymn* – Sing a hymn based on Psalm 42, 84, or 137, reflecting a *longing for encounter with God* while exiled from the familiar center of worship.

❧ *Lifting Hearts To God* – Offer a prayer of desire for *God's nearness* in the midst of circumstances in which God seems distant. Include the needs of participants who may be experiencing difficult circumstances.

▨ ENCOUNTERING THE WORD   (40 to 45 minutes)

➪ Invite participants to share their psalms (or perhaps just a phrase or two) from Search Sheet 21. Share from your own.

➪ Invite someone to read about the Northern Kingdom (Israel) falling to Assyria in 2 Kings 17:1-6. *Distribute copies of* **Exile Map.** Locate **Samaria, Haran, Nineveh** and **Ecbatana**. Look at the scale. Try to figure out how many miles the exiles had to march.

⇨ Invite someone to read about the Southern Kingdom (Judah) falling to Babylon in 2 Kings 24:1-4, 10-14, 20b-25:21. Locate **Jerusalem, Babylon, Susa** and **Ur** on the map. Again, try to figure how many miles these exiles marched.

The covenantal people believed **Mt. Zion,** the mountain upon which their temple was built (where Abraham's faith was tested when he was told to sacrifice Isaac), to be **indestructible** because of the presence of the Lord in the temple where they sacrificed and worshipped the God of the Covenant. Now that they had seen the temple destroyed, they had a **major faith crisis.** Did this mean God was no longer all-powerful? That God had forsaken them?

⇨ The prophetic writer of 2 Kings and 2 Chronicles knew why God's judgment of the exile had befallen the covenantal people. Read 2 Kings 17:7-23 and 2 Chronicles 36: 11-21, and *create your own list of reasons **WHY** God's people were exiled. Record them* on chalkboard or newsprint.

⇨ **Discuss** these reasons from the perspective of God's holiness vs. God's steadfast love and faithfulness. What might have happened to the covenantal people if God had not judged and sent the people into exile?

⇨ *Distribute copies of **Illustration 22A**.* This Illustration depicts the journey of the people of God in the Hebrew Scriptures and suggests that **"The Exile"** is their **valley experience** – a painfully difficult yet necessary stage on the way to Shalom. *It is in the valley that faith is refined, love is purified, and hope is born anew.* Immaturity avoids the valley because it fears pain; maturity is willing to endure pain to bring healing and renewed vision. Allow time for reading, comments and questions.

⇨ *Distribute copies of **Illustration 22B**.* The **exile** or **valley** itself contains stages; maturity of faith is a process with some recognizable recurring features. Allow time for reading, comments and questions.

▨ GOING FORTH IN GOD'S NAME   (5 to 10 minutes)

❥ Read (or ask a participant to read) a portion of Psalm 22, 77, or 88 – **"prayers from the pits."** Option: Sing a hymn which reflects the themes of these Psalms. End the session by noting that the **duty** and **privilege** of God's people is to **cry out** when they are in distress.

❥ Distribute copies of:
   Search Sheet 22
   Daily Scripture Readings For Week 22

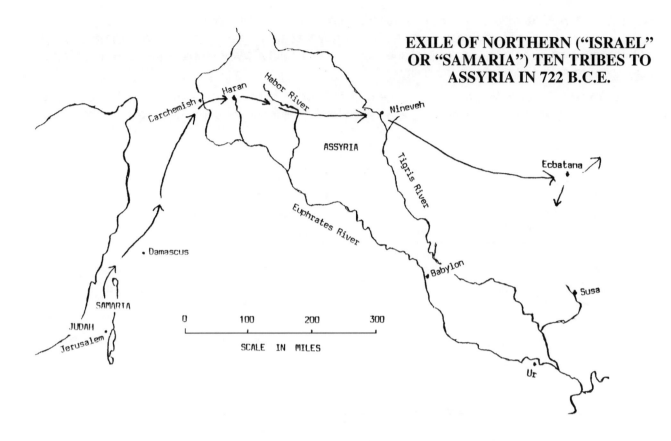

EXILE OF NORTHERN ("ISRAEL" OR "SAMARIA") TEN TRIBES TO ASSYRIA IN 722 B.C.E.

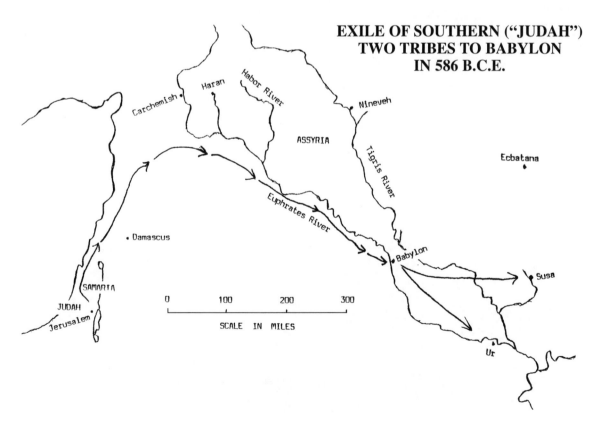

EXILE OF SOUTHERN ("JUDAH") TWO TRIBES TO BABYLON IN 586 B.C.E.

Psalms 22, 77, and 88 reflect the **cries of people experiencing exile**. Where is God when the covenantal people are in the pits? Why does God seem silent? What about the minority who remained faithful to God but were taken into exile because of the sins of the majority? Why would a just and holy God allow the innocent to suffer as much as the guilty?

Read Psalms 22, 77, and 88. Then choose one of the above questions (or a burning question of your own) and write your response below, including how these Psalms illumine (or complicate) your response.

_____

_____

_____

_____

_____

_____

_____

_____

_____

_____

_____

_____

DAILY SCRIPTURE
READINGS • WEEK 22

THE **AWE REVERENCE WONDER** AT THE **NEARNESS HOLINESS BEAUTY** OF GOD = THE BEGINNING OF **WISDOM**

(PROVERBS 1:7A)

	HEBREW SCRIPTURE	NEW TESTAMENT	PSALM	PROVERBS
Day 1	2 Samuel 13:1-39	John 17:1-26	119:81-96	16:6-7
Day 2	2 Samuel 14:1-15:22	John 18:1-24	119:97-112	16:8-9
Day 3	2 Samuel 15:23-16:23	John 18:25-19:22	119:113-128	16:10-11
Day 4	2 Samuel 17:1-29	John 19:23-42	119:129-152	16:12-13
Day 5	2 Samuel 18:1-19:10	John 20:1-31	119:153-176	16:14-15
Day 6	2 Samuel 19:11-20:13	John 21:1-25	120:1-7	16:16-17
Day 7	2 Samuel 20:14-22:20	Acts 1:1-26	121:1-8	16:18

Personal Notes and Glimpses of Wisdom:

"I wonder if God's scattered sheep will ever be happy again..."

**STAGES
OF THE
HEBREW PEOPLE**

Growth in Goshen's
fertile farmland
1876 – 1446 B.C.E.

The Wilderness Years,
Law and Tabernacle, inheriting
the land through time of judges
1446 – 1050 B.C.E.

Receiving the Sacred Covenant –
the early Patriarchal Years
2250 – 1876 B.C.E.

Shalom!
Awaiting the Lord's reign of
peace and justice
432 – 5 B.C.E.

The United Monarchy
1050 – 930 B.C.E.
The Divided Monarchy
930 – 586 B.C.E.
1050 – 586 B.C.E.

Restoration and
Rebuilding
538 – 432 B.C.E.

The Exile
Northern (Israel)
to Assyria in 722 B.C.E.
Southern (Judah)
to Babylon in 586 B.C.E.
586 – 538 B.C.E.

STAGES OF THE EXILE

Initial shock gives way to the green pastures of new growth in faith

Still waters of reflection on where people went wrong, re-focusing on the One who is leading

Belonging includes the "tough love" of God's judgment (pain) as God intervenes in the downward spiral of the people's apostasy

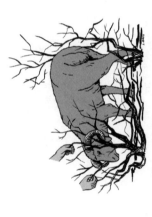

Repentance, cleansing, and purifying bring restoration; the people are restored to right paths through the Good Shepherd's leading

Return to their homeland with shouts of joy

The prophets point to renewed hope and widened vision of God's grace and blessing

Bitter reality and homesickness lead to crying out from the depths – the people's right and responsibility during times of trouble

SESSION 23 • WISDOM IN THE NIGHT

The aim of this session is to search for the wisdom of God in the midst of suffering.

MATERIALS NEEDED

Hymnals
Accompaniment
Bibles
Completed Search Sheet 22
Completed Insights from Daily Scripture Readings For Week 22
Copies for each participant of:
    "Wisdom In The Night" Script
    Search Sheet 23
    Daily Scripture Readings For Week 23

▣ ASSEMBLING

Although the **story of Job** has its setting in the era of the patriarchs, it is a **timeless search for God from the depths of despair.** The questions Job asks and the theology offered by his friends are certainly akin to our struggles and the struggles of the covenantal people during the **exile.** In this session, participants are invited to join Job and the exiled people in the **drama of despair and hope.**

▣ THE APPROACH TO GOD   (5 to 10 minutes)

❧ *Singing a hymn* – Sing a hymn which searches for God's nearness in the midst of life's difficulties. *"Jesus, Lover Of My Soul"* is a possibility.

❧ *Prayer* – Offer a prayer expressing concern for participants or their relatives and friends who may be searching for meaning and truth in the midst of unanswered questions, like Job and "The Exiles."

▣ ENCOUNTERING THE WORD   (40 to 45 minutes)

⇨ Invite participants to share their reflections on the questions and Psalms of Search Sheet 22. Share your own reflections. Make the transition to the "Wisdom In The Night" Playlet.

⇨ *Distribute copies of the "Wisdom In The Night" Script.* Assign the parts of Narrator, Job, Eliphaz, Bildad, Zophar, Elihu and God. Enjoy the playlet together. Use the following **Questions For Reflection** after the playlet:

1. Which of the friends' arguments about why Job suffers makes the most sense? Which argument do you most frequently hear?

2. How do you feel about God allowing Satan to inflict pain and suffering on an innocent person to prove or disprove theories?

3. If God is just and good, why are a country's own soldiers killed by "friendly fire?" Innocent bystanders and children killed by bullets intended for someone else? Children born with AIDS, etc.?

4. Why live a godly life if "the rain falls on the just and the unjust?"

5. Why should One-Who-Is-Innocent suffer for the sins of those who are guilty? (Foreshadows Christ's suffering)

▨ GOING FORTH IN GOD'S NAME   (5 to 10 minutes)

❧ *Singing a Hymn* – Sing a hymn which reflects trust in God when we cannot see the way ahead. *"I Will Trust When I Cannot See"* or *"Sometime We'll Understand"* are possibilities.

❧ *Prayer* – Offer a prayer of trust in God whose ways are unfathomable to people, especially in times of deep distress.

❧ Distribute copies of:
  Search Sheet 23
  Daily Scripture Readings For Week 23

"Wisdom In The Night" Playlet

Narrator: In the days of the patriarchs, in the land of Uz, there lived a man named Job. Job worshipped God and lived in obedience to God. He had many sheep and cattle (which is the way wealth was determined in those days); he was influential and well respected in his community; and he enjoyed his wife and large family of seven sons and three daughters. At each family celebration, Job would offer a burnt offering sacrifice to God for purification in case any of his children had sinned in their hearts.

Unbeknown to Job and his family and friends, he was the subject of a conversation in the heavenly council. God asked Satan if he had noticed Job's piety and integrity before God. But Satan said, "He only worships and serves you for what he gets out of it – you've made him rich!" So God said, "You may test your theory on Job as long as you do no harm to him."

Before long there came a day in which Job lost his flocks and herds, his servants and his sons and daughters in sudden disasters. Then Job tore his robes, shaved his head, and worshipped God, "The Lord gave, and the Lord has taken away; blessed be the Name of the Lord." In all this, Job did not sin.

Back in the heavenly council, Satan had lost face when his first theory failed. So he proposed another: "Job is only concerned about his own skin. Take away his health, and he'll curse you." So God said, "You may test this theory also, as long as you spare Job's life."

Soon Job broke out with open running skin sores over his entire body. This great man sat on a pile of ashes, an outcast of society. Even his wife begged him to curse God and die rather than suffer. Still Job did not sin.

After a while three of Job's best friends, Eliphaz, Bildad and Zophar – and a young friend named Elihu – came to visit him. They hardly recognized Job – so great was his suffering. They sat in silence for a long time, pondering how such terrible things could happen to such a good and God-fearing man. Then they began a theological discussion seeking an answer to this dilemma:

Debate Cycle 1

Job: Life is so bitter. I wish I had never been born!

Eliphaz: Job, you've helped many people; now it's your turn to let others help you. By special revelation I have learned that God punishes those who sin – but not the innocent. Everyone sins! So my advice is that you accept this trouble in silence – because no one likes a complainer. Accept trouble as an inevitable part of life, and you'll have better days ahead. This too shall pass.

Job: It's sickening to be told to be patient and silent when I'm nearly dead! I just wish I could die. And where is your sympathy when I need it most? I've done nothing wrong to deserve such pain and suffering! I toss and turn all night – No, I will not be silent. I will cry out to God against this injustice. "O God, I'd rather die than suffer like this. If I have sinned, why don't you forgive?"

Bildad: Job, God is a just God. Tradition has proven that God always rewards those who do good and punishes those who do evil.

Job: I believe God is just – but not in my case! I am innocent; yet I suffer. The innocent suffer as much as the guilty. "Why, O God, do you create and then destroy? If you would leave me alone, I might find some comfort before I die!"

Zophar: So you think you're innocent, Job? One of the secrets of wisdom is that God gives everyone less punishment than they deserve. Confess your sins, and God will heal and restore you.

Job: Well, aren't you the wise guys! Why don't YOU be silent? THAT would be wise! And if God has changed the ways of wisdom – that is, punishment of the wicked and blessing the righteous – can you do anything to change that? Your rigid rules and "wise" advice don't fit my situation, so I'll bring my case directly to God; for life is short and death is so final. "O God, let me just die until this nightmare is over; and then restore me to life again. What other hope is there?"

Debate Cycle 2

Eliphaz: Listen to yourself, Job. Your attempts to justify yourself only prove your guilt! Are you the authority on wisdom? The sages and their ancestors have always taught that those who stubbornly defy God will be punished horribly; they will not be successful.

Job: It's easy for you to talk when I'm the one who's in pain. God has worn me out with pain, and those who see my anguish just stare open-mouthed, poke fun of me and walk away. I've become a symbol of scorn in the community. Now I feel even God has given up on me. Still, I believe God is just. Surely there must be someone who will plead my cause in heaven and give me some hope before I die!

Bildad: Well, I resent you belittling our advice. You're getting emotional – self-centered and irrational! You're wrong to say the righteous suffer while evildoers prosper. The fate of the wicked is horrible – they become weak-kneed and fearful. Calamity eats away at their skin. They become insecure, and so do their children!

Job: So my friends are now my accusers! Blame the victim! My conduct is a matter between me and God – not for you to judge. Go ahead, find fault and bring charges. But after my skin has fallen off, God will vindicate me, and I'll be there to see it. All those who have wrongly accused me will have to answer to God!

Zophar: I am insulted also, Job. Don't you know that ever since mortals were placed on this earth the prosperity of the wicked is temporary but their punishment is severe? This is the heritage of the wicked decreed by God!

Job: Your theology is wonderful . . . it just doesn't fit my situation. Why shouldn't I cry out or be impatient? I am a righteous man and I'm suffering horribly while the wicked live in their nice homes, enjoy raising their families and watching their flocks and herds increase! When they die they're fondly remembered. They don't need God for anything! I suppose next you'll say that God's judgment will fall on their children – but what kind of justice is that? All your attempts to "comfort" me are empty lies!

Debate Cycle 3

Eliphaz: Job, of what use is all your piety to God? Does God punish people for their piety? No! So then it must be because of your wickedness that you suffer. Let me point out your sins to you: 1) You demanded collateral from your own family for a loan, 2) You stripped people of their clothing and gave no water to the weary and withheld food from the hungry, and 3) Although you were a powerful landowner, you sent widows away empty-handed and crushed the spirit of orphans. Again I say, confess your sin and repent. Submit to God, and God will bless you again.

Job: I search for God. I want to reason with God and plead my own case. God knows my heart. I have always submitted to God. God is testing me — but not to purge sin. I cannot seem to understand God's ways. Look what goes on in the world – the wicked steal, oppress the poor, rebel against God, murder and commit adultery. Yet God blesses and prospers them. Nothing is black and white anymore; everything seems gray.

Bildad: Nobody's perfect, Job. We're all sinners in God's sight. Viewed from the high heavens we're nothing but worms!

Job: Some help all of you are! As long as I live I will maintain my innocence, my integrity and godly living in spite of this affliction. And I will continue my faith in God my Creator and Judge even though I do not understand how God created and even though I am denied justice in this situation. May the wicked be punished even more severely!

God alone is wise, and no one on earth can find wisdom. It cannot be mined from the earth or bought with all the wealth in the world. Wisdom is God's secret. People become wise by reverencing God and rejecting evil.

Ah, I remember the good old days of happy family celebrations, prosperity, and respect in the community. But now I'm society's outcast, the butt of their jokes. My skin turns black and falls off, and I am in deep grief even though I am a righteous man. I was fair to my employees. I gave generously to charity and was not overly consumed with success. As God is my witness, I kept no secrets from God, and I did not try to please people more than God.

Elihu's Speech

Elihu: Hold on a minute! I'm the youngest, so I've been watching and listening as I should. But now I have something to say: Job, you maintain your innocence; however, God does not answer you. I know that God speaks through suffering to correct, not to destroy. I believe God's angel will heal you – but only when you admit you've sinned.

Job, you say God isn't fair and there's nothing to be gained by serving God. But God is the Supreme Judge, and God's judgments ARE just! You have now added resentment and rebellion against God to your list of sins.

"Good vs. bad" is a human matter; God remains high above! And when people cry to God it is because of their own need – God gets nothing out of it! That's why you get no reply.

Since God uses suffering to teach people where they've gone wrong, you should be learning your lesson, not sitting around wishing you were dead! We are nothing in comparison to God's awesome power in thunder and lightning, rain and snow. And God is holy, so we do well to reverence God. But this great and holy God does not pay attention to those who are arrogant about their own wisdom!

God Breaks Into The Debate

God: You ask many questions of me, Job. But I am the Creator, and you are the creature, so I will ask the questions. Can you create as I have created and put the stars in their courses? Can you make a lion or an ostrich? Tame them? Feed them? Is it by your wisdom that birds fly? Can you control a hippo or a crocodile? Are you my equal that you question my justice?

Job: I know, Lord, that you can do all things and no one can get in the way of your purpose for all that you created. I have spoken of things too wonderful for me – things I did not understand. In the past I had known ABOUT you, but now I have ENCOUNTERED you face to face. Please forgive my bitter and ignorant questioning of your justice.

God: And now, Eliphaz, Bildad, and Zophar, I am angry with you for speaking only your rigid rules ABOUT me to Job rather than honestly searching to ENCOUNTER me as he did. Go to him, sacrifice, and ask him to pray for your forgiveness.

Epilogue

Narrator: Job prayed for the forgiveness of his three friends, and God accepted his prayer on their behalf. God restored Job's health and wealth, giving him twice as many sheep and cattle as he had before. The community once again respected him, and he had many happy family feasts with seven sons and three daughters who were the fairest women in the land. Job gave his daughters an inheritance as well as his sons. And Job lived to enjoy his great-great-grandchildren before he died old and full of years.

SEARCH SHEET 23

Throughout the journey of the "Mysterious Melchizedek" (priestly) people, Scripture provides glimpses of **women,** often unnamed, who provided **wise leadership** in various situations. Some have already been noted. This Search Sheet invites a look at some others. Look up the following and briefly summarize their contributions to family, community, or tribe:

1. **Abigail** (1 Samuel 25)_____

2. **The Wise Woman Of Tekoa** (2 Samuel 14:1-21 _____

3. **The Woman With A Well At Bahurim** (2 Samuel 17:17-20) _____

4. **The Wise Woman Of Abel** (2 Samuel 20:14-22) _____

5. **The Woman Of Shunem** (2 Kings 8:1-6) _____

6. **Sheerah** (1 Chronicles 7:24) _____

7. **Achsah** (Joshua 15:16-19) _____

8. **Sisters Mahlah, Noah, Hoglah, Milcah, and Tirzah** (Joshua 17:1-6) _____

9. **Daughters Of Shallum** (Nehemiah 3:12) _____

10. **Mother Of King Lemuel** (Proverbs 31:1) _____

SEARCH SHEET 23
ANSWER GUIDE

Throughout the journey of the "Mysterious Melchizedek" (priestly) people, Scripture provides glimpses of **women,** often unnamed, who provided **wise leadership** in various situations. Some have already been noted. This Search Sheet invites a look at some others. Look up the following and briefly summarize their contributions to family, community, or tribe:

1. **Abigail** (1 Samuel 25) *Took a peace offering to David after her husband Nabal insulted him, thus preventing violence*

2. **The Wise Woman Of Tekoa** (2 Samuel 14:1-21) *Went to King David via Joab's engineering and told a story which reunited him with his estranged son Absolom*

3. **The Woman With A Well At Bahurim** (2 Samuel 17:17-20) *Hid Jonathan and Ahimaaz in a well covered with cloth and grain, to help crush Absolom's rebellion*

4. **The Wise Woman Of Abel** (2 Samuel 20:14-22) *Saved the city of Abel from destruction by having rebel Sheba's head thrown over the wall*

5. **The Woman Of Shunem** (2 Kings 8:1-6) *After leaving her land during a famine, she went to the King, asked, and got it back*

6. **Sheerah** (1 Chronicles 7:24) *Daughter of Ephraim who built both Lower and Upper Beth-horon and Uzzen-sheerah*

7. **Achsah** (Joshua 15:16-19) *Assertive daughter of Caleb who asked for and received springs and a field upon her marriage to the victorious Othniel (later a judge)*

8. **Sisters Mahlah, Noah, Hoglah, Milcah, and Tirzah** (Joshua 17:1-6) *Claimed their inheritance of land, thus increasing the tribe of Manasseh's land allotment*

9. **Daughters Of Shallum** (Nehemiah 3:12) *Worked with their father to repair a section of the walls and gates of Jerusalem after the exile*

10. **Mother Of King Lemuel** (Proverbs 31:1) *Taught her son the way to distinguish between wise and foolish women before he married*

DAILY SCRIPTURE
READINGS • WEEK 23

THE **AWE REVERENCE WONDER** AT THE **NEARNESS HOLINESS BEAUTY** OF GOD = THE BEGINNING OF **WISDOM**

(PROVERBS 1:7A)

	HEBREW SCRIPTURE	NEW TESTAMENT	PSALM	PROVERBS
Day 1	2 Samuel 22:21-23:23	Acts 2:1-47	122:1-9	16:19-20
Day 2	2 Samuel 23:24-24:25	Acts 3:1-26	123:1-4	16:21-23
Day 3	1 Kings 1:1-53	Acts 4:1-37	124:1-8	16:24
Day 4	1 Kings 2:1-3:3	Acts 5:1-42	125:1-5	16:25
Day 5	1 Kings 3:4-4:34	Acts 6:1-15	126:1-6	16:26-27
Day 6	1 Kings 5:1-6:38	Acts 7:1-29	127:1-5	16:28-30
Day 7	1 Kings 7:1-51	Acts 7:30-50	128:1-6	16:31-33

Personal Notes and Glimpses of Wisdom:

"I wonder how wise it is for sheep to suffer..."

SESSION 24 • WOMEN OF WISDOM

The aim of this session is to see the wisdom of Ruth and Esther among the people of God.

MATERIALS NEEDED

Hymnals
Accompaniment
Bibles
Plenty of space for mime
Completed Search Sheet 23
Completed Insights from Daily Scripture Readings For Week 23
Copies for each participant of:
    Search Sheet 24
    Daily Scripture Readings For Week 24

▨ ASSEMBLING

The wisdom of women and their place in Scripture as well as among the whole people of God is often understated. In many hymnals it may be difficult to find even one hymn which celebrates the special place of women among the people of God. This session invites a look at two women for whom books of the Bible were named. It offers an opportunity for participants to discover their contributions to the covenantal community.

▨ THE APPROACH TO GOD   (5 to 10 minutes)

❧ *Singing a hymn* which celebrates the faith of women. *"The First One Ever"* and *"Women In The Night"* are possibilities.

❧ *Offer a Prayer* of thanksgiving for the special gifts God gives to women, and give thanks for their contribution to the community of faith.

▨ ENCOUNTERING THE WORD   (40 to 45 minutes)

➪ Invite participants to share from Search Sheet 23. Which of these women did you admire the most? Which one seemed wisest to you?

➪ Proceed with *"Stories With Mime."* Read each story as participants mime. Invite their responses to the reflection questions which follow.

▨ GOING FORTH IN GOD'S NAME   (5 to 10 minutes)

❧ *Sing a Hymn* which speaks of the total (and priestly) commitment to God demonstrated by Ruth and Esther. *"I Surrender All"* and *"Is Your All On The Altar?"* are possibilities.

❥ ***Offer a Prayer*** of thanksgiving for Ruth and Esther as role models of the wholehearted response God loves and rewards in the community of faith.

❥ Distribute copies of:
    Search Sheet 24
    Daily Scripture Readings For Week 24

Stories With Mime

The Story Of Ruth

Elimelech and Naomi, of the tribe of Judah, lived in Bethlehem with their two sons Mahlon and Chilion during the days of the judges. There was a famine in Israel, so the family moved 50 miles away to the land of Moab, on the eastern side of the Dead Sea, where there was food. Not long after they moved, Elimelech died. After a while Mahlon and Chilion married Moabite women, Ruth and Orpah. Before either couple was blessed with children, Mahlon and Chilion died. Naomi, widowed and bereft of her sons and the possibility of grandchildren (thus without heirs), decides to return to Bethlehem where she has heard there will be an abundant harvest. She says goodbye to daughters-in-law Ruth and Orpah, advising them to return to their families and to marry again. *(Allow plenty of space. Invite all participants to act the role of grieving Naomi, widowed and childless, saying goodbye to Ruth and Orpah.)*

Ruth and Orpah had learned of the God of the Covenant during their marriages to Naomi's sons. This One True God was different than the many gods of Moab. Ruth and Orpah's love and devotion for Naomi and her God was deep, and there was much weeping at the thought of parting. Eventually, Orpah did what Naomi asked. She kissed her mother-in-law goodbye and turned to go back to her own family and her own land. *(Invite all participants to act the role of Orpah, doing as Naomi asked, saying goodbye and returning to her own land and her own family.)*

Naomi urged Ruth to follow Orpah's example, make the best of the situation and return to her home. But Ruth understood that her husband's responsibility to his widowed mother was vital in the eyes of the One True God. Now that he was dead, she takes this task as her own. Ruth refuses to do as Naomi asks – there is something far more important to her than obeying her mother-in-law, and that is <u>obedience</u> to the One True God. Ruth vows, "Where you go, I will go; where you lodge, I will lodge; your people shall be my people, and your God my God." *(Invite participants to act the role of Ruth leaving behind her homeland and her people and their gods to be faithful to the One True God and to care for Naomi.)*

As Naomi and Ruth arrived in Bethlehem, the whole town was stirred at learning of the calamities which had befallen Naomi in the past ten years. Naomi (which means sweetness) even changed her name to Mara (which means bitterness) because God had dealt bitterly with her. The townsfolk were equally amazed at the devotion of Naomi's widowed Moabite daughter-in-law. Ruth set out early in the morning to glean in the barley fields – one of the few ways a widow could earn a living. She worked hard until evening and then threshed out the barley she had gleaned, and it measured three-fifths of a bushel – an unusually large amount for a day's gleaning!

The wealthy and prominent landowner Boaz, in whose field Ruth happened to glean, noticed her hard work and asked about the new gleaner. His servants told him she was the widowed Moabite daughter-in-law of the widow Naomi. Boaz went to Ruth and said, "Stay in my fields with my reapers, and I will protect you." Ruth was surprised at his kindness. She bowed and asked, "Why are you being so kind to me, a foreigner?" Boaz answered, "I have heard of your devotion to Naomi, how even when you were widowed you left your family and your homeland and came to live among people you didn't know to help your mother-in-law. May the Lord repay you for what you have done. And may you be richly rewarded by the Lord, the God of Israel, under whose wings you have come to take refuge." *(Invite participants to act the role of Boaz noticing Ruth for her hard work and devotion to her mother-in-law, and blessing her.)*

When Ruth brought home such large gleanings, Naomi asked her in whose field she had gleaned. Naomi explained that Boaz was a relative of Elimelech and that Israel's law required that a close male relative had the responsibility to buy back land which a poor relative sold and to provide an heir for a close male relative who had died. Naomi advised Ruth to go to the threshing floor where Boaz would be sleeping and to lie down at his feet to signal her request that he act as redeemer for Elimelech's family. Boaz was startled at first. Then he blessed Ruth for the nobleness of her concern. "But there is a relative who is closer than I," he said. "The matter will have to be decided by him with the elders at the city gate tomorrow. If he is not willing to redeem the property and provide an heir, I will do it." Boaz gave Ruth grain from the threshing floor as a token of his pledge.

At the city gate the next morning, the closest male relative declined to buy Naomi's land when he learned that the responsibility to provide an heir went with the purchase or land. He said, "I cannot redeem it for myself without endangering my own inheritance." Then, in keeping with tradition, he finalized the transfer of property by taking off his sandal and giving it to Boaz, the relative who was next in line. *(Invite participants to act the role of the closest relative who removed his sandal because he would not risk his own inheritance to redeem Elimelech's family.)*

At the city gate the elders witnessed Boaz' redemption of Elimelech's family by purchasing the property from Naomi and taking Mahlon's widow Ruth as his wife. The elders blessed the union, "May the Lord make the woman who is coming into your home like Rachel and Leah, who together built up the house of Israel. May you produce children in Ephrathah and be famous in Bethlehem!" *(Invite participants to act the role of the elders witnessing the legal transaction and blessing the marriage of Boaz and Ruth.)*

The Lord blessed the union of Ruth and Boaz with a son, Obed, who by Israelite law became Elimelech and Mahlon's heir. Naomi smiled as she held Obed close. When the women of Bethlehem saw Naomi holding Obed, they said, "Blessed be the Lord who has redeemed your family and given you an heir. May this child renew and sustain you in your old age; for your daughter-in-law who loves you, who is more to you than seven sons, has borne him!" *(Invite participants to act the role of the women of Bethlehem praising God and blessing Naomi upon the birth of Obed.)*

Epilogue: Obed became the father of Jesse, the father of David.

Questions For Reflection

1. What did it feel like to act the part of:
   A. Bereaved Naomi saying goodbye to Ruth and Orpah in Moab, the land of her sorrow?
   B. Orpah, obeying Naomi's request to return to her family?
   C. Ruth, disobeying Naomi, leaving her homeland and family for a land she had never seen, to be faithful to her departed husband's God?
   D. Boaz, noticing Ruth and her hard work and devotion to Naomi?
   E. The relative who wouldn't risk his own inheritance to redeem Elimelech's family?
   F. The women of Bethlehem praising God and blessing Naomi upon the birth of Obed?

2. Who do you think risked the most to be a redeemer in this story? Tell why you think this is so.

3. How does Ruth's total commitment to God compare with the commitment of Abram and Sarai to do God's will? Mary, the mother of Jesus? The self-giving love of Jesus?

4. The name of Ruth and Boaz's new little son spells the first four letters of the way of wisdom. Name it: O B E D _ _ _ _ _.

5. What does the inclusion of a Moabite woman in this story of redemption of an Israelite family say about the nature of the people of God? (Romans 1:5, 13:10)

6. I wonder who shepherded the events of this story?

The Story of Esther

In the year 483 BCE, when many of the exiled Jews still lived away from their homeland, Persian King Ahasuerus (or Xerxes) held a six-month-long banquet at his palace in Susa, a city 150 miles east of Babylon, to show off his wealth and power. During the last seven days, he invited all the people of Susa, great and small, to join in the celebration. Queen Vashti gave a special banquet for the women. After he had had much to drink, the King sent for Queen Vashti so he could show off her beauty to the people. Queen Vashti, not wishing to be put on display, refused to come. *(Invite everyone to act the role of Queen Vashti refusing to be put on display before a drunken audience.)*

The King was angry. Upon the advice of his sages, he deposed Queen Vashti so other noble ladies in his vast empire from India to Ethiopia would not follow her example and rebel against their husbands. Then he began a year-long beauty pageant, seeking the most beautiful women in the land. He planned to sample them all and then select a new queen. One of these women was Hadassah (Jewish name) or Esther (Persian name), who had been brought up by her cousin Mordecai after her parents' early death. Esther quickly won the favor of everyone at the palace, and when her turn came the King loved her and made her his queen. *(Everyone acts the role of Esther being crowned Queen of the vast Persian empire.)*

Esther's cousin Mordecai came daily to the palace court to ask about Esther. He advised her not to disclose her racial identity. One day while Mordecai was waiting for Esther he learned of a plot to assassinate the King. He told Esther, who told the King, who had the would-be assassins hanged. *(Everyone acts the part of Mordecai advising and protecting his lovely cousin and her new husband.)*

Soon King Ahasuerus promoted a man named Haman as his highest ranking official and commanded that everyone bow to him. But Mordecai would not bow. When questioned, he said it was against his Jewish faith. Haman was furious. He plotted to kill not only Mordecai but all people of the Jewish race. To set a date for the mass extermination, Haman and friends cast the pur (lot or die). They wrote letters to be circulated throughout the empire. King Ahasuerus agreed to the law and stamped his official seal on the letters. *(Everyone acts the part of Haman gloating over his anti-Semitic power play.)*

When Mordecai and Jews everywhere learned of the plot, they tore their clothes, put on sackcloth and ashes, wailed and mourned, fasted, wept and lamented. Mordecai sent a copy of the letter to Esther requesting her to act on their behalf. Esther sent a message back, "If anyone goes to the King in the inner court without being sent for, he or she will be put to death – unless the King holds out his golden scepter." She added a PS, "I have not been sent for in 30 days." Mordecai sent word back. "This includes you and your family as well! Perhaps you have become royalty for just such a time as this." Esther wondered. Then she sent word to Mordecai: "Gather all the Jews in Susa to fast for three days. After that, I will go to the King, though it is against the law, and if I perish, I perish." *(Everyone acts the part of Esther, wondering, then deciding to risk her life for the sake of Jews everywhere.)*

On the third day, Esther put on her royal robes and stood in the inner court of the King's palace. King Ahasuerus saw her. Then he held out his golden scepter. *(Everyone acts the part of King Ahasuerus holding out his golden scepter to Esther.)*

The King told Esther he would give her any request, even if it were half of his kingdom. Esther requested the honor of the King and Haman in attending a banquet she had prepared for them. While they were drinking wine at the banquet, the King again asked Esther for her request. She requested the King and Haman to come to another banquet. As they left the banquet, Haman saw Mordecai, still refusing to bow. He was infuriated! His wife and friends urged him to build gallows for Mordecai.

That night the King could not sleep and ordered the book of records to be read to him. He discovered that no honor had been given Mordecai for thwarting an assassination plot. The King called Haman and asked, "What should be done for a man the King chooses to honor?" And Haman replied, "Let him wear the King's robes and crown and ride the King's horse through the city square." King Ahasuerus said to Haman, "Do this for Mordecai the Jew." . . . Haman went home and sulked to his wife Zeresh and their friends. This time Zeresh said, "If Mordecai is a Jew, you cannot stand against him." *(Everyone acts the part of Zeresh warning Haman of the mysterious power of the Jews.)*

Meanwhile, at Esther's second feast, the King again asked her what she wished for. Esther said, "My life and lives of my people!" The King asked, "Who has plotted against you and your people?" Esther said, "This wicked Haman." The King left the banquet and paced in the palace garden. Haman, not knowing Queen Esther was the cousin of Mordecai the Jew, begged for mercy. When the King returned, he ordered Haman to be hanged on the gallows he had prepared for Mordecai.

Esther begged the King to revoke the letters ordering the destruction of the Jews. But the King said, "A letter sealed with the seal of the King of Persia cannot be revoked. (A law of the Medes and Persians cannot be changed!) But you can write a new letter and seal it with my ring." *(Everyone acts the part of King Ahasuerus, powerless to change the law of destruction, but empowering Esther to make a new letter, a new law, a new beginning.)*

The King promoted Mordecai to the high position Haman had held; and Haman was hanged on the gallows he had built for Mordecai. Together, Esther and Mordecai wrote a new letter, sealed with the King's ring, granting the Jews the right to organize and defend anyone who attacked them on the 13th day of the 12th month - the date set for their destruction by Haman's casting the pur. This letter was circulated through all 127 provinces of the Persian empire from India to Ethiopia.

The Jews defended themselves well and gained power over their enemies. Everyone in the whole city of Susa shouted their favor, for a day of mourning and death was turned into a day of light and gladness, joy and honor. The Jews feasted and gave gifts of food to each other and presents to the poor. *(Everyone acts the part of the Jews feasting and giving gifts of food to each other and presents for the poor.)*

Epilogue: Queen Esther instituted the Feast of Purim (from "pur") for the 14th and 15th days of the 12th month, preceded by a fast. This became a law which has not been changed to this day!

Questions For Reflection

1. How did you feel when acting the role of:
    A. Queen Vashti refusing to be put on display for her beauty amid a drunken audience?
    B. Esther being crowned Queen of the Persian Empire?
    C. Mordecai, advising and protecting?
    D. Haman gloating?
    E. Esther, fasting and deciding to risk her life?
    F. King Ahasuerus holding out the golden scepter?
    G. Zeresh warning Haman of the mysterious power of the Jews?
    H. King Ahasuerus empowering Esther to write a new law?
    I. The Jews feasting and giving gifts upon their victorious deliverance?

2. Who do you think risked the most to be a redeemer in this story? Tell why you think this is so.

3. How does Esther's wholehearted commitment to the people of God (Jews) compare with the commitment of Ruth? Joseph in Egypt? With the self-giving love of Jesus?

4. How is King Ahasuerus' inability to change a sealed law like God's predicament in not going back on the curses contained in the covenant? How is the King's decision to empower a new law like the new covenant (New Testament) God gave?

5. I wonder who shepherded the events of this story?

The northern ten tribes (referred to as "Israel" and also as "Ephraim") went into exile in Assyria (whose capital was Nineveh) in 722 BCE. The southern two tribes (Benjamin and Judah, known as "Judah") were exiled to Babylon in 586 BCE – although some of them were taken in 597 BCE. God's intent was that the exile would last for 70 years (see Jeremiah 25:11 and 2 Chronicles 36:21) – one-seventh of the 490 years from the beginning of the United Kingdom to the fall of Jerusalem. (See Search Sheet 2, Question 9)

Most of the people adapted to their new homes throughout the Assyrian empire which later became part of the Babylonian empire. Many of them continued to worship God even though they were far away from their destroyed center of worship in Jerusalem. A whole new generation was born - people who had never seen Jerusalem or the temple. The prophet Ezekiel encouraged the exiles. In Ezekiel 37:15-28, he makes known the will of God for the exiled people.

1. What is God's will for the northern tribes ("Ephraim")?

2. What is God's will for the southern tribes ("Judah")?

3. A descendant of _____ will rule over them. (vs. 24)

4. Where will they live? (vs. 25)

5. How will they live? (vss. 23-24)

6. What is God's plan for them? (vs. 26)

7. What message will God thus give all nations? (vs. 28)

While some of the people adapted to foreign culture, others retained their unique identity by continuing to worship God although they were far away from their homeland. Within the hearts of a tenth of the exiles, there was a burning desire to return to Jerusalem, rebuild its walls and temple, and worship God as before. When Persia conquered Babylon, King Cyrus issued a decree which allowed and assisted the Hebrew people to return to their homeland. The first group returned under the leadership of Zerubbabel and Jeshua. The year was 538 BCE, 48 years from the time they left Jerusalem. **Imagine yourself as one of that first group.** How would you feel about returning? What do you think you will find when you arrive in Jerusalem? How do you think you will feel then? Jot down ways you might feel (use reverse side if needed), and be prepared to share them in Session 25.

_____

_____

_____

_____

_____

_____

_____

_____

_____

_____

The northern ten tribes (referred to as "Israel" and also as "Ephraim") went into exile in Assyria (whose capital was Nineveh) in 722 BCE. The southern two tribes (Benjamin and Judah, known as "Judah") were exiled to Babylon in 586 BCE – although some of them were taken in 597 BCE. God's intent was that the exile would last for 70 years (see Jeremiah 25:11 and 2 Chronicles 36:21) – one-seventh of the 490 years from the beginning of the United Kingdom to the fall of Jerusalem. (See Search Sheet 2, Question 9)

Most of the people adapted to their new homes throughout the Assyrian empire which later became part of the Babylonian empire. Many of them continued to worship God even though they were far away from their destroyed center of worship in Jerusalem. A whole new generation was born – people who had never seen Jerusalem or the temple. The prophet Ezekiel encouraged the exiles. In Ezekiel 37:15-28, he makes known the will of God for the exiled people.

1. What is God's will for the northern tribes ("Ephraim")? _Reunification_

2. What is God's will for the southern tribes ("Judah")? _Reunification_

3. A descendant of _David_ will rule over them. (vs. 24)

4. Where will they live? (vs. 25) _In the land God gave Jacob_

5. How will they live? (vss. 23-24) _As cleansed and obedient people, faithful to God_

6. What is God's plan for them? (vs. 26) _To bless and multiply them in peace, with God at their center_

7. What message will God thus give all nations? (vs. 28) _God has made Israel holy and put a sanctuary among them forever_

While some of the people adapted to foreign culture, others retained their unique identity by continuing to worship God although they were far away from their homeland. Within the hearts of a tenth of the exiles, there was a burning desire to return to Jerusalem, rebuild its walls and temple, and worship God as before. When Persia conquered Babylon, King Cyrus issued a decree which allowed and assisted the Hebrew people to return to their homeland. The first group returned under the leadership of Zerubbabel and Jeshua. The year was 538 BCE, 48 years from the time they left Jerusalem. **Imagine yourself as one of that first group.** How would you feel about returning? What do you think you will find when you arrive in Jerusalem? How do you think you will feel then? Jot down ways you might feel (use reverse side if needed), and be prepared to share them in Session 25.

_____

_____

_____

_____

_____

_____

_____

_____

_____

_____

_____

DAILY SCRIPTURE
READINGS • WEEK 24

The **AWE REVERENCE WONDER** at the **NEARNESS HOLINESS BEAUTY** of God = the beginning of **WISDOM**

(PROVERBS 1:7A)

	HEBREW SCRIPTURE	NEW TESTAMENT	PSALM	PROVERBS
Day 1	1 Kings 8:1-66	Acts 7:51-8:13	129:1-8	17:1
Day 2	1 Kings 9:1-10:29	Acts 8:14-40	130:1-8	17:2-3
Day 3	1 Kings 11:1-12:19	Acts 9:1-25	131:1-3	17:4-5
Day 4	1 Kings 12:20-13:34	Acts 9:26-43	132:1-18	17:6
Day 5	1 Kings 14:1-15:24	Acts 10:1-23a	133:1-3	17:7-8
Day 6	1 Kings 15:25-17:24	Acts 10:23b-48	134:1-3	17:9-11
Day 7	1 Kings 18:1-46	Acts 11:1-30	135:1-21	17:12-13

Personal Notes and Glimpses of Wisdom:

"I wonder if sheep can be redeemers like Ruth or Esther..."

SESSION 25 • RESTORATION WISDOM

he aim of this session is to experience the wisdom of God in "The Restoration."

MATERIALS NEEDED

Hymnals
Accompaniment
Bibles
Lego or other plastic bricks in a variety of sizes
Completed Search Sheet 24
Completed Insights From Daily Scripture Readings For Week 24
Copy of "Restoration Building Project" for each group of builders
Copies for each participant of:
    Search Sheet 25
    Daily Scripture Readings For Week 25

▦ ASSEMBLING

For nearly 50 years the people of God had lived away from their homeland and center of worship, but hope had not been lost. Encouraged by the prophet Ezekiel, a faithful remnant still looked forward to the day they would be able to return and rebuild Jerusalem's walls and temple. That day came in 538 BCE after the Babylonian empire fell to Persia and King Cyrus issued a decree allowing God's people to return to Jerusalem. Survivors who did not wish to return gave financial assistance to those who went. **God in mercy had heard and answered the cries of the people** and shortened the 70-year exile. This session looks at the wisdom of God in leading the people through **"The Restoration,"** a time between 538 and 432 BCE.

▦ THE APPROACH TO GOD   (5 to 10 minutes)

❥ *Sing a hymn* of joyous pilgrimage such as *"We're Marching To Zion."*

❥ *Offer a Prayer* of thanksgiving to God for shortening the time of the exile – and for not rewarding us according to our transgressions!

▦ ENCOUNTERING THE WORD   (40 to 45 minutes)

⇨ Review Search Sheet 24. Invite participants' response to the way they think they might feel when returning home after nearly 50 years of exile. Then read (or invite a participant to read) Psalm 126 which expresses the height and depth of the feelings of the returning exiles. Distribute copies of "Restoration Building Project" to each group of builders. Read *"Days Of Our Restoration,"* a first-person narrative, while participants build with bricks, etc. Invite comments or questions as participants reflect on the rebuilding.

▦ GOING FORTH IN GOD'S NAME   (5 to 10 minutes)

❥ *Read Psalm 147* responsively or sing a hymn based on this Psalm as a closing prayer of thanksgiving to God who heals and restores!

❥ Distribute copies of:
Search Sheet 25
Daily Scripture Readings For Week 25

"Days Of Our Restoration"

It was hard to believe it was really happening! We had been dreaming of returning for nearly 50 years. We were so excited about **returning to Jerusalem** – even though we had to walk hundreds of miles to get there. We sang as we walked so the trip didn't seem so long.

Finally, we arrived in Jerusalem. There were thousands of us – family heads, priests and Levites, servants, singers – all whose hearts God had moved to come. We had horses and mules and camels and donkeys. We had with us the gold and silver dishes and bowls from our temple which Nebuchadnezzar had taken to Babylon. King Cyrus had returned them to us when he set us free. We shouted and danced and laughed and sang and wept – **we were so happy!**

We all settled in our hometowns. Then **reality** set in. **Our temple was in ruins**. So were the walls of our Holy City. King Cyrus had sent us to do a difficult task: rebuild our temple. (*Distribute Illustration 25 and plastic bricks among participants, and invite them to work together in small groups to rebuild.*) The first thing we built was the **altar** (*invite participants to build an altar*) so we could **sacrifice to God** according to the Law of Moses. We celebrated the Feast of Tabernacles.

In the second year after our return, Zerubbabel and Jeshua, our leaders, organized workers and supplies to begin rebuilding the temple. We worked on the **foundation** first (*invite participants to "lay the foundation," and allow some time for them to complete this*). When the foundation was laid, the priests sounded their trumpets and the Levites clashed their cymbals, and the singers led us in songs of praise and thanksgiving, **"God's love endures forever!"** We shouted our joy! There was also weeping – those who had seen the richness of Solomon's temple wept at the comparison. The singing and shouting and weeping made so much noise it could be heard for miles away! (*Invite participants to sing "God Is So Good" or a praise chorus of their choice – with motions, clapping, hand "trumpets," etc.*)

When our **enemies** heard that we were rebuilding the temple of the Lord, they offered "help." But Zerubbabel said it was our task and we would do it. This offended our enemies, and they organized opposition to our rebuilding. Eventually they sent a letter to King Artaxerxes warning him that Jerusalem was a rebellious city and if it were rebuilt the people would revolt and not pay taxes. King Artaxerxes thus issued an order to use force to stop the rebuilding of Jerusalem.

For the next 16 years, we worked on **rebuilding our own houses**. Then in 520 BCE the prophets Haggai and Zechariah came to us and prophesied in the name of our God and challenged us to **put God first** and **rebuild the temple**. (*Invite participants to resume building the temple.*) Zerubbabel and Jeshua led us, and we began the work. Haggai and Zechariah worked with us and **encouraged** us. Tattenai, governor of Trans-Euphrates, wrote a letter to Darius, new King of Persia, informing him of the rebuilding and our elders' using King Cyrus' edict as authorization. King Darius checked the records, found King Cyrus' edict, and ordered Tattenai not to interfere with the rebuilding of the temple. In fact, King Darius even ordered Governor Tattenai to pay us workers out of the royal treasury and to provide animals for our sacrifices. The King wanted us to pray for him and his sons! (*Allow time for completion of the temple.*)

Four years later, in 516 BCE, the **temple was completed**. We celebrated with **great joy**! We offered sacrifices and held installation ceremonies for the priests and Levites who would serve God in the temple according to the Law of Moses. Then we **celebrated the Passover** with great joy, **giving thanks to God** for changing the attitude of those who opposed rebuilding!

In 483 BCE our restoration community was **shocked** to receive a letter sealed with Persian King Ahasuerus' seal saying that all Jews would be killed by their enemies on the 13th day of the 12th month. We put on sackcloth and ashes, fasted and prayed, mourned and wailed. Had God brought us here to rebuild only to be killed? . . . Then came an **answer**. Queen Esther, our Jewish sister, had risked her life by going to the King uninvited – to save our lives – and the King had listened! Since no law of the Persians can be changed,

Queen Esther wrote a new letter, sealed with the King's seal, giving us the right to defend ourselves on the 13th day of the 12th month. **God gave us victory**, and we celebrated with great joy! Queen Esther wrote another letter, sealed with the King's seal, making this an annual feast, the **Feast of Purim** (because the **"pur"** was thrown to determine the date) which is observed to this day!

In 458 BCE, a great teacher, **Ezra**, of the Levitical priestly heritage, and other priests and Levites, singers, gatekeepers and temple servants came to Jerusalem. Once again, God caused King Artaxerxes and his advisers to be generous to us, sending temple treasures and gold and silver from Babylon for offerings and other needs. Ezra's main task was to appoint judges who knew God's laws and to **teach these laws** to all of us.

Shortly after Ezra arrived, he learned that our leaders and officials were marrying Canaanite and other foreign women. Some had even divorced their older Hebrew wives to marry younger foreign women. When Ezra heard this, he tore his coat and pulled hair out of his head and sat down appalled. This was the same kind of **unfaithfulness** that caused our exile to Babylon! Please don't think this is a matter of racial prejudice – it goes much deeper than that! The practice of intermarriage led to **idolatry**, and that is what caused the exile!

This was a very difficult time for our restoration community. Ezra prayed a prayer of confession to God for our corporate sin of intermarriage/idolatry. Then he called all the people together. The offenders were notified that if they did not come to the meeting they would forfeit all their property and be expelled from the community. Family heads were selected to investigate the cases of intermarriage one by one. Those who were found guilty had to divorce their foreign wives. Ezra **fasted** and **wept** at the temple, and the people in the crowd **mourned** and **wept**. The **acts of repentance** were painful to our whole community; but this was necessary if we were to continue to receive God's blessings and be the **holy priestly people God** called us to be. (Invite participants to silently kneel and confess individual or corporate unfaithfulness to God and decide upon appropriate acts of repentance – turning away from the unfaithfulness and back toward God to once again receive blessing and direction.)

Thirteen years later (in 445 BCE), **Nehemiah**, a cupbearer to King Artaxerxes at the palace in Susa, heard that Jerusalem's walls and gates were still broken down. He began to weep and mourn at this disgrace to our city. Once again, the Persian King and Queen helped us by providing Nehemiah with building supplies to rebuild Jerusalem's walls and gates. The people readily joined in the work, each family or group taking a section. (Invite participants to build Jerusalem's walls and gates as on Illustration 25.)

When Governor Sanballat, Tobiah the Ammonite and others heard what we were doing, they laughed and ridiculed. **We prayed to God and kept on working.** They plotted to fight against us and stir up trouble. Nehemiah **organized** us, assigning families to all of the exposed places in the wall, arming them with swords, spears and bows. Half of us worked while the other half defended. Our enemies challenged us to meet them on the plains to fight. We declined four times because we were busy doing God's work. They accused Nehemiah of planning to become king and lead a revolt. This was a discouraging time, but **we kept on keeping on**, knowing that **God was giving us strength** to continue. With God's help, the wall was **completed in 52 days!**

After the walls were built, we had a **great assembly**, and Ezra read the entire Book of the Law given to Moses by God. He read aloud from daybreak until noon. We all **stood** and **wept** as he read. When the reading was complete, we lifted our hands and said **"Amen! Amen!"** Then we **bowed** down and **worshipped** the Lord with our faces to the ground. The Levites explained the meaning of the Law to us. Ezra and Nehemiah told us to weep no more. They told us to **celebrate by eating together** and **sharing** with those who had nothing – because **the joy of the Lord is our strength!** As part of the celebration, we built booths from tree branches and lived in these booths. Our **joy** was greater than it had ever been!

After the celebration, we met for worship and **confessed** the sins of our ancestors – how they broke God's laws until God punished us with the exile. We **renewed** the covenant God had given our ancestors long ago, promising **obedience** and **faithfulness.**

Nehemiah and Ezra carried out some final **reforms** – rebuking those who did not keep the Sabbath holy, purifying the priesthood from further mixed marriages, and stopping the practice of usury among us.

We held a great celebration **dedicating** the **walls**. Two choirs walked along the top of the wall in opposite directions and met at the **temple**. Our **shouting** and **singing** could be heard for miles around! *(Invite participants to sing, "The Joy Of The Lord Is Our Strength.")*

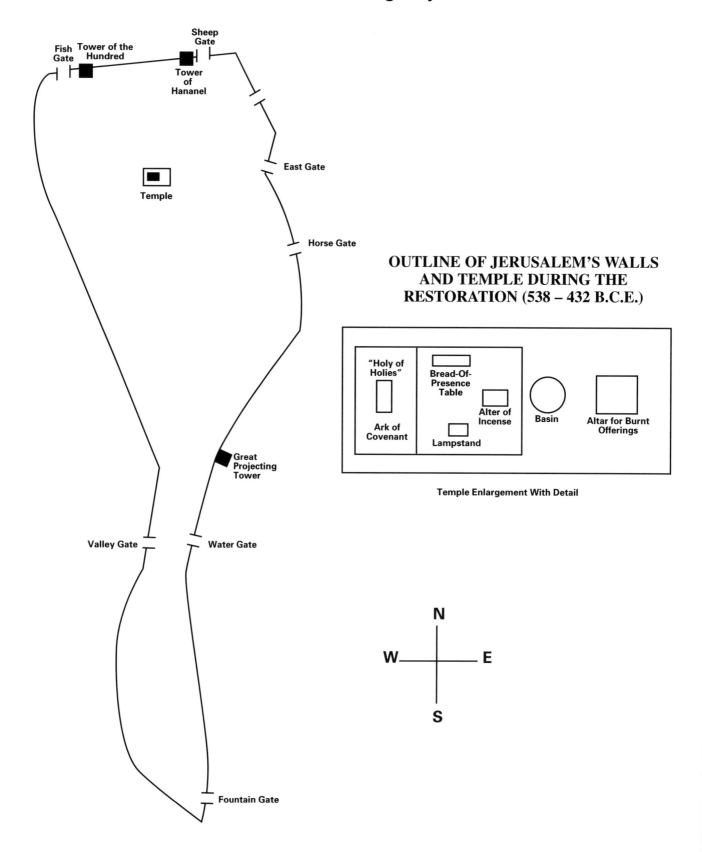

"Restoration Building Project"

Fish Gate

Tower of the Hundred

Sheep Gate

Tower of Hananel

East Gate

Temple

Horse Gate

OUTLINE OF JERUSALEM'S WALLS AND TEMPLE DURING THE RESTORATION (538 – 432 B.C.E.)

"Holy of Holies"

Bread-Of-Presence Table

Alter of Incense

Basin

Altar for Burnt Offerings

Ark of Covenant

Lampstand

Temple Enlargement With Detail

Great Projecting Tower

Valley Gate

Water Gate

N
W — E
S

Fountain Gate

SEARCH SHEET 25

Next week's session covers the Psalms – wisdom's songs – the heartcries of the people of God through the ages – words and melodies that shepherd us through daily living. In preparation for a session on the Psalms, read the following Psalms and jot down your answers to the following questions:

1. **Psalm 1** – How do you find peace, contentment and fulfillment in life? _____
   _____

2. **Psalm 19** – When life seems gray and meaningless and you want to know what's right and what isn't, how can you find out? _____
   _____

3. **Psalm 31** – When you're the victim of a horrendous injustice, what can you do? _____
   _____

4. **Psalm 32** – When you've said or done something you shouldn't have and feel awful about it, what can you do? _____
   _____
   _____

5. **Psalm 42** – When depression settles in and won't go away, what can you do? _____
   _____
   _____

6. **Psalm 46** – When the storms and stresses of life seem stronger than your faith, name three things you can do: _____
   _____
   _____

7. **Psalm 51** – When you feel worthless, what can God do for you? _____
   _____

8. **Psalm 77** – When you cry out to God and feel your prayers are not being answered, what can you do?
   _____
   _____

9. **Psalm 121** – When you feel fearful and vulnerable, what assurance does Psalm 121 offer?_____
   _____
   _____

10. **Psalm 136** – What is a perpetual reason for giving thanks to God? _____
    _____
    _____

11. **Psalm 139** – When God seems far away, what does this Psalm assert? _____
    _____
    _____

12. **Psalm 150** – On what note do the Psalms conclude? _____
    _____
    _____

Next week's session covers the Psalms – wisdom's songs – the heartcries of the people of God through the ages – words and melodies that shepherd us through daily living. In preparation for a session on the Psalms, read the following Psalms and jot down your answers to the following questions:

1. **Psalm 1** – How do you find peace, contentment and fulfillment in life? _By following God's wise way, not the way of the ungodly_

2   **Psalm 19** – When life seems gray and meaningless and you want to know what's right and what isn't, how can you find out? _By meditating on God's perfect Law_

3   **Psalm 31** – When you're the victim of a horrendous injustice, what can you do? _Trust God; commit your life to God_

4   **Psalm 32** – When you've said or done something you shouldn't have and feel awful about it, what can you do? _Tell God; receive God's forgiveness, and live it_

5   **Psalm 42** – When depression settles in and won't go away, what can you do? _Ask, seek, hope in God, await the day you will again praise God_

6   **Psalm 46** – When the storms and stresses of life seem stronger than your faith, name three things you can do: _1) Announce God's strength, 2) Look at God's power on earth, and 3) Be still and remember God is with us_

7   **Psalm 51** – When you feel worthless, what can God do for you? _Recreate, restore, renew, deliver_

8. **Psalm 77** – When you cry out to God and feel your prayers are not being answered, what can you do? _Meditate on God's mighty works, God's holiness, God's unfailing leadership (shepherding)_

9. **Psalm 121** – When you feel fearful and vulnerable, what assurance does Psalm 121 offer? _God is ever present, watching over and protecting from harm_

10. **Psalm 136** – What is a perpetual reason for giving thanks to God? _God's steadfast love endures forever_

11. **Psalm 139** – When God seems far away, what does this Psalm assert? _God knows us intimately and leads and guides us_

12. **Psalm 150** – On what note do the Psalms conclude? _Wholehearted praise_

Daily Scripture Readings • Week 25

The **Awe / Reverence / Wonder** at the **Nearness / Holiness / Beauty** of God = the beginning of **Wisdom**

(Proverbs 1:7a)

	Hebrew Scripture	New Testament	Psalm	Proverbs
Day 1	1 Kings 19:1-21	Acts 12:1-23	136:1-26	17:14-15
Day 2	1 Kings 20:1-21:29	Acts 12:24-13:15	137:1-9	17:16
Day 3	1 Kings 22:1-53	Acts 13:16-41	138:1-8	17:17-18
Day 4	2 Kings 1:1-2:25	Acts 13:42-14:7	139:1-24	17:19-21
Day 5	2 Kings 3:1-4:17	Acts 14:8-28	140:1-13	17:22
Day 6	2 Kings 4:18-5:27	Acts 15:1-35	141:1-10	17:23
Day 7	2 Kings 6:1-7:20	Acts 15:36-16:15	142:1-7	17:24-25

Personal Notes and Glimpses of Wisdom:

"I wonder what sheepfold I can help restore today..."

SESSION 26 • WISDOM'S SONGS

The aim of this session is to view the wisdom of God in the Psalms.

MATERIALS NEEDED

Hymnals
Accompaniment
Bibles
Chalkboard or Newsprint
Completed Search Sheet 25
Completed Insights from Daily Scripture Readings For Week 25
Copies for each participant of:
    "Write-Along Sheets"
    Search Sheet 26
    Daily Scripture Readings For Week 26

▦ ASSEMBLING

The Psalms offer brief and easy reading, inspiration and comfort, pardon and mercy, and expressions of praise and thanksgiving. But there's more! This session looks at the organization and themes of the Psalms, the Gospel Message contained in them, and the wisdom they offer – **ways to encounter God and enjoy the peace of God-related living** – rather than creeds or laws or formulas. Through the ages the Psalms have been a rich resource for prayer, chanting, singing or liturgical expression.

▦ THE APPROACH TO GOD   (5 to 10 minutes)

❧ *Sing, chant or read* a Psalm of praise as preparation for encountering the Word.

▦ ENCOUNTERING THE WORD   (40 to 45 minutes)

⇨ Using the *"Lecturette"* with *"Write-Along Sheets,"* lead participants through the themes of Wisdom's Songs.

▦ GOING FORTH IN GOD'S NAME   (5 to 10 minutes)

❧ *Invite participants* to select and sing a closing hymn from Wisdom's Songs, the Psalms.

❧ Distribute copies of:
    Search Sheet 26
    Daily Scripture Readings For Week 26

"Lecturette"

The Book of Psalms is divided into **150 poems or songs,** each a complete expression of faith in God. The Psalms are written in a kind of poetry that does not depend on rhyme or a certain number of syllables. Rather, there is a **rhythm and repetition** which **contrasts, complements or deepens** the meaning of the original phrase. This style of poetry can be translated into any language and not lose its beauty or meaning.

Example of repetition: (Psalm 91:1)

"You who live in the shelter of the Most High,
who abide in the shadow of the Almighty,"

Division Into Five Books:

Although the Book of Psalms is a complete book, it has been divided into five "books," perhaps to correspond with and balance the five Books of the Law. *(Illustrate the following on chalkboard or newsprint.)*

Book 1	Psalms 1 – 41
Book 2	Psalms 42 – 72
Book 3	Psalms 73 – 89
Book 4	Psalms 90 – 106
Book 5	Psalms 107 – 150

The Psalms were written to accompany worship among the people of God. Jeremiah 18:18 suggests three types of worship leaders and three types of literature. *(Illustrate the following on chalkboard or newsprint.)*

Types Of Leaders And Literature

Leader	Literature
Priest	The Law
Sage (The Wise)	The Writings (stories, poetry, proverbs)
Prophet	Prophecy and Prophetic History

Themes In The Psalms

Among the Psalms, there are various themes. (Illustrate the following on chalkboard or newsprint. Option: Invite participants to name an example.)

1. **Hymns of Praise** — Composed for use in worship. These include hymns of praise for creation, God's leadership and kingship, Zion as the Holy City and center of worship. (8, 19, 29, 68, 100, 103, 105, etc.)

2. **Laments** — Individual (3, 5-7, 22, 42, 43, 51, 88, etc.)
Corporate (44, 74, etc.) – all cries to God for help in times of distress.

3. **Songs of Trust** — Expressions of confidence in God's nearness, desire and willingness to help. (27, 46, etc.)

4. **Petitions** — Requests for help from God (38, 70)

5. **Penitential Hymns**	Confession of sin to God with request for forgiveness and new beginnings. (6, 32, 38, 51, 102, 130, 143)
6. **Hymns of Thanksgiving**	Individual (30, 32, 34, etc.) Corporate (18, 116, 118, etc.) – thanks to God for deliverance.
7. **Royal Psalms**	Written for some special royal celebration. (2, 18, 20, 45, etc.)
8. **Pilgrimage Songs**	Or "Songs of Ascent" as people "went up to Jerusalem" for worship. (120 – 134)
9. **Liturgical**	Psalm with a ritually repeated theme. (136)
10. **Instructional**	Instruction based on reflection of God's ways of leading in daily life. (1, 34, 37, 73, 78, 112, 119, 128, 133, etc.)
11. **Peace and Justice**	Hymns celebrating God's universal rule with peace and justice. (47, 93-99, etc.)
	Note: The above listings include some overlapping. Also, many psalms contain a combination of these themes.

The Gospel Message

While the Psalms contain many themes for practical faith, they also announce the **Gospel Message** – the Word of Life who became flesh. Find these elements of the Gospel Message in the Psalms:

The Holy Birth (Psalm 2:7) _You are my son; today I have begotten you_

God's salvation for all (Psalm 98:2) _Lord's victory in the sight of the nations_

Recognition of the One who comes in the name of the Lord (Psalm 118:26-27) _Blessed is the one who comes . . . with branches_

The suffering and death of the Righteous One (Psalm 22:1-2 and 31:5) _Why have you forsaken me? Into your hand I commit my spirit_

The resurrection (Psalm 118:14-24) _Vs. 17, I shall not die, but I shall live; Vs. 19, Open to me the gates of righteousness_

The ascension (Psalm 47, esp. vs. 5) _God has gone up with a shout_

The second coming (Psalm 96:, esp. vss. 10-13) _He will judge the world with equity, righteousness, truth_

The Psalms sing God's Wisdom in **The Law** and in **The Gospel Of Grace**. In the beauty of poetry, they illustrate that **The Law** does not exist apart from **Grace**. In "The Wisdom Series" they form a perfect bridge to the New Testament which shows that **Grace** does not exist apart from **The Law**.

A Look At A Cry Of Wisdom

Many of the more familiar Psalms are hymns of praise and shouts of thanksgiving. Perhaps less familiar are the laments, the cries of wisdom. Let's take a closer look at one of them:

Psalm 130 is a cry of someone in distress. Read verses 1 and 2. What would be the opposite of crying out to God in a time of distress? _Repression, stifling self_ Why might a person feel he or she did not have the right and privilege of crying out to God in a time of distress? (See verse 3) _Because of iniquities_
What does God do that makes it possible for sinful people to talk with Holy God? (See verse 4) _Forgives_

Often in the midst of a Psalm of distress there is a transformation (moving **from** orientation, **through** dis-orientation, **to** reorientation). Where do you find a transformation in Psalm 130? _After the waiting (vss. 5-6), hope, steadfast love_
What decision and recommendation does the author make as a result of this prayer while in distress? _Put your trust and hope in the Lord who is powerful and faithful to redeem_

It has been observed by many that we live in a dysfunctional society – one in which "political correctness" and instruction such as "if you can't say something nice don't say it" bids us to deny our true feelings. How does Psalm 130 offer wholeness in the midst of such repression? _By crying out to God in times of distress, waiting, hoping, trusting, focusing on God alone to act_

Wisdom For Daily Living

Take up Search Sheet 25. Ask the 12 questions and invite participants to be the experts, offering wisdom for daily living.

"Write-Along Sheet"

Number of Psalms? _____

Style of Poetry _____

Division Into Five Books:

Book 1	Psalms _____
Book 2	Psalms _____
Book 3	Psalms _____
Book 4	Psalms _____
Book 5	Psalms _____

Types Of Leaders And Literature

Leader	Literature
Priest	_____
Sage (The Wise)	_____
Prophet	_____

Themes In The Psalms

1. _____
2. _____
3. _____
4. _____
5. _____
6. _____
7. _____
8. _____
9. _____
10. _____
11. _____

The Gospel Message

While the Psalms contain many themes for practical faith, they also announce the **Gospel Message** – the Word of Life who became flesh. Find these elements of the Gospel Message in the Psalms:

The Holy Birth (Psalm 2:7) _____

God's salvation for all (Psalm 98:2) _____

Recognition of the One who comes in the name of the Lord (Psalm 118:26-27) _____
_____

The suffering and death of the Righteous One (Psalm 22:1-2 and 31:5) _____
_____

The resurrection (Psalm 118:14-24) _____

The ascension (Psalm 47, esp. vs. 5) _____

The second coming (Psalm 96:, esp. vss. 10-13) _____
_____

The Psalms sing God's Wisdom in _____ and in _____. In the beauty of poetry, they illustrate that _____ does not exist apart from _____. In "The Wisdom Series" they form a perfect bridge to the New Testament which shows that _____ does not exist apart from _____.

A Look At A Cry Of Wisdom

Many of the more familiar Psalms are hymns of praise and shouts of thanksgiving. Perhaps less familiar are the laments, the cries of wisdom. Let's take a closer look at one of them:

Psalm 130 is a cry of someone in distress. Read verses 1 and 2. What would be the opposite of crying out to God in a time of distress? _____ Why might a person feel he or she did not have the right and privilege of crying out to God in a time of distress? (See verse 3) _____
_____

What does God do that makes it possible for sinful people to talk with Holy God? (See verse 4) _____
_____

Often in the midst of a Psalm of distress there is a transformation (moving **from** orientation, **through** disorientation, **to** reorientation). Where do you find a transformation in Psalm 130? _____
_____

What decision and recommendation does the author make as a result of this prayer while in distress? __
_____

Session 26 ends The Wisdom Series' study of the Hebrew Scriptures. Before moving on to the New Testament, it is helpful to look at the 400+ years which lie between the testaments – "The Inter-Testamental Years." Before Session 27, it would be helpful to scan-read 1 and 2 Maccabees ("Apocryphal Books" – which are included in the Catholic Bible but not in the Protestant). These, although gory, give additional stories of the people of God during these 400+ years. Below is a historical sketch of some main events and major eras during the inter-testamental years.

450 – 330 BCE – THE PERSIAN ERA

The prophet Malachi (last book in the Hebrew Scriptures) ministered around 430 BCE while Judah was under Persian rule. The Persian kings were tolerant of the Hebrew faith, and the Jews were allowed religious self-rule by a high priest.

330 – 168 BCE – THE HELLENISTIC (GREEK) ERA

Between 334 and 323 BCE, Alexander the Great conquered the East. To unite all the people he conquered, Alexander forced Greek language and culture on everyone. The Jews were allowed to observe their own religious laws within that context. The Hebrew Scriptures were translated into Greek around 250 BCE.

When Alexander the Great died, his empire was divided among his generals. Ptolemy ruled Egypt and "Palestine," as Judah and its surrounding area came to be called. Seleucus ruled Syria and Mesopotamia. The Ptolemies and Seleucids fought for control of Palestine for over 100 years, the Seleucids (Syria) gaining control in 198 BCE. When Antiochus (IV) Epiphanes ruled Syria from 175-164 BCE, the practice of Judaism was prohibited. Antiochus tried to destroy all copies of the Torah (The Law), put up a statue of the Greek god Zeus in the temple in Jerusalem, and sacrificed a pig in the temple. Priest Mattathias and his five sons, including Judas (Maccabeus), led a 24-year war (166-142 BCE).

166 – 63 BCE – THE HASMONEAN (MACCABEAN) ERA

In a time of extreme cruelty to the Hebrew people, when many Jews compromised their faith with Greek culture, one Jewish family (known as the Maccabees or Hasmoneans) fought fiercely to preserve the Hebrew Scriptures and pure worship in Jerusalem. This family began a dynasty which lasted until the Roman general Pompey conquered Jerusalem in 63 BCE and Judah or Palestine came under Roman rule. (Their struggle is described in 1 and 2 Maccabees)

63 BCE – 30 CE (or AD) – THE ROMAN ERA

Pompey conquered Jerusalem after a three-month siege during which he massacred priests in the Holy of Holies. Palestine was ruled by procurators, such as Herod the Great (ruler when Jesus was born), and the people longed for deliverance from cruel Roman rule.

DAILY SCRIPTURE
READINGS • WEEK 26

THE **AWE REVERENCE WONDER** AT THE **NEARNESS HOLINESS BEAUTY** OF GOD = THE BEGINNING OF **WISDOM**

(PROVERBS 1:7A)

	HEBREW SCRIPTURE	NEW TESTAMENT	PSALM	PROVERBS
Day 1	2 Kings 8:1-9:13	Acts 16:16-40	143:1-12	17:26
Day 2	2 Kings 9:14-10:31	Acts 17:1-34	144:1-15	17:27-28
Day 3	2 Kings 10:32-12:21	Acts 18:1-22	145:1-21	18:1
Day 4	2 Kings 13:1-14:29	Acts 18:23-19:12	146:1-10	18:2-3
Day 5	2 Kings 15:1-16:20	Acts 19:13-41	147:1-20	18:4-5
Day 6	2 Kings 17:1-18:12	Acts 20:1-38	148:1-14	18:6-7
Day 7	2 Kings 18:13-19:37	Acts 21:1-16	149:1-9	18:8

Personal Notes and Glimpses of Wisdom:

"I wonder if sheep can be psalmists..."

SESSION 27 • INTER-TESTAMENTAL WISDOM

The aim of this session is to explore the developments among the covenantal people of God during the 400+ years between the prophet Malachi and the birth of Christ.

MATERIALS NEEDED

Hymnals
Accompaniment
Bibles
Inter-Testamental Scripts, copied for assigning
Chalkboard or Newsprint
Search Sheet 26 for reference
Completed Insights from Daily Scripture Readings For Week 26
Copies for each participant of:
    Search Sheet 27
    Daily Scripture Readings For Week 27

▦ ASSEMBLING

This session briefly scans the inter-testamental years showing God's leadership of the covenantal people through dark and difficult times – while preparing the way for the arrival of the long-awaited Messiah. Participants are invited to read scripts representing four groups of God's people, each with pre-conceived ideas of what the Messiah *should* be like.

▦ THE APPROACH TO GOD   (5 to 10 minutes)

❧ *Sing a hymn* of encouragement in the midst of difficult times – such as *"Never Give Up"* or a hymn which expresses longing for the coming of the Messiah such as *"Come Thou Long Expected Jesus."*

❧ *Offer a prayer* for guidance in this session, especially for openness to pre-conceived ideas we may have about what the Messiah *should* be like.

▦ ENCOUNTERING THE WORD   (40 to 45 minutes)

⇨ Invite participants to have Search Sheet 26 available for easy reference as you tell about some inter-testamental developments. Have copies of the Inter-Testamental scripts ready for distribution. Give the *"Inter-Testamental Lecturette,"* writing headings on chalkboard or newsprint as you go along.

▦ GOING FORTH IN GOD'S NAME   (5 to 10 minutes)

❧ *Sing a hymn* of God's all-inclusive love, such as "In Christ There Is No East Or West."

❧ *Offer a prayer* of thanksgiving for the wisdom of the inter-testamental years.

❧ Distribute copies of:
    Search Sheet 27
    Daily Scripture Readings For Week 27

"Inter-Testamental Lecturette"

When the people of God were exiled – the Northern (Israel) ten tribes to Assyria and the Southern (Judah) two tribes to Babylon – they were scattered throughout the cities and countrysides of these foreign empires. They found homes, and raised families who had never seen Jerusalem or the temple. For the most part, their captors were tolerant of their religious beliefs. So when King Cyrus of Persia made it possible for them to return, many chose to stay where they were instead of returning and rebuilding.

One big change during those 400+ years between the testaments is that of the **TEMPLE.** After Solomon's temple stood from 959 BCE to 586 BCE (nearly 400 years), the post-exilic temple (encouraged by Haggai and Zechariah) was built and dedicated in 516 BCE. It stood about 450 years (through the Hasmonean or Maccabean era) until it was destroyed by Pompey's invasion of Jerusalem in 63 BCE. Herod the Great began rebuilding the temple in 19 BCE to gain favor with the Jewish people. Building continued until 64 CE (or AD). The Romans destroyed the temple in 70 CE because of the Zealots' revolt. It was never rebuilt.

How did the people of God "keep the faith" without the **temple**, their center of worship – the only place sacrifice was allowed by their law? Loss of the temple as a center of worship gave rise to **synagogues**, local centers of worship. Although there was no sacrificing at synagogues, they were local centers for prayer, singing, reading and exposition from the Law and the Prophets. These synagogues also became Jewish community centers, which functioned as local schools and governmental centers. This is why Jesus and the Apostles could find a ready-made Jewish audience – people **expecting the Messiah** – in each community. The elders of each Jewish community became civil authorities and moral counselors. **Scribes** studied, copied and preserved the Law and Prophets, teaching, explaining and developing religious tradition (and eventually **over-regulating**!). Alexander the Great's insistence on use of the **Greek Language** facilitated translation of the Hebrew Scriptures into a common language, making them available to all who could read.

When Asia Minor came under Roman rule, a network of **roads** was built to facilitate ease of travel between communities. Although these roads were built for governmental and military purposes, they became the pathway for the **Good News of New Beginnings** to spread throughout the world.

During the 400+ inter-testamental years, four distinct groups of Jews emerged. These groups were intolerant of each other; each believed itself to be the **greatest** among the people of God, while all others were "outsiders" to God's care and blessings. We now have the rare opportunity to hear a representative of each of the four groups – **SADDUCEES, PHARISEES, ESSENES,** and **ZEALOTS** – and to hear them respond to a few pertinent questions.

Distribute the four scripts for reading. After each is read, ask questions as follows:

FOR THE SADDUCEE REPRESENTATIVE:

1. How would you feel about someone who said, "Happy are those who grieve, for they shall be comforted?" *(The Sadducees do not believe in a resurrection. That's why they are **"sad-you-see."**)*

2. How would you feel about the following statement? "Happy are those who are humble before God; the whole world and heaven also belong to them." *(The Sadducees were wealthy and wielded power with Roman rulers; they had to get all they could now, because they didn't believe in a future life!)*

3. How would you feel about this statement? "The least shall be greatest in God's kingdom, and the greatest shall be least."

4. How would you feel about someone saying, "Don't store up treasures here on earth where they can erode or be stolen. Store them in heaven where they will never lose their value and are safe from thieves. If your profits are in heaven, your heart will be there too."

FOR THE PHARISEE REPRESENTATIVE:

1. How would you feel about someone who said, "Be careful not to do your good deeds and acts of kindness publicly so others will admire you. Do your acts of kindness secretly, and God who knows all secrets will reward you." *(The Pharisees were popular among the Jews and enjoyed the praise they received for doing their good deeds in public.)*

2. How do you feel about the following statement? "The whole law of Moses can be summarized like this – do for others what you want them to do for you." *(The Pharisees were careful to keep every law plus many traditions, but their focus was on **performance** rather than an **attitude of the heart**.)*

3. How do you feel about someone who said, "Don't pray publicly where people can see you; go away by yourself to pray. And when you fast, put on brightly colored clothing so no one else will know you're fasting." *(The Pharisees enjoyed religious people-pleasing.)*

FOR THE ESSENE REPRESENTATIVE:

1. How would you feel about someone who said, "Happy are those who work for peace – they shall be called the children of God." *(The Essenes were anticipating a war between the children of Darkness and the children of Light which they, the children of Light, would win.)*

2. How would you feel about someone who said, "You are the world's light. Don't hide your light, but let your good deeds shine so that people everywhere will praise God." *(The Essenes had isolated themselves from the other Jewish groups because of religious corruption. They strictly observed the Law or Torah.)*

FOR THE ZEALOT REPRESENTATIVE:

1. How would you feel about someone who said, "Don't resist violence; if you are slapped on one cheek, turn the other too." *(The Zealots believed in using violence to overthrow Roman rule because allegiance to Caesar was treason to God.)*

2. How would you feel about someone saying, "Love your enemies and pray for those who persecute you?"

3. How do you feel about the following statement? "Happy are those who are persecuted and lied about because they do what is right and good; they, like the ancient prophets, will receive a great reward in heaven."

EPILOGUE:

The **Sadducee** group ended in 70 CE (or AD) with the fall of Jerusalem.

The **Essene** community at Qumran was destroyed by an earthquake around 60 BCE, and they moved into the Hasmonean area of Jerusalem. It was most likely in an Essene monastery that Jesus hosted the disciples at The Last Supper (see Luke 22:10 "man carrying jar of water" – women traditionally carried water – except in a monastic community such as that of the Essenes). In 1947 CE, a shepherd boy accidentally discovered jars containing manuscripts of Hebrew Scriptures – copied and hidden by Essenes 2000 years earlier — in a cave at Qumran. The destruction of the temple in 70 CE seems to have put an end to their apocalyptic expectations.

Jesus was born into a **Pharisee** family and taught pure rabbinical Pharisaic Judaism. Although some of his harshest criticism was directed at the Pharisees (Matthew 23), it was not on the basis of their orthodoxy but for the unloving and unjust ways they practiced it. The Pharisaic orthodoxy laid the foundation for Judaism beyond the destruction of Jerusalem in 70 CE.

Of the **Zealot** group, Jesus chose at least one disciple, Simon. The group ended when the Romans used Jewish slaves to build a siege ramp to Masada in 73 CE, and the Zealots chose to kill themselves rather than kill their Jewish brothers or be killed by the Romans.

Thank the representatives of the four groups for sharing their views. Write the four following groups on chalkboard or newsprint. Then discuss the ways they view Christ's message.

Intellectuals	Charismatics
Mystics	Social Pietists

How do they compare with the **Sadducees, Pharisees, Essenes** and **Zealots?**

INTER-TESTAMENTAL SCRIPTS

THE SADDUCEE REPRESENTATIVE:

I am a Sadducee. That is, I am one of the **wealthy upper class of Jews** – the land owners who emerged from the Hasmonean or Maccabean Era when we Jews were independent from foreign rule. We are not mystics and visionaries like the Essenes who separated themselves from their Jewish brothers and sisters. We do not believe in fighting the Romans who rule over us like the Zealots are doing. We don't like being under Roman rule any better than the other Jews, but we are **realists** – we make the best of things as they are. We entertain the Roman officials in our homes and try to get them to see things from our point of view. We've done quite well. We've gained considerable influence with them. We know how to get things done – you catch more flies with honey than with vinegar, you know.

We believe in the **Written Law** that our God gave to Moses, but we do not believe in all the tradition that other Jews like the Pharisees have added to the Law. We believe in the here and now, but not in a here-after in which people will be rewarded for their good deeds, prayer, fasting, or heaven forbid, suffering! God gave us a free will, and we believe God intends that we use it to enjoy life now.

While we enjoy life here, socializing with the Romans, we believe God will send a Messiah, a **good and gracious King**, who will be **like us, enjoying wealth and prominence here and now.**

THE PHARISEE REPRESENTATIVE:

I am a Pharisee – one of the **religious priests and scribes** – an orthodox Jew – believer in our people as a holy priestly nation. The Pharisees began as a group during the Hasmonean or Maccabean Era when we were independent from foreign rule. We are God's loyal ones, faithfully keeping the Law **AND** our traditions in exact detail. We even added some laws and traditions of our own to make sure there won't be another exile like that of our ancestors who did not keep the Law God gave to Moses.

We Pharisees live a temperate lifestyle and are not overly concerned with wealth and pleasure like the Sadducees. Perhaps that is because we believe in life in a future world, unlike them. We are very strict about keeping **Sabbath laws** and worshipping at the **temple,** and we do not affiliate with Gentiles or Greeks because they could influence us away from our high standards the way our ancestors were influenced by pagan people and their religions. We are also strict about observing Jewish **dietary laws**. We carry our own food when we travel through Gentile land so we won't have to eat food that may have been offered to pagan gods or food which has not been tithed to our God.

We believe God will send a Messiah like the prophets said, a descendant of King David. This Messiah will be **one of us**, a **priestly teacher of the Law, a Rabbi who will understand the importance of observing all the laws and traditions — especially temple worship, Sabbath observance and dietary laws.**

THE ESSENE REPRESENTATIVE:

I am an Essene. Our group formed during the Maccabean Era over a hundred years ago. We took part in the Maccabean revolt to keep from having Greek religion forced on us. But after our people had won independence, many of us were disgusted with our own religious corruption. Priests were more interested in money than in serving God in the temple. There were special interest groups always trying to gain power by giving gifts to religious and civic officials. So our group moved to Qumran, south of Jericho along the Dead Sea where we formed a monastic community. Marriage was discouraged because it left too little time for prayer and study. So we men had to do our share of cooking and carrying water. We soon developed a cistern and aqueduct system to carry water throughout the community.

While we were at Qumran, we diligently obeyed the laws of God, studied the Scriptures, carefully copying and preserving them on papyrus with our own special ink made from charcoal. We wrote our own elaborate commentaries on the Scriptures. We had common ownership of property, and we celebrated sacramental meals each day, washing and dressing in white robes before each meal. We followed a strict vegetarian diet. We saw ourselves as the **Children of Light**, the true people of God who must always keep ourselves separated from the Children of Darkness.

A generation ago, our monastic community at Qumran was destroyed by an earthquake. Our water system especially was un-usable. So we moved back to Jerusalem where Herod eventually gave us the buildings used by the Hasmoneans – Herod hated them! That's why we're in Jerusalem now, still carrying out our own monastic lifestyle. We believe there will be a life after this life – but not in our human bodies.

We look forward to the coming of the Messiah God promised in the Scriptures. The Messiah will be **one of us** – a **Child of Light, who will lead all Children of Light to victory in a great battle** against the Children of Darkness. And we will **win!**

THE ZEALOT REPRESENTATIVE:

I am a Zealot. That is, I am a **nationalist Jew**. Our group formed just a few years ago because none of the other groups seemed to realize that if we're going to be free of those bloody Romans we're going to have to fight! Fight, I say! The Essenes have separated themselves from the rest of us Jews so they can pray and write and dream of the time when God will send Someone to save us from these dark days. The Sadducees and Pharisees are so immersed in politics and religion that they don't know how to fight for what is right.

We Zealots clearly see that paying taxes to Rome is treason to God who is the true King of Israel. So we fight against what is wrong and stand up for what is right. We actively resist paying taxes to Rome. We organize and carry out acts of defiance against Roman rule. We fiercely defend Jewish tradition; therefore, we oppose the use of Greek language in our land. We are revolutionaries – freedom fighters who actively seek the salvation which God promised to our people.

Our God promised a Messiah, a descendant of that great guerrilla fighter King David. This Messiah will be **one of us** – a **revolutionary** – a **military general who will lead us to victory over Rome and set us free at last!**

After hundreds of years of expecting the Messiah God promised, and after many years of struggle since the exile, hope for a Deliverer descendant of King David was still alive among four groups of the people of God. While chafing under cruel Roman rule, the people of God could not see how a strong central government with its **unity, freedom from wars, network of military roads, common language and culture** could be a part of God's plan. Nor did they realize the depth of corruption in their own religious system and their **need to get ready for Someone Special** whom God was preparing to send. So God sent someone to help them prepare for the Messiah's coming.

John the Baptist, cousin of Jesus, was born to an elderly and barren couple, the priest Zechariah and his wife Elizabeth, who was Mary's cousin. Read the story of his birth in Luke 1:5-80.

1. What special instructions were given to Zechariah and Elizabeth regarding raising John? (vs. 15)
   _____

2. Compare these instructions with Numbers 6:1-5. _____

3. What other Hebrew parents had received such instructions? (Judges 13:2-13) _____
   _____ What other Hebrew parents were given a child in their
   "senior" years? (Genesis 18:1-15) _____

4. Extraordinary births were announced by angels/prophets and required special responses by the parents. Intertwined with the story of John's birth is the promise of Jesus' birth. Read Mary's response in Luke 1:46-55. Then read Hannah's prayer after she gave little Samuel to God for lifelong service (1 Samuel 2:1-10). What similarities do you find in these prayers?_____
   _____
   _____

5. Along with the promise of special births, certain responsibilities were given to the child. What was the purpose of John the Baptist's life? (Luke 1:16-17, 76-79) _____
   _____
   _____

6. What was the purpose of Jesus' life? (Luke 1:32-33, 2:10-11, 28-32) _____
   _____
   _____

7. When was John the Baptist filled with the Holy Spirit? (Luke 1:15) _____

8. To what ancient prophet was he likened? (vs. 17) _____

9. What special circumstances surrounded your birth? _____
   _____

10. To what special task has God called you? _____
    _____

After hundreds of years of expecting the Messiah God promised, and after many years of struggle since the exile, hope for a Deliverer descendant of King David was still alive among four groups of the people of God. While chafing under cruel Roman rule, the people of God could not see how a strong central government with its **unity, freedom from wars, network of military roads, common language and culture** could be a part of God's plan. Nor did they realize the depth of corruption in their own religious system and their **need to get ready for Someone Special** whom God was preparing to send. So God sent someone to help them prepare for the Messiah's coming.

John the Baptist, cousin of Jesus, was born to an elderly and barren couple, the priest Zechariah and his wife Elizabeth, who was Mary's cousin. Read the story of his birth in Luke 1:5-80.

1. What special instructions were given to Zechariah and Elizabeth regarding raising John? (vs. 15) _John was to drink no wine or strong drink_

2. Compare these instructions with Numbers 6:1-5. _Nazirites had no haircuts or strong drink_

3. What other Hebrew parents had received such instructions? (Judges 13:2-13) _Manoah and his wife before the birth of Samson_ What other Hebrew parents were given a child in their "senior" years? (Genesis 18:1-15) _Abram and Sarai were given Isaac_

4. Extraordinary births were announced by angels/prophets and required special responses by the parents. Intertwined with the story of John's birth is the promise of Jesus' birth. Read Mary's response in Luke 1:46-55. Then read Hannah's prayer after she gave little Samuel to God for lifelong service (1 Samuel 2:1-10). What similarities do you find in these prayers? _Praise to God, praise of God's holiness, faithfulness, mercy; raising up of the lowly, humble, feeble while putting down the proud, mighty, rich, wicked_

5. Along with the promise of special births, certain responsibilities were given to the child. What was the purpose of John the Baptist's life? (Luke 1:16-17, 76-79) _To turn the people of Israel to God, hearts of parents to children, disobedient to wisdom of righteousness, make ready a people prepared for the Lord, give knowledge of salvation by forgiveness of sins, guide to peace_

6. What was the purpose of Jesus' life? (Luke 1:32-33, 2:10-11, 28-32) _To take the throne of David, reign over the house of Jacob forever, give peace via salvation, light for revelation to Gentiles and for glory to Israel_

7. When was John the Baptist filled with the Holy Spirit? (Luke 1:15) _Before his birth_

8. To what ancient prophet was he likened? (vs. 17) _Elijah_

9. What special circumstances surrounded your birth? _____

_____

10. To what special task has God called you? _____

_____

DAILY SCRIPTURE
READINGS • WEEK 27

THE **AWE REVERENCE WONDER** AT THE **NEARNESS HOLINESS BEAUTY** OF GOD = THE BEGINNING OF **WISDOM**

(PROVERBS 1:7A)

	HEBREW SCRIPTURE	NEW TESTAMENT	PSALM	PROVERBS
Day 1	2 Kings 20:1-22:2	Acts 21:17-36	150:1-6	18:9-10
Day 2	2 Kings 22:3-23:30	Acts 2:37-22:16	1:1-6	18:11-12
Day 3	2 Kings 23:31-25:30	Acts 22:17-23:10	2:1-12	18:13
Day 4	1 Chronicles 1:1-2:17	Acts 23:11-35	3:1-8	18:14-15
Day 5	1 Chronicles 2:18-4:4	Acts 24:1-27	4:1-8	18:16-18
Day 6	1 Chronicles 4:5-5:17	Acts 25:1-27	5:1-12	18:19
Day 7	1 Chronicles 5:18-6:81	Acts 26:1-32	6:1-10	18:20-21

Personal Notes and Glimpses of Wisdom:

"I wonder how sheep survived those 400+ inter-testamental years..."

SESSION 28 • PREPARING WISDOM'S WAY

The aim of this session is to see how John the Baptist prepared people to receive Wisdom.

MATERIALS NEEDED

Hymnals
Accompaniment
Bibles
Chalkboard or Newsprint
Completed Search Sheet 27
Completed Insights from Daily Scripture Readings For Week 27
Copies for each participant of:
   "The Ministry Of John The Baptist"
   Search Sheet 28
   Daily Scripture Readings For Week 28

▒ ASSEMBLING

This session of getting ready for the Messiah's coming, like the previous inter-testamental study, helps bridge the gap in Messianic expectations between the Hebrew Scriptures' prophecy and the New Testament fulfillment. Carefully and prayerfully consider the role of John the Baptist in his time and what it means for disciples today.

▒ THE APPROACH TO GOD   (5 to 10 minutes)

❧ *Sing* (or sing along with a tape of) *"Prepare Ye The Way Of The Lord"* from *Godspell* or a hymn calling for social holiness.

❧ *Offer a prayer* asking God's help in preparing a place in each heart for the Messiah.

▒ ENCOUNTERING THE WORD   (40 to 45 minutes)

⇨ With Search Sheet 27 in hand, review the story of the birth of John the Baptist, noting the ways in which the story of his birth and Jesus' birth draw on the familiar stories of the Hebrew tradition. Then invite participants to share their uniqueness in God's sight and the tasks they feel God calls them to do.

⇨ Distribute copies of "The Ministry Of John The Baptist" to each participant, and use as a guide for discussion.

▒ GOING FORTH IN GOD'S NAME   (5 to 10 minutes)

❧ *Close with a prayer* which incorporates participants' responses to ways we get ready to be with God.

❧ Distribute copies of:
   Search Sheet 28 (This forms the backdrop for next session; no answer guide provided)
   Daily Scripture Readings For Week 28

"The Ministry Of John The Baptist"

1. Read Matthew 3:1-12. How did John the Baptist tell people to get ready for the kingdom (kin-dom) of heaven which was near? (see especially vss. 3, 6, 11)

2. Why was John angry at the Pharisees and Sadducees who came for baptism? (vss. 7-10)

3. What did John say about the limitations of the baptism he gave? (vss. 11-12)

4. Read Luke 3:1-18. What does John tell the people to do to get ready for the Messiah's coming? (vss. 3-4, 8)

5. When the crowds asked John to be more specific about how to get ready, what did he tell them? (vss. 10-14)

6. What might we do the night before worship to get ready to be with God?

7. What do we do in the worship service to get ready to be with God?

8. What can we do to prepare the way of God in our homes?

   In our churches?

   In our communities?

   In our nation?

   In the world?

"The Ministry Of John The Baptist" (Answer Guide)

1. Read Matthew 3:1-12. How did John the Baptist tell people to get ready for the kingdom (kin-dom) of heaven which was near? (see especially vss. 3, 6, 11)
Make paths straight, confess sins, be baptized with water, anticipate baptism of Holy Spirit

2. Why was John angry at the Pharisees and Sadducees who came for baptism? (vss. 7-10)
Their repentance was superficial; they "did not bear fruits of repentance" but trusted in their blood line

3. What did John say about the limitations of the baptism he gave? (vss. 11-12)
The baptism of water is for repentance; baptism of Holy Spirit empowers for ministry

4. Read Luke 3:1-18. What does John tell the people to do to get ready for the Messiah's coming? (vss. 3-4, 8)
Repent, be baptized for forgiveness of sins, make paths straight, bear fruits of repentance rather than rely on blood line of Abraham

5. When the crowds asked John to be more specific about how to get ready, what did he tell them? (vss. 10-14)
Share food and possessions, be financially honest, no stealing or violence or false accusations; be content with wages

6. What might we do the night before worship to get ready to be with God?
Make the night before worship a quiet time without TV or social events, focus on God and what God has done, be thankful, forgive, confess sins

7. What do we do in the worship service to get ready to be with God?
Praise, confess sins, sing

8. What can we do to prepare the way of God in our homes?
Work for greater honesty in relationships, refocus on God's will and way . . .

In our churches?
Pray together; keep God in Center

In our communities?
Outreach and service

In our nation?
Prayer, participation in decision-making process, etc.

In the world?
Take time to pray for the universal church, the global community; listen to international guests; travel

Read the story of Jesus' coming to earth in each of the gospels as listed below. Make your own notes of similarities and differences. What does one writer include that another does not? How might one writer's purpose in telling the story be different from another's?

Matthew 1 and 2

Mark 1:1-14

Luke 1:1-4, 26-56, 2:1-40

John 1:1-18

DAILY SCRIPTURE
READINGS • WEEK 28

THE **REVERENCE** AT THE **HOLINESS** OF GOD = THE BEGINNING OF **WISDOM**
AWE / WONDER ... NEARNESS / BEAUTY

(PROVERBS 1:7A)

	HEBREW SCRIPTURE	NEW TESTAMENT	PSALM	PROVERBS
Day 1	1 Chronicles 7:1-8:40	Acts 27:1-20	7:1-17	18:22
Day 2	1 Chronicles 9:1-10:14	Acts 27:21-44	8:1-9	18:23-24
Day 3	1 Chronicles 11:1-12:18	Acts 28:1-31	9:1-12	19:1-3
Day 4	1 Chronicles 12:19-14:17	Romans 1:1-17	9:13-20	19:4-5
Day 5	1 Chronicles 15:1-16:36	Romans 1:18-32	10:1-15	19:6-7
Day 6	1 Chronicles 16:37-18:17	Romans 2:1-24	10:16-18	19:8-9
Day 7	1 Chronicles 19:1-21:30	Romans 2:25-3:8	11:1-7	19:10-12

Personal Notes and Glimpses of Wisdom:

"I wonder how sheep could prepare the way of the Messiah..."

SESSION 29 • WISDOM'S NEW BIRTH

The aim of this session is to see Jesus' coming to earth through the windows of the four gospel writers.

MATERIALS NEEDED

Bibles
Accompaniment
Advent wreath, matches, glass container for used matches, individual candle for each participant
One copy of each Gospel writer's script
Completed Search Sheet 28
Completed Insights from Daily Scripture Readings For Week 28
Copies for each participant of:
    "Order of Worship for Celebrating Wisdom's New Birth"
    Search Sheet 29
    Daily Scripture Readings For Week 29

▓ ASSEMBLING

When the world was ready to receive the mysterious new birth of wisdom, God sent the Promised One to live among people who longed to be close to God. This session is designed as a worship service celebrating Wisdom's New Birth. Enjoy!

▓ THE APPROACH TO GOD   (5 to 10 minutes)

❥ *Sing* a favorite Christmas carol selected by participants.

❥ *Invite participants* to share their discoveries of the similarities and differences in the Gospel readings listed on Search Sheet 28. Incorporate their insights into a **litany or prayer**, giving thanks for each insight.

▓ ENCOUNTERING THE WORD   (40 to 45 minutes)

⇨ Distribute a copy of the "Order of Worship for Celebrating Wisdom's New Birth" to each participant. Assign someone the task of lighting the advent wreath candles as indicated on the Order of Worship. Assign four participants to read the Gospel writers' scripts. Celebrate the worship service together!

▓ GOING FORTH IN GOD'S NAME   (5 to 10 minutes)

❥ *Give each participant* an opportunity to share what was meaningful to them in the worship service, and give thanks to God.

❥ Distribute copies of:
    Search Sheet 29
    Daily Scripture Readings For Week 29

Order of Worship
For Celebrating Wisdom's New Birth

Introduction

MATTHEW SPEAKS

Lighting Of First Advent Candle

Hymn: *"O Little Town Of Bethlehem"*

MARK SPEAKS

Lighting of Second Advent Candle

Hymn: *"Silent Night"*

LUKE SPEAKS

Lighting Of Third Advent Candle

Hymn: *"Hark! The Herald Angels Sing"*

JOHN SPEAKS

Lighting of Fourth Advent Candle

Hymn: *"O Word Of God Incarnate"*

READING OF LUKE 2:1-7 IN UNISON

Lighting of The Christ Candle

Receiving The Light Of Christ *(Individual candles are lit)*

Hymn: *"Joy To The World"*

BENEDICTION *(In Unison)* *"Let us go forth to enjoy the Light of Wisdom's New Birth, letting our Light so shine that it will bring glory to God in the highest!"*

Matthew's Script

I am Matthew, author of the Gospel which appears **first** in your Bibles. I viewed Jesus' birth through the window of the Hebrew Scriptures which record **God's promise to send a Messiah** who would be born of the lineage of David. Beginning with Abraham, I recorded the genealogy of Jesus Christ, son (or descendant) of David, the son (or descendant) of Abraham. I recorded 14 generations from Abraham to David and 14 generations from David to the time of the Jewish exile to Babylon, and 14 generations from the exile to Jesus.

I looked at Jesus' birth through the eyes of Joseph, a righteous man who discovered his fiancée Mary was pregnant before they had become intimate. That's why the angel appeared to Joseph in a dream – to convince Joseph not to divorce Mary as he had planned. This was important, you see, so that the word of God spoken by the prophet Isaiah would be fulfilled: "The virgin will be with child and will give birth to a son, and they will call him Immanuel" (Isaiah 7:14), which means "God with us."

Although I wrote to show my Jewish brothers and sisters that **Jesus was the Messiah God had promised,** I realized that God sent Jesus for the whole world. That is why I told the story of the visit of the Magi, people from far away who came to Jerusalem to worship because of a star they had seen in the east.

The angel of the Lord appeared to Joseph again, telling him to take Mary and Jesus to Egypt so Jesus would be spared when Herod ordered all baby boys in Bethlehem killed. After Herod's death, the angel told Joseph it was safe to return. This was necessary to fulfill the word of the Lord through the prophet Hosea, "Out of Egypt I called my son."

Through the window of the Gospel I wrote, Jesus shines clearly as the Messiah God promised long ago, born of the lineage of David in the little town of Bethlehem.

Mark's Script

I am Mark, author of the **second** Gospel in your Bible. Mine is the **shortest** of the Gospels. As you look at Jesus' coming through the window of my writing, you will see that I record none of the details surrounding Jesus' birth. Mine is an action Gospel, written from the stories of Jesus which I heard from Peter's preaching. Instead of writing for Jewish readers, as Matthew did, I wrote for Gentiles, particularly those who might be **suffering** for believing in Jesus.

I wrote of the One who is more powerful than John the Baptist, the One who would baptize not with water but with the Holy Spirit of God. I show Jesus as God's Son, born also of the Holy Spirit who descended visibly upon him when he was baptized by John in the Jordan.

Jesus was borne by the Holy Spirit through temptations by the Evil One in the desert. When John the Baptist was put in prison, Jesus took up his ministry of announcing the Good News of God: "The time has come. The kingdom (kin-dom) of God is near. Repent and believe the Good News!"

By showing the Spirit-empowered **self-giving lifestyle** of Jesus and the **persecution and rejection** that he endured, I teach the **necessity of adversity in discipleship**. For in the midst of every **dark and silent night**, there comes a **new and holy birth**.

Luke's Script

I am Luke, author of the **third** Gospel in your Bible. I look at Jesus' coming through the window of a **physician** who has attended many births and thus has gained an admiration for the wisdom and courage of women. While Matthew records Joseph's genealogy, I trace Mary's as a descendant of David. Although I have witnessed the miracle of birth many times, the birth of Jesus outshines them all! It is surrounded by supernatural events beginning with the birth of Jesus' forerunner, John the Baptist — the angel appearing to Zechariah in the temple, the advanced age of Zechariah and Elizabeth, the meeting of Elizabeth and her cousin Mary, and Elizabeth's baby leaping in her womb with the knowledge of Mary's expected child.

Then the birth of Jesus was announced by the angel Gabriel to Mary, a poor and humble young woman. Mary sang a **song of wisdom**, praising God for **putting down the mighty** but **lifting up the lowly** – thus re-creating **equality.** In the fullness of time, Jesus was born in Bethlehem in a cave where the animals were kept. Heaven's **angels** appeared to rugged **shepherds** in the fields around Bethlehem and announced "Good News of great joy for all people – in the town of David a Savior has been born to you. You will find him wrapped in cloths and lying in a manger."

Never in all my years as a **physician** have I known of such a **wonderful birth** – a birth which touched the **whole universe**, bringing together angels and shepherds, heaven and earth! That beautiful melody of herald angels' voices is with us whenever we sing of Jesus' coming to earth.

John's Script

I am John, author of the **fourth** Gospel in your Bible. Through the window of the Gospel I wrote, you can see Jesus' coming as **the birth of a "new creation."** As Moses began the Book of Genesis with the words, "In the beginning," so I began my Gospel:

"In the beginning was the Word, and the Word was with God, and the Word was God. He was in the beginning with God. All things came into being through him, and without him not one thing came into being. What has come into being in him was life, and the life was the light of all people. The **light shines in the darkness,** and the darkness did not overcome it."

Jesus is that One True Light which enlightens everyone, a Light which cannot be overcome by darkness. At creation God said, "Let there be light." Again God speaks saying, "Let there be Light," and God's "Word became flesh and lived among us, and we have seen his glory, the glory as of a father's only son, full of grace and truth." "The law indeed was given through Moses; **grace and truth** came through Jesus Christ."

I wrote this Gospel **so that everyone might "believe that Jesus is the Christ (Messiah), the Son of God, and that by believing all may have life in his name."** (20:31)

In his birth, Jesus is the **"Word of God Incarnate,"** the **Wisdom** from on high, the **Truth** unchanged, unchanging, the **Light** in our dark sky." (William W. How, 1867)

Matthew wrote the Gospel to show that Jesus is the Messiah, King David's descendant, promised by the Hebrew prophets. The Gospel of Matthew is sprinkled with nine texts emphasizing God's fulfillment of prophecies in Jesus. Look them up, take notes, and list the prophet who announced each:

1:22-23 _____
_____

2:15 _____
_____

2:17-18 _____
_____

2:23 _____
_____

4:14-16 _____
_____

8:17 _____
_____

12:17-21 _____
_____

13:35 _____
_____

27:9-10 _____
_____

(Did you remember to identify the ancient prophets?)

Matthew wrote the Gospel to show that Jesus is the Messiah, King David's descendant, promised by the Hebrew prophets. The Gospel of Matthew is sprinkled with nine texts emphasizing God's fulfillment of prophecies in Jesus. Look them up, take notes, and list the prophet who announced each:

1:22-23 *The Virgin shall conceive and bear a son, and they shall name him Emmanuel." (Isaiah 7:14)*

2:15 *Out of Egypt I have called my son. (Hosea 11:1)*

2:17-18 *A voice was heard in Ramah, wailing and loud lamentation, Rachel weeping for her children . . ." (Jeremiah 31:15)*

2:23 *He will be called a Nazorean (branch) (Isaiah 11:1)*

4:14-16 *(Of the Gentiles in Galilee) The people who sat in darkness have seen a great light." (Isaiah 9:1-2)*

8:17 *(At the healing of Peter's mother-in-law) He took our infirmities and bore our diseases." (Isaiah 53:4)*

12:17-21 *Here is my servant, I will put my Spirit upon him, and he will proclaim justice to the Gentiles. (Isaiah 42:1-4)*

13:35 *I will speak in parables, proclaim what has been hidden from the foundation of the world. (Asaph the seer, (2 Chronicles 29:30), and a quote from Psalm 78;2)*

27:9-10 *They took thirty pieces of silver, the price of the one on whom a price had been set . . . (Jeremiah 18;1-3)*

DAILY SCRIPTURE
READINGS • WEEK 29

THE **AWE REVERENCE WONDER** AT THE **NEARNESS HOLINESS BEAUTY** OF GOD = THE BEGINNING OF **WISDOM**

(PROVERBS 1:7A)

	HEBREW SCRIPTURE	NEW TESTAMENT	PSALM	PROVERBS
Day 1	1 Chronicles 22:1-23:32	Romans 3:9-31	12:1-8	19:13-14
Day 2	1 Chronicles 24:1-26:11	Romans 4:1-12	13:1-6	19:15-16
Day 3	1 Chronicles 26:12-27:34	Romans 4:13-5:5	14:1-7	19:17
Day 4	1 Chronicles 28:1-29:30	Romans 5:6-21	15:1-5	19:18-19
Day 5	2 Chronicles 1:1-3:17	Romans 6:1-23	16:1-11	19:20-21
Day 6	2 Chronicles 4:1-6:11	Romans 7:1-13	17:1-15	19:22-23
Day 7	2 Chronicles 6:12 -8:10	Romans 7:14-8:8	18:1-15	19:24-25

Personal Notes and Glimpses of Wisdom:

"I wonder how God gets inside my wool when I read the Gospels..."

SESSION 30 • WISDOM'S PROMISE FULFILLED

*he aim of this session is to see in Matthew's Gospel,
The Messiah — the fulfillment of God's promise.*

MATERIALS NEEDED

Hymnals
Accompaniment
Bibles
Completed Search Sheet 29
Completed Insights from Daily Scripture Readings For Week 29
Copies for each participant of:
  Illustration 30A
  "A Closer Look At Matthew's Gospel" (Two pages)
  Search Sheet 30
  Daily Scripture Readings For Week 30

▦ ASSEMBLING

Having celebrated Wisdom's New Birth in all the Gospels, "The Wisdom Series" now looks at the uniqueness of each Gospel, beginning with the Gospel of Matthew.

▦ THE APPROACH TO GOD   (5 to 10 minutes)

❧ *Describe* the session theme to participants, and invite them to select an appropriate hymn to sing.

❧ Invite a participant to *offer a prayer* for God's guidance in this session.

▦ ENCOUNTERING THE WORD   (40 to 45 minutes)

⇨ Refer to Search Sheet 29. Invite participants to summarize the themes of the Hebrew prophecies Matthew quotes. Ask, "Which prophecies include the Gentiles?"

⇨ Distribute copies of Illustration 30A and "A Closer Look at Matthew's Gospel." Invite participants (or teams) to select, read and summarize the passages and questions listed. Then share the results as a group.

▦ GOING FORTH IN GOD'S NAME   (5 to 10 minutes)

❧ *Offer a prayer* of thanksgiving for the Hebrew faith which extends to include all people through the person, life and ministry of Jesus Christ.

❧ Distribute copies of:
    Search Sheet 30
    Daily Scripture Readings For Week 30

"A Closer Look At Matthew's Gospel"

Take a look at "Matthew's Gospel – An Outline." Notice the **"Introduction"** (Matthew 1 and 2) in which Matthew uses a genealogy, neatly divided into three 14-generation parts, to introduce the birth of Jesus, the Messiah promised by God to the Hebrew people.

The body of Matthew's Gospel is woven around **five sections** which correspond to the **five books of Hebrew Law**. Jesus is the fulfillment of The Law, a living illustration of the Secrets of Wisdom given to God's people.

1. The first of the five sections is Matthew 5-7, **The Sermon On The Mount**. This might correspond to the first book of Hebrew Law, Genesis, meaning "beginnings." Read these chapters and note ways the Sermon on the Mount may be like the **"new beginnings"** of Genesis and the **"green pastures"** of Psalm 23. _____

    _____

    _____

    _____

2. The second of the sections is Matthew 10, **The Commissioning of the Twelve Apostles** which correspond to **The Twelve Tribes of the Hebrew people**. Read this chapter and tell how it may be like the Book of Exodus in which the Twelve Tribes become the foundation for a new nation in which worship of God is central. _____

    _____

    _____

    _____

    How might Matthew 10 be like the **"still waters"** of Psalm 23? _____

    _____

3. The third section is Matthew 13, **Parables of the Kingdom (kin-dom).** Read these parables. How might they be like the Book of Leviticus which contains lifestyle wisdom for the holy priestly "Mysterious Melchizedek" people? _____

    _____

    _____

    How might these parables be like the restoration and right paths of Psalm 23? _____

    _____

    _____

4. The fourth section is Matthew 18 which teaches how to live in the kingdom (kin-dom). Read this chapter. Then tell how it might be like the Book of Numbers which tells how God's people lived during their **Wilderness years** (Session 14). _____

    _____

    _____

    _____

    How might the wisdom of living in the kingdom (kin-dom) be like **going through the valley of the shadow of death** in Psalm 23? _____

    _____

    _____

5. The fifth section is Matthew 24-25, the "Olivet Discourse," when Jesus sat with his disciples in a small cave on the Mount of Olives and instructed them about the end of the age and the struggles that lay ahead. Read these chapters. Then tell how they may be like Deuteronomy 30:15-20 where Moses gives parting wisdom to the covenant people. _____

_____

_____

_____

How might Matthew 24-25 be like **the table** the Good Shepherd prepares for the sheep **in the presence of the enemies** in Psalm 23? _____

_____

_____

Conclusion: Matthew's Gospel concludes with "The Great Commission," Matthew 28:16-20. Read this. Then tell what it may have to do with the **goodness and mercy** described at the end of Psalm 23. _____

_____

_____

_____

"A Closer Look At Matthew's Gospel" (Answer Guide)

1. Practicing the wisdom of the Sermon, summarized in the Lord's Prayer, and the "Be (happy) Attitudes" fulfills the Law (and prophets), nourishes us via new beginnings ("green pastures"), and transforms us into a "new creation."

2. The Twelve Tribes and Twelve Apostles were each called "out from" one lifestyle "into" another for a special task – announcing the nearness of God's Kingdom (kin-dom).

   Jesus' words nourish, refresh and cause growth, like still waters for sheep.

3. A holy, righteous, obedient lifestyle is the seed from which the Kingdom (kin-dom) grows to fullness.

   Wayward lifestyles lead to ruin, self-destruction; parables invite reconsideration of lifestyles, and offer restoration to God's way – transformation.

4. In the midst of many confusing voices and choices after deliverance, Moses and Jesus teach the way of humility, relational wisdom and forgiveness in everyday living.

   Living kingdom (kin-dom) wisdom will result in resistance and opposition; it will be difficult to see the way ahead – so disciples will need to trust and follow the Good Shepherd.

5. Jesus challenges followers to remain faithful in loving service and proclamation of the Gospel just as Moses urged obedience to God as the way to eternal blessing.

   Jesus warns of persecution and false leaders; these can weaken the faith of those who do not remain near the Shepherd. Following Jesus and his teachings is **The Way** through the valley.

Conclusion: Loving service and proclamation of the Gospel is **The Way** Christ bids disciples to live so that the Kingdom (kin-dom) may be brought to fullness and all people brought to Christ as the Shepherd brings sheep into the sheepfold to enjoy goodness and mercy forever.

SEARCH SHEET 30

The Gospels of Matthew, Mark and Luke are quite similar in content and sequence as they record Jesus' teachings and actions. The Gospel of John is noticeably different. Thus, the first three Gospels have become known as "The Synoptic Gospels." Scholars have puzzled over an explanation for the similarities – well developed oral tradition, eyewitness testimony, a common source or a sharing of writings among the three authors. In this exercise, you are the experts as you examine the context of Jesus' miracle of calming the storm in the Synoptic Gospels and compare similarities and differences.

READ:	Matthew 8:23-27	Mark 4:36-41	Luke 8:22-25

What happens before each?

_____

After?

What words or actions are the same in all three Gospels? _____

_____

_____

_____

_____

_____

What differences do you find? _____

_____

_____

_____

_____

_____

_____

SEARCH SHEET 30
ANSWER GUIDE

The Gospels of Matthew, Mark and Luke are quite similar in content and sequence as they record Jesus' teachings and actions. The Gospel of John is noticeably different. Thus, the first three Gospels have become known as "The Synoptic Gospels." Scholars have puzzled over an explanation for the similarities – well developed oral tradition, eyewitness testimony, a common source or a sharing of writings among the three authors. In this exercise, you are the experts as you examine the context of Jesus' miracle of calming the storm in the Synoptic Gospels and compare similarities and differences.

READ:	**Matthew 8:23-27**	**Mark 4:36-41**	**Luke 8:22-25**
What happens before each?	_Crowds pressing after healing of a leper, Gentile and woman; rebuke of half-hearted followers._	_Teaching a large crowd with parables they were unable to understand._	_Teaching with parables, then stating his "relatives" were those who heard God's Word and did it._
After?	_Healing Gadarene demoniac_	_Healing Gerasene demoniac_	_Healing Gerasene demoniac_

What words or actions are the same in all three Gospels? _They were all in the same boat, the disciples woke Jesus up because of the storm, the disciples cried out for help, Jesus rebukes the wind and sea AND questions the disciples' lack of faith. All conclude with a question, "Who is this that even the winds and sea obey?" (with only slight variations)_

What differences do you find? _Only Mark tells us it's evening, that there were other boats, and that Jesus said, "Peace! Be still!" The phrasing of the disciples' cry is different in all. Matthew says Jesus first rebukes the disciples; Mark and Luke say that he first rebuked the wind and the sea. Only Luke mentions "sailing" in the boat. Only Mark tells that Jesus was in the stern. Matthew and Mark describe a "dead calm" while Luke says "calm." Matthew and Mark say the boat was swamped; Luke says it filled with water. Matthew and Mark say a windstorm arose; Luke says it swept down on the lake. Reaction of disciples: amazed, awed, afraid and amazed._

DAILY SCRIPTURE
READINGS • WEEK 30

THE **AWE REVERENCE WONDER** AT THE **NEARNESS HOLINESS BEAUTY** OF GOD = THE BEGINNING OF **WISDOM**

(PROVERBS 1:7A)

	HEBREW SCRIPTURE	NEW TESTAMENT	PSALM	PROVERBS
Day 1	2 Chronicles 8:11-10:19	Romans 8:9-21	18:16-36	19:26
Day 2	2 Chronicles 11:1-13:22	Romans 8:22-39	18:37-50	19:27-29
Day 3	2 Chronicles 14:1-16:14	Romans 9:1-21	19:1-14	20:1
Day 4	2 Chronicles 17:1-18:34	Romans 9:22-10:13	20:1-9	20:2-3
Day 5	2 Chronicles 19:1-20:37	Romans 10:14 -11:12	21:1-13	20:4-6
Day 6	2 Chronicles 21:1-23:21	Romans 11:13-36	22:1-18	20:7
Day 7	2 Chronicles 24:1-25:28	Romans 12:1-21	22:19-31	20:8-10

Personal Notes and Glimpses of Wisdom:

"I wonder how God remembers such long-ago promises..."

30.8

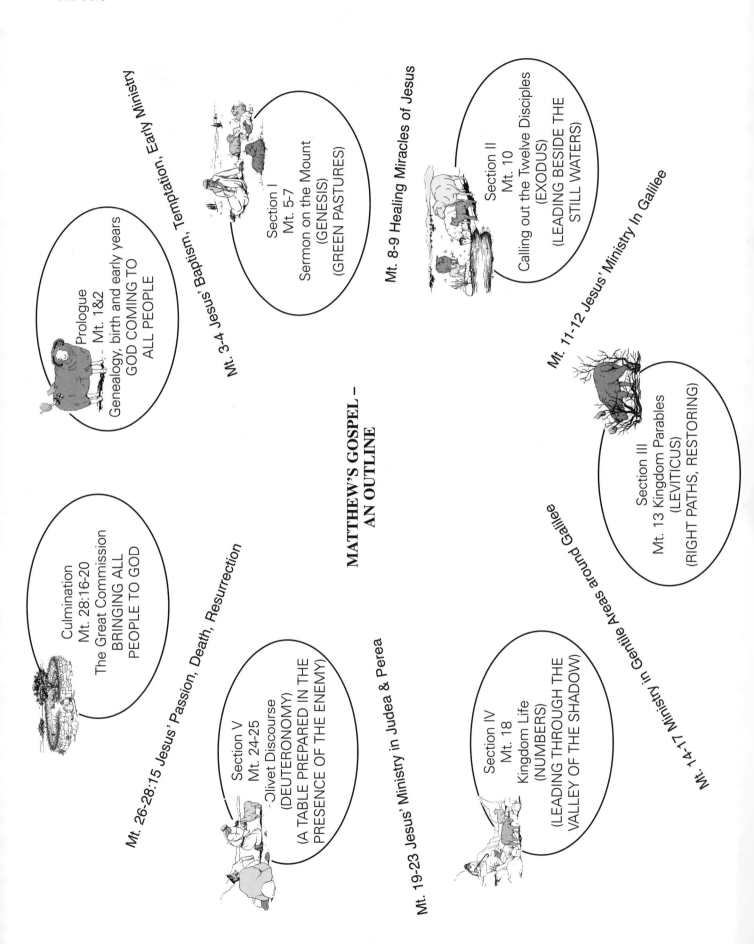

Prologue
Mt. 1&2
Genealogy, birth and early years
GOD COMING TO
ALL PEOPLE

Section I
Mt. 5-7
Sermon on the Mount
(GENESIS)
(GREEN PASTURES)

Section II
Mt. 10
Calling out the Twelve Disciples
(EXODUS)
(LEADING BESIDE THE
STILL WATERS)

Section III
Mt. 13 Kingdom Parables
(LEVITICUS)
(RIGHT PATHS, RESTORING)

Section IV
Mt. 18
Kingdom Life
(NUMBERS)
(LEADING THROUGH THE
VALLEY OF THE SHADOW)

Section V
Mt. 24-25
Olivet Discourse
(DEUTERONOMY)
(A TABLE PREPARED IN THE
PRESENCE OF THE ENEMY)

Culmination
Mt. 28:16-20
The Great Commission
BRINGING ALL
PEOPLE TO GOD

MATTHEW'S GOSPEL –
AN OUTLINE

Mt. 3-4 Jesus' Baptism, Temptation, Early Ministry

Mt. 8-9 Healing Miracles of Jesus

Mt. 11-12 Jesus' Ministry In Galilee

Mt. 14-17 Ministry in Gentile Areas around Galilee

Mt. 19-23 Jesus' Ministry in Judea & Perea

Mt. 26-28:15 Jesus' Passion, Death, Resurrection

SESSION 31 • WISDOM'S SELF-GIVING SERVANT

T*he aim of this session is to see Jesus as the Self-Giving Servant of God in the Gospel of Mark.*

MATERIALS NEEDED

Bibles
Hymnals
Accompaniment
Plain paper for journaling
Completed Search Sheet 30
Completed Insights from Daily Scripture Readings For Week 30
Copies for each participant of:
    Search Sheet 31
    Daily Scripture Readings For Week 31

▨ ASSEMBLING

While Matthew's Gospel presents Jesus as the Messiah God promised to the Hebrew people, Mark's short Gospel portrays Jesus as the Self-Giving Servant of God. Since Mark's Gospel is an "action" Gospel, this session calls for action (mime) by participants.

▨ THE APPROACH TO GOD   (5 to 10 minutes)

❧ Introduce this session on the Gospel of Mark by describing it as an ***action*** Gospel. Invite participants to select and ***sing a hymn*** which speaks of Jesus as a person of action, a Self-Giving Servant.

❧ Invite a participant to ***offer a prayer*** requesting God's movement in this session.

▨ ENCOUNTERING THE WORD   (40 to 45 minutes)

⇨ Refer to Search Sheet 30. Invite participants to share the events which took place before Jesus' miracle of calming the storm. Ask: "How might this change the way one sees the miracle?" (Like changing the frame around a picture?) Invite them to share other similarities and differences. This exercise is its own reward; everyone's understanding of the story and the Synoptic Gospels is enhanced by shared insights.

⇨ Proceed to "Acting Out The Gospel Of Mark."

▨ GOING FORTH IN GOD'S NAME   (5 to 10 minutes)

❧ *Offer a prayer* of thanksgiving for Jesus showing us God's way to joy and peace through self-giving servanthood.

❧ Distribute copies of:
    Search Sheet 31
    Daily Scripture Readings For Week 31

"Acting Out The Gospel Of Mark"

Mark skips over the details of Jesus' birth, beginning with John the Baptist, Jesus' forerunner, who baptizes Jesus. A voice from heaven announces Jesus as the Son of God. The Holy Spirit descends like a dove on Jesus, empowering him to withstand temptation and begin his ministry in Galilee. Jesus proclaims John the Baptist's message with a new authority, "The time has come. The Kingdom of God is near. Repent and believe the Good News."

Beside the Sea of Galilee, Jesus called the first disciples from among the fishermen, "Come, follow me, and I will make you fish for people." That call comes to each of us: *(call each participant by name, inviting them to walk to a designated place as their names are called, "_____, come follow Jesus.")*

You and I are called, as Jesus' disciples, to leave our own work, follow Jesus, see and hear him teaching in the synagogue. We hear people express amazement at his teaching, for he teaches with an authority not seen in other teachers of the Law. As we watch, a man with an evil spirit disrupts. Jesus commands the demon to come out. The man shakes violently *(participants mime the shaking),* and the demon comes out with a shriek! The people are really amazed. Word spreads quickly, and soon there are many people coming to Jesus for healing and deliverance.

As we stay with Jesus in the insular complex at Capernaum, we notice that he is often missing early in the morning. When we go looking, we find him outside in the garden alone, praying. *(Leader and participants kneel.)* Prayer – talking, listening, and humbly obeying God – is **The Source** of Jesus' power and ours. *(Allow time for silent prayer.)*

(While continuing to kneel —) Remember the time people were bringing their little children to Jesus to have him bless them? Some of us disciples discouraged their parents. But Jesus said, "Let the little children come to me. Anyone who will not receive the kingdom of God like a little child will never enter it..." While we're kneeling and feeling short like children, let's allow ourselves to receive the kingdom of God *as little children . . . letting Jesus take us as children in his arms, put his hands on us and bless us. (Allow a few moments; then invite participants to rise.)*

Because of his miracles, Jesus is very popular around Capernaum; but he insists on moving about Galilee preaching, teaching, healing the sick and delivering the demon-possessed. Often when he heals he says, "Don't tell this to anyone." But people always tell – and then more people come. When he heals, Jesus asks the person seeking healing to do something. *(Invite participants to mime the following actions Jesus called for)* To a leper he says, **"Go, show yourself to the priest and offer the sacrifices Moses commanded for your cleansing."** To a paralytic he says, **"Get up, take up your mat, and walk."** On the Sabbath, he tells a man with a shriveled hand, **"Stand up** in front of everyone. **Stretch out your hand."** After healing the demon-possessed man in the region of the Gerasenes, Jesus says, **"Go home** to your family and **tell them how much the Lord has done for you,** and how he has had mercy on you." One woman does the action before Jesus tells her. She *touches* his robe. He singles her out in the crowd and says, "Daughter, your faith has healed you. **Go in peace and be freed from your suffering.**" Jesus even tells a dead little girl to **"Get up."** Then he tells those around her, **"Give her something to eat."**

As Jesus heals and delivers people, preaches and teaches with an authority beyond anything we disciples and the Galileans have ever heard, more and more people follow him. The scribes and Pharisees and Sadducees feel Jesus' popularity is a threat to their religious authority. They try to discredit Jesus: "He is possessed by a demon! By the prince of demons he drives out demons!" *(Participants mime the religious leaders trying to discredit Jesus.)* It was a cheap shot. We watch to see how Jesus handles it... He does not get angry or confront them directly. He speaks in parables and asks questions: "How can Satan drive out Satan? A kingdom divided against itself cannot stand."

Once some Pharisees and teachers of the law who came from Jerusalem noticed that Jesus and you and I, his disciples, don't ceremonially wash our hands before eating or keep other traditions such as washing cups, pitchers and kettles. *(Participants mime the Pharisees and teachers of the law properly and ceremonially washing their hands where everyone can see them.)* They asked Jesus, "Why don't your disciples live according to the traditions of the elders?" We listen as Jesus replies, "Isaiah was right about you hypocrites when he wrote, 'These people honor me with their lips, but their hearts are far from me.' You have let go of the commands of God and are holding on to the traditions of men. Nothing from the outside can make you unclean. It is what comes out of the evil thoughts of your hearts that makes you unclean."

Another time, Jesus drove the merchants and moneychangers from the temple courts, quoting Isaiah, "My house will be called a house of prayer for all nations," and accusing the people of making the temple a "den of robbers." *(Participants mime Jesus' action of turning the tables and driving out the merchants.)* The chief priests, teachers of the law and the elders came to him and asked, "By what authority are you doing these things? Who gave you authority to do this?" – since Jesus had no official status in Jerusalem's religious system. *(Participants mime the Sanhedrin officials confronting Jesus . . . then mime Jesus standing before the confronting officials – does he seem afraid of them?)* As we watch, Jesus says, "I will answer your question if you answer this question: 'Was John's baptism from heaven or from men?'" The religious leaders get in a huddle and discuss the question. *(Participants mime the religious leaders in a huddle discussing the question: "If we say 'from heaven,' he'll ask why we didn't believe him. If we say 'from men' the people will be angry because everyone knows John really was a prophet.")* The religious leaders answer Jesus, "We don't know." And Jesus says, "Neither will I tell you by what authority I am doing these things."

Again, Jesus speaks in parables, this time telling a story about a landowner who rented his land to farmers and then went away on a journey. At three different times, he sent three different servants to collect the rent. The farmers beat the first, hit the second on the head, and killed the third. Other servants met with similar fate. One day the owner sent his son whom he loved, thinking, "They'll respect my son." But the farmers killed him for the inheritance. What do you think the owner will do to the tenant farmers? *(Participants mime the owner's response.)* Jesus answers, "He will come and kill the tenants and give the farmland to others. Haven't you read this Scripture: 'The stone the builders rejected has become the capstone; the Lord has done this, and it is marvelous in our eyes.'"

Now the religious leaders are angry with Jesus for cleansing the temple, foiling them on their trick questions, and speaking the truth in a parable against them. Jesus knows it won't be long before this prophecy is fulfilled. There is much we disciples need to learn before that time. We enjoyed the time of popularity; now we must learn about rejection, betrayal, suffering and death in the journey of discipleship. But we are not ready or willing to learn. As Jesus begins talking about such difficulties, Peter takes him aside and rebukes him. *(Participants mime Peter taking Jesus aside and "teaching" him about positive thinking . . .)* Jesus rebukes Peter, "Get behind me, Satan! You do not have in mind the things of God, but the things of men." *(Participants mime Jesus rebuking Peter.)*

Jesus teaches about the self-giving nature of God's love to which mature discipleship leads: "If any want to become my followers, let them deny themselves and take up their cross and follow me. For those who want to save their life will lose it, and those who lose their life for my sake, and for the sake of the gospel, will save it." *(Leader asks participants: "Are you still willing to follow?")*

Jesus continues, "The Son of Man is to be betrayed into human hands, and they will kill him, and three days after being killed, he will rise again." *(Participants mime the disciples hearing but not understanding what Jesus was saying, afraid to ask.)*

Jesus, knowing we disciples do not understand, takes us aside again, on the road to Jerusalem. "The Son of Man will be handed over to the chief priests and the scribes, and they will condemn him to death; then they will hand him over to the Gentiles; they will mock him, and spit upon him, and flog him, and kill him; and after three days he will rise again." *(Participants mime the disciples looking at each other, then at Jesus, still not comprehending.)*

James and John ask, "Grant us to sit, one at your right hand and one at your left, in your glory." *(Participants mime James and John, seeking the honor and power positions in Jesus' kingdom.)* Jesus, realizing they are still thinking of earthly power and status, chides them, "You do not know what you are asking. Are you able to drink the cup that I drink, or be baptized with the baptism that I am baptized with?"

While we as disciples struggle with our human nature to please people and get power for ourselves, Jesus teaches, "The Son of Man came not to be served but to serve, and to give his life a ransom for many." Then, as we are eating, Jesus takes a loaf of bread, and after blessing it he breaks it, gives it to us, and says, "Take; this is my body." *(Participants mime receiving the body of Christ.)* Then he takes a cup, and after giving thanks he gives it to us, and we all drink from it as he says, "This is my blood of the covenant, which is poured out for many." *(Mime receiving Jesus' blood of the covenant, poured out for us and many.)*

Later, when Jesus' prophecy about rejection, betrayal, mocking, suffering, and death was fulfilled, all of us deserted him and fled. *(Participants mime running away from the time of trial and suffering.)* And from the cross, Jesus cried, "My God, my God, why have even you forsaken me?" Then Self-Giving Servanthood was accomplished.

REFLECTING ON THE WORD:

Invite participants to reflect and journal on the following question: Where do you think God may be seeking to accomplish self-giving servanthood in your life? (Option: Type or write the question on 3 x 5 cards or lined paper.) Then begin journaling yourself. Allow time for journaling and then for voluntary sharing of insights received through journaling.

The Gospel of Luke, subject of Session 32, portrays Jesus as "The Seeking Savior." In preparation, this Search Sheet invites discovery of **WHAT** the Savior seeks to bring to all people. *(All references are from the Book of Luke.)*

1. The W_ _ _ _ _ of G _ _
    (2:40, 52, 11:49)

2. G _ _ _ N _ _ _
    (2:20, 4:18, 4:43)

3. S _ _ _ _ _ _ _ _
    (1:77, 3:6)

4. F _ _ _ _ _ _ _ _ _ _ of S _ _ _
    (7:48-49, 17:3-4, 24:47)

5. R _ _ _ _ _ _ to the C _ _ _ _ _ _ _,
    F _ _ _ _ _ _ to the O _ _ _ _ _ _ _ _
    (4:18)

6. L _ _ _ _ to the G _ _ _ _ _ _ _
    (2:32)

7. C _ _ _ _ _ _ _ _ _ _ _ for I _ _ _ _ _ (2:25)
    R _ _ _ _ _ _ _ _ for J _ _ _ _ _ _ _ _ (2:38)

8. Stories and pictures of the K _ _ _ _ _ _ of G _ _
    (13:18, 20)

9. The N _ _ C _ _ _ _ _ _ _ (22:20) of the
    K _ _ _ _ _ _ of G _ _ (22:16, 18)

10. H _ _ _ _ _ _ for all our D _ _ _ _ _ _ _
    (5:15, 17b)

11. The P _ _ _ _ of the H _ _ _ S _ _ _ _ _
    (3:16, 22, 4:14-15)

12. P _ _ _ _ (1:79, 2:14, 24:36)
    J _ _ (2:10, 24:52)
    B _ _ _ _ _ _ _ (24:50)

13. E _ _ _ _ _ _ L _ _ _ (10:25, 18:29-30)

14. Read Luke 12:49-53 and be prepared for discussion.

SEARCH SHEET 31
ANSWER GUIDE

The Gospel of Luke, subject of Session 32, portrays Jesus as "The Seeking Savior." In preparation, this Search Sheet invites discovery of **WHAT** the Savior seeks to bring to all people. *(All references are from the Book of Luke.)*

1. The W _ISDOM_ of G _OD_
    (2:40, 52, 11:49)

2. G _OOD_ N _EWS_
    (2:20, 4:18, 4:43)

3. S _ALVATION_
    (1:77, 3:6)

4. F _ORGIVENESS_ of S _INS_
    (7:48-49, 17:3-4, 24:47)

5. R _ELEASE_ to the C _APTIVES,_
    F _REEDOM_ to the O _PPRESSED_
    (4:18)

6. L _IGHT_ to the G _ENTILES_
    (2:32)

7. C _ONSOLATION_ for I _SRAEL_ (2:25)
    R _EDEMPTION_ for J _ERUSALEM_ (2:38)

8. Stories and pictures of the K _INGDOM_ of G _OD_
    (13:18, 20)

9. The N _EW_ C _OVENANT_ (22:20) of the
    K _INGDOM_ of G _OD_ (22:16, 18)

10. H _EALING_ for all our D _ISEASES_
    (5:15, 17b)

11. The P _OWER_ of the H _OLY_ S _PIRIT_
    (3:16, 22, 4:14-15)

12. P _EACE_ (1:79, 2:14, 24:36)
    J _OY_ (2:10, 24:52)
    B _LESSING_ (24:50)

13. E _TERNAL_ L _IFE_ (10:25, 18:29-30)

14. Read Luke 12:49-53 and be prepared for discussion.

DAILY SCRIPTURE
READINGS • WEEK 31

THE **REVERENCE** AT THE **HOLINESS** OF GOD = THE BEGINNING OF **WISDOM**

AWE / WONDER — NEARNESS / BEAUTY

(PROVERBS 1:7A)

	HEBREW SCRIPTURE	NEW TESTAMENT	PSALM	PROVERBS
Day 1	2 Chronicles 26:1-28:27	Romans 13:1-14	23:1-6	20:11
Day 2	2 Chronicles 29:1-36	Romans 14:1-23	24:1-10	20:12
Day 3	2 Chronicles 30:1-31:21	Romans 15:1-22	25:1-15	20:13-15
Day 4	2 Chronicles 32:1-33:13	Romans 15:23-16:7	25:16-22	20:16-18
Day 5	2 Chronicles 33:14-34:33	Romans 16:8-27	26:1-12	20:19
Day 6	2 Chronicles 35:1-36:23	1 Corinthians 1:1-17	27:1-6	20:20-21
Day 7	Ezra 1:1-2:70	1 Corinthians 1:18-2:5	27:7-14	20:22-23

Personal Notes and Glimpses of Wisdom:

"I wonder how someone can keep giving and still have so much..."

SESSION 32 • WISDOM'S SEEKING SAVIOR

The aim of this session is to see Jesus as the Seeking Savior in the Gospel of Luke.

MATERIALS NEEDED

Bibles
Hymnals
Accompaniment
Completed Search Sheet 31
Completed Insights From Daily Scripture Readings For Week 31
Copies for each participant of:
    "The Seeking Savior"
    Search Sheet 32
    Daily Scripture Readings For Week 32

▦ ASSEMBLING

From Matthew's "Promised Messiah," and Mark's "Self-Giving Servant," The Wisdom Series moves to Luke's "Seeking Savior." Search Sheet 31 invites a look at **WHAT** the Seeking Savior came to bring. This session looks at the recipients – **WHO** the Savior seeks.

▦ THE APPROACH TO GOD　(5 to 10 minutes)

❧ Invite participants to suggest and *sing a hymn* which portrays Jesus as The Seeking Savior.

❧ Lead, or ask a participant to lead in a *prayer* which includes all people the Savior may be seeking through us.

▦ ENCOUNTERING THE WORD　(40 to 45 minutes)

⇨ Invite sharing from Search Sheet 31 of all that the Savior came to bring. Then refer to Luke 12:49-53, and ask: "If Jesus came to bring peace (Number 12), why would he say this?" Allow the group to grapple with the question. *(Note for Leader: While it is true that Jesus came to bring peace in interpersonal relationships and peace between people and God, there is still a cosmic battle between Christ and the forces of evil which are opposed to God and God's purpose on earth. This conflict will be experienced even within families.)*

⇨ Distribute copies of **"The Seeking Savior,"** inviting participants to select, look up and share answers from the passages listed. Use **"The Seeking Savior" (Answer Guide and Commentary)** to supplement.

▦ GOING FORTH IN GOD'S NAME　(5 to 10 minutes)

❧ *Offer a prayer* of thanksgiving for God's love reaching to all people through The Seeking Savior.

❧ Distribute copies of:
    Search Sheet 32 **(Note: No answer guide is provided. It's easy and invites personal response.)**
    Daily Scripture Readings For Week 32

"The Seeking Savior"

Look up the references – all from the Gospel of Luke – and make notes on the back of this page for group sharing. What are they like – these people *The Savior is seeking?*

1. The L _ _ _ (19:10, 15:11-32)

2. A _ _ F _ _ _ _ (3:6, 4:25-27, 43,
   10:30-37, 17:11-19)

3. W _ _ _ _ (7:36-50, 8:2-3, 43-48,
   10:38-42, 23:49, 24:1-10)

4. S _ _ _ _ _ _ (5:32, 15:1-2),
   T _ _ C _ _ _ _ _ _ _ _ _
   (5:27-32, 18:9-14, 19:1-10)

5. C _ _ _ _ _ _ _ (8:40-42, 49-56,
   9:37-43, 46-48, 18:15-17)

6. The P _ _ _ (6:20, 21:1-4) and
   The H _ _ _ _ _ ((6:21)

7. The S _ _ _ (5:12-26, 31, 6:6-10,
   8:26-39, 13:10-17, 14:1-6, 18:35-43)

8. The B _ _ _ _, the L _ _ _, L _ _ _ _ _,
   D _ _ _, D _ _ _, and P _ _ _ (7:22)

9. S _ _ _ _ _ O _ _ _ _ _ _ _ (14:12-24)

10. A _ _ N _ _ _ _ _ _ (24:47)

11. Why do you think Jesus is seeking these people (rather than the social and religious elite)? _____
    _____
    _____

12. Who is the Savior seeking through you? _____

"The Seeking Savior" (Answer Guide and Commentary)

1. The theme of the Gospel of Luke, "The Son of Man came to seek and save what is **LOST**." (19:10) Luke 15:11-32 tells the story of the **Lost Son** also known as "The Prodigal Son."

2. (3:6) **ALL FLESH** – non-Jews as well as Jews. In 4:43, Jesus does not stay in Capernaum where he has lodging and is popular but goes to other cities to proclaim the Good News of the Kingdom (kin-dom) of God, for this is his purpose. In 10:30-37, the Parable of the Good Samaritan is difficult for an Israeli lawyer to hear – it speaks of a "despised person" (Samaritan) as being the "Good Neighbor" rather than the religious elite – priest and Levite. In 17:11-19, of ten lepers cleansed, only one, a Samaritan (again, a socially despised person in Israel) returns to praise and thank God.

3. **WOMEN**. In 7:36-50, a sinful woman anoints Jesus' feet while he is a guest at Simon's house. In 8:2-3, many women – Mary Magdalene, Joanna, Susanna and others – follow Jesus along with the 12 disciples. In 8:43-48, a woman who had hemorrhaged for 12 years touched Jesus' robe and was healed and commended for her faith. In 10:38-42, Martha is chided for her busyness while Mary is commended for listening to Jesus. In 23:49, women were near the cross when Jesus died. In 24:1-10, women coming to embalm Jesus are the first to learn of the resurrection. **Note: Traditional Judaism at that time might not have considered women worth seeking.**

4. **SINNERS** (5:32), "not the righteous" are the ones Jesus came to call to repentance. In 15;1-2, tax collectors and sinners listen to Jesus while Pharisees grumble that Jesus eats with sinners.

   TAX COLLECTORS (5:27-32). Jesus calls Levi, a tax collector, who leaves all to follow Jesus and throws a banquet for tax collectors and sinners while Pharisees and scribes grumble that Jesus eats with such. In 18:9-14 is the story of the Pharisee and tax collector praying – one showy and grateful that he is not like other sinners, the other in a corner pleading for God's mercy. In 19:1-10, Zaccheus, chief tax collector, climbs up to see Jesus; and Jesus dines with repentant Zaccheus.

5. **CHILDREN**. In 8:40-42, 49-56, Jesus heals Jairus' 12-year-old daughter. In 9:37-43, Jesus heals the boy with an unclean spirit/convulsions. In 9:46-48, in an argument of who is the greatest, Jesus takes a child beside him. In 18:15-17 the disciples rebuke people who bring children for blessing. Jesus says, "Let the children come to me."

6. **POOR**. In 6:20, Jesus says, "Blessed are you who are poor, for yours is the kingdom of God. In 21:1-4, the poor widow's two small coins are commended over the rich and their gifts.

7. **SICK**. In 5:31, Jesus says, "Those who are well have no need of a physician, but those who are sick." In 5:12-26, Jesus heals a leper. In 6:6-10, Jesus heals a withered hand on the Sabbath. In 8:26-39, Jesus heals the Gerasene demoniac. In 13:10-17, Jesus heals a crippled woman on the Sabbath. In 14:1-6, Jesus heals a man with dropsy on the Sabbath. In 18:35-43, Jesus heals a blind man.

8. **BLIND, LAME, LEPERS, DEAF, DEAD, POOR.** (7:22)

9. **SOCIAL OUTCASTS**. In 14:12-24, Jesus describes the guests at the great banquet.

10. **ALL NATIONS.** (24:47)

11. (1:38, 45, 48a) Jesus comes for willing servants who know their need, not for the self-sufficient.

In the Gospel of John, Jesus reveals God to the people who listened to him, for Jesus is the Son of God. What is God like? Go search as Jesus reveals God:

I AM THE _____ (John 6:35-40)

I AM THE _____ (John 8:12, 9:1-11)

I AM THE _____ (John 10:7-10)

I AM THE _____ (John 10:11-18)

I AM THE _____ (John 11:25-27)

I AM THE _____ (John 14:6-7)

I AM THE _____ (John 15:1-11)

Select the **"I AM"** statement above which best reveals God to you. Write a paragraph describing how you experience God in this way in your life:

_____

_____

_____

_____

_____

_____

_____

_____

_____

_____

_____

_____

_____

DAILY SCRIPTURE
READINGS • WEEK 32

THE **AWE REVERENCE WONDER** AT THE **NEARNESS HOLINESS BEAUTY** OF GOD = THE BEGINNING OF **WISDOM**

(PROVERBS 1:7A)

	HEBREW SCRIPTURE	NEW TESTAMENT	PSALM	PROVERBS
Day 1	Ezra 3:1-4:24	1 Corinthians 2:6-3:4	28:1-9	20:24-25
Day 2	Ezra 5:1-6:22	1 Corinthians 3:5-23	29:1-11	20:26-27
Day 3	Ezra 7:1-8:20	1 Corinthians 4:1-21	30:1-12	20:28-30
Day 4	Ezra 8:21-9:15	1 Corinthians 5:1-13	31:1-8	21:1-2
Day 5	Ezra 10:1-44	1 Corinthians 6:1-20	31:9-18	21:3
Day 6	Nehemiah 1:1-3:14	1 Corinthians 7:1-24	31:19-24	21:4
Day 7	Nehemiah 3:15-5:13	1 Corinthians 7:25-40	32:1-11	21:5-7

Personal Notes and Glimpses of Wisdom:

"I wonder if sheep could help the Savior seek and find someone..."

SESSION 33 • WISDOM IN HUMAN FLESH

*T*he aim of this session is to encounter Wisdom in Human Flesh
(Jesus, the Son of God) in the Gospel of John.

MATERIALS NEEDED

Bibles
Hymnals
Accompaniment
Completed Search Sheet 32
Completed Insights from Daily Scripture Readings For Week 32
Copies for each participant of:
    Search Sheet 33
    Daily Scripture Readings For Week 33

▓ ASSEMBLING

This session looks at the Gospel of John. After a brief introductory lecturette showing how this Gospel differs from the Synoptic Gospels, participants will be invited to encounter Jesus as did Nathanael, Nicodemus, the Samaritan woman at the well, and Martha.

▓ THE APPROACH TO GOD   (5 to 10 minutes)

❧ *Sing a hymn* of trust and petition for greater insight, such as "Be Thou My Vision" or "Open My Eyes That I May See."

❧ *Offer a prayer* for God's leading in encountering Jesus in the stories of the Gospel of John.

▓ ENCOUNTERING THE WORD   (40 to 45 minutes)

➪ Give the "Lecturette On The Gospel Of John," and invite responses to Search Sheet 32. Let participants select which encounter(s) they wish to work with. Allow time for discussion and feedback following the encounters. Do not rush or try to include all of them, but simply proceed as time permits.

▓ GOING FORTH IN GOD'S NAME   (5 to 10 minutes)

❧ Invite participants to name new ways they may have seen Jesus in the encounters of this session. Incorporate their responses into a ***prayer of thanksgiving*** to God for Jesus, the Son of God, who came in human flesh and is with us always in the person of the Holy Spirit.

❧ Distribute copies of:
    Search Sheet 33
    Daily Scripture Readings For Week 33

Lecturette On The Gospel Of John

The Synoptic Gospels – Matthew, Mark and Luke – give us pictures of Jesus' life and ministry, miracles, parables, teachings and challenge. They show us the human side of Jesus, his birth, temptations, agony in the garden and cries from the cross.

The Gospel of John is different. It is more concerned with interpretation of the events of Jesus' life than historical events. John doesn't begin with Jesus' birth on earth; he begins with Creation, revealing Jesus as the One who was with God in the beginning (1:2-4), came to be with us in the flesh as the Messiah (1:41, 4:29, 7:26, 10:24-30, 11:27), the Son of God, and continues ministry among us through the Holy Spirit (14:26). Thus, John reveals Jesus' **eternal** nature whereas the Synoptics illustrate his **human** nature.

(Invite participants to take up completed Search Sheet 32 and share the "I AM" that best reveals Christ to them.)

John's purpose in writing is found in 20:31: "But these are written so that you may come to believe that Jesus is the Messiah, the Son of God, and that through believing you may have life in his name."

(Invite participants to select from the following, as time permits, first reading the passage with someone as NARRATOR, another as NICODEMUS, etc., and one as JESUS. Then invite role play by putting the Scripture into their own words, drawing from their own understanding of what is happening in this encounter. After the role play, ask, "What was Nicodemus' (etc.) need or burning question?" "How was that need met by Jesus?" (or "How was that burning question answered?") "What happened in Nicodemus' (etc.) life as a result of that encounter?" (Or, "What did an encounter with THE ETERNAL accomplish that was humanly impossible?")

The Passages:

NATHANAEL (John 1:43-51)

NICODEMUS (John 3:1-21) Later: 7:50-51, 19:38-42

SAMARITAN WOMAN (John 4:1-42)

MARTHA (John 11:1-44)

Next week's session invites wonder at the mystery of Christ's humanity and divinity. In preparation, this Search Sheet invites comparison of the first human being with Jesus. How were they alike? How were they different? Look up the following verses and see:

ADAM	JESUS
Gen. 1:26-27, 5:1 _____	Col. 1:15a _____
Gen. 2:25 _____	2 Cor. 5:21 _____
Gen. 31:1-5 _____	Mt. 4:1-11, Heb. 2:18 _____
Gen. 2:18 _____	John 6:66 _____
Gen. 1:29-30 _____	Mt. 4:2 _____
Gen. 2:16-17 _____	Mt. 24:36 _____
Gen. 3:5, 22a _____	Phil. 2:6 _____
Gen. 3:6 _____	Phil 2:7-8 _____
Gen. 3:7-10 _____	Mk. 1:35, 6:46 _____

Next week's session invites wonder at the mystery of Christ's humanity and divinity. In preparation, this Search Sheet invites comparison of the first human being with Jesus. How were they alike? How were they different? Look up the following verses and see:

ADAM	**JESUS**
Gen. 1:26-27, 5:1 *Created in the image of God*	Col. 1:15a *"image of the invisible God"*
Gen. 2:25 *naked but not ashamed*	2 Cor. 5:21 *Jesus had no sin*
Gen. 31:1-5 *tempted*	Mt. 4:1-11, Heb. 2:18 *tempted as we are*
Gen. 2:18 *not good to be alone – God saw loneliness*	John 6:66 *When many disciples left him, Jesus must have felt lonely*
Gen. 1:29-30 *God provided plants "good for food"*	Mt. 4:2 *Jesus was hungry*
Gen. 2:16-17 *Tree of knowledge of good and evil was an exception to the freedom God gave*	Mt. 24:36 *Even Jesus does not know all that the Father knows – when end will come*
Gen. 3:5, 22a *desired to be like God, knowing good and evil*	Phil. 2:6 *did not grasp at being equal with God*
Gen. 3:6 *Actively reached for "wisdom" like God*	Phil 2:7-8 *Made himself nothing, humbled self, obedient even unto death*
Gen. 3:7-10 *Grasping leads to shame, fear, hiding from God*	Mk. 1:35, 6:46 *Realizing his dependence on God, Jesus prayed*

DAILY SCRIPTURE
READINGS • WEEK 33

THE **REVERENCE** AT THE **HOLINESS** OF GOD = THE BEGINNING OF **WISDOM**

AWE / WONDER — NEARNESS / BEAUTY

(**PROVERBS 1:7A**)

	HEBREW SCRIPTURE	NEW TESTAMENT	PSALM	PROVERBS
Day 1	Nehemiah 5:14-7:60	1 Corinthians 8:1-13	33:1-11	21:8-10
Day 2	Nehemiah 7:61-9:21	1 Corinthians 9:1-18	33:12-22	21:11-12
Day 3	Nehemiah 9:22-10:39	1 Corinthians 9:19-10:13	34:1-10	21:13
Day 4	Nehemiah 11:1-12:26	1 Corinthians 10:14-11:2	34:11-22	21:14-16
Day 5	Nehemiah 12:27-13:31	1 Corinthians 11:3-16	35:1-16	21:17-18
Day 6	Esther 1:1-3:15	1 Corinthians 11:17-34	35:17-28	21:19-20
Day 7	Esther 4:1-7:10	1 Corinthians 12:1-26	36:1-12	21:21-22

Personal Notes and Glimpses of Wisdom:

"I wonder if I have wisdom under my wool..."

_____
_____
_____
_____
_____
_____
_____
_____
_____
_____

SESSION 34 • WISDOM'S PARADOX

The aim of this session is to explore the mystery of Jesus' human and divine nature and to wonder about the potential available to us.

MATERIALS NEEDED

Bibles
Hymnals
Accompaniment
Chalkboard or Newsprint
Completed Search Sheet 33
Completed Insights from Daily Scripture Readings For Week 33
Copies for each participant of:
    "Jesus' Humanity and Divinity"
    Search Sheet 34
    Daily Scripture Readings For Week 34

▨ ASSEMBLING

One of the great mysteries of faith in the Gospels is the portrayal of Jesus as both human and divine. How much was human? How much was divine? This session invites questions as leader and participants wonder together at this mystery.

▨ THE APPROACH TO GOD   (5 to 10 minutes)

❥ **Sing a hymn** which expresses the human and divine nature of Jesus, such as *"Love Divine All Loves Excelling."*

❥ **In a prayer,** ask for the Spirit's leading as you explore together a great mystery of the faith.

▨ ENCOUNTERING THE WORD   (40 to 45 minutes)

⇨ Explore Search Sheet 33 together. How were the first human being and Jesus alike? How were they different?

⇨ Explore "Jesus' Humanity and Divinity" together. Look up the passages. What does each passage reveal about Jesus humanity? Divinity? (Option: List responses on chalkboard or newsprint under the headings of **HUMANITY** and **DIVINITY**). Then ask for a group consensus on the following question: ***"On what basis did Jesus calm the waters, heal, deliver, and raise the widow's son and Lazarus from the dead – his DIVINITY or OBEDIENT HUMANITY?"***

If they answer **DIVINITY,** ask how Elijah raised the widow's son and how the Apostles did miracles. If they answer **OBEDIENT HUMANITY**, ask if we then could do such miracles. How?

⇨ Be ready to quote:

Matthew 7:7 – "Ask, and it will be given you; search and you will find; knock, and the door will be opened for you."

Matthew 17:20 – "If you have faith the size of a mustard seed, you will say to this mountain, 'Move from here to there,' and it will move; and nothing will be impossible for you."

Mark 11:24 – "Whatever you ask for in prayer, believe that you have received it, and it will be yours."

John 14:12 – "The one who believes in me will also do the works that I do and, in fact, will do greater works."

⇨ If we can do greater things, how will this happen? Read, or have a participant read:

John 14:15-21

John 15:1-17

▦ GOING FORTH IN GOD'S NAME   (5 to 10 minutes)

❥ *Sing a hymn* based on any of the above Scripture.

❥ *Offer a prayer,* inviting the Spirit of Wisdom to bear fruit in and through each one by divine mystery.

❥ Distribute copies of:
    Search Sheet 34
    Daily Scripture Readings For Week 34

"Jesus' Humanity And Divinity"

Look up the following passages. What does each passage reveal about Jesus' humanity? Divinity?

	HUMANITY	DIVINITY
Matthew 1:18-25		
Matthew 3:13-17		
Matthew 4:1-2, 6, 11		
Matthew 7:21-22		
Matthew 7:28-29		
Matthew 8:20		
Matthew 8:29		
Matthew 9:36		
Matthew 11:25-30		
Matthew 12:1-8		
Matthew 14:9-21		
Matthew 16:13-20		
Matthew 27:50, 54		
Matthew 28:1-7		
John 1:1-5, 14, 18		
John 1:29-34		
John 4:6-7		
John 5:17-24		
John 6:2, 14		
John 10:30		
John 12:27		
John 13:3-5, 12-15		
John 14:6-7		
John 18:11		
John 19:7, 33-34		

"Jesus' Humanity And Divinity" (Answer Guide)

Look up the following passages. What does each passage reveal about Jesus' humanity? Divinity?

	HUMANITY	DIVINITY
Matthew 1:18-25	*Born of Mary*	*Mary with child from the Holy Spirit*
Matthew 3:13-17	*Baptized by John*	*Heavenly voice: "This is my Son."*
Matthew 4:1-2, 6, 11	*Tempted, fasted, famished*	*Victorious over temptation*
Matthew 7:21-22		*Calls God "Father," self "Lord"*
Matthew 7:28-29		*Teaches with super-human authority*
Matthew 8:20	*No place to sleep*	*Calls self "Son of Man" (Messianic)*
Matthew 8:29		*Demons call Jesus "Son of Man"*
Matthew 9:36	*Compassion for crowds*	*Sees "sheep without shepherd"*
Matthew 11:25-30	*Gentle, humble, helps weary*	*Calls God "Father"*
Matthew 12:1-8	*Goes thru grainfields on Sabbath*	*"Son of Man" is lord of Sabbath*
Matthew 14:9-21	*Grieves at John's death*	*Feeds 5,000 with 5 loaves, 2 fish*
Matthew 16:13-20		*Reveals Messiahship*
Matthew 27:50, 54	*Cries; died*	*Watchmen: "Jesus is God's Son"*
Matthew 28:1-7		*Angel: "Jesus has been raised"*
John 1:1-5, 14, 18	*Became human, lived among us*	*Was in the beginning with God*
John 1:29-34		*At baptism: "Jesus is God's Son"*
John 4:6-7	*Tired, asks for drink*	
John 5:17-24	*Breaks Sabbath tradition*	*Calls himself God's Son*
John 6:2, 14		*Miracles prove Messiahship*
John 10:30		*"The Father and I are one"*
John 12:27	*"My soul is troubled"*	*Addresses God as "Father"*
John 13:3-5, 12-15	*Washes disciples feet*	*Father had given all things to Jesus*
John 14:6-7		*Way, Truth, Life, One with Father*
John 18:11	*Accepts pain and suffering*	*as "cup" Father has given him*
John 19:7, 33-34	*Dies, exudes blood and water*	*Claimed to be "Son of God"*

Jesus, fully HUMAN and fully DIVINE, taught "The Law – Wisdom's Secrets" (see Session 11) as "attitudes" for the people of God. **The Beatitudes**, as we know them, are found in Matthew 5:3-12.

Was Jesus teaching something **new**? Or was he teaching what was taught in the Hebrew Scriptures? Form your answer as you read each of the following Beatitudes and compare them with the Hebrew Scripture references given:

1. ***Blessed are the meek, for they will inherit the earth.*** "Happy are those who make _____ _____, who do not turn to the _____, to those who go astray after _____." (Psalm 40:4)

2. ***Blessed are those who hunger and thirst for righteousness, for they will be filled.*** "Blessings are on the head of the _____, but the mouth of the _____ conceals _____." (Proverbs 10:6) "Happy are those who _____, who greatly delight in _____." (Psalm 112:1)

3. ***Blessed are the merciful, for they will receive mercy.*** "Happy are those who consider the _____; the Lord _____ them in the day of _____." (Psalm 41:1)

4. ***Blessed are the pure in heart, for they will see God.*** "Happy are those who do not follow _____ . . . but their delight is in the _____." (Psalm 1:1-2) They are like _____ . . . In all that they do, they _____." (1:3) "For _____ watches over the _____, but the way of the _____ will _____." (1:6)

5. ***Blessed are the peacemakers, for they will be called children of God.*** "Happy are those whose way is _____, who walk in the _____." (Psalm 119:1) "Happy is the _____ whose God is _____." (Psalm 33:12)

6. ***Blessed are those who are persecuted for righteousness' sake, for theirs is the kingdom of heaven.*** "Happy are those whom you _____, O Lord, and whom you teach out of _____, giving them respite from days of _____." (Psalm 94:12-13)

Jesus, fully HUMAN and fully DIVINE, taught "The Law – Wisdom's Secrets" (see Session 11) as "attitudes" for the people of God. ***The Beatitudes***, as we know them, are found in Matthew 5:3-12.

Was Jesus teaching something ***new***? Or was he teaching what was taught in the Hebrew Scriptures? Form your answer as you read each of the following Beatitudes and compare them with the Hebrew Scripture references given:

1. ***Blessed are the meek, for they will inherit the earth.*** "Happy are those who make <u>the Lord their trust</u>, who do not turn to the <u>proud</u>, to those who go astray after <u>false gods</u>." (Psalm 40:4)

2. ***Blessed are those who hunger and thirst for righteousness, for they will be filled.*** "Blessings are on the head of the <u>righteous</u>, but the mouth of the <u>wicked</u> conceals <u>violence</u>." (Proverbs 10:6) "Happy are those who <u>fear the Lord</u>, who greatly delight in <u>his commandments</u>." (Psalm 112:1)

3. ***Blessed are the merciful, for they will receive mercy.*** "Happy are those who consider the <u>poor</u>; the Lord <u>delivers</u> them in the day of <u>trouble</u>." (Psalm 41:1)

4. ***Blessed are the pure in heart, for they will see God.*** "Happy are those who do not follow <u>the advice of the wicked</u> . . . but their delight is in the <u>law of the Lord</u>" (Psalm 1:1-2) They are like <u>trees planted by streams of water</u> . . . In all that they do, they <u>prosper</u>." (1:3) "For <u>the Lord</u> watches over the <u>way of the righteous</u>, but the way of the <u>wicked</u> will <u>perish</u>." (1:6)

5. ***Blessed are the peacemakers, for they will be called children of God.*** "Happy are those whose way is <u>blameless</u>, who walk in the <u>law of the Lord</u>." (Psalm 119:1) "Happy is the <u>nation</u> whose God is <u>the Lord</u>." (Psalm 33:12)

6. ***Blessed are those who are persecuted for righteousness' sake, for theirs is the kingdom of heaven.*** "Happy are those whom you <u>discipline</u>, O Lord, and whom you teach out of <u>your law</u>, giving them respite from days of <u>trouble</u>." (Psalm 94:12-13)

DAILY SCRIPTURE
READINGS • WEEK 34

THE **AWE** **REVERENCE** **WONDER** AT THE **NEARNESS** **HOLINESS** **BEAUTY** OF GOD = THE BEGINNING OF **WISDOM**

(PROVERBS 1:7A)

	HEBREW SCRIPTURE	NEW TESTAMENT	PSALM	PROVERBS
Day 1	Esther 8:1-10:3	1 Corinthians 12:27 – 13:13	37:1-11	21:23-24
Day 2	Job 1:1-3:26	1 Corinthians 14:1-17	37:12-29	21:25-26
Day 3	Job 4:1-7:21	1 Corinthians 14:18-40	37:30-40	21:27
Day 4	Job 8:1-11:20	1 Corinthians 15:1-28	38:1-22	21:28-29
Day 5	Job 12:1-15:35	1 Corinthians 15:29-58	39:1-13	21:30-31
Day 6	Job 16:1-19:29	1 Corinthians 16:1-24	40:1-10	22:1
Day 7	Job 20:1-22:30	2 Corinthians 1:1-11	40:11-17	22:2-4

Personal Notes and Glimpses of Wisdom:

"I wonder what mysterious things we can do when Jesus gets into our wool..."

SESSION 35 • WISDOM'S SECRET ATTITUDES

The aim of this session is to discover Wisdom's Secret Attitudes, their connection with the Hebrew Scriptures and their relatedness to all Scripture.

MATERIALS NEEDED

Bibles (various translations helpful for this session)
Hymnals
Accompaniment
Chalkboard or Newsprint
Commentaries and Thesauruses for group use
Completed Search Sheet 34
Completed Insights from Daily Scripture Readings For Week 34
Copies for each participant of:
    Search Sheet 35
    Daily Scripture Readings For Week 35

▨ ASSEMBLING

After looking at the person of Jesus Christ, fully human and fully divine, this session invites a look at the summaries of Jesus' teachings in the Beatitudes, Summary of the Law, and Summary of Scripture, The Lord's Prayer. The "Secret Attitudes" guide us as Wisdom's disciples.

▨ THE APPROACH TO GOD   (5 to 10 minutes)

❧ *Sing a hymn* of pilgrimage in need of Wisdom – such as *"Guide Me O Thou Great Jehovah."*

❧ *Offer (or invite a participant beforehand to offer) a prayer* of petition for Wisdom in the earthly pilgrimage of faith.

▨ ENCOUNTERING THE WORD   (40 to 45 minutes)

⇨ With Search Sheet 34 in hand, ask for participants' responses to the questions there: "Did Jesus teach something new? Or was he teaching what was taught in the Hebrew Scriptures?" Why do they think so? Accept and commend all responses and insights.

⇨ Invite participants to turn to Matthew 5:3-12 (in a variety of translations). Taking one Beatitude at a time, have them read from various translations – then as a group formulate their own paraphrase of each "attitude." Record (or have a participant record) these paraphrases on chalkboard or newsprint. (Option: Type participants' paraphrase, copy and distribute during Session 36.)

⇨ Referring to Matthew 22:34-40, Mark 12:28-31, or Luke 10:25-28, or memory, ask participants to give Jesus' summary of the Law (the "Secrets of Wisdom" given by God to Moses – Session 11). Once again, invite the group to put these into their own words and print them on newsprint or chalkboard. (Option: If time permits, compare the scenes (settings) into which each Gospel writer puts this summary.)

⇨ Another Summary of Wisdom's Secret Attitudes was given to Jesus' disciples in the form of a prayer. It was customary for every Jewish rabbi to formulate a prayer which was the summary of all his teachings. So when Jesus' disciples said, "Lord, teach us to pray, just as John taught his disciples," (Luke 11:1), Jesus gave a prayer which was the summary of all his teachings (Luke 11:2-4, Matthew 6:9-13) – which is also a summary of all Scripture. Once again, invite participants to turn to this prayer in Matthew 6:9-13, and put this prayer into their own words. Record, or have a participant record this on newsprint or chalkboard.

▣ GOING FORTH IN GOD'S NAME   (5 to 10 minutes)

❧ *Read (or have a participant read)* John 21:19-26. Ask other participants to listen for a phrase which Jesus says three times in this passage (vss. 19, 21, 26). Ask: "Based on this passage, what do you think was Jesus' purpose in all his life and teaching?"

❧ *Sing* "The Lord's Prayer" or a hymn which speaks of the peace Christ came to bring through his life and teaching.

❧ Distribute copies of:
   Search Sheet 35
   Daily Scripture Readings For Week 35

SEARCH SHEET 35

In addition to teaching Wisdom's Secret Attitudes, Jesus had another unique way of teaching about the mysterious kingdom (kin-dom) of God – he told **parables.**

When an "expert in the law" tested Jesus by asking how to "inherit eternal life," Jesus answered first with a question about the Law. The "expert" answered by giving the summary of the Law: "Love God; Love Neighbor." When Jesus commended him, he asked, "Who is my neighbor?" This time Jesus answered with a parable. Read this **parable** in Luke 10:25-37.

1. Why do you suppose Jesus used a parable here? (vss. 25a, 29a) _____

_____

2. Which character in the story/parable do you think the expert in the law would identify with? _____

_____

3. What do you think Jesus was trying to teach the "expert" by telling this story? _____

_____

4. What does Jesus do at the end of the story? (vs. 36) _____

_____

5. Why do you think Jesus does this? _____

_____

6. Do you think the parable was effective? _____
   Why or why not? _____

_____

7. Look up the following passages and list other reasons Jesus had for using parables to teach about the mysterious kingdom (kin-dom) of God:

   Mark 4:10-12 _____

   Mark 12:12 _____

   Luke 7:36-50 _____

8. How was Jesus' purpose in telling the parable in Luke 7:40-42 similar to Nathan's purpose in telling the parable to David in 2 Samuel 12:1-4? _____

_____

In addition to teaching Wisdom's Secret Attitudes, Jesus had another unique way of teaching about the mysterious kingdom (kin-dom) of God – he told **parables.**

When an "expert in the law" tested Jesus by asking how to "inherit eternal life," Jesus answered first with a question about the Law. The "expert" answered by giving the summary of the Law: Love God; Love Neighbor. When Jesus commended him, he asked, "Who is my neighbor?" This time Jesus answered with a **parable.** Read this parable in Luke 10:25-37.

1. Why do you suppose Jesus used a parable here? (vss. 25a, 29a) *To indirectly confront an "expert" who wanted to test Jesus*

2. Which character in the story/parable do you think the expert in the law would identify with? *The priest or Levite*

3. What do you think Jesus was trying to teach the "expert" by telling this story?
    *The **heart** of all law is love, compassion and mercy*

4. What does Jesus do at the end of the story? (vs. 36) *Asks the expert his own question, "Who is a neighbor?"*

5. Why do you think Jesus does this? *Jesus is practicing "tough love" – confronting in a way which brings healing by change of attitude and patterns of thinking*

6. Do you think the parable was effective? *Yes*
    Why or why not? *The "expert" answers on the side of mercy. Jesus affirms and challenges him to live this way*

7. Look up the following passages and list other reasons Jesus had for using parables to teach about the mysterious kingdom (kin-dom) of God:

    Mark 4:10-12 *To keep it a secret from those who would not receive it*

    Mark 12:12 *An indirect way of conveying an unpopular truth*

    Luke 7:36-50 *"Tough love," confronting Simon with his own need for forgiveness*

8. How was Jesus' purpose in telling the parable in Luke 7:40-42 similar to Nathan's purpose in telling the parable to David in 2 Samuel 12:1-4? *The parable overcame the natural resistance to hearing words which convict of sin and the need for forgiveness*

DAILY SCRIPTURE
READINGS • WEEK 35

THE **AWE REVERENCE WONDER** AT THE **NEARNESS HOLINESS BEAUTY** OF GOD = THE BEGINNING OF **WISDOM**

(PROVERBS 1:7A)

	HEBREW SCRIPTURE	NEW TESTAMENT	PSALM	PROVERBS
Day 1	Job 23:1-27:23	2 Corinthians 1:12-2:11	41:1-13	22:5-6
Day 2	Job 28:1-30:31	2 Corinthians 2:12-17	42:1-11	22:7
Day 3	Job 31:1-33:33	2 Corinthians 3:1-18	43:1-5	22:8-9
Day 4	Job 34:1-36:33	2 Corinthians 4:1-12	44:1-8	22:10-12
Day 5	Job 37:1-39:30	2 Corinthians 4:13-5:10	44:9-26	22:13
Day 6	Job 40:1-42:17	2 Corinthians 5:11-21	45:1-17	22:14
Day 7	Ecclesiastes 1:1-3:22	2 Corinthians 6:1-13	46:1-11	22:15

Personal Notes and Glimpses of Wisdom:

"I wonder how many secret attitudes will fit under my wool..."

SESSION 36 • WISDOM'S MYSTERIOUS GROWTH STORIES

The aim of this session is to search three parables for the mysterious ways Wisdom's kin-dom comes and grows.

MATERIALS NEEDED

Bibles
Hymnals
Accompaniment
Chalkboard or Newsprint
Crayons, colored markers, pencils
Completed Search Sheet 35
Completed Insights from Daily Scripture Readings For Week 35
Copies for each participant of:
    The group's paraphrase of "The Beatitudes" from Session 35
    "Of Hearts And Soils"
    "Of Small and Secret Seeds"
    Search Sheet 36
    Daily Scripture Readings For Week 36

▓ ASSEMBLING

Jesus gives us "Wisdom's Secret Attitudes," summaries of Scripture, and prayer. Then, in unique stories, Jesus illustrates the transforming power these attitudes have in daily life. This session invites encounter with Jesus in stories of the mysterious kin-dom's coming and its growth.

▓ THE APPROACH TO GOD   (5 to 10 minutes)

❧ *Select and sing a hymn* which speaks of the coming and/or growth of the mysterious kin-dom of God.

❧ *Offer a prayer* for new wisdom and insight into the stories of the kin-dom.

▓ ENCOUNTERING THE WORD   (40 to 45 minutes)

⇨ Using Search Sheet 35, invite participants to share their responses to the parable of the Good Samaritan in Luke 10:25-37. Then read, or (have a participant read) 2 Chronicles 28:8-15. What relationship might these stories have? How does this change the way participants may see the parable of the Good Samaritan? Invite participants to share from their Search Sheets the reasons Jesus may have had for teaching with parables.

⇨ Jesus gave the parable of the "Four Kinds of Soil" to a large crowd which included his disciples. Matthew tells us this took place at the Sea of Galilee where there were many farm workers present. Jesus sat in a boat to tell the story while the crowd stood on shore. *Distribute "Of Hearts And Soils,"* along with crayons, colored markers and pencils. *Read Matthew 13:3-8.* Invite participants to draw a picture of each kind of soil in the "hearts" as you read the verse describing each. (Assure participants that sharing completed pictures is optional.)

⇨ When pictures have been drawn, *read the interpretation of the parable in Matthew 13:18-23.* Then go back and *read the verse corresponding to the meaning of each kind of soil* as listed on Illustration 36A. Invite participants to describe in their own words the kind of heart which corresponds to the soil Jesus described. List these on chalkboard or newsprint.

Optional: How might these four kinds of hearts and soils correspond to the four groups studied in Session 27? (Essenes, Zealots, Sadducees, Pharisees) or (Mystics, Charismatics, Intellectuals, Social Pietists) **Note:** *Do not force a comparison here - inviting* **wonder** *is sufficient!*

⇨ *Distribute "Of Small and Secret Seeds,"* crayons, markers and pencils. *Read the Parable of the Mustard Seed from Matthew 13:31-32.* Invite participants to draw this story in the space provided. (Remember that the mustard seed of which Jesus spoke was not like the ones we may have seen as jewelry, etc. The mustard seed of which Jesus spoke was the size of a dot of finely ground pepper found in pods on shrub-like trees.)

⇨ When drawings are completed, ask: "What does this story tell about the beginnings of God's kin-dom?" "What clues does it give about the way the kin-dom grows to maturity?" "How different will its size be in the end compared to the beginning?"

Jesus gave another parable about the nature of the kin-dom's growth. *Read Mark 4:26-29.* Invite participants to draw this seed and the plant which grows from it. You may wish to re-read it as they draw. When drawings are completed, ask: "What makes the seed grow?" "Who makes it grow?" "The one who planted it?" "What stages does the seed grow through before it is ripe?" "Could the one who sowed the seed have stopped it from growing to maturity?"

▨ GOING FORTH IN GOD'S NAME   (5 to 10 minutes)

❧ *Sing a hymn* which speaks of the wonder and mystery of God's kin-dom as it comes and grows.

❧ *Close with a prayer* of thanksgiving for the insights these parables give into the nature and growth of the kin-dom.

❧ Distribute copies of:
    The group's paraphrase of "The Beatitudes" from Session 35
    Search Sheet 36
    Daily Scripture Readings For Week 36

OF HEARTS AND SOILS
Matthew 13:3-8

A.

13:4

13:19_____

_____
_____
_____

B.

13:5-6

13:20-21 _____

_____
_____
_____

C.

13:7

13:22_____

_____
_____
_____

D.

13:8

13:23_____

_____
_____
_____

OF SMALL AND SECRET SEEDS

THE MUSTARD SEED
(Matthew 13:31-32, Mark 4:30-32, Luke 13:18-19)

THE SEED GROWING SECRETLY
(Mark 4:26-29)

Jesus has given summaries and attitudes of the kin-dom and glimpses into its mysterious beginnings and growth. This Search Sheet invites a look at divine love and mercy in the kin-dom and the people who make up the kin-dom of God.

Read each of the parables listed below. Then, record your insights and observations as follows:

A. What the parable reveals about divine love and mercy.

B. What the parable reveals about those who are welcomed into the kin-dom.

1. **The Unforgiving Debtor** (Matthew 18:23-35)
    A. _____
    _____
    B. _____
    _____

2. **The Owner And Vineyard Workers** (Matthew 20:1-16)
    A. _____
    _____
    B. _____
    _____

3. **Simon, The Woman, and the Two Debtors** (Luke 7:36-50)
    A. _____
    _____
    B. _____
    _____

4. **The Lost Sheep and the Lost Coin** (Luke 15:1-10)
    A. _____
    _____
    B. _____
    _____

5. **The Pharisee and the Publican** (Luke 18:9-14)
    A. _____
    _____
    B. _____
    _____

Jesus has given summaries and attitudes of the kin-dom and glimpses into its mysterious beginnings and growth. This Search Sheet invites a look at divine love and mercy in the kin-dom and the people who make up the kin-dom of God.

Read each of the parables listed below. Then, record your insights and observations as follows:

A. What the parable reveals about divine love and mercy.

B. What the parable reveals about those who are welcomed into the kin-dom.

1. **The Unforgiving Debtor** (Matthew 18:23-35)
   A. *God's mercy and forgiveness are gifts which need to go forward (or the recipient faces perilous consequences)*
   B. *Sinners and debtors, whether the sin/debt is great or small, can receive God's forgiving love*

2. **The Owner And Vineyard Workers** (Matthew 20:1-16)
   A. *Divine love may be generous but unconventional, free to make different contracts and fulfill them*
   B. *They may be the "idle" (unemployed), the "last" people in society you'd expect to be in the kin-dom*

3. **Simon, The Woman, and the Two Debtors** (Luke 7:36-50)
   A. *Jesus uses "tough love" to show Simon his need for forgiveness. God's love reaches out to the "superior," the judgmental, and the sinner*
   B. *A judgmental man is lovingly confronted, and a sinful woman is commended for her faith; both are welcomed into the kin-dom*

4. **The Lost Sheep and the Lost Coin** (Luke 15:1-10)
   A. *Angels rejoice and people celebrate when the lost one is found*
   B. *Tax collectors and sinners, shepherd and homemaker alike are welcome. The "righteous" may miss it.*

5. **The Pharisee and the Publican** (Luke 18:9-14)
   A. *God's love and mercy are for those who acknowledge their sinfulness and need for divine mercy*
   B. *Thieves, rogues, adulterers, and tax collectors who know who they are in God's sight (the humble) may enter ahead of the self righteous*

DAILY SCRIPTURE
READINGS • WEEK 36

THE **AWE** **REVERENCE** AT THE **NEARNESS** **HOLINESS** OF GOD = THE BEGINNING OF **WISDOM**
WONDER **BEAUTY**

(PROVERBS 1:7A)

	HEBREW SCRIPTURE	NEW TESTAMENT	PSALM	PROVERBS
Day 1	Ecclesiastes 4:1-6:12	2 Corinthians 6:14-7:7	47:1-9	22:16
Day 2	Ecclesiastes 7:1-9:18	2 Corinthians 7:8-16	48:1-14	22:17-19
Day 3	Ecclesiastes 10:1-12:14	2 Corinthians 8:1-15	49:1-20	22:20-21
Day 4	Song of Songs 1:1-4:16	2 Corinthians 8:16-24	50:1-23	22:22-23
Day 5	Song of Songs 5:1-8:14	2 Corinthians 9:1-15	51:1-19	22:24-25
Day 6	Isaiah 1:1-2:22	2 Corinthians 10:1-18	52:1-9	22:26-27
Day 7	Isaiah 3:1-5:30	2 Corinthians 11:1-15	53:1-6	22:28-29

Personal Notes and Glimpses of Wisdom:

_____

_____

_____

_____

_____

_____

_____

_____

_____

_____

"I wonder how many small and secret seeds could grow in a sheep's heart..."

SESSION 37 • WISDOM'S MYSTERIOUS LOVE STORIES

The aim of this session is to look at the nature of divine love and of the people this love seeks to bring into the mysterious kin-dom of God.

MATERIALS NEEDED

Bibles
Hymnals
Accompaniment
Chalkboard or Newsprint
Completed Search Sheet 36
Completed Insights from Daily Scripture Readings For Week 36
Copies for each participant of:
    "Questions For Interpreting Parables"
    (Optional) Parable Interpretation Exercise
    Search Sheet 37
    Daily Scripture Readings For Week 37

▦ ASSEMBLING

After reflecting on attitudes, summaries, beginnings and growth, this session focuses on the stories of the mysterious kin-dom which illustrate the nature of divine love and the nature of those who are sought for the kin-dom. This session also illustrates a way of interpretation which can be applied to all parables.

▦ THE APPROACH TO GOD   (5 to 10 minutes)

❧ *Sing a hymn* of divine love which seeks those who need and will receive the love of the kin-dom. *"The Shepherd Of Love"* is one possibility.

❧ *Offer a prayer* for awakening to the divine love that calls people into the kin-dom.

▦ ENCOUNTERING THE WORD   (40 to 45 minutes)

⇨ Using Search Sheet 36, invite participants to share their insights into the **nature of divine love** and the **nature of kin-dom people.** Make two headings on chalkboard or newsprint, and list their responses.

   Another of Jesus' stories which illustrates the nature of divine love and the nature of kin-dom people is found in Luke 15:11-32. Read this. Invite further responses to the list you began on chalkboard or newsprint.

⇨ *Distribute "Questions For Interpreting Parables"* and guide participants through this process with Bibles open to Luke 15:11-32. You may wish to illustrate this process on chalkboard or newsprint.

⇨ If time permits, *distribute copies of "(Optional) Parable Interpretation Exercise" and guide participants through this process.* One of them may be willing to do a sermon on this parable. Encourage this! If time does not permit, distribute copies of this exercise at the end of the session.

▨ GOING FORTH IN GOD'S NAME   (5 to 10 minutes)

❧ *Sing a hymn* which expresses the wonder of God's love.

❧ *Offer a prayer* of thanksgiving for divine love mysteriously given to those who have not earned it and do not deserve it – a love available to all who will humbly receive it.

❧ Distribute copies of:
 "(Optional) Parable Interpretation Exercise" (if not used during the session)
 Search Sheet 37
 Daily Scripture Readings For Week 37

Questions For Interpreting Parables

1. **What is the original setting of the parable?** (What is going on among the people to whom the parable is given? What is going on between the people and Jesus?)

2. **What seems to be the main point of the parable?** (Why did Jesus tell it?)

3. **How does the Gospel writer interpret the parable?** (To discover this, it is helpful to know the main theme of each Gospel as summarized in Session 29 and studied in Sessions 30-33. It may also be helpful to compare the parable with the other Gospels which record it – if it was given in more than one Gospel.)

4. **What do you think God may be saying to us through the parable?** (How is our culture similar to the culture into which Jesus spoke the parable? How is it different? How is human nature the same or different?)

5. **What does the parable tell about the kin-dom of God in our lives, our homes, our communities, our nations?**

(Condensed from *An Introduction To The Parables Of Jesus*, by Robert H. Stein, The Westminster Press, 1981, pp. 53-81)

(Optional) Parable Interpretation Exercise

Read Matthew 7:24-27 and Luke 6:47-49. What does Jesus assume will happen in each builder's life? (Clue: John 16:33 – "In the world you _____."

Using "Questions For Interpreting Parables" from Session 37, interpret the parable of "The Two Builders:"

1. _____
   _____
   _____
   _____
   _____

2. _____
   _____
   _____
   _____
   _____

3. _____
   _____
   _____
   _____
   _____

4. _____
   _____
   _____
   _____
   _____

5. _____
   _____
   _____
   _____

How does James teach the message Jesus taught in the parable of The Two Builders? (James 1:22-25)

_____

(Now you are ready to preach a sermon on this parable.)

As Jesus walked the countryside, seaside and villages around the Sea of Galilee, he chose ordinary people and familiar scenes as illustrations of the mysterious kin-dom of God – seeds, farmers, women, yeast. Look around your home, your place of work, nature – what do you see? How could this be an illustration of the kin-dom of God?

What ordinary people or things do you see around your home? _____
_____
_____

At work? _____
_____
_____

In nature? _____
_____
_____

What might these tell us about the nature of the kin-dom of God?

The kin-dom of God is like a _____
_____
_____

The kin-dom of heaven is like a _____
_____
_____

The kin-dom of God is like _____
_____
_____

(If your imagination isn't working well – or if you have "writer's block," invite a child to wonder with you: "I wonder how _____ could be like the kin-dom of God . . .")

DAILY SCRIPTURE
READINGS • WEEK 37

THE **AWE REVERENCE WONDER** AT THE **NEARNESS HOLINESS BEAUTY** OF GOD = THE BEGINNING OF **WISDOM**

(PROVERBS 1:7A)

	HEBREW SCRIPTURE	NEW TESTAMENT	PSALM	PROVERBS
Day 1	Isaiah 6:1-7:25	2 Corinthians 11:16-33	54:1-7	23:1-3
Day 2	Isaiah 8:1-9:21	2 Corinthians 12:1-10	55:1-23	23:4-5
Day 3	Isaiah 10:1-11:16	2 Corinthians 12:1-21	56:1-13	23:6-8
Day 4	Isaiah 12:1-14:32	2 Corinthians 13:1-14	57:1-11	23:9-11
Day 5	Isaiah 15:1-18:7	Galatians 1:1-24	58:1-11	23:12
Day 6	Isaiah 19:1-21:17	Galatians 2:1-16	59:1-17	23:13-14
Day 7	Isaiah 22:1-24:23	Galatians 2:17-3:9	60:1-12	23:15-16

Personal Notes and Glimpses of Wisdom:

"I wonder why the Good Shepherd keeps on loving and seeking wandering sheep..."

SESSION 38 • WISDOM'S MYSTERIOUS CENTER

T*he aim of this session is to take a new look at Wisdom's Mysterious Center.*

MATERIALS NEEDED

Bibles
Hymnals
Accompaniment
Chalkboard or Newsprint
Session 12 for reference
Picture of Tabernacle and Temple
Completed Search Sheet 37
Completed Insights from Daily Scripture Readings For Week 37
Copies for each participant of:
    "Wisdom's Mysterious Center"
    Search Sheet 38
    Daily Scripture Readings For Week 38

▦ ASSEMBLING

The kin-dom of God has secret attitudes, mysterious beginnings and growth, and a mysterious love. This session focuses on the kin-dom's mysterious center. (Review Session 12, and have tabernacle and temple pictures available for use in this session.)

▦ THE APPROACH TO GOD   (5 to 10 minutes)

❧ *Sing the familiar children's hymn,* "The Wise Man Built His House Upon The Rock" (with motions!) or a hymn which speaks of choosing between God's way and the other way of living (disaster).

❧ *Offer a prayer* for awakening to the divine love that calls people into the kin-dom.

▦ ENCOUNTERING THE WORD   (40 to 45 minutes)

⇨ Review Search Sheet 37 (and Optional Parable Exercise if used). Commend participants on their search, insight and sharing in the group which enriches everyone's understanding.

⇨ *Distribute copies of "Wisdom's Mysterious Center" and pencils.* Give the "Lecturette." Invite participants to sketch the CENTER described in each of the seven frames. Invite comments and questions. Allow time for optional sharing of sketches and insights gained in the process.

▦ GOING FORTH IN GOD'S NAME   (5 to 10 minutes)

❧ *Sing a hymn/prayer* which speaks of the church as a people, such as "We Are The Church."

❧ Distribute copies of:
    Search Sheet 38
    Daily Scripture Readings For Week 38

Lecturette for
"Wisdom's Mysterious Center"

FRAME 1 – In the beginning, when God brought forth light from darkness, the firmament, the waters, and vegetation, God formed people from the elements of the earth, male and female in the likeness of God. God breathed life into them (Genesis 1 and 2) and crowned them with glory and honor (Psalm 8:5). People became living breathing **CENTERS** for God's wisdom and glory. *(In Frame 1, invite participants to make a quick sketch of people receiving the lifebreath, wisdom and glory of God, becoming living breathing CENTERS of God's wisdom and glory.)*

NOTE: Stick people are fine, and "show and tell" is optional!

FRAME 2 – People did not always obey God (Genesis 3). They put their own limited wisdom in the place of God's wisdom and glory. Gone was the ONENESS, wisdom and glory they first enjoyed with God. But God still loved people and wanted to walk and talk with them. God washed the sinful earth with a flood and offered a **new beginning** to the faithful Noah family (Genesis 7-9). Later, God gave a **covenant of blessing** to faithful Abram and Sarai (Genesis 12:1-3). As people went where God called them, they had special encounters with God. At each place of encounter, they built an **altar of stone** to mark the **CENTER** where they encountered God (Genesis 12:7-9, 28:10-22, Exodus 24:3-8). *(In Frame 2, invite participants to make a quick sketch of an altar of stones as a CENTER of encounter with God's wisdom and glory.)*

FRAME 3 – After many years of slavery in Egypt, God led the people through the waters of the Red Sea on dry ground, to safety on the other side. But, having been shepherds and farmers, they didn't know how to live in a wilderness. God called them to Mt. Sinai where they had a special encounter with God, and Moses received "The Secrets of Wisdom," **wise ways of living**, written by the finger of God on stone tablets. Under Moses' leadership, the people built an Ark of the Covenant and a **Tabernacle** or Tent of Meeting. The Ark containing "The Secrets Of Wisdom" was placed in the Tabernacle's Most Holy Place – its **CENTER**. At this **CENTER**, Moses and Aaron met with God to learn **God's Way** in daily life decisions. *(In Frame 3, invite participants to make a quick sketch of the new CENTER of God's wisdom and glory — the TABERNACLE with its Most Holy Place containing the Ark of the Covenant in which the tablets of "Wisdom's Secrets" were kept.)*

FRAME 4 – After their wilderness years and early years in the promised land, the people were led by King David who longed for a more permanent **CENTER** for God's wisdom and glory. His son, King Solomon, asked God for wisdom; and under his leadership a beautiful **CENTER, the Temple**, was built. As the Ark of the Covenant with its "Secrets of Wisdom" was placed in the Holy of Holies of the Temple, God's glory filled the new **CENTER** (1 Kings 8:10-11, 2 Chronicles 7:1-3). *(Invite participants to make a quick sketch of the TEMPLE, the new CENTER of God's wisdom and glory. Note: You may wish to have pictures of the Temple from Bibles or Bible reference books available — or sketches from Session 12.)*

FRAME 5 – The united monarchy became divided, and after 400 years its Northern and Southern Kingdoms crumbled. The beautiful Temple was destroyed. After the exile, a smaller Temple was built. This was also destroyed. Twenty years before Jesus' birth, Herod the Great, in an attempt to gain favor with the Jews, began building a third Temple. This is the Temple which Jesus visited, the place where he encountered the moneychangers. Although there was a temple and an established religious system in Jerusalem, Jesus did not seem to be a part of it. He did not choose any of the 12 disciples from the religious ruling class in Jerusalem. He did most of his three years of ministry in Galilee, 70 miles north of Jerusalem. **Wherever Jesus went**, people experienced transformation and growth from his wise teaching, healing by his love and touch, and deliverance by his power. A **mysterious transition** was taking place. No longer was a **place** like the Temple the center of God's wisdom and glory; now God's wisdom and glory were centered in the **person of Jesus the Christ**, the New Creation, God in human flesh. **(In Frame 5, invite participants to sketch Jesus as the CENTER of God's wisdom and glory.)**

(As they sketch, you may wish to read John 2:13-22, emphasizing verse 21. Note the progression: A) Jesus' anger at a "just-a-business" (corrupt) religious system, B) The "sign" he cites as his authority to rid the temple of moneychangers (verse 21) – "signs" were evidence of God's presence in Jesus per verse 11, and C) The fulfillment of Jesus' prophecy by his resurrection – see verse 22.)

FRAME 6 – Threatened by Jesus' popularity and power, Jerusalem's angry religious leaders put him to death. After Jesus' death, resurrection and ascension, where was the **CENTER** of God's wisdom and glory? On Pentecost, after much prayer and faithful waiting, the prophecies of Ezekiel (36:25-27) and Joel (2:28-32) were fulfilled. With the sound of a mighty rushing wind, **the Holy Spirit of Jesus filled all who believed.** Women, children and men became living portable **CENTERS** for God's wisdom and glory. **(In Frame 6, invite participants to make a sketch of the Spirit of Jesus filling believers, making them living portable CENTERS of God's wisdom and glory.)**

FRAME 7 – All those who believe, the people of God around the world, are called to be a **priestly kin-dom**, built together like "living stones" into a holy temple or **CENTER** of God's wisdom and glory (1 Corinthians 3:16, 6:19, Ephesians 2:19-22, 1 Peter 2:4-5) of which Jesus is the **"Cornerstone."** And in that Holy City to which our earthly journey leads, there is no temple. All the people of God will be **ONE-WITH-CHRIST-THE-CENTER** (Revelation 21:22-23). **(In Frame 7, invite participants to make a sketch of all believers as ONE-WITH-CHRIST-THE-CENTER.)**

(Frame 7 recalls a childhood song, "Jesus Loves The Little Children, All the children of the world, Red and yellow, black and white, they are precious in his sight – Jesus loves the little children of the world.")

Closing Exercise: Invite participants to sit quietly, close their eyes, and become aware of God's Wisdom and Glory in their **CENTERS**. (Allow several minutes) Close the experience by giving thanks to God for filling our **CENTERS** with Wisdom and Glory so we can live as the faithful people (kin-dom) of God.

Questions For Reflection:

1. Has the **CENTER** changed? Or has human **AWARENESS OF THE CENTER** changed? Both?
2. What does a growing awareness of the **CENTER** of God's Wisdom and Glory mean in your life? In the lives of the whole people (kin-dom) of God?

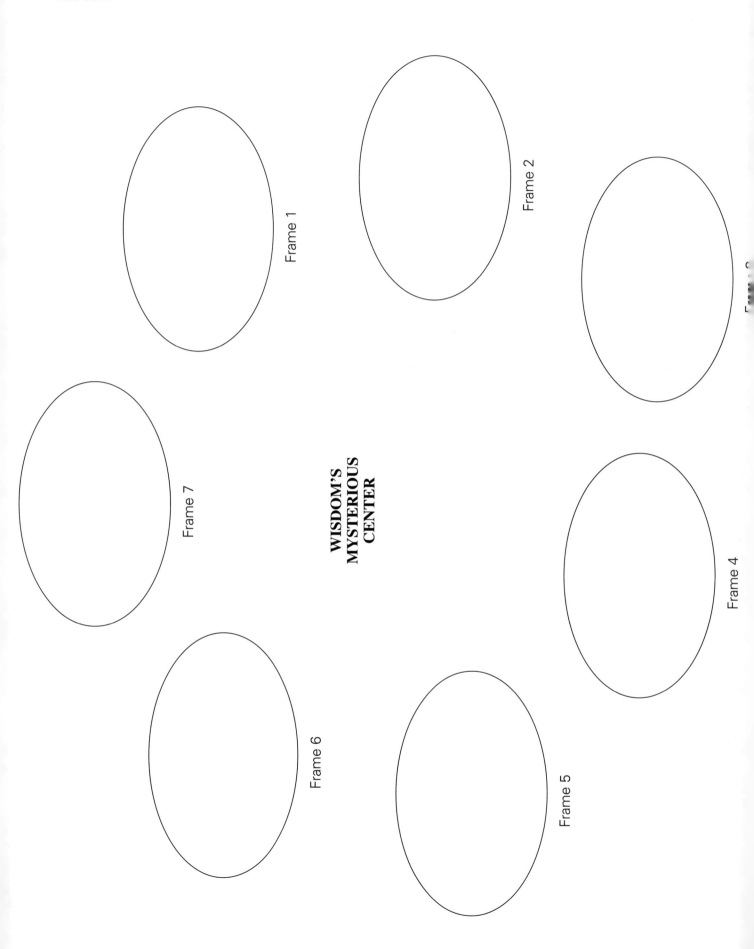

Frame 1

Frame 2

Frame 7

WISDOM'S
MYSTERIOUS
CENTER

Frame 4

Frame 6

Frame 5

Session 36 provided a glimpse of the kin-dom's beginning and growth. Session 37 looked at the mysterious unconditional love of the kin-dom. This Search Sheet invites a look at the **cost of discipleship** for those who decide to follow Jesus, the central figure in the mysterious kin-dom of God.

Read the parables listed below. Briefly describe what the parable tells about the **cost of discipleship** for people of the kin-dom.

The Hidden Treasure (Matthew 13:44) _____

_____

_____

The Precious Pearl (Matthew 13:45-46) _____

_____

_____

The Friend At Midnight (Luke 11:5-8) _____

_____

_____

The Tower Builder (Luke 14:27-30, 33) _____

_____

_____

The Warring King (Luke 14:31-33) _____

_____

_____

The Farmer And His Servant (Luke 17:7-10) _____

_____

_____

The Persistent Widow (Luke 18:2-8) _____

_____

_____

Session 36 provided a glimpse of the kin-dom's beginning and growth. Session 37 looked at the mysterious unconditional love of the kin-dom. This Search Sheet invites a look at the **cost of discipleship** for those who decide to follow Jesus, the central figure in the mysterious kin-dom of God.

Read the parables listed below. Briefly describe what the parable tells about the **cost of discipleship** for people of the kin-dom.

The Hidden Treasure (Matthew 13:44)   *Disciples find joy in the kin-dom of heaven, a joy that causes willingness to give all for it*

The Precious Pearl (Matthew 13:45-46)   *Finding the kin-dom is worth selling one's all*

The Friend At Midnight (Luke 11:5-8)   *Finding/receiving the kin-dom may require some persistence*

The Tower Builder (Luke 14:27-30, 33)   *Discipleship requires consideration of cost before commitment and a willingness to give up all possessions for Christ*

The Warring King (Luke 14:31-33)   *Disciples need to consider the terms of discipleship before commitment*

The Farmer And His Servant (Luke 17:7-10)   *Receiving God's forgiving love and welcome into the kin-dom makes obedience a "must," not an occasion for commendation or reward*

The Persistent Widow (Luke 18:2-8)   *Disciples need to pray always, be persistent, and not lose heart*

DAILY SCRIPTURE
READINGS • WEEK 38

THE **REVERENCE** AT THE **HOLINESS** OF GOD = THE BEGINNING OF **WISDOM**

THE **AWE REVERENCE WONDER** AT THE **NEARNESS HOLINESS BEAUTY** OF GOD = THE BEGINNING OF **WISDOM**

(PROVERBS 1:7A)

	HEBREW SCRIPTURE	NEW TESTAMENT	PSALM	PROVERBS
Day 1	Isaiah 25:1-28:13	Galatians 3:10-22	61:1-8	23:17-18
Day 2	Isaiah 28:14-30:11	Galatians 3:23-4:31	62:1-12	23:19-21
Day 3	Isaiah 30:12-33:12	Galatians 5:1-12	63:1-11	23:22
Day 4	Isaiah 33:13-36:22	Galatians 5:13-26	64:1-10	23:23
Day 5	Isaiah 37:1-38:22	Galatians 6:1-18	65:1-13	23:24-25
Day 6	Isaiah 39:1-41:16	Ephesians 1:1-23	66:1-20	23:26-28
Day 7	Isaiah 41:17-43:13	Ephesians 2:1-22	67:1-7	23:29-35

Personal Notes and Glimpses of Wisdom:

"I wonder how much wisdom and glory will fit in my Center..."

SESSION 39 • WHEN WISDOM SEEMED SILENT

The aim of this session is to explore that time when Wisdom seemed silent.

MATERIALS NEEDED

Bibles
Hymnals
Accompaniment
Chalkboard or Newsprint
Completed Search Sheet 38
Completed Insights from Daily Scripture Readings For Week 38
Copies for each participant of:
    "When Wisdom Seemed Silent"
    Search Sheet 39
    Daily Scripture Readings For Week 39

▦ ASSEMBLING

What was it like to recognize Jesus as The Messiah, The Center and Embodiment of the Kin-dom of God, and then see him betrayed, accused of a felony, condemned falsely, executed? Had Wisdom been silenced? This session invites participants to walk in the sandals of the disciples through the events of Christ's Passion.

▦ THE APPROACH TO GOD   (5 to 10 minutes)

❧ *Sing a hymn* such as *"Were You There When They Crucified My Lord?"* to invite participants into the sandals of the disciples as they experience with dread and fear the events of Christ's Passion.

❧ *Offer a prayer* for insight into the events of Christ's Passion from the viewpoint of a close follower.

▦ ENCOUNTERING THE WORD   (40 to 45 minutes)

⇨ Discipleship in the Kin-dom offers unmatched purpose and meaning in this life plus eternal life with Christ beyond. But discipleship has a cost. (Invite participants to share from Search Sheet 38 the cost of discipleship they saw in the parables listed. Commend each insight.)

⇨ *Distribute copies of "When Wisdom Seemed Silent."* Invite participants to read, imagine themselves as close followers of Jesus, and participate in exploring that painful but necessary time when life didn't make sense and Wisdom seemed silent.

▦ GOING FORTH IN GOD'S NAME   (5 to 10 minutes)

❧ *Sing* *"What Wondrous Love Is This"* as a **hymn** and **prayer.**

❧ Distribute copies of:
    Search Sheet 39
    Daily Scripture Readings For Week 39

"When Wisdom Seemed Silent"

THE WEEK BEFORE PASSION WEEK: Christ's ***Passion*** begins at a ***mountain-like*** rock north of the Sea of Galilee at Caesarea Philippi (now Banias) where the following conversation took place: Read Matthew 16:13-20 and ***SUMMARIZE:*** _____

_____

Why do you think this conversation was so necessary at this time? _____

_____

After that revelation, Jesus speaks more of his forthcoming suffering, emphasizing the cost of believing Jesus is the Messiah, the Son of God. Jesus and the disciples journeyed toward Jerusalem, staying at the home of friends, Mary, Martha and Lazarus in Bethany (Mark 11:12) which is two miles east of Jerusalem at the Mount of Olives. They visited a special cave on the Mount of Olives where Jesus had taught the disciples privately. Once, after Jesus finished praying, his disciples asked him for a prayer which summarized all his teachings. Jesus gave them this prayer which summarizes all Scripture, illustrating all that is necessary to bring about ***Shalom*** (peace, wholeness). Read Luke 11:1-4 and ***SUMMARIZE:***_____

_____

_____

_____

SABBATH (Saturday) – Jesus and the disciples apparently spent a quiet Sabbath in and around Bethany.

SUNDAY – This was "Palm Sunday," the day Jesus made his Triumphal Entry into Jerusalem. Read Matthew 21:1-11. With someone looking at Mark 11:1-10, Luke 19:29-44, and John 12:12-19 (noting the context of each), note the following:

How Jesus Felt About This Event _____

_____

How The Disciples Felt _____

_____

How The Religious Leaders Felt _____

_____

MONDAY – Jesus gave the disciples his parting teaching on the Temple's south side "teaching steps." As the leaders of the Religious Sanhedrin listened in from doorways above, Jesus said: (Read Matthew 23:2-4, Mark 12:38-40) ***SUMMARIZE:*** _____

_____

How do you think the religious leaders felt about this? _____

_____

Later on Monday, Jesus drove the moneychangers from the Temple. (Read Matthew 21:12-13, Mark 11:15-18). Why did Jesus do this? _____

_____

How did the religious leaders react? _____

_____

TUESDAY – Jesus returned to the Temple to teach. Here his authority was questioned by religious leaders (Matthew 21:23-27, Mark 11:27-33, Luke 20:1-8). Jesus directed some of his most transparent parables and harshest criticism at the hypocrisy of religious leaders (Matthew 21:28 – 23:39, Mark 12:1-44, Luke 20:9 – 21:4).

It is highly likely that Jesus and the disciples celebrated Passover at an Essene monastery on **Tuesday** according to the custom of the Essenes who celebrated Passover two to three days early in protest of religious corruption in Jerusalem. Scripture's clue is in Mark 14:13 and Luke 22:10 where Jesus instructs the disciples to look for "a man carrying water." Men in traditional Jewish culture did not carry water; women did. But in a monastic community, such as that of the Essenes, men did carry water.

The Passover meal was eaten at a triclinium table (see sketch) at which everyone reclined on the left elbow (Matthew 26:20, Mark 14:17-18, Luke 22:14). Jesus was the Host and thus was in Position 2. The assistant who got up to pour wine and get bread was in Position 1. We know from John 13:23 that John was reclining next to Jesus and leaned back against Jesus (John 13:25). Since everyone reclined on their left

elbows, this means John was the assistant. On the other side of the host, in Position 3, was the guest of honor, often thought to have been Peter. However, we read that Simon Peter (John 13:24) motioned to John to ask Jesus who was going to betray him. If Peter were on the other side of Jesus, he couldn't have motioned to John. Also, only two people could sit close enough to Jesus to have dipped with him – the assistant host and the guest of honor. We read (Matthew 26:23) that Judas dipped with Jesus. This means that Jesus made Judas, the betrayer, the **guest of honor** at this holy meal, fulfilling Jesus' teaching, "Love your enemies, do good to those who hate you" (Luke 6:27) and his role as Good Shepherd who "prepares a table before me in the presence of my enemies" (Psalm 23:5). Where, then was Simon Peter? Perhaps he was sulking (as was his nature) over having been called a **stumblingblock** so soon after being called **The Rock** upon whom Christ would build the church. Or perhaps he remembered Jesus' teaching about the first being last and the last being first and about not assuming the place of honor at a banquet – and took the last place, Position 13, the towel-and-basin position. When he neglected **doing** the task that went with the lowest position, Jesus , The Host, became the Servant, washing feet while Peter protested.

Towel & Basin

TRICLINIUM TABLE

From the Passover, Jesus and the disciples (minus Judas) went to the Garden of Gethsemane on the Mount of Olives where Jesus prayed his High Priestly Prayer: (Read John 17) **SUMMARIZE:** _____

_____

_____

In the Garden of Gethsemane, Jesus was betrayed by Judas, arrested, bound and taken to Annas, father-in-law of the high priest, Caiaphas (John 18:12-24). After an informal hearing, Annas sent Jesus, bound, to Caiaphas (John 18:24) for formal trial before the Civil Sanhedrin at the House of Caiaphas (Matthew 26:57-68, Mark 14:53-65).

     What was the Civil Sanhedrin's charge against Jesus? _____

     The penalty? _____

WEDNESDAY – After spending the night in the felony pit (a deep pit in the quarry with a small hole in the top through which the felon was lowered by a rope which was then removed), Jesus was taken before the Religious Sanhedrin which met at the Temple. Read Luke 22:66-71.

What was the Religious Sanhedrin's charge against Jesus? _____

From the Religious Sanhedrin, Jesus was taken to Pilate (Luke 23:1-5), the Roman governor of Judea, since Jews did not have authority to carry out a death penalty. The charge presented to Pilate was that of **treason** (Jesus' claim to be The Messiah, "King of the Jews"). After Pilate questioned Jesus and learned Jesus was a Galilean (thus under Herod's jurisdiction), he sent Jesus to Herod Antipas (son of Herod the Great) who happened to be in Jerusalem at the time (Luke 23:6-12). Herod "rubber-stamped" the decision of the other Jewish leaders and thus became friends with his former enemy, Pilate.

THURSDAY – Herod sent Jesus back to Pilate. Pilate conducted a trial in three parts:

Part I – (Luke 23:13-19) – Pilate confers with the chief priests, leaders and the people. What was the leaders' response: _____

Part II – (Luke 23:20-21) – Pilate addresses the mob and holds a second conference. What was the leaders' response? _____

Part III – (Luke 23:22-23) – Pilate questions the leaders again and offers to flog and release Jesus. What was the leaders' response? _____

Pilate's Final Verdict – (Luke 23:24-25) _____
_____

After this lengthy trial, Jesus was handed over to the Roman guards. The roughest Roman guards were assigned to Judea because the Jews were so insubordinate. The guards had a cruel game known as "The King's Game" which they played with victims of capital offenses just before executing them. (This game was so cruel it was outlawed everywhere except Judea because of the unconquerable spirit of Judea's people.) Using a gameboard on the floor of the Antonio Fortress courtyard, soldiers rolled dice and moved the victim around the board. When the victim landed on a certain square, the soldiers could do something cruel – press a crown of thorns on his head, spit on him, mock him like a burlesque king – anything except kill him because they had to make an example of him publicly. (Matthew 27:27-31, Mark 15:16-20, John 19:1-3)

It is likely that the soldiers (the "whole cohort" was probably about 500 soldiers) played this game all Thursday night. In the morning, they led Jesus out to crucify him in daylight so all could see.

FRIDAY – The events of Jesus' execution are recorded in Matthew 27:32-54, Mark 15:21-39, Luke 23:16-49, and John 19:16-30. *How do you picture yourself during the execution? Choose from among the following, and write a brief description of how you might have felt if you had been in their sandals:*

As Simon of Cyrene? (Matthew 27:32) _____

As the Roman soldiers? (Matthew 27:34-37) _____

As those who passed by? (Matthew 27:39-40 _____

As the chief priests, scribes, elders? (Matthew 27:41-43) _____

As the two bandits? (Luke 23:39-43) _____

As the disciples? (Matthew 26:56) _____

As Jesus' mother Mary? (John 19:25-27) _____

As "the disciple Jesus loved?" (John 19:26-27) _____

As Joseph of Arimathea? (Matthew 27:57-60) _____

As the women? (Matthew 27:55-56, 61) _____

In the absence of the disciples, Jesus was buried by **Joseph of Arimathea** (Matthew 27:57-61, Mark 15:42-47, Luke 23:50-54, John 19:38-42 which includes Nicodemus), assisted by the **women** who had followed and supported him (Matthew 27:55-56, Mark 15:40-41, Luke 23:49, 55-56, John 19:25-26).

The story of Christ's Passion, having begun at a rock in Caesarea Philippi, ends with his **body** buried in a **rock** at the quarry where stones for the **temple** had been hewn. Jesus words, for which he was executed, echo from the quarry tomb: **"Destroy this temple and in three days I will raise it up"** (Matthew 26:59-61, John 2:19). **Had WISDOM really been silenced?** What happened to the **CENTER OF WISDOM AND GLORY** at Christ's execution? (Reflect on the words: **ROCK, TEMPLE, BODY**)

"When Wisdom Seemed Silent" (Answer Guide)

THE WEEK BEFORE PASSION WEEK

Matthew 16:13-20 — Jesus asks who people say he is. Peter says, "You are the Christ."

Discussion might include the necessity of the disciples being convinced of Jesus' Messiahship before the events of his passion, which could make them wonder – if they were not sure beforehand.

Luke 11:1-4 – Awe and wonder at the holiness of God, preparing a Center within ourselves where God can reign, making the kin-dom of God Central in our lives, receiving forgiveness, forgiving others, openness to God's leading and guiding in all of life.

SUNDAY

How Jesus felt – Jesus is ready to publicly acknowledge his Messiahship, even though he knows he will be rejected on this basis. He wept over the city because of its refusal to accept the One-Who-Came-To-Bring-Peace.

How the disciples felt – They did as they were told but did not understand the full significance of the events until after Christ's resurrection.

How the religious leaders felt – The leaders were angry at their powerlessness to control Jesus and the crowds who followed him.

MONDAY

Matthew 23:2-4, Mark 12:38-40 – Jesus condemns religious leaders for not practicing what they teach, for placing heavy burdens on others which they themselves are not willing to bear, and for doing their religious deeds "for the sake of appearance."

How religious leaders felt – They felt "exposed," threatened, angry, determined to kill Jesus.

Why Jesus drove out moneychangers – Jesus saw that the Temple, designated as a Holy Center, had fallen from its "God first" calling to "money first" – business as usual.

How religious leaders reacted – They plotted to kill Jesus – after challenging his authority.

TUESDAY

John 17 theme – "That they may all be one." Jesus prayed for the protection of disciples who will undergo suffering, oppression. Compare the "unity theme" of John 17 with the goal of "The Wisdom Series" (John 10:16), "So there will be one flock, one shepherd."

The Civil Sanhedrin's charge: Blasphemy and sedition, a felony, for his statement about the temple.

The penalty? Death!

WEDNESDAY

The Religious Sanhedrin's charge: Blasphemy, sedition.

THURSDAY

Part I – "Away with Jesus, release Barabbas"

Part II – "Crucify him"

Part III – Loudly demanded crucifixion

Pilate's Verdict: He gave the crowd their demand, released Barabbas and turned Jesus over to be crucified.

FRIDAY *– (Personal Response)*

SEARCH SHEET 39

Imagine that you and a close friend had great plans for opening a new business. After three years of planning and preparation, your partner is accused of a crime he or she didn't commit, arrested, tried and convicted of a felony, placed on death row and executed. How would you feel? What would you do? What would you wonder about?

When it is all over and you looked back, you could see how someone was carefully planning for months to frame your partner. The warning signs were there all along, but you and your partner were so focused on your own plans that you missed these signs.

Jesus' disciples were like that – human! They were training and preparing to assume key positions in the Kingdom of God. Jesus gave many prophetic "clues" that establishing this Kin-dom would involve suffering. Some of these clues are listed below. Read them. Then note how the disciples responded:

PROPHECY	RESPONSE
Matthew 16:21-28	16:22-23 _____
Matthew 17:22-23	17:23 _____
	20:20-28 _____
Matthew 26:31-32, 34	26:33-35 _____
	26:56 _____
Mark 9:30-31	9:32 _____
Mark 10:32-34	10:32 _____
	10:35-40 _____
Luke 9:44	9:45 _____
Luke 18:31-33	18:34 _____
John 2:17-21	2:22 _____
John 16:12-16	16:17-18 _____

SEARCH SHEET 39
ANSWER GUIDE

Imagine that you and a close friend had great plans for opening a new business. After three years of planning and preparation, your partner is accused of a crime he or she didn't commit, arrested, tried and convicted of a felony, placed on death row and executed. How would you feel? What would you do? What would you wonder about?

When it is all over and you looked back, you could see how someone was carefully planning for months to frame your partner. The warning signs were there all along, but you and your partner were so focused on your own plans that you missed these signs.

Jesus' disciples were like that – human! They were training and preparing to assume key positions in the Kingdom of God. Jesus gave many prophetic "clues" that establishing this Kin-dom would involve suffering. Some of these clues are listed below. Read them. Then note how the disciples responded:

PROPHECY	RESPONSE
Matthew 16:21-28	16:22-23 *Peter says, "God forbid!"*
Matthew 17:22-23	17:23 *They were greatly distressed.*
	20:20-28 *Mother asks for sons' power positions*
Matthew 26:31-32, 34	26:33-35 *Peter, all say, "I will never deny/desert."*
	26:56 *All disciples deserted and fled.*
Mark 9:30-31	9:32 *They did not understand and were afraid to ask.*
Mark 10:32-34	10:32 *They were amazed / afraid.*
	10:35-40 *Two disciples ask for political favors.*
Luke 9:44	9:45 *They did not understand; meaning was concealed.*
Luke 18:31-33	18:34 *Understood nothing, hidden, did not grasp.*
John 2:17-21	2:22 *After Jesus was raised, disciples remembered / believed.*
John 16:12-16	16:17-18 *Disciples ask each other, "What does he mean?"*

DAILY SCRIPTURE
READINGS • WEEK 39

THE **AWE REVERENCE WONDER** AT THE **NEARNESS HOLINESS BEAUTY** OF GOD = THE BEGINNING OF **WISDOM**

(PROVERBS 1:7A)

	HEBREW SCRIPTURE	NEW TESTAMENT	PSALM	PROVERBS
Day 1	Isaiah 43:14-45:10	Ephesians 3:1-21	68:1-18	24:1-2
Day 2	Isaiah 45:11-48:11	Ephesians 4:1-16	68:19-35	24:3-4
Day 3	Isaiah 48:12-50:11	Ephesians 4:17-32	69:1-18	24:5-6
Day 4	Isaiah 51:12-53:12	Ephesians 5:1-33	69:19-36	24:7
Day 5	Isaiah 54:1-57:13	Ephesians 6:1-24	70:1-5	24:8
Day 6	Isaiah 57:14-59:21	Philippians 1:1-26	71:1-24	24:9-10
Day 7	Isaiah 60:1-62:5	Philippians 1:27-2:18	72:1-20	24:11-12

Personal Notes and Glimpses of Wisdom:

SESSION 40 • WISDOM'S JOYOUS SURPRISE

The aim of this session is to discover the joy of the risen Christ – Wisdom's Joyous Surprise!

MATERIALS NEEDED

Bibles
Hymnals
Accompaniment
Chalkboard or Newsprint
"Wisdom's Joyous Surprise Puzzle," copied, mounted and cut
Completed Search Sheet 39
Completed Insights for Daily Scripture Readings For Week 39
Copies for each participant of:
    Search Sheet 40
    Daily Scripture Readings For Week 40

▦ ASSEMBLING

Jesus' followers weren't ready for his suffering and death. And while they were still in a state of shock, denial and disbelief, there was another surprise – the joyous mystery of the resurrection! Like Jesus' followers, we become lost in pain, suffering or bereavement, temporarily forgetting these are necessary preludes to maturity of faith, wisdom and joy. This session explores Christ's surprising resurrection appearances through the eyes of disciples.

▦ THE APPROACH TO GOD   (5 to 10 minutes)

➧ Invite participants to *select and sing* a favorite Easter hymn. Then *offer a prayer* for new insights into the joyous mystery of the resurrection.

▦ ENCOUNTERING THE WORD   (40 to 45 minutes)

⇨ Take up Search Sheet 39. Invite participants to share their insights and discoveries into Jesus' prophecies of his suffering and death – and the disciples' reactions. How do participants think they would have reacted? . . . Denial has a God-given purpose – to protect and cushion us from events in life which are too shocking to absorb immediately. But if Christ's followers were to bear the "Good News" to all nations, they needed to take in the truth, the actuality of Christ's death and resurrection. To accomplish this, Jesus makes many appearances after his resurrection. Each encounter is a piece to this joyous and puzzling mystery of our faith. Put puzzle pieces on table. Invite participants to take up pieces to the puzzle, share the "clues" on the faces of the pieces, and assemble them to discover the mystery of faith printed on the puzzle's border.

▓ GOING FORTH IN GOD'S NAME   (5 to 10 minutes)

❧ Close by *singing* another favorite Easter hymn selected by participants.

❧ Distribute copies of:
   Search Sheet 40
   Daily Scripture Readings For Week 40

"Wisdom's Joyous Surprise Puzzle"

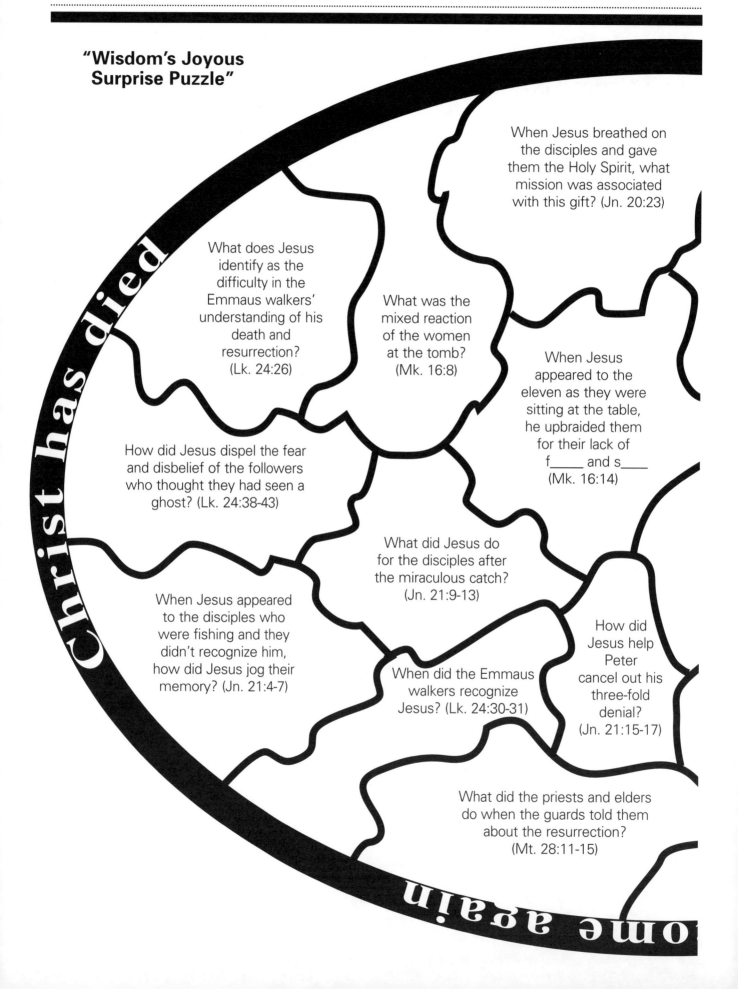

Christ has died

When Jesus breathed on the disciples and gave them the Holy Spirit, what mission was associated with this gift? (Jn. 20:23)

What does Jesus identify as the difficulty in the Emmaus walkers' understanding of his death and resurrection? (Lk. 24:26)

What was the mixed reaction of the women at the tomb? (Mk. 16:8)

When Jesus appeared to the eleven as they were sitting at the table, he upbraided them for their lack of f____ and s____ (Mk. 16:14)

How did Jesus dispel the fear and disbelief of the followers who thought they had seen a ghost? (Lk. 24:38-43)

What did Jesus do for the disciples after the miraculous catch? (Jn. 21:9-13)

When Jesus appeared to the disciples who were fishing and they didn't recognize him, how did Jesus jog their memory? (Jn. 21:4-7)

When did the Emmaus walkers recognize Jesus? (Lk. 24:30-31)

How did Jesus help Peter cancel out his three-fold denial? (Jn. 21:15-17)

What did the priests and elders do when the guards told them about the resurrection? (Mt. 28:11-15)

ome again

"Wisdom's Joyous Surprise Puzzle"

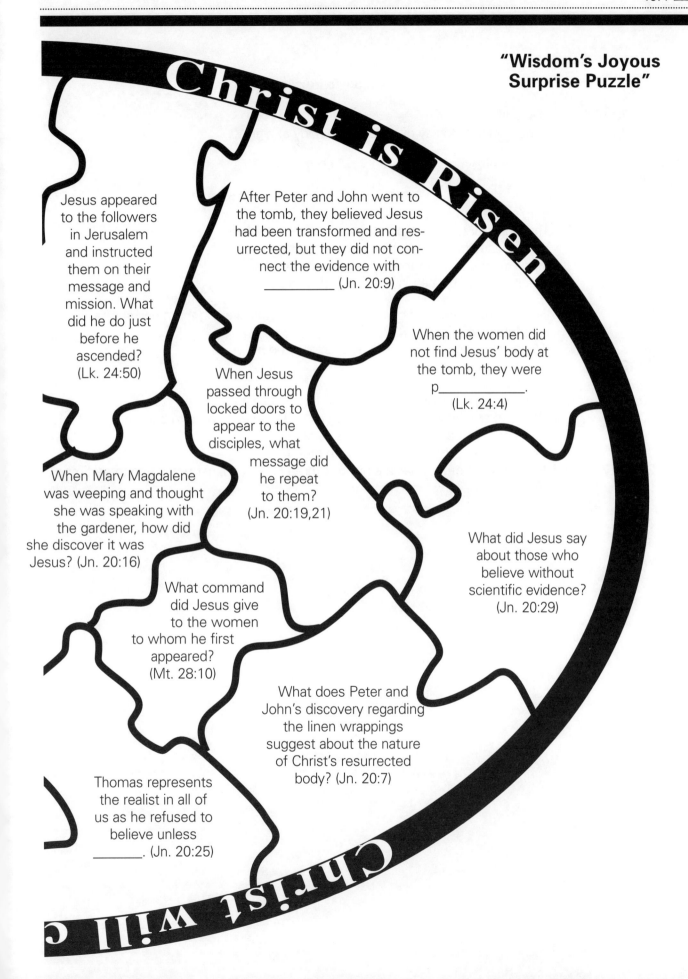

Christ is Risen

Jesus appeared to the followers in Jerusalem and instructed them on their message and mission. What did he do just before he ascended? (Lk. 24:50)

After Peter and John went to the tomb, they believed Jesus had been transformed and res-urrected, but they did not con-nect the evidence with _____ (Jn. 20:9)

When the women did not find Jesus' body at the tomb, they were p_____. (Lk. 24:4)

When Jesus passed through locked doors to appear to the disciples, what message did he repeat to them? (Jn. 20:19,21)

When Mary Magdalene was weeping and thought she was speaking with the gardener, how did she discover it was Jesus? (Jn. 20:16)

What did Jesus say about those who believe without scientific evidence? (Jn. 20:29)

What command did Jesus give to the women to whom he first appeared? (Mt. 28:10)

What does Peter and John's discovery regarding the linen wrappings suggest about the nature of Christ's resurrected body? (Jn. 20:7)

Thomas represents the realist in all of us as he refused to believe unless _____. (Jn. 20:25)

Christ will c

Scripture Guide To Puzzle

Matthew 28:10	"Go tell"
Matthew 28:11-15	Bribed soldiers to say disciples stole body at night
Mark 16:8	Terror, amazement
Mark 16:14	Faith, stubbornness
Luke 24:4	Perplexed
Luke 24:26	Their inability to understand the necessity of the Messiah's suffering
Luke 24:30-31	When Jesus took bread, blessed, broke and gave it
Luke 24:38-43	Jesus invites them to touch him, eats broiled fish
Luke 24:50	Jesus lifted up his hands and blessed them
John 20:7	Jesus' resurrected body went through the cloths, leaving them undisturbed
John 20:9	Scripture's prophecies
John 20:16	When Jesus spoke her name, she recognized his voice
John 20:19, 21	"Peace be with you!"
John 20:23	Forgiveness
John 20:25	He sees and touches
John 20:29	"Blessed are those who have not seen and yet have come to believe"
John 21:4-7	Jesus guides them to a miraculous catch
John 21:9-13	Jesus cooked fish and served it with bread
John 21:15-17	Jesus asked Peter to declare his love three times and instructed him three times to "Feed my sheep"

1. How would our faith be different if Jesus was not raised? (1 Corinthians 15:12-19) _____
    _____

2. What does Christ's resurrection mean to us in our life and our death? (1 Corinthians 15:50-58) _____
    _____

3. Read the following passages and tell whether you believe the resurrection is a **historical event** or an **ongoing process** – and why: Romans 12:2, Ephesians 2:4-7, Colossians 2:12, 3:1-4 _____
    _____
    _____

    "Christ has died. Christ is risen. Christ will come again." This is the mystery of our faith. Since we cannot fully explain a mystery, we simply announce and affirm it.

    Christ's resurrection is one of the reasons for worship on the first day of the week. Another reason is because Creation began on the first day of the week – and with his resurrection Christ ushers in a New Creation. A third reason for worship on the first day of the week is because **our Gospel is a Gospel of New Beginnings**. True worship with repentance and forgiveness makes us clean and new again; this is central to the Gospel Message (Luke 24:47, John 20:22-23).

4. After Jesus' ascension (Luke 24:50-53), the disciples were instructed to wait in Jerusalem until they "have been clothed with power from on high" (Luke 24:49). What are some of the **benefits** of receiving that power? (John 14:15-31) _____
    _____
    _____

    What are some of the disciples' **responsibilities** in receiving that power? (John 14:15-31) _____
    _____
    _____

5. What is the mission/purpose for which Jesus lived, died, rose, ascended and presently empowers us? (Matthew 28:18-20, Luke 24:47) _____
    _____
    _____

1. How would our faith be different if Jesus was not raised? (1 Corinthians 15:12-19)
   Preaching and faith are in vain if Christ has not been raised.

2. What does Christ's resurrection mean to us in our life and our death? (1 Corinthians 15:50-58)
   Our perishable nature puts on the imperishable, and then death is swallowed up in victory.

3. Read the following passages and tell whether you believe the resurrection is a historical event or an ongoing process – and why: Romans 12:2, Ephesians 2:4-7, Colossians 2:12, 3:1-4
   Both – we're being transformed daily, raised with Christ so we can set our minds on things that are above.

   "Christ has died. Christ is risen. Christ will come again." This is the mystery of our faith. Since we cannot fully explain a mystery, we simply announce and affirm it.

   Christ's resurrection is one of the reasons for worship on the first day of the week. Another reason is because **Creation** began on the first day of the week – and with his resurrection Christ ushers in a New Creation. A third reason for worship on the first day of the week is because **our Gospel is a Gospel of New Beginnings**. True worship with repentance and forgiveness makes us clean and new again; this is central to the Gospel Message (Luke 24:47, John 20:22-23).

4. After Jesus' ascension (Luke 24:50-53), the disciples were instructed to wait in Jerusalem until they "have been clothed with power from on high" (Luke 24:49). What are some of the **benefits** of receiving that power? (John 14:15-31) *The Spirit of truth is with us always, giving us power to love one another and keep commandments so we can realize God's peace – eternal life.*

   What are some of the disciples' **responsibilities** in receiving that power? (John 14:15-31) *Keeping the commandments, the heart of which is love for God and neighbor.*

5. What is the mission/purpose for which Jesus lived, died, rose, ascended and presently empowers us? (Matthew 28:18-20, Luke 24:47) *Making disciples of all nations, baptizing, teaching repentance and the forgiveness of sins.*

DAILY SCRIPTURE
READINGS • WEEK 40

THE **AWE** **REVERENCE** AT THE **NEARNESS** **HOLINESS** OF GOD = THE BEGINNING OF **WISDOM**
WONDER **BEAUTY**

(PROVERBS 1:7A)

	HEBREW SCRIPTURE	NEW TESTAMENT	PSALM	PROVERBS
Day 1	Isaiah 62:6-65:25	Philippians 2:19-3:4a	73:1-28	24:13-14
Day 2	Isaiah 66:1-24	Philippians 3:4b-21	74:1-23	24:15-16
Day 3	Jeremiah 1:1-2:30	Philippians 4:1-23	75:1-10	24:17-20
Day 4	Jeremiah 2:31-4:18	Colossians 1:1-20	76:1-12	24:21-22
Day 5	Jeremiah 4:19-6:14	Colossians 1:21-2:7	77:1-20	24:23-25
Day 6	Jeremiah 6:15-8:7	Colossians 2:8-23	78:1-31	24:26
Day 7	Jeremiah 8:8-9:26	Colossians 3:1-17	78:32-55	24:27

Personal Notes and Glimpses of Wisdom:

_____

_____

_____

_____

_____

_____

_____

_____

_____

"I wonder what joyous surprises will come after my suffering..."

SESSION 41 • WISDOM'S POWER UNLEASHED

*T*he aim of this session is to see Wisdom's power unleashed to spread the Gospel.

MATERIALS NEEDED

Bibles
Hymnals
Accompaniment
Candle, matches, etc.
Chalkboard or Newsprint
Blank sheets of paper, pencils
Completed Search Sheet 40
Completed Insights for Daily Scripture Readings For Week 40
Copies for each participant of:
    Wisdom's Spread Sheet
    Search Sheet 41
    Daily Scripture Readings For Week 41

▨ ASSEMBLING

Jesus' suffering and death took place during the Jewish celebration of Passover; Jesus became the Passover lamb, the firstborn, sacrificed to heal and save all who believe. Seven weeks later came the Jewish Feast of Weeks (or Harvest, or Firstfruits) when the Law was given and the people brought offerings of new grain. Because it began on the 50th day after the Sabbath of Passover week, it came to be called Pentecost (from the Greek "Pente" meaning fifty). The Law and Pentecost take on new meaning as the gift of Christ's Holy Spirit is poured out to empower its recipients for the task of spreading Wisdom's secrets fulfilled in Jesus the Christ.

▨ THE APPROACH TO GOD   (5 to 10 minutes)

❧   Invite participants to *select and sing* a favorite Pentecost hymn.

❧   Invite participants to sit quietly for five minutes to focus on Christ and be aware of the Holy Spirit's presence within and among the group. You may wish to light a candle and place it in the Center of the group to symbolize the mysterious living presence of Christ among you.

▨ ENCOUNTERING THE WORD   (40 to 45 minutes)

➪ Invite participants to share their insights from Search Sheet 40. (A suggested method would be to have one participant share on each question and invite others to add to this). On the last question, invite participants to jointly state the mission as you write it on chalkboard or newsprint.

➪ *Distribute blank sheets of paper and pencils.* Invite participants to make a diagram of how the Gospel would spread as you read Acts 1:8, "But you will receive power when the Holy Spirit has come upon you; and you will be my witnesses in Jerusalem, in all Judea and Samaria, and to the ends of the earth."

⇨ Provide time for voluntary sharing of diagrams.

⇨ *Distribute copies of "Wisdom's Spread Sheet,"* illustrating the threefold thrust of the Gospel message (Illustration A) and the network model (Illustration B). After participants have had time to look over the diagrams, invite their comments. The group may wish to combine ideas and create a composite.

⇨ Finally, invite participants to put their name or initials in one of the 12 circles and then think of 6-12 people they might invite into a Bible study such as "The Wisdom Series" upon completion of this course. Invite them to write the names or initials of these people in the circles surrounding the circle with their own name. End by wondering, "I wonder how many circles like this there could be . . ."

▨ GOING FORTH IN GOD'S NAME   (5 to 10 minutes)

❧ Invite participants to *select and sing* a hymn of mission / obedience to the Great Commission.

❧ *Close with a prayer* which petitions the movement of the Holy Spirit within all whose names have been written in the circles of faith for the spread of wisdom.

❧ *Reminder:* Search Sheet 41 was designed to be used with the New Revised Standard Version (NRSV). Other translations may not work well for an exercise of this type.

❧ Distribute copies of:
　　Search Sheet 41
　　Daily Scripture Readings For Week 41

WISDOM'S SPREAD SHEET

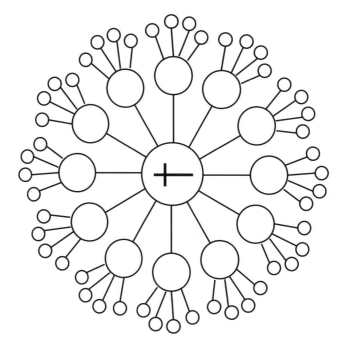

Networking Style:
Jesus – 12 Disciples – Others

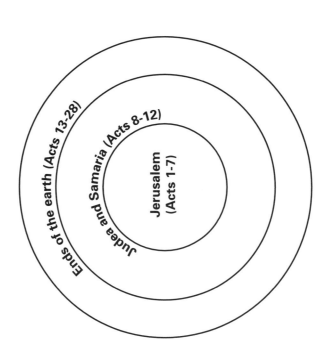

Three-fold spread of Wisdom – Acts 1:8

SEARCH SHEET 41

1. Obedient to Christ's command (Acts 1:4-5), the disciples and followers waited in Jerusalem for the baptism of the Holy Spirit. What did they do while they waited? (1:12-26) _____

    _____

2. What amazed God-fearing Jews most following the outpouring of the Holy Spirit? (2:5-12) _____

    _____

3. What happened as a result of Peter's empowered preaching? (2:41) _____

    _____How did the believers show their love for Christ and for one another? (2:42-47)

    _____

4. The indwelling Spirit gave the apostles power over _____(3:10). The Holy Spirit gave believers b_____ (4:13) in the midst of opposition and persecution, and they continued to speak the Word of God with b_____ (4:31), asserting, "We must o_____ God rather than any h_____ a_____!" (5:29)

5. Opposition and persecution continued until S_____ became the first martyr (7:54-60), beginning a severe p_____ against the church in J_____ (8:1). This caused believers to be s_____ from place to place (8:4). P_____ proclaimed the Good News in S_____ (8:5) where he was joined by P_____ and J_____ (8:14).

6. An encounter with Jesus on the way to D_____ changed S_____ (9:1-9), the worst persecutor of the church, into its greatest trailblazer. P_____'s vision on a rooftop in Joppa coincided with an angel's visit to C_____ in Caesarea (10:1-33), resulting in the Gospel being extended to the Gentiles because "God shows no p_____" (10:34).

7. A Hellenist plot to kill Saul caused him to be sent off to T_____ (9:30), and King Herod Agrippa's murder of J_____ and imprisonment of P_____ (12:1-3) brought the church again into fervent prayer. "But the Word of God continued to a_____ and gain a_____ (12:24), spreading as far as R_____ (28:16) as Paul proclaimed the k_____ and taught about the Lord Jesus Christ with all b_____ (28:31).

And the Gospel continues to advance through the **ACTS** of believers everywhere!

SEARCH SHEET 41
ANSWER GUIDE

1. Obedient to Christ's command (Acts 1:4-5), the disciples and followers waited in Jerusalem for the baptism of the Holy Spirit. What did they do while they waited? (1:12-26) *Prayed, cast lots and selected Matthias as apostle in place of Judas Iscariot*

2. What amazed God-fearing Jews most following the outpouring of the Holy Spirit? (2:5-12) *It caused Galileans to speak in many different languages*

3. What happened as a result of Peter's empowered preaching? (2:41) *Three thousand souls were added to Christ's followers* How did the believers show their love for Christ and for one another? (2:42-47) *Prayer, teaching, worship, sharing possessions*

4. The indwelling Spirit gave the apostles power over *illness* (3:10). The Holy Spirit gave believers b*oldness* (4:13) in the midst of opposition and persecution, and they continued to speak the Word of God with b*oldness* (4:31), asserting, "We must o*bey* God rather than any h*uman* a*uthority*!" (5:29)

5. Opposition and persecution continued until S*tephen* became the first martyr (7:54-60), beginning a severe p*ersecution* against the church in J*erusalem* (8:1). This caused believers to be s*cattered* from place to place (8:4). P*hilip* proclaimed the Good News in S*amaria* (8:5) where he was joined by P*eter* and J*ohn* (8:14).

6. An encounter with Jesus on the way to D*amascus* changed S*aul* (9:1-9), the worst persecutor of the church, into its greatest trailblazer. P*eter*'s vision on a rooftop in Joppa coincided with an angel's visit to C*ornelius* in Caesarea (10:1-33), resulting in the Gospel being extended to the Gentiles because "God shows no p*artiality*" (10:34).

7. A Hellenist plot to kill Saul caused him to be sent off to T*arsus* (9:30), and King Herod Agrippa's murder of J*ames* and imprisonment of P*eter* (12:1-3) brought the church again into fervent prayer. "But the Word of God continued to a*dvance* and gain a*dherents* (12:24), spreading as far as R*ome* (28:16) as Paul proclaimed the k*in-dom of God* and taught about the Lord Jesus Christ with all b*oldness* (28:31).

And the Gospel continues to advance through the **ACTS** of believers!

DAILY SCRIPTURE
READINGS • WEEK 41

THE **AWE REVERENCE WONDER** AT THE **NEARNESS HOLINESS BEAUTY** OF GOD = THE BEGINNING OF **WISDOM**

(PROVERBS 1:7A)

	HEBREW SCRIPTURE	NEW TESTAMENT	PSALM	PROVERBS
Day 1	Jeremiah 10:1-11:23	Colossians 3:18-4:18	78:56-72	24:28-29
Day 2	Jeremiah 12:1-14:10	1 Thessalonians 1:1-2:9	79:1-13	24:30-34
Day 3	Jeremiah 14:11-16:15	1 Thessalonians 2:10-3:13	80:1-19	25:1-5
Day 4	Jeremiah 16:16-18:23	1 Thessalonians 4:1-5:3	81:1-16	25:6-7
Day 5	Jeremiah 19:1-21:14	1 Thessalonians 5:4-28	82:1-8	25:8-10
Day 6	Jeremiah 22:1-23:20	2 Thessalonians 1:1-12	83:1-18	25:11-14
Day 7	Jeremiah 23:21-25:38	2 Thessalonians 2:1-17	84:1-12	25:15

Personal Notes and Glimpses of Wisdom:

"I wonder how many sheep can be touched with Wisdom's power..."

SESSION 42 • WISDOM'S BOUNDLESS GRACE

*T**he aim of this session is to explore the mystery of Wisdom's boundless grace.***

MATERIALS NEEDED

Bibles
Hymnals
Accompaniment
Chalkboard or Newsprint
Completed Search Sheet 41
Completed Insights for Daily Scripture Readings For Week 41
Copies for each participant of:
    "The Grace Quiz"
    Search Sheet 42
    Daily Scripture Readings For Week 42

▓ ASSEMBLING

So much had happened – Christ's suffering and death, resurrection, ascension, the outpouring of the Holy Spirit, and growth in faith and numbers in spite of intense persecution and oppression. But during the twenty years that followed, questions arose among believers. Was there a difference in the way Jews and Gentiles received salvation and lived by faith? Should the Law still be central to faith as it had been for hundreds of years? A scholarly Jew with Roman citizenship, Paul started churches and visited them. When he saw that a carefully written statement of the Gospel was needed, he put himself to this task. The result is the Epistle of Paul to the Romans – a book which has been central to every major reform and renewal of Christian faith and life.

▓ THE APPROACH TO GOD   (5 to 10 minutes)

❧   Invite participants to *select and sing* a favorite hymn of praise for the boundless grace God has given to us in Christ Jesus.

❧   Invite a participant to *offer a prayer* of thanksgiving for God's boundless grace.

▓ ENCOUNTERING THE WORD   (40 to 45 minutes)

➪ Invite participants to take turns reading Search Sheet 41, a summary of how the message of Wisdom's boundless grace spread from Jerusalem into Judea and Samaria and to "the ends of the earth."

    As Wisdom's boundless grace spread throughout the world, there were naturally some distortions, misunderstandings, and differences of interpretation. The Apostle Paul saw the need for a carefully written statement of the meaning of the Gospel message. The Epistle of Paul to the Romans is the result.

➪ *Write a large "A" on each "Grace Quiz;" then distribute copies.* Invite participants to decide how they would like to approach the open-book quiz – individually, as teams, dividing the questions among group members, etc. When completed, discuss the questions together, remembering there may be different ways of interpreting questions and answers. Celebrate points of unity in the midst of diversity!

▨ GOING FORTH IN GOD'S NAME   (5 to 10 minutes)

❧ Invite participants to *select and sing* another hymn as a *prayer* celebrating God's boundless grace.

❧ Distribute copies of:
  Search Sheet 42
  Daily Scripture Readings For Week 42

The Grace Quiz
(An Open-Book Quiz on the Book of Romans)

You have already received an **"A"** for "The Grace Quiz." Why take it then? Because taking it will help in understanding the meaning of the **"A"** you have received. Living what you learn will result in growing more **"A-like"** in every area of your life! So give it a try – you've got nothing to lose – your **"A"** is yours to keep forever!!!

1. Read Romans 1:16-17, and state the theme of the epistle: _____
    _____

2. All who believe in Christ are, like Paul, c_____ and s___ a_____ (1:1), empowered by the s_____ of h_____ (1:4), given g_____ (1:5), and like the believers in Rome are b_____ (1:7) by God.

3. What happens to those who know God but do not honor God or give thanks? (1:21-23) _____
    _____

4. Does God force people to serve and follow? (1:24, 26, 28) _____
    _____

5. What is the status of all people (Jew and Greek) before God? (3:9-10, 23) _____
    _____

6. How did Abraham come to be right (or righteous) in God's sight? (4:1-23) _____
    _____How do we get right with God? (4:24 – 5:1)
    _____

7. What is the blessedness of those who are put right with God by believing rather than achieving? (4:6-8) _____

8. After we are put right with God, we have p_____ with God (5:1), and we receive the gift of r_____ (5:11). How are we sure God loves us? (5:7-8) _____
    _____

9. God's grace is an undeserved gift to sinners. If we sin more, will we get more grace? (6:15-23) _____ How would Christ have us walk? (6:4) "In n_____ of l_____."

10. Paul speaks of two kinds of slavery: (6:15-23)
    Slavery to s___ which leads to d_____ (6:16)
    Slavery to o_____ which leads to r_____, or enslaved to G_____ where the advantage is s_____ which leads to e_____ l_____ (6:22).

11. In Christ, there is a "new world order" – the new law of the S_____ of life sets us free from the law of s____ and d_____. (8:2)

12. The indwelling S_____ gives us power over the things of the f_____ so we can experience l_____ and p_____. (8:5-6)

13. Although the Spirit gives faith new dimension, there will still be s_____ as c_____ waits eagerly for a still-unrevealed dimension of g_____. (8:18-19)

14. Because the Spirit i_____ for us according to the will of God, all things work together for g_____, we are not eternally condemned, and nothing can separate us from _____
    _____ (8:27-39)

15. In Chapters 9-11, Paul discusses the problem of the people of the first covenant (Israel) being rejected because of their unbelief while other people (Gentiles) are included in the new covenant. Is God unjust? (9:14-16) _____ What was Israel's stumblingblock? (9:30-33, 10:21) _____ God's rejection is not total; there is a r_____ chosen by g_____, not w_____. (11:5-6) What purpose does Paul suggest the non-total rejection of Israel might serve? (11:15) _____ _____Is God's non-total rejection of Israel final? (11:23) What does Paul suggest as God's ultimate purpose in this non-total rejection? (11:32) _____

_____

16. How does Paul invite members of the new covenant (the church) to live with one another? (Chapter 12)
    A. Present your bodies as l_____ s_____, holy and acceptable to God.
    B. Do not be conformed to this world but be t_____ by the r_____ of your mind.
    C. L_____ one another.
    D. S_____ the Lord.
    E. R_____ in h_____, be patient in s_____, persevere in p_____.
    F. Contribute to the n_____ of the saints; extend h_____ to strangers.
    G. B_____ those who persecute you . . . If your e_____ are hungry, f_____ them.
    H. Overcome e_____ with g_____.

17. How do **"New Covenant" people** live with the government? (Chapter 13)
    A. Be s_____ to governing authorities.
    B. Pay t_____.
    C. Fulfill the law by l_____ one another.

18. How do "New Covenant" people live together amid strengths and weaknesses?
    A. W_____ those who are weak in faith (14:1)
    B. Do not p_____ j_____ on one another, and never put a h_____ in the way of another (14:13).
    C. Those who are strong ought to p___ u___ with the failings of the w_____ and b_____ u____ the neighbor (15:1-2).

19. Summarize Paul's warning (16:17-20): _____
    Summarize his blessing (16:25-27): _____

The Grace Quiz (Answer Guide)

1. *Salvation by grace through faith*

2. *Called, set apart, spirit of holiness, grace, beloved.*

3. *Become futile in thinking, fools*

4. *No, God "gives them up" or as we would say, "lets go"*

5. *All are sinners whose words show it*

6. *Abraham believed God and was made righteous through faith*
    By believing Christ's death and resurrection are for us

7. *The blessing of forgiveness*

8. *Peace, reconciliation; God sent his Son Jesus who loved us enough to die for us*

9. *By no means! "In newness of life."*

10. *Sin . . . death*
    Obedience . . . righteousness, God . . sanctification . . eternal life

11. *Spirit, sin and death*

12. *Spirit . . . flesh . . . life and peace*

13. *Sufferings as creation . .. glory*

14. *Intercedes . . . good; the love of God in Christ Jesus our Lord*

15. *By no means! . . . Not accepting Jesus as their Messiah – disobedience to God . . . remnant . . grace, not works. Reconciliation of the world. No – grafted in by belief. Mercy for all.*

16. A. *Living sacrifice*
    B. *Transformed by the renewing of your mind*
    C. *Love*
    D. *Serve*
    E. *Rejoice in hope, patient in suffering, persevere in prayer*
    F. *Needs . . . hospitality*
    G. *Bless . . . enemies . . . feed*
    H. *Evil . . . good*

17. A. *Subject*
    B. *Taxes*
    C. *Loving*

18. A. *Welcome*
    B. *Pass judgment . . . hindrance*
    C. *put up . . . weak . .. build up*

19. *Warning: Avoid self-seeking people who cause dissension.*
    Blessing: Praise be to God who brings about obedience of faith through the Gospel of Jesus Christ!

The Apostle Paul often contrasts the works of "the flesh" (human desire apart from God) with the works of "the Spirit" (human desire transformed by the indwelling Spirit). Using Galatians 5:19-21, list the obvious "works of the flesh:" _____

_____

In contrast, the "fruit of the Spirit" is: (5:22-23) _____

_____

Those who receive the indwelling Spirit of God receive "spiritual gifts" – special abilities to be used in building up "the body of Christ" (the faith community, kin-dom of God, or the church universal). Most of the gifts are listed in Romans 12, 1 Corinthians 12, and Ephesians 4. Others can be found in 1 Corinthians 7, 13 and 14, Ephesians 3, and 1 Peter 4. Read these passages, and make your own list of "spiritual gifts" below:

_____

_____

_____

_____

_____

What additional gifts do you see at work in your faith community? _____

_____

_____

_____

_____

The Apostle Paul often contrasts the works of "the flesh" (human desire apart from God) with the works of "the Spirit" (human desire transformed by the indwelling Spirit). Using Galatians 5:19-21, list the obvious "works of the flesh:" *Fornication, impurity, licentiousness, idolatry, sorcery, enmities, strife, jealousy, anger, quarrels, dissensions, factions, envy, drunkenness, carousing*

In contrast, the "fruit of the Spirit" is: (5:22-23) *Love, joy, peace, patience, kindness, generosity, faithfulness, gentleness, self-control*

Those who receive the indwelling Spirit of God receive "spiritual gifts" – special abilities to be used in building up "the body of Christ" (the faith community, kin-dom of God, or the church universal). Most of the gifts are listed in Romans 12, 1 Corinthians 12, and Ephesians 4. Others can be found in 1 Corinthians 7, 13 and 14, Ephesians 3, and 1 Peter 4. Read these passages, and make your own list of "spiritual gifts" below:

Given in "Wisdom's Gift List," Session 43

What additional gifts do you see at work in your faith community? *Music, art, etc.*

DAILY SCRIPTURE
READINGS • WEEK 42

THE REVERENCE AT THE HOLINESS OF GOD = THE BEGINNING OF WISDOM

AWE / REVERENCE / WONDER   NEARNESS / HOLINESS / BEAUTY

(PROVERBS 1:7A)

	HEBREW SCRIPTURE	NEW TESTAMENT	PSALM	PROVERBS
Day 1	Jeremiah 26:1-27:22	2 Thessalonians 3:1-8	85:1-13	25:16
Day 2	Jeremiah 28:1-29:32	1 Timothy 1:1-20	86:1-17	25:17
Day 3	Jeremiah 30:1-31:26	1 Timothy 2:1-15	87:1-7	25:18-19
Day 4	Jeremiah 31:27-32:44	1 Timothy 3:1-16	88:1-18	25:20-22
Day 5	Jeremiah 33:1-34:22	1 Timothy 4:1-16	89:1-13	25:23-24
Day 6	Jeremiah 35:1-36:32	1 Timothy 5:1-25	89:14-37	25:25-27
Day 7	Jeremiah 37:1-38:28	1 Timothy 6:1-21	89:38-52	25:28

Personal Notes and Glimpses of Wisdom:

"I wonder how much more grace-full I can be..."

SESSION 43 • WISDOM'S GIFTS

T he aim of this session is to discover
Wisdom's gifts, their meaning, and their purpose.

MATERIALS NEEDED

Bibles
Hymnals
Accompaniment
Chalkboard or Newsprint
Gift wrapping paper (boxes optional)
"Wisdom's Gifts Puzzle," copied, mounted, cut, pieces gift-wrapped
Completed Search Sheet 42
Completed Insights from Daily Scripture Readings For Week 42
Copies for each participant of:
    "Wisdom's Gifts List"
    Search Sheet 43
    Daily Scripture Readings For Week 43

▥ ASSEMBLING

Christ's followers were commissioned to "go tell" the joyous news of the resurrection – a new dimension in God's grace – to all the world. They were empowered by the indwelling Spirit who equips believers by giving them spiritual gifts. This session explores Wisdom's gifts, their meaning and purpose.

▥ THE APPROACH TO GOD   (5 to 10 minutes)

❧ ***Sing a hymn*** such as *"Many Gifts, One Spirit"* or a hymn selected by participants.

❧ Invite a participant to ***offer a prayer*** of praise and thanksgiving for Wisdom's gifts and petition for sensitivity to the leading of the Spirit in this session.

▥ ENCOUNTERING THE WORD   (40 to 45 minutes)

Using Search Sheet 42, note the works of the flesh and the fruits of the Spirit. Invite participants to share from their lists of spiritual gifts while you or a participant record the gifts on chalkboard or newsprint.

⇨ *Distribute gift-wrapped puzzle pieces.* Invite each participant to read about the gift/s he or she received. Invite participants to put the pieces together to "build up the body of Christ" and experience the unity of all Wisdom's gifts.

Invite reflection on the "puzzle experience." What might be the significance of the lamb shape? What insights into the nature, meaning and purpose of Wisdom's gifts did participants discover?

⇨ *Distribute copies of "Wisdom's Gifts List."* If time permits, invite participants to name gifts they have received from God and to name and affirm gifts in each other. If there is uncertainty, encourage them to try using the gift and evaluating the results (trial-and-error method). Also, any of the gifts may be given for a specific need at a given time (always leave room for mystery!).

▣ GOING FORTH IN GOD'S NAME   (5 to 10 minutes)

❥   Invite participants to *select and sing* another hymn as a *prayer* affirming and dedicating their spiritual gifts. (This could be *"The Doxology"*)

❥   Distribute copies of:
   Search Sheet 43
   Daily Scripture Readings For Week 43

"Wisdom's Gifts Puzzle"

TONGUES – speaking or hearing from God in an unlearned language.

LEADERSHIP – voluntarily setting goals and harmoniously working with others to reach goals.

EXHORTATION – comfort, encouragement.

EVANG sharing with l

MIRACLES – being God's agents in powerful supernatural acts for Christ.

PROPHECY – sharing messages received from God.

MARTYRDOM– joyous suffering for the sake of Christ.

ADMINIST understan planning range

APOSTLE – spiritual leadership of many churches.

KNOWLEDGE – discovering, analyzing and sharing information for growth.

FA dis Go and pu in futu

SERVICE – identifying and filling unmet needs.

INTERPRETATION– "translating" tongues' messages.

SERVICE– identifying and filling unmet needs.

PASTOR– respon- sibility for a group of believers.

"Wisdom's Gifts Puzzle"

GELIST– ... the gospel ... believers.

MERCY – empathetically and compassionately alleviating suffering.

EXORCISM – casting out demons in Jesus' name.

INTERCESSION – frequent extended prayer for specific needs.

HELPS– assisting others in using spiritual gifts.

TRATION– ...nding and ...for long-...goals.

CELIBACY – joyous singlehood for the sake of Christ.

GIVING – cheerfully contributing material resources.

DISCERNING SPIRITS – knowing difference between divine and satanic acts.

WISDOM – receiving and sharing insight from the mind of Christ.

ITH – ...cerning ...d's will ...rposes ...re work.

MISSIONARY – ministry for Christ in another culture.

HOSPITALITY – warmly welcoming, housing, feeding those in need.

TEACHING – making disciples.

VOLUNTARY POVERTY – chosen poverty to serve God more effectively.

HEALING – being God's agents of supernatural restoration of health.

Wisdom's Gifts List

Administration – Understanding and planning for long-range goals.

Apostle – Spiritual leadership of many churches.

Celibacy – Joyous singlehood for the sake of Christ.

Discerning Spirits – Knowing the difference between divine and satanic acts.

Evangelist – Sharing the gospel with unbelievers.

Exhortation – Comfort, encouragement.

Exorcism – Casting out demons in Jesus' name.

Faith – Discerning God's will and purposes in future work.

Giving – Cheerfully contributing material resources.

Healing – Being God's agents of supernatural restoration of health.

Helps – Assisting others in using their spiritual gifts.

Hospitality – Warmly welcoming, housing, and feeding those in need.

Intercession – Frequent extended prayer for specific needs.

Interpretation – "Translating" tongues' messages.

Knowledge – Discovering, analyzing and sharing information for growth.

Leadership – Voluntarily setting goals and harmoniously working with others to reach these goals.

Martyrdom – Joyous suffering for the sake of Christ.

Mercy – Empathetically and compassionately alleviating suffering.

Miracles – Being God's agents in powerful supernatural acts for Christ.

Missionary – Ministry for Christ in another culture.

Pastor – Responsibility for a group of believers.

Prophecy – Sharing messages received from God.

Service – Identifying and filling unmet needs.

Teaching – Making disciples.

Tongues – Speaking or hearing from God in an unlearned language.

Voluntary Poverty – Chosen poverty to serve God more effectively.

Wisdom – Receiving and sharing insight from the mind of Christ.

Source: Adapted from *Your Spiritual Gifts Can Help Your Church Grow*, by C. Peter Wagner, Regal Books (Ventura, California), 1982.

With people receiving, developing and using their **spiritual gifts** for **building the body/community of God**, one would imagine there would be peace and harmony – like the peace Israel enjoyed during the reign of Kings David and Solomon. But even with the outpouring of the Holy Spirit and the gifts of the Spirit, Christians then and now are called to **live their faith** in the midst of an **unredeemed** and even **hostile** world where other spirits still work to subvert the ultimate plan and purpose of God.

Such was the case in the ancient Greek city of **Corinth,** a commercial center which controlled trade between the Aegean and Adriatic Seas. Corinthians were proud of their learning and philosophy which brought together people of many races and countries. However, the city was dominated by the temple of Aphrodite, the "goddess of love" whose worship included temple prostitution, gross sexual immorality and self-indulgence (much like Israel's Baalism).

Paul established a church in Corinth on his **second missionary journey**. From here the Good News of Christ could spread quickly to many nations. But Greek philosophy subtly twisted the Gospel message, and the immoral practices of Aphrodite worship gradually became acceptable in the Corinthian church. A delegation from Corinth came to Paul and asked his advice. Paul's epistles to the Corinthians grew out of that encounter.

Scan-read through the books of 1 and 2 Corinthians (noting headings and sub-headings if your Bible has them). List the main issues Paul addresses:

_____   _____
_____   _____
_____   _____
_____   _____
_____   _____

Look at your faith community or church through the eyes of Paul. What are the difficulties in the area **around** it? _____
_____

What are the difficulties **within** your faith community or church? _____
_____

The next session looks at the task of "Living As Wisdom's People" in the midst of evils **within** and **around** the people of God.

With people receiving, developing and using their **spiritual gifts** for **building the body/community of God**, one would imagine there would be peace and harmony – like the peace Israel enjoyed during the reign of Kings David and Solomon. But even with the outpouring of the Holy Spirit and the gifts of the Spirit, Christians then and now are called to **live their faith** in the midst of an **unredeemed** and even **hostile** world where other spirits still work to subvert the ultimate plan and purpose of God.

Such was the case in the ancient Greek city of **Corinth,** a commercial center which controlled trade between the Aegean and Adriatic Seas. Corinthians were proud of their learning and philosophy which brought together people of many races and countries. However, the city was dominated by the temple of Aphrodite, the "goddess of love" whose worship included temple prostitution, gross sexual immorality and self-indulgence (much like Israel's Baalism).

Paul established a church in Corinth on his **second missionary journey**. From here the Good News of Christ could spread quickly to many nations. But Greek philosophy subtly twisted the Gospel message, and the immoral practices of Aphrodite worship gradually became acceptable in the Corinthian church. A delegation from Corinth came to Paul and asked his advice. Paul's epistles to the Corinthians grew out of that encounter.

Scan-read through the books of 1 and 2 Corinthians (noting headings and sub-headings if your Bible has them). List the main issues Paul addresses:

Divisions in the church   *Marriage and single life*
Quarreling among members   *Food offered to idols; social events in temples*
A case of incest   *Women veiled, etc.*
Court cases between members   *Pride/abuse of spiritual gifts*
Abuse of Christian freedom   *Misunderstandings about resurrection*

Look at your faith community or church through the eyes of Paul. What are the difficulties in the area **around** it? *(Personal response)*

What are the difficulties **within** your faith community or church? *(Personal response)*

The next session looks at the task of "Living As Wisdom's People" in the midst of evils **within** and **around** *the people of God.*

DAILY SCRIPTURE
READINGS • WEEK 43

THE **REVERENCE** AT THE **HOLINESS** OF GOD = THE BEGINNING OF **WISDOM**

AWE / **WONDER** / **NEARNESS** / **BEAUTY**

(PROVERBS 1:7A)

	HEBREW SCRIPTURE	NEW TESTAMENT	PSALM	PROVERBS
Day 1	Jeremiah 39:1-41:18	2 Timothy 1:1-18	90:1-91:16	26:1-2
Day 2	Jeremiah 42:1-44:23	2 Timothy 2:1-21	92:1-93:5	26:3-5
Day 3	Jeremiah 44:24-47:7	2 Timothy 2:22-3:17	94:1-23	26:6-8
Day 4	Jeremiah 48:1-49:22	2 Timothy 4:1-22	95:1-96:13	26:9-12
Day 5	Jeremiah 49:23-50:46	Titus 1:1-16	97:1-98:9	26:13-16
Day 6	Jeremiah 51:1-53	Titus 2:1-15	99:1-9	26:17
Day 7	Jeremiah 51:54-52:34	Titus 3:1-15	100:1-5	26:18-19

Personal Notes and Glimpses of Wisdom:

"I wonder how spiritual gifts can make me grow..."

SESSION 44 • LIVING AS WISDOM'S PEOPLE

*T*he aim of this session is to glean wisdom for living as
God's people from Paul's epistles to the Corinthians.

MATERIALS NEEDED

Bibles
Hymnals
Accompaniment
Chalkboard or Newsprint
Completed Search Sheet 43
Completed Insights from Daily Scripture Readings For Week 43
Copies for each participant of:
    "Church Council Agenda"
    Search Sheet 44
    Daily Scripture Readings For Week 44

ASSEMBLING

As Christ's followers spread the Good News of the **resurrection** and **new beginnings,** new communities of faith were founded and equipped with the Spirit and the gifts. These communities of faith, or churches, grew in number and in maturity of faith. The Corinthian believers were in a city which was a cultural and commercial center – an excellent place from which faith could radiate. But there were problems within and surrounding the faith community, problems which threatened to choke the spread of its message. This grieved the Apostle Paul. When a delegation of Corinthian believers came to him in Ephesus for advice, he penned the letter of **1 Corinthians**. This was followed by a difficult and painful visit to the church, a sharp letter, and then **2 Corinthians** which looks forward to another (and happier) visit after the crisis.

THE APPROACH TO GOD   (5 to 10 minutes)

❧ *Sing a hymn* of pardon and repentance such as *"Grace Greater Than Our Sin."*

❧ *Offer a prayer* (or invite a participant to offer prayer) asking the Spirit's leading in this session, gently guiding and providing insight into living as Wisdom's people.

ENCOUNTERING THE WORD   (40 to 45 minutes)

⇨ Invite participants to share from Search Sheet 43 their lists of issues Paul addresses in 1 and 2 Corinthians. Write them on chalkboard or newsprint.

⇨ While displaying the list, *distribute copies of "Church Council Agenda."* Inform participants that this session has become a **Church Council Meeting** in which they will need to make some difficult decisions about how to live as Wisdom's people. (If the group is larger than four, invite members to decide whether they would like to subdivide. If subdividing, assign the various issues, allow time for work, and then reconvene to share recommendations.) Either way, allow time for discussion of recommendations.

Ask:

1) What spiritual gifts have been at work in this process?

2) How have they worked to build up the community of faith (body of Christ)?

3) What insights can we glean for living as Wisdom's people today?

▨ GOING FORTH IN GOD'S NAME   (5 to 10 minutes)

❥ *Sing a hymn* of rededication to God's plan and purpose, such as *"God Of Love And God Of Power."*

❥ *Offer a prayer* of thanksgiving for the wisdom God gave in this session.

❥ Distribute copies of:
   Search Sheet 44
   Daily Scripture Readings For Week 44

Church Council Agenda

ISSUE A – It has come to our attention that there are **divisions** in the church. We know it is the will of God that we be **united** in Christ's love. In order to move from disunity to unity, it is necessary to identify the cause of the divisions. To help in this task, please read the Scripture passages and make a summary statement under the headings below:

1. Misunderstanding of the Christian message (1 Corinthians 1:18 – 3:4) _____
   _____
   _____
   _____

2. Misunderstanding of the role of ministers in Christian growth (1 Corinthians 3:5 – 4:5) _____
   _____
   _____
   _____

3. Misunderstanding of mature Christianity (1 Corinthians 4:6-13) _____
   _____
   _____
   _____

Please recommend ways these insights could be shared with the congregation to bring about healing of divisions: _____
_____
_____

ISSUE B — It has come to our attention that one of our members is having an affair with his father's wife. Many people know about this but complacently say, "Everybody's doing it," or "Let those who are without sin cast the first stone." The church is called to **"be holy."** We need to take a strong stand **against immorality**. How can we do this in a way that fulfills our call to **holiness** and still shows Christ's **love and grace** toward sinners? (See 1 Corinthians 5:1-13, 6:12-20, 2 Corinthians 5:11-21, 7:1) _____
_____
_____
_____
_____
_____
_____

ISSUE C – One of our members cheated another member in a business deal. Unable to settle their differences, they did not seek the advice of someone in the church who has the gift of wisdom or discernment but took the matter to court in a civil lawsuit. This shows those outside the church that church members are unable to practice the love of Christ in daily life. How can the Council assist in reconciling these two members? (See 1 Corinthians 6:1-8, Matthew 18:15-20) _____

_____
_____
_____

What policy can the Council recommend to prevent further civil lawsuits among members? (Mt. 18:15-17, 1 Cor. 6:4-5) _____

_____
_____
_____

Why is it important to settle problems among believers? (Mt. 18:18-20, 1 Cor. 6:2-3) _____

_____
_____

ISSUE D – For some time now, members who host social events and raise money for the missionaries have been "lording it over" those who are less visible – those who study the Scriptures, intercede, and teach in the Church School. And those who speak in tongues put down those who preach and teach but do not have the gift of tongues. How can the Council guide the congregation to a more **loving** and **united** way of **using spiritual gifts?** (See 1 Corinthians 12 – 14)* _____

_____
_____
_____
_____
_____
_____
_____

__Note:__ Use care in interpreting 1 Cor. 14:34-36. It may be that women in Corinth were unfamiliar with orderly procedures and were disturbing worship by asking questions at inappropriate times from the separate section where they sat. Chapter 11:5 indicates that women in Corinth did prophesy; thus 14:34-36 is not intended to forever forbid women a voice in the church. Compare with Galatians 3:28.

SEARCH SHEET 44

1. In addressing the problems of the church at Corinth, Paul begins with _____ (1 Cor. 1:4) to God for the _____ (1:4) which has already been given and is in evidence among them.

2. Paul points the troubled Corinthians to the **power** and **wisdom** of God which is centered in _____ (1:24, 30). How is the secret and hidden wisdom of God revealed to believers? (2:10) _____ When this wisdom is revealed to believers, what can they understand? (2:12) _____

3. Those who have received God's grace and gifts have a common purpose. What is it? (3:8-10) _____ _____ You and I (the community of faith) are G___ t_____ because G____ S_____ lives within us (3:16). When we are jealous and quarrel among ourselves, we are not s_____ p_____ but p_____ of the f_____, i_____ in Christ (3:1). This destroys God's t_____ (the community of faith) which is h_____ (3:17).

4. Paul instructs the Corinthian faith community to discern between the "w_____ of this w_____ (3:19) and G_____ w_____ (2:7), taught by the _____ (2:13) and understood by those who are s_____ (2:13) and m_____ (2:6).

5. In stressing the importance of moral behavior, Paul likens the relationship of God with believers to a marriage: "Anyone united to the Lord becomes o____ s_____ with him" (6:17). "Your b_____ is a t_____ of the H____ S_____ within you" (6:19). We have been w_____, s_____, and j_____ in the name of the Lord Jesus Christ and in the Spirit of our God (6:11); thus we are "n____(our) o_____" (6:19) and are called to g_____ God in our bodies (6:20).

6. Our bodies have a purpose beyond what we can see and know: "God r_____ the Lord and will also r_____ us by his power" (6:14). The Christian body/temple of faith is built on the cornerstone of Christ's r_____ and ours! (1 Corinthians 15, especially verses 12-19)

1. In addressing the problems of the church at Corinth, Paul begins with _thanks_ (1 Cor. 1:4) to God for the _grace of God_ (1:4) which has already been given and is in evidence among them.

2. Paul points the troubled Corinthians to the **power** and **wisdom** of God which is centered in _Jesus Christ_ (1:24, 30). How is the secret and hidden wisdom of God revealed to believers? (2:10) _Through the Spirit_ When this wisdom is revealed to believers, what can they understand? (2:12) _Gifts given us by God_

3. Those who have received God's grace and gifts have a common purpose. What is it? (3:8-10) _To be God's servants together building God's building/body/temple._ You and I (the community of faith) are G_od's temple_ because G_od's_ S_pirit_ lives within us (3:16). When we are jealous and quarrel among ourselves, we are not s_piritual_ p_eople_ but p_eople_ of the f_lesh_, i_nfants_ in Christ (3:1). This destroys God's t_emple_ (the community of faith) which is h_oly_ (3:17).

4. Paul instructs the Corinthian faith community to discern between the "w_isdom_ of this w_orld_ (3:19) and G_od's_ w_isdom_ (2:7), taught by the S_pirit_ (2:13) and understood by those who are s_piritual_ (2:13) and m_ature_ (2:6).

5. In stressing the importance of moral behavior, Paul likens the relationship of God with believers to a marriage: "Anyone united to the Lord becomes o_ne_ s_pirit_ with him" (6:17). "Your b_ody_ is a t_emple_ of the H_oly_ S_pirit_ within you" (6:19). We have been w_ashed_, s_anctified_, and j_ustified_ in the name of the Lord Jesus Christ and in the Spirit of our God (6:11); thus we are "n_ot_ (our) o_wn_" (6:19) and are called to g_lorify_ God in our bodies (6:20).

6. Our bodies have a purpose beyond what we can see and know: "God r_aised_ the Lord and will also r_aise_ us by his power" (6:14). The Christian body/temple of faith is built on the cornerstone of Christ's r_esurrection_ and ours! (1 Corinthians 15, especially verses 12-19)

DAILY SCRIPTURE
READINGS • WEEK 44

THE **AWE REVERENCE WONDER** AT THE **NEARNESS HOLINESS BEAUTY** OF GOD = THE BEGINNING OF **WISDOM**

(PROVERBS 1:7A)

	HEBREW SCRIPTURE	NEW TESTAMENT	PSALM	PROVERBS
Day 1	Lamentations 1:1-2:19	Philemon 1:1-25	101:1-8	26:20
Day 2	Lamentations 2:20-3:66	Hebrews 1:1-14	102:1-28	26:21-22
Day 3	Lamentations 4:1-5:22	Hebrews 2:1-18	103:1-22	26:23
Day 4	Ezekiel 1:1-3:15	Hebrews 3:1-19	104:1-23	26:24-26
Day 5	Ezekiel 3:16-6:14	Hebrews 4:1-16	104:24-25	26:27
Day 6	Ezekiel 7:1-9:11	Hebrews 5:1-14	105:1-15	26:28
Day 7	Ezekiel 10:1-11:25	Hebrews 6:1-20	105:16-36	27:1-2

Personal Notes and Glimpses of Wisdom:

_____

_____

_____

_____

_____

_____

_____

_____

_____

SESSION 45 • FOUR HYMNS OF WISDOM

The aim of this session is to celebrate the wisdom of the Pauline epistles to the Galatians, Ephesians, Philippians and Colossians.

MATERIALS NEEDED

Bibles
Hymnals
Accompaniment
Chalkboard or Newsprint
Completed Search Sheet 44
Completed Insights from Daily Scripture Readings For Week 44
Copies for each participant of:
   "Four Hymns Of Wisdom" Worship Service
   Search Sheet 45
   Daily Scripture Readings For Week 45

▦ ASSEMBLING

In his letters and visits to the Corinthians, Paul corrects their theology and advises them on practical matters of faith. There were also problems in interpretation and living out of faith in Galatia, Ephesus, Philippi and Colossae. Paul addresses these in epistles or letters, the latter three of which were written from prison. In this session they have been incorporated into a worship service celebrating *"four hymns of wisdom."*

▦ THE APPROACH TO GOD   (5 to 10 minutes)

❧ The usual hymn and prayer can be omitted here as *"Encountering The Word"* is presented in a worship format.

▦ ENCOUNTERING THE WORD   (40 to 45 minutes)

⇨ Briefly review Search Sheet 44. Inform participants that Paul addressed problems similar to those of the Corinthians in Galatia, Ephesus, Philippi and Colossae. These have been incorporated into a worship service for this session. *Distribute copies of* **"Four Hymns Of Wisdom,"** designate a "worship leader" for each epistle, select hymns (if the hymns listed are not in your hymnal, look in the Scripture reference or topical index of your hymnal for appropriate hymns), provide accompaniment, and celebrate the service.

▦ GOING FORTH IN GOD'S NAME   (5 to 10 minutes)

❧ Invite informal feedback on the worship experience. Give thanks for insights of wisdom.

❧ Distribute copies of:
   Search Sheet 45
   Daily Scripture Readings For Week 45

"FOUR HYMNS OF WISDOM"

Greeting
L. Grace to you and peace from God our Father and the Lord Jesus Christ,

P. *Who gave himself for our sins to set us free from the present evil age,*

L. According to the will of our God and Father,

P. *To whom be the glory forever and ever. Amen.*

Opening Prayer (In Unison)
O God who searches and knows our innermost secrets, like the Galatians we daily forget Your Self-Giving Love for us in Christ Jesus. We seek human approval rather than the approval You have given us. We act inconsistently with the truth of the Gospel of salvation by grace through faith in Christ alone. We spend our time seeking temporary "security" rather than giving thanks for the Eternal Reality of our faith. We try to confine You in systems of rules and rituals of our own making. We "clone" others into our system rather than share with them the freedom of living by the Grace-Full Spirit You have put within and among us. Renew in us the joy of Eternal Acceptance as Your beloved children. Amen.

A Responsive Reading On Paul's Epistle To The Galatians
L. At Galatia the Jewish Christians were insisting that the Gentile converts had to follow the ceremonial laws Moses received from God.

P. *This was upsetting to the Apostle Paul who taught that repentance, forgiveness and faith are God's gifts in Christ. The Galatians were exchanging their new freedom through faith in Christ for the old slavery of "legalism."*

L. Now that we are justified through faith in Christ, what is the purpose of The Law – the "Secrets of Wisdom?"

P. *The Law – the "Secrets of Wisdom" – was given to get ready for the blessed event of God's coming to earth in human flesh – Christ, the embodiment of Wisdom.*

L. While The Law taught from outside and beyond ourselves, The Spirit of Wisdom leads us from within so we can obey the heart of The Law. What is the heart of The Law?

P. *The Royal Law of Love – "Love God most of all; love your neighbor as much as you love yourself."*

L. We can abuse this new freedom of the Royal Law of Love by using God's gift for selfish purposes – "living by the flesh."

P. *Or we can truly love and serve one another – "life in the Spirit."*

L. What is the result of living by the flesh?

P. *Immorality, jealousy, anger, quarreling, addictions, divisions.*

L. What is the result (or "fruit") of living by the Spirit?

P. *Love, joy, peace, patience, kindness, generosity, faithfulness, gentleness and self-control. These cannot be legislated!*

L. There is a key verse which summarizes Paul's message to the Galatians – Galatians 2:16 -

P. *"Yet we know that a person is justified not by the works of the law but through faith in Jesus Christ. And we have come to believe in Jesus Christ, so that we might be justified by faith in Christ, and not by doing the works of the law, because no one will be justified by the works of the law."*

L. The Epistle of Paul to the Galatians has been called the "Magna Charta of the Church" because it lifts up Christian liberty over observance of ceremonial law. If Paul's Epistle to the Galatians could be summarized in one word, what would that word be?

P. *Freedom!*

L. We sing together of that **FREEDOM** in Christ:

Hymn "Freely, Freely," "Once For All," "Love Divine All Loves Excelling," "And Can It Be That I Should Gain?" "There's A Wideness In God's Mercy," "When I Survey The Wondrous Cross," "In Christ There Is No East Or West."

A Responsive Reading On Paul's Epistle To The Ephesians

L. Paul's Epistle to the Ephesians was written from prison as a circular letter to the churches in Asia Minor (now western Turkey). What difficulties were these churches facing?

P. *There was a division between Jewish and Gentile Christians.*

L. Paul addresses this division by saluting all believers with grace and peace, giving thanks for them to God who has given them every spiritual blessing, and reminding them of Christ's death to reconcile to God sinners of all races, religions, cultures and social standing.

P. *Paul then invites the believers to try to glimpse the vast scope of God's plan and purpose. As people of all nations come together in Christ, they demonstrate God's wisdom to earthly and heavenly powers. Paul reminds them he is praying that God may fill them with love so they can carry out their task as united people of God.*

L. That was Paul's doctrinal statement. His style was to give a theological or doctrinal statement first and then offer practical wisdom. What practical advice does Paul give?

P. *Paul calls believers to live a new life worthy of God's great gift of salvation. This means letting go of old habits and selfish ways of living, giving up grudges, anger, spite and bitterness. Imitating Christ's character means seeking truth, peace and justice in family life and all relationships.*

L. Letting go of our old ways of thinking and acting and letting new life in Christ change our thinking and behavior is an ongoing struggle – "spiritual warfare." To win, we need to put on the "armor of God." What is this armor?

P. *The helmet of salvation, breastplate of righteousness, belt of truth, shoes of peace, shield of faith and sword of the Spirit which is the Word of God.*

L. If you could summarize Paul's message to the Jewish and Gentile Christians in Ephesus and Asia Minor in one word, what would that word be?

P. *Unity!*

L. We sing a hymn of UNITY for all believers:

Hymn "They'll Know We Are Christians By Our Love," "Many Gifts, One Spirit," "One Bread, One Body," "We Are The Church," "Jesus, United By Thy Grace," "The Church's One Foundation."

A Responsive Reading On Paul's Epistle To The Philippians

L. Near the end of his life, after shipwrecks and beatings, confinement to prison and facing possible execution, Paul wrote a letter to the believers at Philippi, a city in Macedonia on one of the main East-West roads. What was his main concern for the Philippians?

P. *Paul wanted to thank them for the gifts they sent with Epaphroditus who became very ill while delivering them. As Epaphroditus returns to Philippi, Paul uses the occasion to talk about persisting in faith through hardships.*

L. How does Paul encourage the Philippians (and all believers) to "hang in there" when the going gets tough?

P. *He tells believers to stand firm, continuing to live lives worthy of the Gospel of Christ, even when we face tough opposition. As people who are united in Christ, we follow the example of Christ who let go of his divinity to be human, humbled himself as a servant, became obedient to a degrading execution and thus became Lord of earth and heaven.*

L. It sounds like humility is wisdom's secret to unity.

P. *Selfish ambition and conceit are the enemies of harmony and unity among believers. "The mind of Christ" is an attitude of humility and obedience to God; this is Wisdom's secret!*

L. What happens when we walk humbly with God through the sufferings of life?

P. **When we allow our focus to shift from our pain to sharing the Gospel with others, we experience the joy of Christ's resurrection.**

L. Paul warns the Philippians to watch out for "the Judaizers" – a group of Jewish Christians who followed him and told Gentile converts they had to follow Jewish ceremonial law. Then, he provides us with a "pilgrim perspective" of mature Christian living:

P. **"Forgetting what lies behind and straining forward to what lies ahead, I press on toward the goal for the prize of the heavenly call of God in Christ Jesus." (Philippians 3:13b-14)**

L. If you could summarize Paul's Epistle to the Philippians in one word, what would that word be?

P. **Joy!**

L. We sing a hymn of JOY:

Hymn "Joyful, Joyful We Adore Thee," "He Is Lord," "At The Name Of Jesus," "There's Within My Heart A Melody," "I Come With Joy," "He Touched Me," "Rejoice Ye Pure In Heart."

A Responsive Reading On Paul's Epistle To The Colossians

L. The church in Colossae was started by Epaphras, a convert from nearby Ephesus. Soon after its beginning, other teachers established strict Jewish dietary and ceremonial rules. Gnosticism was also beginning with its "secret knowledge" and insistence that spirit was good and matter was evil.

P. **Like a drop of food coloring in a glass of pure water, the church at Colossae became tainted as it mixed other teachings with the Gospel of Jesus Christ.**

L. To correct the Colossian compromise with legalism and philosophy, Paul lifts up the all-sufficiency of Christ to them.

P. **Christ's divine glory was present in creation, and Christ has first place in the lives of the new creation – the forgiven people who make up the church. New life in the risen and glorious Christ takes people beyond mere human regulations.**

L. To humbly follow Christ means to "put to death" the old self with its lust, greed, anger, slander and dishonesty.

P. **New and victorious life in Christ means practicing forgiveness, compassion, kindness, humility, meekness, patience, love and peace.**

L. There is a glorious promise for those who live the new life in Christ:

P. **"So if you have been raised with Christ, seek the things that are above, where Christ is, seated at the right hand of God. Set your minds on things that are above, not on things that are on earth, for you have died, and your life is hidden with Christ in God. When Christ who is your life is revealed, then you also will be revealed with him in glory." (Colossians 3:1-4)**

L. If you could summarize Paul's epistle to the Colossians in one word, what would that word be?

P. **Glory!**

L. Let us sing a hymn of **GLORY:**

Hymn "In The Cross Of Christ I Glory," "To God Be The Glory," "Christ Whose Glory Fills The Skies," "Christ Is The World's Light," "My Tribute," "Gloria Patri."

Thanksgiving (In Unison)

Thanks be to God who has come in person and now lives within to bring us **FREEDOM, UNITY, JOY** and **GLORY.**

Benediction

L. "Peace be to the whole community, and love with faith, from God the Father and the Lord Jesus Christ.

P. **Grace be with all who have an undying love for our Lord Jesus Christ." AMEN.**

(Ephesians 6:23-24)

In Colossians 1:15-20, Paul has written a hymn to the glory of Christ in the universe – creation and in the body (church):

"He is the image of the invisible God, the firstborn of all creation; for **in him all things in heaven and on earth were created,** things visible and invisible, whether thrones or dominions or rulers or powers – all things have been created through him and for him. He himself is before all things, and in him all things hold together. **He is the head of the body, the church;** he is the beginning, the firstborn from the dead, so that he might come to have first place in everything. For in him all the fullness of God was pleased to dwell, and through him God was pleased to reconcile to himself all things, whether on earth or in heaven, by making peace through the blood of his cross."

Imagining the church as a **body** must have been difficult for people who lived in a monarchy or kingdom. Jesus spoke and taught much about the mysterious "Kingdom (Kin-dom) of God." Jesus was crucified because of a charge of "sedition" – speaking of a **kin-dom** by which he meant his **body** – which those in power misunderstood or misconstrued to be a threat to the Roman emperor. Perhaps we still misunderstand. Perhaps the following comparison of characteristics will illustrate:

Kingdom	Body (Kin-dom)
Power Over	Power With
Oppresses Others	Empowers Others
Competes	Cooperates
Polarizes	Synchronizes
Motive: To Get	Motive: To Give
Political	Relational
Acts of Power/Control/Violence	Acts of Kindness/Nonviolence/Peace

On the lines below (or on reverse side or separate paper), write a psalm, hymn, poem (or draw a picture) illustrating the glory of Christ in creation and in the church **AND/OR** a story, statement or creed illustrating the human understanding of **KINGDOM** (kin-dom) and Christ's meaning of **BODY.**_____

_____
_____
_____
_____
_____
_____
_____
_____
_____
_____

DAILY SCRIPTURE
READINGS • WEEK 45

THE **AWE REVERENCE WONDER** AT THE **NEARNESS HOLINESS BEAUTY** OF GOD = THE BEGINNING OF **WISDOM**

(PROVERBS 1:7A)

	HEBREW SCRIPTURE	NEW TESTAMENT	PSALM	PROVERBS
Day 1	Ezekiel 12:1-14:11	Hebrews 7:1-17	105:37-45	27:3
Day 2	Ezekiel 14:12-16:42	Hebrews 7:18-28	106:1-12	27:4-6
Day 3	Ezekiel 16:43-17:24	Hebrews 8:1-13	106:13-31	27:7-9
Day 4	Ezekiel 18:1-19:14	Hebrews 9:1-10	106:32-48	27:10
Day 5	Ezekiel 20:1-49	Hebrews 9:11-28	107:1-43	27:11
Day 6	Ezekiel 21:1-22:31	Hebrews 10:1-17	108:1-13	27:12
Day 7	Ezekiel 23:1-49	Hebrews 10:18-39	109:1-31	27:13

Personal Notes and Glimpses of Wisdom:

"Freedom!"
"Unity!"
"Joy!"
"Glory!"

SESSION 46 • WISDOM'S ENCOURAGING WORDS

*T*he aim of this session is to experience the encouragement of Paul's epistles to the Thessalonians.

MATERIALS NEEDED

Bibles
Hymnals
Accompaniment
Chalkboard or Newsprint
Completed Search Sheet 45
Completed Insights from Daily Scripture Readings For Week 45
Copies for each participant of:
    "Wisdom's Encouraging Words"
    Search Sheet 46
    Daily Scripture Readings For Week 46

▦ ASSEMBLING

After being beaten and imprisoned in Philippi in the Roman province of Macedonia, Paul and Silas went on to Thessalonica, the capital of Macedonia, about 100 miles from Philippi. Here they met with Jews at the synagogue to proclaim Jesus as the Messiah who suffered as Scripture foretold. A church of Jewish and Gentile Christians was established and immediately subjected to opposition and persecution by Judaizers who followed Paul and Silas. Paul, Silas and Timothy had to leave town quickly for their safety. Would the newly established church survive? Paul yearned for news and finally sent Timothy. His epistles to the Thessalonians – encouragement in times of persecution – are in response to Timothy's report that the church had indeed survived.

▦ THE APPROACH TO GOD   (5 to 10 minutes)

❧ *Sing a hymn* of conviction such as *"I Know Whom I Have Believed."*

❧ *Offer a prayer* of thanksgiving for the faithfulness of the people of God (including yourself and participants).

▦ ENCOUNTERING THE WORD   (40 to 45 minutes)

⇨ Invite participants to share their responses from Search Sheet 45. Thank them for sharing. *Distribute copies of "Wisdom's Encouraging Words,"* assign parts, and proceed with the story. Allow time for insights and sharing.

▨ GOING FORTH IN GOD'S NAME　　(5 to 10 minutes)

❥　Close with a ***hymn of thanksgiving*** for those who lived and died faithfully – such as *"For All The Saints."* ***Offer a prayer*** of encouragement and petition that God will keep us faithful.

❥　Distribute copies of:
　　Search Sheet 46
　　Daily Scripture Readings For Week 46

"Wisdom's Encouraging Words"

On his second missionary journey, while in Troas, Paul had a vision of someone in **Macedonia** begging, "Come over to Macedonia and help us." Sharing the vision with others on the journey confirmed the vision to be God's call.

In the city of **Philippi** in the **Greek province of Macedonia,** Paul, Silas and Timothy spoke with **women** at the place of prayer. Lydia, a businesswoman who dyed and sold purple cloth, believed the gospel and invited the missionaries to stay at her home. But after Paul and Silas **exorcised** a fortune-telling slave girl (which ruined her owners' economy), the owners incited a **mob scene**. Paul and Silas were arrested, stripped, severely flogged and imprisoned. In prison, they sang hymns: **(Sing a chorus or hymn together such as "The Joy Of The Lord Is My Strength")** While they were singing there was an earthquake which shook off their chains, shook up the jailer who became a believer and was baptized with his household. In the morning, Paul and Silas were escorted out of town.

One hundred miles from Philippi was the **Macedonian capital city of Thessalonica**. Still aching from the beating in Philippi, Paul and Silas went to the synagogue in **Thessalonica** and started a conversation with the Jews and Greeks who met there:

Paul: We have come here to share with you the Good News of Jesus, the Messiah, who lived among us, died for us, and was raised from the dead.

Jew: Our Messiah will set us free from foreign rule – not be a phantom who is here one day and gone the next!

Greek: A Messiah who suffers and dies? Sounds masochistic to me!

Paul: The prophets foretold that our Messiah would suffer and die for us. I did not understand this at first – it was not until I had an **encounter** with the risen Jesus on the way to Damascus that I began to search the Scriptures. And this is what I found:

David, ancestor of our Messiah, went through suffering while he was king. Psalm 69:20-21 says, "Insults have broken my heart, so that I am in despair. I looked for pity, but there was none; and for comforters, but I found none. They gave me poison for food, and for my thirst they gave me vinegar to drink." That's exactly what the Roman soldiers did to Jesus on the cross – gave him vinegar to drink. The prophet **Isaiah** said of our Messiah, "He was wounded for our transgressions, crushed for our iniquities; upon him was the punishment that made us whole, and by his bruises we are healed. All we **like sheep** have gone astray; we have all turned to our own way, and the Lord has laid on him the iniquity of us all." (Isaiah 53:5-6)

On three Sabbath days Paul and Silas explained the Scriptures, showing that it was necessary for the Messiah to suffer and to rise from the dead. Some of the Jews believed Jesus was their Messiah; many Greeks believed, including some prominent Greek women. One believer, Jason, entertained Paul and Silas as guests.

But the other Jews became jealous and felt threatened by the "new doctrine" Paul and Silas were teaching. They went to the marketplaces, collected some ruffians, and formed a mob which set the city in an uproar. Because they could not find Paul and Silas, they hauled Jason and other believers before the city authorities. These were the charges:

Jews: 1) " These people who have been turning the world upside down have come here also, 2) Jason has entertained them as guests, and 3) They are all acting contrary to the decrees of the emperor, saying that there is another king named Jesus." (Acts 17:6-7)

City Authority: This is most disturbing! Jason, do you realize your new beliefs and the company you've been keeping has caused this mob scene?

Jason: I am very sorry for any trouble my beliefs or my guests may have caused this city.

City Authority: We are ordering you to post bail. You realize that if you cause further trouble you will be put in jail.

That night the **believers met for prayer** and discussed the mob scene. They realized Paul and Silas' presence in Thessalonica would certainly provoke future uproars. They thought it wise for Paul and Silas to move on. So that very night the believers said farewell to Paul and Silas and escorted them safely out of the city.

Paul and Silas went on to **Beroea** where the Jews were more receptive than in Thessalonica. But the Judaizers who were in Thessalonica soon came to Beroea. Silas and Timothy stayed in Beroea while Paul went to **Athens.** Paul sent for Timothy to meet him in Athens.

Paul: Timothy, I'm concerned about the believers in Thessalonica. We had such a short stay there, and there was trouble from the very start.

Timothy: You're concerned that the tempter may have caused them to abandon their faith and make our efforts useless?

Paul: Yes – I'd like you to go to Thessalonica and strengthen and encourage the believers in the midst of their trials.

Timothy: I'll go and stay with them as long as I'm needed.

While Timothy went to **Thessalonica,** Paul went to **Corinth** where he stayed a year and a half with tent-makers Aquila and Priscilla who were forced from their home when Claudius expelled all Jews from Rome.

After some time, Silas and Timothy each arrived from Macedonia. Paul couldn't wait to hear Timothy's report from Thessalonica:

Paul: Tell me, how are they? How are the believers getting along?

Timothy: I bring good news! Their faith has held fast in the midst of persecution and their many difficulties.

Paul: Timothy, how do they feel about me – teaching them such a short time and then having to leave because of the mob?

Timothy: They talked often and fondly of your ministry among them. They long to see you again!

Paul: How I give thanks to God for the joy of hearing that!

Timothy: They have a **love for one another** which can only be the fruit of the Spirit of Christ who lives within them.

Paul: It's a blessing to know the message has taken root and survived through suffering! I can't wait to write them a **letter of encouragement**!

Timothy: There are some other things you will need to know before you write – the opposition is saying you are just another slick teacher preying on gullible people. You tell them what they want to hear and flatter them so they give money, and then you take their money and run. There is a certain **distrust of leaders** which is being stirred by the opposition.

Paul: So they know how to survive persecution and opposition but it is difficult for them to trust human leaders . . . where have we heard that before? Is there anything else I should know?

Timothy: Well, you remember from being there that Thessalonica has temples for worship of Dionysus and Orpheus. At these temples there are "sacred prostitutes," and these gods are supposedly pleased by sexual orgies. When people become believers in Jesus as the Messiah, the Christ, they often bring some of these practices into the church.

Paul: I shall write to them about showing *love for God* through *moral and holy living.*

Timothy: There also seems to be some confusion about Christ's promise to return – like, why work? And what about believers who die before Christ comes again?

Paul: Ah! The promise of Christ's return is sweetest to those who suffer most – and the Thessalonians have had their share of trials! But so have I, and I still work for a living while I travel and teach. *Suffering is part of the faith* – it seems to be the way in which God works most effectively and powerfully. It is the way God worked in Christ. Yes, I will write them a letter! And thank you, Timothy, for your faithful work and insightful report!

And so Paul wrote a *letter of encouragement* to the Thessalonian believers who struggled amid intense persecution. He reminds them of the ways he is *not* like "the other slick teachers," instructs them in *holy* and *moral* living, *encourages* them to work faithfully, and *assures and teaches* believers about Christ's promise and their future with Christ after physical death.

Read 1 Thessalonians 5:11-22. Put it into your own words and *make a list* of wisdom's practical and encouraging words:

_____   _____
_____   _____
_____   _____
_____   _____
_____   _____
_____   _____
_____   _____
_____   _____
_____   _____
_____   _____

A few months after writing the first letter or epistle to the Thessalonians, Paul received further word from them and wrote a *second letter*. The second letter reinforces the first with encouraging words of faith, hope and love – but also has some sharp words for laziness. In his second letter, Paul clears up some remaining misunderstandings about Christ's return.

As is his style, Paul concludes his letters with a *blessing or benediction*. Read 1 Thessalonians 5:23-28 and 2 Thessalonians 3:16-18. Summarize these in your own words and share them in unison as a blessing and benediction of *Wisdom's Encouraging Words:*

_____
_____
_____
_____
_____
_____
_____
_____

In his first letter to the Thessalonians, Paul gives a concise statement of the Gospel message. Read 1 Thessalonians 1:9-10 and put it into your own words:

_____

_____

_____

In his travels and in his letters, Paul tells the **Gospel message**. When people become believers, he challenges them to live what they believe – even in the face of difficulties. The Gospel, like the seeds in Jesus' parables, needs to take root and **grow** – or it will shrivel and die. Those who are members of Christ's body need to **continue learning and growing in their faith.**

One way to continue learning and growing is to **teach others**. When you have completed "The Wisdom Series" (and there are only six more sessions . . .), you can teach it. The following questions encourage you to reflect on yourself as a leader:

1. Everyone has a **"leadership style"** (caring, encouraging, bold and up-front, carefully organizing and researching, trial-and-error, skillfully and logically presenting, entertaining, etc.). How would you describe your leadership style? _____

2. What are your **strengths** for leadership? _____

    _____

    _____

3. What are your **weaknesses** in leadership? _____

    _____

    _____

Next week's session invites a look at "pastoral wisdom" from Paul's letters to Timothy, Titus and Philemon. These letters contain a wealth of **wisdom for leaders!** (You may wish to re-read them before next session.)

DAILY SCRIPTURE
READINGS • WEEK 46

THE **AWE REVERENCE WONDER** AT THE **NEARNESS HOLINESS BEAUTY** OF GOD = THE BEGINNING OF **WISDOM**

(PROVERBS 1:7A)

	HEBREW SCRIPTURE	NEW TESTAMENT	PSALM	PROVERBS
Day 1	Ezekiel 24:1-26:21	Hebrews 11:1-16	110:1-7	27:14
Day 2	Ezekiel 27:1-28:26	Hebrews 11:17-31	111:1-10	27:15-16
Day 3	Ezekiel 29:1-30:26	Hebrews 11:32-12:13	112:1-10	27:17
Day 4	Ezekiel 31:1-32:32	Hebrews 12:14-29	113:1-114:8	27:18-20
Day 5	Ezekiel 33:1-34:31	Hebrews 13:1-25	115:1-18	27:21-22
Day 6	Ezekiel 35:1-36:38	James 1:1-18	116:1-19	27:23-27
Day 7	Ezekiel 37:1-38:23	James 1:19-2:17	117:1-2	28:1

Personal Notes and Glimpses of Wisdom:

SESSION 47 • PASTORAL WISDOM

The aim of this session is to discover wisdom for leadership from Paul's letters to Timothy, Titus and Philemon.

MATERIALS NEEDED

Bibles
Hymnals
Accompaniment
Chalkboard or Newsprint
Completed Search Sheet 46
Completed Insights from Daily Scripture Readings For Week 46
Copies for each participant of:
"Follow-Along Page"
"Pastoral Wisdom's Pathway"
Search Sheet 47
Daily Scripture Readings For Week 47

▓ ASSEMBLING

While many of Paul's letters were sent to churches, some were sent to *individuals.* The letters to Timothy, Titus and Philemon contain wisdom which is still valuable to *those who lead.* This session invites participants to discover what may be helpful as they prepare for leadership. Participants may need encouragement to share "The Wisdom Series" with others.

▓ THE APPROACH TO GOD   (5 to 10 minutes)

❧ *Sing a hymn* which petitions God for wisdom in leadership, such as *"God Of Love and God of Power"* (or select from the "Ordination" category in the topical index of your hymnal).

❧ Like Solomon, *ask God for wisdom* for yourself as you lead and for participants who are leaders-in-training.

▓ ENCOUNTERING THE WORD   (40 to 45 minutes)

⇨ Invite participants to share the Gospel message *summary* they have written from 1 Thessalonians. Option: Formulate a consolidated "group statement" and write this on chalkboard or newsprint.

⇨ Invite participants to share their insights into their *leadership style, strengths* and *weaknesses* in leadership. Invite affirmation from other participants. Affirm and encourage everyone. Share a leadership weakness of your own. (This exercise calls for great caring and *sensitivity*.)

⇨ *Distribute copies of "Follow-Along Pages"* and proceed with the Lecturette. Invite comments and questions as needed and as time permits. Offer to remain after the session for questions which require more time.

⇨ *Distribute copies of "Pastoral Wisdom's Pathway."* Allow participants time to look it over and ask questions or share insights.

▦ GOING FORTH IN GOD'S NAME   (5 to 10 minutes)

❧   *Sing a hymn* of pastoral wisdom such as *"Beside The Still Waters," "Lead Me, O Lead Me," "The New 23rd,"* or other hymn on Psalm 23.

❧   *Close with a prayer* of thanksgiving for the Good Shepherd who leads all sheep and shepherds – and for the wisdom of Paul's epistles to Timothy, Titus and Philemon.

❧   Distribute copies of:
      Search Sheet 47
      Daily Scripture Readings For Week 47

Lecturette

This session may recall Session 9, "Shaping a Wise Leader," and the stages Moses went through as God shaped him into a **wise leader** – one who taught "The Law – Wisdom's Secrets" (Session 11). The aim of Session 47 is to discover **wisdom** for **leadership** from Paul's letters to Timothy, Titus and Philemon.

The **FIRST** step in leadership is for leaders to **love themselves**. Proverbs 19:8 says "To get wisdom is to love oneself." Paul says, "The aim of such instruction (sound teaching and preaching) is love that comes from a pure heart, a good conscience, and sincere faith" (1 Timothy 1:5). This love comes by **humbly** receiving God's love and grace. Paul shares his own humble self love in 1 Timothy 1:12-14 where he describes himself as a blasphemer, persecutor and a violent man who was shown **grace** and **mercy** from God who **loved** us by sending Christ Jesus. In Titus 3:3-7, Paul describes himself and other leaders as once being "foolish, disobedient, led astray, slaves to various passions and pleasures, passing our days with malice and envy, despicable, hating one another." After the "goodness and loving kindness of God our Savior appeared," they were saved **not by works of righteousness** but according to **God's mercy** through the water of rebirth and renewal by the Holy Spirit. Now, justified by God's grace, they **belong** to God, walk and talk with God through **prayer**, are constantly being **renewed** within by the Holy Spirit, enjoy the **hope** of eternal life, and extend that **Good News** to others.

SECONDLY, good leaders lead by **example**. Women (1 Timothy 3:11) and men who lead need to **bear the fruits of faith**. Leaders model good works and demonstrate **integrity** (Titus 2:7) between what they say and what they do.

(Read 1 Timothy 3:2-7 and Titus 1:5-9 and **list the qualities of good leaders**. As participants list these qualities on their Follow-Along Page, make a list on chalkboard or newsprint. The list may include the following:

self-control	**hospitality**	**ability to teach**
gentleness (non-violence)	**sensibility**	**respectability**
temperate	**not quarrelsome**	**not a new convert**
not a lover of money	**good reputation**	**not overbearing**
not quick-tempered	**lover of goodness**	**upright, holy**
disciplined	**clear conscience**	**monogamous**
honest	**steadfast faith**	**orderly family**
family leader	**sincere**	**tested**

THIRDLY, good leaders need to lead **quiet** and **peaceable** lives, praying and **interceding** for "everyone" (1 Timothy 2:1-2). Like sheep who need still water to drink, those who lead need **times of retreat** from daily busyness to reflect on the Word of God, to pray for the needs of believers locally and everywhere, and to listen for the voice of God which can best be heard in the stillness.

FOURTHLY, leaders need gifts and abilities of **restoring** those who wander or stray from wisdom's way. This means knowing the difference between pure and false teachings.

(Invite participants to read 1 Timothy 1:3-11, 4:1-5, 6:3-10, 2 Timothy 4:3-5 and Titus 1:10-16 and list the qualities of "pure" and "false" teachings. Again, you may wish to **list these** on chalkboard or newsprint.) The list may include the following:

Pure Teachings	False Teachings
divine training known by faith	*myths and genealogies*
characterized by love	*speculation, meaningless talk*
gospel-consistent teaching	*fornication, lying*
thanksgiving and prayer	*hypocrisy, demonic teaching*
godliness and contentment	*envy, dissension, slander*
sound doctrine	*love of money*
soberness, truth	*crowd-pleasing*
endures suffering	*idle talk, rebellious, lying*
evangelizes	*actions deny faith*
obedient to God	*disobedient to God*

In the story of Philemon and his run-away slave Onesimus, Paul demonstrates **mature leadership by mutual submission**. Philemon was the leader of a house church in Colossae. His slave Onesimus ran away from Philemon. In Ephesus (or possibly Rome), Onesimus encountered Paul, received the grace and freedom of Christ, and assisted Paul. Paul had declared slaves and free as "one in Christ" (Galatians 3:28), but Roman law required that slaves be returned to their masters. Although Paul outranked Philemon, Paul **submitted** to Philemon's right of ownership under Roman law. While suggesting a Christ-like way for Philemon to receive Onesimus, Paul leaves the decision to Philemon rather than giving an apostolic order. Paul then urged Onesimus to return to Philemon. Paul **submitted** to Onesimus by offering to pay whatever Onesimus may owe Philemon. Paul's letter to Philemon thus **laid the foundation for Philemon's forgiveness** of Onesimus and the **acceptance of Onesimus** into the church as an equal in Christ. In **leading by mutual submission**, Paul imitates Christ who submitted to death on the cross to reconcile all sinners to God. (Christ did not come to exercise **power over** us but to be Immanuel – God **with** us, even in the depths of our human struggles, suffering and death.)

The following diagram illustrates the **wisdom of restoration by mutual submission**. *Draw it on chalkboard or newsprint, and invite participants to sketch it in the margin or on back of their Follow-Along Page):*

Restoration/
Reconciliation
by
Mutual Submission

FIFTHLY, leaders need to be willing to **lead others** through **difficult times**, for they are sure to come. "Indeed, all who want to live a godly life in Christ Jesus will be persecuted" (2 Timothy 3:12). A leader is one who has been **tested** and has **held fast** to the "mystery of the faith" (1 Timothy 3:9-10).

What are some of the difficulties leaders may face? (Read, or have a participant read 2 Timothy 3:1-9, and list the "other ways" people may go rather than "God's Way" or "Wisdom's Way." This list may include the following: **self-centeredness, greed, boasting, arrogance, abuse, disobedience, ungratefulness, unholiness, inhumanity, implacability, slandering, profligacy, brutality, hating good, treachery, recklessness, conceit, pleasure-seeking, outward godliness without inner power.**

Paul's advice regarding those who forsake the Gospel and go their own way is: "Avoid them!" (2 Timothy 3:5). Leaders are to "continue in what you have learned and firmly believed" (2 Timothy 3:14).

SIXTHLY, leaders are called to **give thanks** and **pray** for **everyone** – even those who misuse power and authority (1 Timothy 2:1-2). Human leaders do not always know what role evil and oppression may have in

God's plan. In the midst of opposition, leaders are called to "pursue righteousness, **_godliness_**, **_faith_**, **_love_**, endurance, gentleness. **_Fight_** the good **_fight_** of the **_faith_**; take hold of the **_eternal life_** to which you were called and for which you made the good confession in the presence of many witnesses" (1 Timothy 6:11-12). In so doing, leaders follow Christ who did not compromise his calling even when he was before Pilate.

SEVENTH, leaders are called to **_preach_** and **_teach_** the **_Gospel_** to **_all_** people and bring them at last to the **_glory_** and **_peace (Shalom)_** God is preparing.

(Invite participants to read the following: 1 Timothy 2:4, 4:8-10, and Titus 2:11-15 and make notes on their Follow-Along Page.)

Distribute copies of "Pastoral Wisdom's Pathway." Invite questions and comments.

"Follow-Along Page"

The aim of Session 47 is to discover w_____ for l_____ from Paul's letters to Timothy, Titus and Philemon.

Leaders need **first** to l_____ themselves, h_____ receiving g_____ and m_____ from God who first l_____ us. Knowing they b_____ to God, leaders need to be women and men of p_____, constantly being r_____ by the Holy Spirit, enjoying the h_____ of eternal life, and extending the G_____ N_____ to others.

Secondly, leaders lead by e_____, their lives showing i_____ between what they say and what they do.

Qualities Of Good Leaders
(1 Timothy 3:2-7, Titus 1:5-9)

_____   _____   _____
_____   _____   _____
_____   _____   _____
_____   _____   _____
_____   _____   _____
_____   _____   _____

Thirdly, leaders need to lead q_____ and p_____ lives, i_____ for everyone (1 Timothy 2:1-2).

Fourthly, leaders need gifts and abilities for r_____ those who wander or stray from Wisdom's Way. They know the difference between pure and false teachings. (1 Timothy 1:3-11, 4:1-5, 6:3-10, 2 Timothy 4:3-5, Titus 1:10-16)

Pure Teachings	False Teachings
_____	_____
_____	_____
_____	_____
_____	_____
_____	_____

Fifthly, leaders need to know how to l_____ o_____ through d_____ t_____. A leader is one who has been t_____ and has h_____ f_____ to the "mystery of the faith."

Difficulties Leaders May Face: (2 Timothy 3:1-9) _____
_____
_____

Sixthly, leaders are called to g_____ t_____ and p_____ for e_____ (1 Timothy 2:1-2). Leaders are called to pursue righteousness, g_____, f_____, l_____, endurance, gentleness and to f_____ the good f_____ of the f_____, taking hold of the e_____ l_____ (1 Timothy 6:11-12).

Seventh, leaders are called to p_____ and t_____ the G_____ N_____ to a____ people and bring them at last to the g_____ and p_____ (S_____) God is preparing.

Notes:
1 Timothy 2:4 _____
1 Timothy 4:8-10 _____
Titus 2:11-15 _____

FEEDING IN GREEN PASTURES

Leaders lead by good example and show integrity of words and actions.

STILL WATERS

Leaders live quiet and peaceful lives, interceding for everyone.

BELONGING

Leaders belong to God who loves us so we can love ourselves and others.

PASTORAL WISDOM'S PATHWAY

RESTORING TO RIGHT PATHS

Leaders know the difference between true and false teachings and help restore those who wander.

SAFE SHEEPFOLD

Leaders preach and teach the good news to everyone and bring them to SHALOM.

TABLE IN THE PRESENCE OF ENEMY

Leaders give thanks and pray for everyone – even enemies.

VALLEY OF THE SHADOW

Leaders have been tested and know how to lead others faithfully through difficult times.

SEARCH SHEET 47

The Epistle to the Hebrews, focus of next session, speaks to Jewish Christians about the tendency to fall back into the old system and thus miss the **wisdom** and **power** of the Gospel of Jesus Christ. Scholars are not sure who wrote Hebrews – Barnabas and Apollos are possibilities. The purpose is similar to Paul's Epistles to the Romans and Galatians: To **renew and restore faith** that is in danger of going backward. This Search Sheet will help you become familiar with the letter to the Hebrews in preparation for Session 48.

1. Long ago God spoke to people through p_____, but in Jesus, God has spoken by a S_____ (1:1-2). Jesus is the reflection of God's g_____ and the exact i_____ of God's very being, and he sustains a____ t_____ by his powerful w_____ (1:3). By his death and resurrection Jesus became s_____ to a_____ (1:4).

2. Jesus is worthy of more glory than M_____(3:3) who was a faithful s_____ while Christ was faithful as a s_____(3:5-6). While other high priests offered sacrifices for their own sins as well as those of the people, Jesus is a high priest who has been t_____ but is without s_____ (4:15), a priest f_____ according to the order of M_____ (5:6). With Christ as our high priest, we can go on toward p_____, beyond the basics of our faith (6:1). Jesus is our high priest in the heavenly sanctuary of which our sanctuaries are sketches and s_____ (8:5). Christ has mediated a better c_____(8:6) with laws written in our m_____ and h_____(8:10). While the ancient priestly sacrifices had to be repeated, Christ gave his blood o_____ for a_____, thus obtaining e_____ redemption (9:12). Those who s_____ b_____ into the old system are l_____, while those who have f_____ in Christ are s_____ (10:39).

3. Faith is the a_____ of things h_____ for, the c_____ of things not s_____ (11:1). It is by f_____ that leaders of the past were able to please and obey God (11:2). Since we are surrounded by this great c_____ of w_____ we can run with p_____ the r_____ that is set before us, keeping our eyes on Jesus, the p_____ and p_____ of our faith (12:1-2).

4. List some ways we can live out this victorious faith: (13:1-9, 17-18) _____
   _____
   _____
   _____
   _____

5. "Now may the God of p_____, who brought back from the dead our Lord Jesus, the great s_____ of the s_____, by the b_____ of the eternal c_____, make you complete in everything g_____ so that you may do his w_____, working among us that which is pleasing in his sight, through Jesus Christ, to whom be the g_____ forever and ever. Amen." (13:20-21)

The Epistle to the Hebrews, focus of next session, speaks to Jewish Christians about the tendency to fall back into the old system and thus miss the **wisdom** and **power** of the Gospel of Jesus Christ. Scholars are not sure who wrote Hebrews – Barnabas and Apollos are possibilities. The purpose is similar to Paul's Epistles to the Romans and Galatians: To **renew and restore faith** that is in danger of going backward. This Search Sheet will help you become familiar with the letter to the Hebrews in preparation for Session 48.

1. Long ago God spoke to people through p_rophets_, but in Jesus, God has spoken by a S_on_ (1:1-2). Jesus is the reflection of God's g_lory_ and the exact i_mprint_ of God's very being, and he sustains a_ll_ t_hings_ by his powerful w_ord_ (1:3). By his death and resurrection Jesus became s_uperior_ to a_ngels_ (1:4).

2. Jesus is worthy of more glory than M_oses_ (3:3) who was a faithful s_ervant_ while Christ was faithful as a s_on_ (3:5-6). While other high priests offered sacrifices for their own sins as well as those of the people, Jesus is a high priest who has been t_ested_ but is without s_in_ (4:15), a priest f_orever_ according to the order of M_elchizedek_ (5:6). With Christ as our high priest, we can go on toward p_erfection_, beyond the basics of our faith (6:1). Jesus is our high priest in the heavenly sanctuary of which our sanctuaries are sketches and s_hadows_ (8:5). Christ has mediated a better c_ovenant_ (8:6) with laws written in our m_inds_ and h_earts_ (8:10). While the ancient priestly sacrifices had to be repeated, Christ gave his blood o_nce_ for a_ll_, thus obtaining e_ternal_ redemption (9:12). Those who s_hrink_ b_ack_ into the old system are l_ost_, while those who have f_aith_ in Christ are s_aved_ (10:39).

3. Faith is the a_ssurance_ of things h_oped_ for, the c_onviction_ of things not s_een_ (11:1). It is by f_aith_ that leaders of the past were able to please and obey God (11:2). Since we are surrounded by this great c_loud_ of w_itnesses_ we can run with p_erseverance_ the r_ace_ that is set before us, keeping our eyes on Jesus, the p_ioneer_ and p_erfecter_ of our faith (12:1-2).

4. List some ways we can live out this victorious faith: (13:1-9, 17-18) _Mutual love, hospitality, visiting prisoners, faithfulness in marriage, contentment (not love of money), imitate good leaders, hold fast to teaching of grace (not regulations), obey and submit to leaders, pray for leaders._

5. "Now may the God of p_eace_, who brought back from the dead our Lord Jesus, the great s_hepherd_ of the s_heep_, by the b_lood_ of the eternal c_ovenant_, make you complete in everything g_ood_ so that you may do his w_ill_, working among us that which is pleasing in his sight, through Jesus Christ, to whom be the g_lory_ forever and ever. Amen." (13:20-21)

DAILY SCRIPTURE
READINGS • WEEK 47

AWE
THE **REVERENCE** AT THE **NEARNESS HOLINESS BEAUTY** OF GOD = THE BEGINNING OF **WISDOM**
WONDER

(PROVERBS 1:7A)

	HEBREW SCRIPTURE	NEW TESTAMENT	PSALM	PROVERBS
Day 1	Ezekiel 39:1-40:27	James 2:18-3:18	118:1-18	28:2
Day 2	Ezekiel 40:28-41:26	James 4:1-17	118:19-29	28:3-5
Day 3	Ezekiel 42:1-43:27	James 5:1-20	119:1-16	28:6-7
Day 4	Ezekiel 44:1-45:12	1 Peter 1:1-12	119:17-32	28:8-10
Day 5	Ezekiel 45:13-46:29	1 Peter 1:13-2:10	119:33-48	28:11
Day 6	Ezekiel 47:1-48:35	1 Peter 2:11-3:7	119:49-64	28:12-13
Day 7	Daniel 1:1-2:23	1 Peter 3:8-4:6	119:65-80	28:14

Personal Notes and Glimpses of Wisdom:

"I wonder if I'll ever get enough wisdom to be a wise leader..."

SESSION 48 • RENEWAL WISDOM

The aim of this session is to see the danger of slipping backward in faith and to discover wisdom for renewal in Hebrews (and Galatians and Romans).

MATERIALS NEEDED

Bibles
Hymnals
Accompaniment
Chalkboard or Newsprint
"Pioneers To Perfection" gameboard (colored and mounted) and Clue Cards (laminated and cut)
Assorted coins and/or buttons
Completed Search Sheet 47
Completed Insights from Daily Scripture Readings For Week 47
Copies for each participant of:
  Search Sheet 48
  Daily Scripture Readings For Week 48

▣ ASSEMBLING

When times are difficult, it's always tempting to go back to old and familiar ways. This was the situation of the Jewish Christians for whom the letter to Hebrews was written. When they were being persecuted for their Christian beliefs, they found it comforting to slip back into familiar Jewish tradition. This alarmed the author (as it did Paul regarding the Romans and Galatians) who realized that to go back into the old system threatened loss of the faith for which Christ came, died and rose. The Hebrew Christians, like all Christians, needed to **persevere** in their faith and follow the "great shepherd of the sheep" through the valley of the shadow of death and on to perfection.

▣ THE APPROACH TO GOD   (5 to 10 minutes)

❧ *Sing* "I Have Decided To Follow Jesus" with emphasis on *"no turning back, no turning back."*

❧ *Offer a prayer* for the faithfulness of yourself and each participant in "keeping on keeping on" even when the way is difficult.

▣ ENCOUNTERING THE WORD   (40 to 45 minutes)

⇨ Invite participants to create a skit beginning with the following scenario: A "new member" (played by leader or participant) has just received the grace of God offered in Jesus Christ. He or she is unfamiliar with customs and traditions of the church or group. Other participants welcome the new member **_unconditionally; BUT THEN_** they begin to offer advice – practical or ridiculous – *"In OUR church, we walk with our left hands behind our backs"* etc. – about how the new member can best *"fit in"* to the church or group. The "new member" tries to comply . . .

When the "new member" looks totally bewildered, stop the "advice" and invite participants to reflect on this experience: Do we do these things in OUR church or group? How does this make new members feel? In what ways is OUR church or group like the churches to whom the Epistles of Romans, Galatians and Hebrews were addressed? (Read Galatians 1:10) What can we do to renew and restore faith and growth in grace at OUR church or in OUR group? (Is this really OUR church or group?)

⇨ Introduce "Pilgrims To Perfection" as a game which explores "going forward" and "turning back." Rules are as follows:

1. You are Christians, pilgrims on a journey to perfection. There are "difficulties" or "calamities" on the journey, but the goal is to keep going WITHOUT TURNING BACK until you reach HEAVEN (or Shalom). Select a coin or button as your gamepiece. Take turns drawing "Clue Cards," (one card per pilgrim per turn) and move forward as indicated in Rule 2.

2. Unless otherwise stated, move forward **_two spaces_** for each correct answer you give (you may look at Completed Search Sheet 47), **_one space_** for each correct answer you receive from another pilgrim on the journey, and **_stay in place WITHOUT GOING BACKWARD_** for each answer you or another pilgrim looks up in the Bible.

3. When you land on "A," "B," "C," "D," or "E" (vulnerable times for slipping backward), **_move backward one space._**

Playing proceeds until all pilgrims reach HEAVEN (or Shalom). Reshuffle and reuse cards as needed. When all pilgrims reach HEAVEN, reflect on the experience: How was the game like a life of faith? Was it "fair?" What was "fair;" what was "not-so-fair?" Is a life of faith "fair?" Did Jesus promise that it would be? What helped to "keep on keeping on" when the journey was difficult? Comments can be recorded on chalkboard or newsprint.

▨ GOING FORTH IN GOD'S NAME   (5 to 10 minutes)

❥ Close with a *pilgrim prayer hymn* such as *"Higher Ground" or "One Step At A Time."*

❥ Distribute copies of:
Search Sheet 48
Daily Scripture Readings For Week 48

"Pioneers to Perfection"
Gameboard

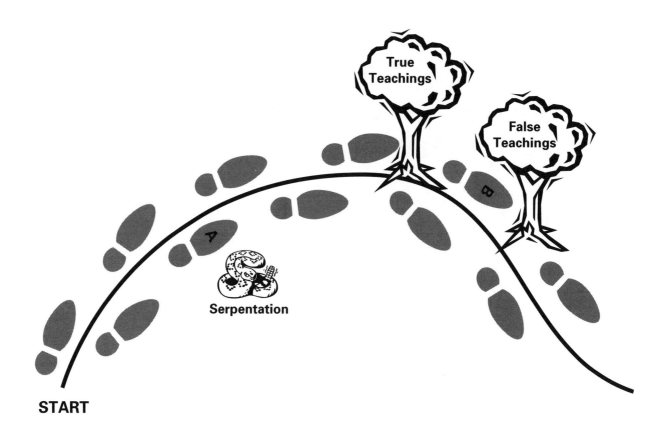

**"Pioneers to Perfection"
Gameboard**

Clue Cards

Faith is the assurance of things h_____ f_____, the c_____ of things not s_____. (Hebrews 11:1)

Moses was God's faithful s_____; Christ was God's faithful s_____. (Hebrews 3:5-6)

Jesus Christ, God's Son, sustains a_____ t_____ by his powerful w_____. (Hebrews 1:3)

Unbelieving hearts are those which t_____ a_____ from the living God. (Hebrews 3:12)

Long ago God spoke to people through p_____, but in Jesus, God has spoken to us by a S____. (Hebrews 1:1)

Hearing God's voice but not obeying is described as r_____. (Hebrews 3:15)

By his death and resurrection Jesus became s_____ to a_____. (Hebrews 1:4)

Why did a generation of Hebrew people who left Egypt in faith die in the wilderness, unable to enter their promised land? (Hebrews 3:7-11, 19, 4:6)

Jesus is the reflection of God's g_____ and the exact i_____ of God's very being. (Hebrews 1:3)

With Christ as our high priest, we can go on toward p_____, beyond the basics of our faith. (Hebrews 6:1)

Those who shrink back after receiving God's grace are l_____, but those who have faith in Christ are s_____. (Hebrews 10:39)

We can persevere in faith because Jesus is the p_____ and p_____ of our faith. (Hebrews 12:2)

While the ancient high priests were chosen among mortals, Christ was appointed by God, a priest f_____ like M_____. (Hebrews 5:6)

Christ endured the cross, disregarding its shame, for the sake of the j_____ that was set before him. (Hebrews 12:2)

In the new covenant mediated by Christ, the laws are written in our m_____ and h_____. (Hebrews 8:10)

We are encouraged, as God's children, to endure trials for the sake of d_____. (Hebrews 12:7)

While ancient priestly sacrifices had to be repeated, Christ gave his blood o_____ for a_____. (Hebrews 9:12)

To bring about renewal in the Corinthian church, Paul taught believers to discern between the w_____ of this world and God's w_____, taught by the S____. (1 Corinthians 2:7, 13, 3:19)

Surrounded by a c_____ of faithful w_____, we can run with p_____ the race that is set before us. (Hebrews 12:1)

The Christian body/temple of faith is built on the cornerstone of Christ's r_____ and ours! (1 Corinthians 15:12-19)

A one-word theme for Paul's Epistle to the Galatians is f_____. (Galatians 5:1, 13)

One key to Paul's joyous faith is that he regards everything as l_____ compared to knowing Christ. (Philippians 3:8)

Name four of the nine fruits of the Spirit: (Galatians 5:22-23)

One secret of joyous faith is f_____ what lies behind and straining f_____ to what lies ahead. (Philippians 3:13-14)

A one-word theme for Paul's Epistle to the Ephesians is u_____. (Ephesians 4:3, 13)

"For to me, l_____ is Christ and d_____ is gain." (Philippians 1:21)

Name three of the six weapons for spiritual warfare: (Ephesians 6:14-17)

A one-word theme for Paul's Epistle to the Colossians is g_____. (Colossians 1:27)

A one-word theme for Paul's Epistle to the Philippians is j_____. (Philippians 1:4)

One way to keep from slipping backward in faith is to set your m_____ on things that are a_____. (Colossians 3:2)

The theme of Paul's Epistle to the Romans is the gospel of grace which is the p_____ of God for s_____ to all who have f_____. (Romans 1:16)

Paul asked the Galatians to discern between seeking h_____ approval and God's approval. (Galatians 1:10)

Paul's advice to lazy people in Thessalonica was, "Anyone unwilling to w_____ should not e_____." (2 Thessalonians 3:10)

If I try to p_____ people, I cannot be a servant of Christ. (Galatians 1:10)

Suffering produces e_____, which produces c_____, which produces h_____ through God's gift of the Holy Spirit. (Romans 5:3-5)

S_____ was the church's first martyr. (Acts 7:54-60)

"Do not be conformed to this world, but be t_____ by the renewing of your minds." (Romans 12:2)

What did the believers do in Jerusalem while they waited for the baptism of the Holy Spirit? (Acts 1:14, 24-26)

Paul's advice to husbands and wives is to be s_____ one to another out of reverence for Christ. (Ephesians 5:21)

The Holy Spirit gave ordinary uneducated people b_____ in the midst of persecution and opposition. (Acts 4:13)

Peter's rooftop vision led to the Gospel being extended to Gentiles because "God shows no p_____." (Acts 10:34)

In spite of p_____, the Thessalonians received the word with joy inspired by the Holy Spirit. (1 Thessalonians 1:6)

In the midst of shipwrecks, imprisonment, persecution and martyrdom, the "word of God continued to a_____." (Acts 12:24)

Paul encouraged Timothy not to be ashamed but to join in s_____ for the gospel. (2 Timothy 1:8)

After we are put right with God (by grace through faith), we have p_____ with God through Christ. (Romans 5:1)

Leaders must hold fast to the faith with a clear c_____. (1 Timothy 3:9)

The law of the S_____ of life sets us free from the law of s____ and d_____. (Romans 8:2)

What can be seen is temporary, but what cannot be seen is e_____. (2 Corinthians 4:18)

■ CLUE CARDS (Answer Guide)

Acts 1:14, 24-26 – prayed, cast lots for Matthias

Acts 4:13 – boldness

Acts 7:54-60 – Stephen

Acts 10:34 – partiality

Acts 12:24 – advance

Romans 1:16 – power, salvation, faith

Romans 5:1 – peace

Romans 5:3-5 – endurance, character, hope

Romans 8:2 – Spirit, sin, death

Romans 12:2 – transformed

1 Corinthians 2:7, 13, 3:19 – wisdom, wisdom, Spirit

1 Corinthians 15:12-19 – resurrection

2 Corinthians 4:18 – eternal

Galatians 1:10 – human

Galatians 1:10 – please

Galatians 5:1, 13 – freedom

Galatians 5:22-23 – love, joy, peace, patience, kindness, generosity, faithfulness, gentleness, self-control

Ephesians 4:3, 13 – unity

Ephesians 5:21 – subject (or submissive)

Ephesians 6:14-17 – belt of truth, breastplate of righteousness, shoes of peace, shield of faith, helmet of salvation, sword of Spirit (word of God)

Philippians 1:4 – joy

Philippians 1:21 – living, dying

Philippians 3:8 – loss

Philippians 3:13-14 – forgetting, forward

Colossians 1:27 – glory

Colossians 3:2 – mind, above

1 Thessalonians 1:6 – persecution

2 Thessalonians 3:10 – work, eat

1 Timothy 3:9 – conscience

2 Timothy 1:8 — suffering

Hebrews 1:1 – prophet, Son

Hebrews 1:3 – glory, imprint

Hebrews 1:3 – all things, word

Hebrews 1:4 – superior, angels

Hebrews 3:5-6 – servant, son

Hebrews 3:12 – turn away

Hebrews 3:15 – rebellion

Hebrews 3:7-11, 19, 4:6 – hardened hearts, turning away, rebellion, unbelief, disobedience

Hebrews 5:6 – forever, Melchizedek

Hebrews 6:1 – perfection

Hebrews 8:10 – minds, hearts

Hebrews 9:12 – once, all

Hebrews 10:39 – lost, saved

Hebrews 11:1 – hoped for, conviction, seen

Hebrews 12:1 – cloud, witnesses, perseverance (or patience)

Hebrews 12:2 – pioneer, perfecter

Hebrews 12:2 – joy

Hebrews 12:7 – discipline

Next week's session will focus on seven "general" letters – universal letters not addressed to a particular faith community like the letters of Paul. Below is a brief description – with some gaps for you to fill in – to familiarize you with these letters:

James – This James is not one of the 12 disciples but rather a half-brother of Jesus who did not b_____ Jesus was the Messiah (John 7:2-5) until he saw Jesus after the r_____ (1 Corinthians 15:7). James is perhaps best known for his statement: "For just as the body without the s_____ is dead, so f_____ without w_____ is also dead" (James 2:26). James also teaches believers to distinguish between two kinds of w_____: 1) that which is evidenced by envy, selfish ambition, disorder, wickedness, partiality and hypocrisy, and 2) that which is pure, peaceable, gentle, willing to yield, full of mercy and good fruits (James 3:13-18).

1 Peter – The Apostle Peter writes from Rome to Christians who are suffering abuse and persecution for their faith. Christians are called to e_____ suffering for doing r_____ (2:20) because C_____ a_____ s_____ f___ y___ (2:21). Those who are r_____ for the sake of Christ are b_____ because the Spirit of God rests upon them (4:14).

2 Peter – The Apostle Peter reminds believers of basic truths of the Christian faith so they will not be led astray by c_____ d_____ m_____ (1:16). He encourages believers to live lives of h_____ and g_____ while waiting for Christ's coming again (3:11).

1 John – The Apostle John, writer of the fourth gospel and of Revelation, also wrote three short letters. In this letter, he wrote about those who might d_____ Christians (2:26). He affirms the message of his gospel – that loving God means to o_____ God's c_____ (5:3).

2 John – While believers are to l_____ o____ a_____ (5), they are to refuse hospitality to d_____ (7, 10).

3 John – This letter is written to an individual, Gaius, who is f_____ to the t_____ (3) and hospitable to co-workers with the t_____ (8). Gaius' exemplary behavior is contrasted with Diotrephes' f_____ c_____ (10), self-seeking, and inhospitality to visiting believers.

Jude – Jude is a younger brother of Jesus and James (above) who warns believers against those who p_____ the g_____ of God and thus d_____ Christ. He points believers to God who is able to k_____ believers from f_____ (24).

SEARCH SHEET 48
ANSWER GUIDE

Next week's session will focus on seven "general" letters – universal letters not addressed to a particular faith community like the letters of Paul. Below is a brief description – with some gaps for you to fill in – to familiarize you with these letters:

James – This James is not one of the 12 disciples but rather a half-brother of Jesus who did not b_elieve_ Jesus was the Messiah (John 7:2-5) until he saw Jesus after the r_esurrection_ (1Corinthians 15:7). James is perhaps best known for his statement: "For just as the body without the s_pirit_ is dead, so f_aith_ without w_orks_ is also dead" (James 2:26). James also teaches believers to distinguish between two kinds of w_isdom_: 1) that which is evidenced by envy, selfish ambition, disorder, wickedness, partiality and hypocrisy, and 2) that which is pure, peaceable, gentle, willing to yield, full of mercy and good fruits (James 3:13-18).

1 Peter – The Apostle Peter writes from Rome to Christians who are suffering abuse and persecution for their faith. Christians are called to e_ndure_ suffering for doing r_ight_ (2:20) because C_hrist_ a_lso_ s_uffered_ f_or_ y_ou_ (2:21). Those who are r_eviled_ for the sake of Christ are b_lessed_ because the Spirit of God rests upon them (4:14).

2 Peter – The Apostle Peter reminds believers of basic truths of the Christian faith so they will not be led astray by c_leverly_ d_evised_ m_yths_ (1:16). He encourages believers to live lives of h_oliness_ and g_odliness_ while waiting for Christ's coming again (3:11).

1 John – The Apostle John, writer of the fourth gospel and of Revelation, also wrote three short letters. In this letter, he wrote about those who might d_eceive_ Christians (2:26). He affirms the message of his gospel – that loving God means to o_bey_ God's c_ommandments_ (5:3).

2 John – While believers are to l_ove_ o_ne_ a_nother_ (5), they are to refuse hospitality to d_eceivers_ (7, 10).

3 John – This letter is written to an individual, Gaius, who is f_aithful_ to the t_ruth_ (3) and hospitable to co-workers with the t_ruth_ (8). Gaius' exemplary behavior is contrasted with Diotrephes' f_alse_ c_harges_ (10), self-seeking, and inhospitality to visiting believers.

Jude – Jude is a younger brother of Jesus and James (above) who warns believers against those who p_ervert_ the g_race_ of God and thus d_eny_ Christ. He points believers to God who is able to k_eep_ believers from f_alling_ (24).

DAILY SCRIPTURE
READINGS • WEEK 48

THE **AWE REVERENCE WONDER** AT THE **NEARNESS HOLINESS BEAUTY** OF GOD = THE BEGINNING OF **WISDOM**

(PROVERBS 1:7A)

	HEBREW SCRIPTURE	NEW TESTAMENT	PSALM	PROVERBS
Day 1	Daniel 2:24-3:30	1 Peter 4:7-5:14	119:81-96	28:15-16
Day 2	Daniel 4:1-37	2 Peter 1:1-21	119:97-112	28:17-18
Day 3	Daniel 5:1-31	2 Peter 2:1-22	119:113-128	28:19-20
Day 4	Daniel 6:1-28	2 Peter 3:1-18	119:129-152	28:21-22
Day 5	Daniel 7:1-28	1 John 1:1-10	119:153-176	28:23-24
Day 6	Daniel 8:1-27	1 John 2:1-17	120:1-7	28:25-26
Day 7	Daniel 9:1-11:1	1 John 2:18 – 3:6	121:1-8	28:27-28

Personal Notes and Glimpses of Wisdom:

_____

_____

"I wonder how I can keep from slipping..."

_____

_____

_____

_____

_____

_____

_____

SESSION 49 • LETTERS OF EVERYDAY WISDOM

The aim of this session is to seek wisdom for everyday life from the Epistles of James, Peter, John and Jude.

MATERIALS NEEDED

Bibles
Hymnals
Accompaniment
Chalkboard or Newsprint
Copy of "Author Scripts," cut for distribution
Completed Search Sheet 48
Completed Insights from Daily Scripture Readings For Week 48
Copies for each participant of:
    Search Sheet 49
    Daily Scripture Readings For Week 49

▦ ASSEMBLING

While Paul's letters were written to certain **groups** or **individuals,** the Epistles of James, Peter, John and Jude were (except for 3 John) written for more **general readership**. To discover their intent and meaning for Christians today, it will be helpful to look at the original setting and purpose. This session explores the wisdom of these epistles via a presentation by each author with an opportunity for "dialogue" afterward . . .

▦ THE APPROACH TO GOD   (5 to 10 minutes)

❧ *Sing a hymn* seeking the wisdom of God in everyday life, such as *"Day By Day And With Each Passing Moment,"* or *"Moment By Moment."*

❧ *Offer a prayer* for God's wisdom and guidance as the group enjoys sharing the wisdom of James, Peter, John and Jude.

▦ ENCOUNTERING THE WORD   (40 to 45 minutes)

⇨ Review Search Sheet 48 with participants. This will introduce the presentations by authors and facilitate dialogue with the authors. *Distribute author scripts.* After each author's presentation, invite participants to ask questions (and try to "stump the author").

▦ GOING FORTH IN GOD'S NAME   (5 to 10 minutes)

❧ *Sing a prayer hymn* which expresses God's undying love, such as *"O Love That Wilt Not Let Me Go."*

❧ Distribute copies of:
    Search Sheet 49
    Daily Scripture Readings For Week 49

Author Scripts

James

I am James – not the disciple who followed Jesus. I'm a half-brother of Jesus. Jesus was a good big brother – so good that the rest of us often felt inadequate. He was different; he seemed to be living out of some inner sense of calling with little concern about earning a living. When he was 30, he started teaching publicly, like a rabbi; but we all knew he didn't take any formal training at the temple in Jerusalem. That didn't seem to matter to the crowds in Galilee. They thought he was wonderful; they loved his stories; many of them claimed he healed them – but we figured it was "just a coincidence." My mother, brothers and sisters and I were concerned that Jesus wasn't taking good care of himself. We went to see him, but he wouldn't talk to us.

His passion for living his beliefs sometimes seemed self-destructive. I wasn't surprised, then, when Jesus got in trouble with the chief priests in Jerusalem. I was surprised at how quickly their anger turned to murder. I didn't think they would go **THAT** far! When the sky turned black while Jesus was hanging and dying, and the veil of the temple split in two – then I finally figured out it couldn't be "just a coincidence" anymore.

After Jesus was buried, I sat alone wondering about my big brother and the things he said and did. I realized then that the words of wisdom Jesus spoke were far more powerful than our family had realized. Looking back, I could also see how painful my attitude must have been to Jesus, and I deeply regretted my failure to understand. I could see that the chief priests' jealousy over Jesus' popularity and their anger at his criticism of their hypocrisy were "human wisdom" like mine.

As I was sitting alone and thinking about these things, Jesus appeared to me. As he looked at me, my inadequacy melted away; I felt so peaceful – the regrets of the past no longer had power over my life. Jesus understood it all and gave me his **mysterious wisdom** in place of my own.

I prayed and waited with other believers in Jerusalem until the Holy Spirit was poured out upon us. Then I received a special desire and energy to teach the difference between **human wisdom** and **God's wisdom.** I taught about a "powerful little rudder" which can steer big ships one way or the other – the tongue. Our faith is known by the **oneness** of our **speech** and our **actions!** I became a leader in the Jerusalem church and at one point wrote down these insights into the wisdom of God to help us all.

(Time For Questions)

Jude

I am Jude – younger brother of Jesus and James whom you just met. As the younger brother, I often got to say little, so my letter is short. I just wanted to warn believers of the danger of **twisting** the gospel. In a big family, there are so many voices that it's sometimes hard to know which one to listen to. This is the way it is among Christian teachers. There needs to be a way to tell the **true** teachers from **false** teachers. I say, **"Look at the way they live."** Do they live what they teach? Do they live moral lives – holy living? Are they mature, prayerful, God-loving, hopeful? I offer believers a way of keeping the gospel pure: **Focus on God** who alone is able to keep you from falling!

(Time For Questions)

Peter

I am Peter, a fisherman from Galilee who became Jesus' disciple. Following Jesus was easier and more fun than fishing – until his ordeal in Jerusalem. It's strange; he talked about it, but I just didn't hear it. I didn't want to hear it – I wanted power and fame like everyone does. I tried to be humble once – I took the last position at the Passover just before Jesus' arrest, but my heart wasn't really in it. I was hoping to get moved up next to Jesus and I forgot to do my job – washing feet. It went downhill from there. I bragged that I could be tough and never deny Jesus no matter how difficult things got. A few hours later I lied about even knowing Jesus. I cowered from the scene of the execution.

After his resurrection, I saw Jesus many times. The time that hurt and healed me most was when Jesus asked me three times, "Do you love me?" And three times I declared my love for him, the One I had identified as the Messiah. Each time he responded, "Feed my sheep," or "Feed my lambs." It finally began to dawn on me that it is by **faithfully doing the humblest tasks of life** and by **faithfully following Christ through life's most difficult ordeals** that we **grow in faith** and at the last inherit the **eternal glory** that God has planned for us from the beginning.

Once I finally learned this **secret of wisdom**, I wrote it out (with Silas' – or Silvanus' help) so it could be shared again and again, especially with those who are going through difficult times. I knew others would be tempted, like me, to quit following Jesus when life got difficult. The evil one is subtle, knows when we're most vulnerable, and appeals to our own desires rather than the covenantal will of God. By **steadfastly doing what is right** and **enduring through times of suffering,** believers emerge **victoriously** from earth's pilgrimage of faith. "God opposes the proud, but gives grace to the humble" (1 Peter 5:5).

(Time For Questions)

John

I am John, the disciple Jesus loved. It was a special privilege for me to be close to Jesus for three years. I learn intuitively; that is, for me, learning is more caught than taught. During those three years with Jesus, I tried to "get inside" his character, to think and feel as he did. The more I tried to do this, the more I knew that what was inside him was **LOVE** – the holiest, kindest love I've ever known. To know the heart of Jesus is to know the heart of God – and God is **LOVE** and yearns to give that love to everyone so that the world at last may be **ONE IN LOVE**.

In my gospel and epistles, I wrote mainly about God's **LOVE** for us which is **intimately entwined with our obedience** to the commandments (or "secrets of wisdom"). I knew it was possible for the evil one to trick Christians, through leaders subtly claiming to be teaching God's love while really seeking to control believers for their own purposes – fame and fortune.

In the three brief epistles I wrote, I tried to teach believers to discern between God's **LOVE** and self-seeking **"counterfeit" love,** between the **Spirit of God** and **false spirits,** between **truth** and **falsehood** – for **power struggles will continue**, even among believers, until Christ returns.

(Time For Questions)

Think of a time you or someone you know experienced the death of a loved one, separation, divorce, financial loss or job loss, robbery, sexual assault, rape, serious auto accident, illness, major life change such as moving, etc. You may wish to include more than one person or experience. Using the following questions, describe the experience as you observed it:

1. How would you describe your (or another's) faith before the loss or difficulty occurred? _____
   _____
   _____
   _____
   _____

2. How would you describe your (or another's) faith during the loss or difficulty? _____
   _____
   _____
   _____
   _____

3. How would you describe your (or another's) faith following the loss or difficulty? _____
   _____
   _____
   _____
   _____

4. How did your (or another's) faith change as a result of the loss or difficulty? _____
   _____
   _____
   _____
   _____

5. Why do you think your (or another's) faith grew (or didn't grow) as a result of the loss or difficulty? ___
   _____
   _____
   _____
   _____

DAILY SCRIPTURE
READINGS • WEEK 49

THE **AWE REVERENCE WONDER** AT THE **NEARNESS HOLINESS BEAUTY** OF GOD = THE BEGINNING OF **WISDOM**

(PROVERBS 1:7A)

	HEBREW SCRIPTURE	NEW TESTAMENT	PSALM	PROVERBS
Day 1	Daniel 11:2-35	1 John 3:7-24	122:1-9	29:1
Day 2	Daniel 11:36-12:13	1 John 4:1-21	123:1-4	29:2-4
Day 3	Hosea 1:1-3:5	1 John 5:1-21	124:1-8	29:5-8
Day 4	Hosea 4:1-5:15	2 John 1:1-13	125:1-5	29:9-11
Day 5	Hosea 6:1-9:17	3 John 1:1-14	126:1-6	29:12-14
Day 6	Hosea 10:1-14:9	Jude 1:1-25	127:1-5	29:15-17
Day 7	Joel 1:1-3:21	Revelation 1:1-20	128:1-6	29:18

Personal Notes and Glimpses of Wisdom:

"I wonder what James, Peter, John and Jude would say if they were preaching in our sheepfold today..."

SESSION 50 • THE WISDOM OF SUFFERING

The aim of this session is to explore various passages to discover the wisdom of suffering.

MATERIALS NEEDED

Bibles
Hymnals
Accompaniment
Chalkboard or Newsprint
Completed Search Sheet 49
Completed Insights from Daily Scripture Readings For Week 49
Copies for each participant of:
    "The Suffering Page"
    Search Sheet 50
    Daily Scripture Readings For Week 50

▥ ASSEMBLING

Like Job, believers can suffer even when they've done no wrong. What is the purpose of suffering in the pilgrimage of faith? What helps faith grow during difficult times? Shared wisdom will enrich each participant's faith journey.

▥ THE APPROACH TO GOD   (5 to 10 minutes)

❧ *Sing a hymn* which speaks of hope and promise during difficult times.

❧ *Offer a prayer* for God's leading, guidance and wisdom in this session.

▥ ENCOUNTERING THE WORD   (40 to 45 minutes)

➪ Invite participants to share insights from Search Sheet 49. Why did they (or others) grow (or not grow) as a result of the loss or difficulty?

➪ *Distribute copies of "The Suffering Page."* Invite participants to look up the Scripture references to discover the purposes and benefits of suffering. You may wish to list them on chalkboard or newsprint as they are "discovered."

▥ GOING FORTH IN GOD'S NAME   (5 to 10 minutes)

❧ *Sing a prayer hymn/prayer* of gratitude for the wisdom and gifts God has given through difficult times – *"Thanks To God"* is a possibility.

❧ Distribute copies of:
    Search Sheet 50
    Daily Scripture Readings For Week 50

The Suffering Page

There are many causes of suffering – for believers and non-believers. We often suffer because of our own human nature, our own mistakes. We also suffer because we are part of a broken world. And we suffer because of the sinful behavior of others. However, we follow a Shepherd who was not exempt from suffering but went **through** it and instructed his followers to do the same. As you look up the following verses, you can discover some **purposes and benefits of suffering:**

Job 23:10 _____

_____

Matthew 5:11-12 _____

_____

Matthew 19:29 _____

_____

John 11:4, 40 _____

_____

Romans 5:3-4 _____

_____

Romans 8:17-18 _____

_____

2 Corinthians 1:3-4 _____

_____

2 Corinthians 4:11 _____

_____

2 Corinthians 12:7 _____

_____

2 Corinthians 12:8-10 _____

_____

Hebrews 12:7 _____

_____

1 Peter 1:6-7 _____

_____

1 Peter 5:10 _____

_____

The Suffering Page (Answer Guide)

There are many causes of suffering – for believers and non-believers. We often suffer because of our own human nature, our own mistakes. We also suffer because we are part of a broken world. And we suffer because of the sinful behavior of others. However, we follow a Shepherd who was not exempt from suffering but went **through** it and instructed his followers to do the same. As you look up the following verses, you can discover some **purposes and benefits of suffering:**

Job 23:10 _Refining (as of gold)_

Matthew 5:11-12 _Assurance of heavenly reward_

Matthew 19:29 _Assurance of eternal life_

John 11:4, 40 _The glory of God is revealed through our suffering_

Romans 5:3-4 _Produces endurance, character, hope, reality of God's love in our hearts through the Holy Spirit_

Romans 8:17-18 _We become heirs, glorified with Christ if we suffer with Christ; the suffering is not worth comparing to the glory_

2 Corinthians 1:3-4 _We are consoled by God so we can console others_

2 Corinthians 4:11 _Through suffering, the life of Christ may be made visible in our mortal flesh_

2 Corinthians 12:7 _Suffering keeps us from becoming too elated/proud_

2 Corinthians 12:8-10 _God's power is made perfect in our weakness_

Hebrews 12:7 _Suffering can be for discipline – which assures me I'm God's child_

1 Peter 1:6-7 _Suffering makes faith more genuine_

1 Peter 5:10 _Suffering allows us to experience Christ's restoring support, strengthening and establishing us for eternal glory_

SEARCH SHEET 50

Through the ages the people of God have **endured** difficult struggles, sufferings, abuse and persecution. What reason does the author of Hebrews give for **enduring**? (Hebrews 10:36) _____

_____

What happens to those who shrink back? (Hebrews 10:39) _____

Read Hebrews 11. Make a list of ten things which God's people were able to do **by faith**:

_____   _____

_____   _____

_____   _____

_____   _____

_____   _____

You are one of the **"people of faith"** – you just weren't around when the Epistle to the Hebrews was written! Think of a difficulty or struggle you have endured **"by faith."** Then complete the following statement:

By faith _____ **endured/suffered** _____

_____

rather than _____.

Not all the people of God who endured suffering by faith realized their reward during their earthly lifetime. Why might that be? (Hebrews 11:39-40) _____

Through the ages the people of God have **endured** difficult struggles, sufferings, abuse and persecution. What reason does the author of Hebrews give for **enduring**? (Hebrews 10:36) _So we may receive what was promised_

What happens to those who shrink back? (Hebrews 10:39) _They're lost_

Read Hebrews 11. Make a list of ten things which God's people were able to do **by faith:**

Understand worlds were prepared by God's Word	_Shut lions' mouths_
Obey God and move – Abraham	_Quench fire_
Conquer kingdoms	_Escape the sword_
Administer justice	_Win strength out of weakness_
Obtain promises	_Put foreign armies to flight, etc._

You are one of the **"people of faith"** – you just weren't around when the Epistle to the Hebrews was written! Think of a difficulty or struggle you have endured **"by faith."** Then complete the following statement:

By faith _____ **endured/suffered** _____

_____

rather than _____.

Not all the people of God who endured suffering by faith realized their reward during their earthly lifetime. Why might that be? (Hebrews 11:39-40) _God has something better_

DAILY SCRIPTURE
READINGS • WEEK 50

THE **AWE REVERENCE WONDER** AT THE **NEARNESS HOLINESS BEAUTY** OF GOD = THE BEGINNING OF **WISDOM**

(PROVERBS 1:7A)

	HEBREW SCRIPTURE	NEW TESTAMENT	PSALM	PROVERBS
Day 1	Amos 1:1-3:15	Revelation 2:1-17	129:1-8	29:19-20
Day 2	Amos 4:1-6:14	Revelation 2:18-3:6	130:1-8	29:21-22
Day 3	Amos 7:1-9:15	Revelation 3:7-22	131:1-3	29:23
Day 4	Obadiah 1:1-21	Revelation 4:1-11	132:1-18	29:24-25
Day 5	Jonah 1:1-4:11	Revelation 5:1-14	133:1-3	29:26-27
Day 6	Micah 1:1-4:13	Revelation 6:1-17	134:1-3	30:1-4
Day 7	Micah 5:1-7:20	Revelation 7:1-17	135:1-21	30:5-6

Personal Notes and Glimpses of Wisdom:

SESSION 51 • PERSEVERING IN WISDOM

The aim of this session is to discover and share ways of persevering in wisdom.

MATERIALS NEEDED

Bibles
Hymnals
Accompaniment
Chalkboard or Newsprint
Completed Search Sheet 50
Completed Insights from Daily Scripture Readings For Week 50
Copies for each participant of:
    "Persevering In Wisdom" Worship Service
    "A Pattern for Perseverance"
    Search Sheet 51
    Daily Scripture Readings For Week 51

▨ ASSEMBLING

When we have received God's gift of grace and begun the journey of faith, how can we keep on keeping on? This session explores ways of persevering in **WISDOM – THE WAY GOD SHEPHERDS US TO SHALOM.**

▨ THE APPROACH TO GOD   (5 to 10 minutes)

❧ *Sing a hymn* of pilgrimage such as *"Higher Ground"* or *"Marching To Zion."*

Invite participants to take up Search Sheet 50. **Begin a prayer** of thanksgiving for the life-giving Spirit who enables saints to do amazing things by faith; then invite participants to name some things they listed that the ancient saints have done by faith – and also the things participants have done by faith. Conclude by asking God's leading in exploring ways of persevering in wisdom.

▨ ENCOUNTERING THE WORD   (40 to 45 minutes)

⇨ *Distribute copies of the "Persevering In Wisdom" worship service.* Assign the various parts and proceed with the worship service, allowing time for reflection and discussion following the service. *Distribute copies of "A Pattern For Perseverance,"* inviting participants to see and discuss the interrelatedness of Psalm 23, The Lord's Prayer, and the pattern for persevering in wisdom.

▨ GOING FORTH IN GOD'S NAME   (5 to 10 minutes)

❧ *"Go Now In Peace,"* spoken or sung, provides an appropriate closing for this worship service.

❧ Distribute copies of:
    Search Sheet 51
    Daily Scripture Readings For Week 51

Persevering In Wisdom
(A Worship Service)

CALL TO WORSHIP:

L: Faith is a gift God has given to shepherd us into eternal life and peace. How do we get to that place?

P: By God's Spirit, we are being transformed into the image of God from one degree of glory to another.

L: What is our responsibility in this ongoing gift and process?

P: We are called to "guard what has been entrusted to us" and to faithfully "endure to the end" with the help of the indwelling Holy Spirit.

HYMN: "Take Time To Be Holy"

NARRATOR: There is a special prayer Jesus gave as a summary of all Scripture. The Lord's Prayer can help us remember how to persevere in wisdom. As we worship together, we will explore its wisdom in seven parts, **using the familiar words**, words adapted from the **Aramaic (inclusive traveler's language)** which Jesus spoke, and a **brief description** of the way each part can help us persevere in wisdom.

Part One

L: "Our Father who art in heaven"

P: Our Mother-Father of the Universe, the One who gave birth to our lifebreath and our heartbeats

NARRATOR: "Abwoon" is the Aramaic word which has been translated as "Our Father." "Abwoon really means much more – it means the Source of Unity from which all creation flowed, the One who gave birth to the whole universe. "Heaven" means the whole universe. Can you picture God giving birth to the whole universe? Nurturing the whole vast universe as if it were a precious baby? The One who created us loves us like a Mother and Father love their baby. We have a special relationship with the One who gave birth to us! This is a bond of belonging that goes beyond our earthly life span.

Part Two

L: "Hallowed be Thy Name."

P: Sweep our hearts clean so your Light can shine freely within us..

NARRATOR: The love of our Creator is like a warm and holy Light that is always shining. We need to sweep our hearts clean of all that clutters and prevents that Light from illuminating the innermost places of our lives.

Part Three

L: "Thy kingdom come. Thy will be done on earth as it is in heaven."

P: Create your united kin-dom now, through our willing hearts and hands. Your desire for justice and peace is then united with ours, bringing together heaven and earth.

NARRATOR: Through the lives of people – past, present and future – who respond to God's love with joyous service, God seeks to bring about unity – weaving individual lives into the fabric of Shalom.

Before we can be used as God's agents in bringing about unity and peace, our wills need to become one with the will of God. We realize that all our possessions and even our very lives are gifts from God. We become willing to use whatever we have to bring about God's purpose of eternal unity and peace. This is a mysterious process called submission – letting go of our own wills so that they become one with the will and purpose of God. Submission, ironically, results in true freedom.

Hymn: "Make Me A Captive, Lord," "Take My Life, and Let It Be" or "Have Thine Own Way, Lord"

Part Four

L: "Give us this day our daily bread."

P: *Grant us what we need each day in food for our bodies and insight for our minds and spirits as we continue to grow in our faith. As you gave manna, we ask only for what is needed, trusting there is enough to sustain all life when everyone shares.*

NARRATOR: Having praised God, swept our hearts clean so God's light may shine into our hearts, and having made our wills one with the will of God, we can ask anything, and God will hear and answer. Our petitions are in accord with God's will – not for things that merely please ourselves or make others say nice things about us – but for what we need to do the will of God: health, physical strength from nourishing food, spiritual strength from the ministry of the Word as it is lived out in community, for vision and insight as we work for God's purpose. We can also give thanks for that which we have already received and learned.

(A time for silent prayer or for sharing needs and giving thanks for what has been received)

Hymn: "What A Friend We Have In Jesus"

Part Five

L: "Forgive us our trespasses as we forgive those who trespass against us."

P: *Loose the tangles of mistakes in our relationships as we release the knots we've made by holding onto others' guilt and shame.*

NARRATOR: Whenever we try to control another person by using our knowledge of their mistakes or failures or sins against them, we form knots or kinks in our relationships with them and with others. This breaks our peace and unity as children of God. To forgive is to let go of the strands we hold of others' guilt and shame – and not use this against them anymore. This straightens and heals our relationships with others and restores the peace and unity with God, the universe and ourselves.

As God forgives our sins and remembers them no more, and as God heals our shameful embarrassing moments so they no longer destroy our peace, we receive courage to let go of the strands we hold that could be used to hurt others. Right relationships with God and others bring peace and unity.

Hymn: "Let There Be Peace On Earth"

Part Six

L: "And lead us not into temptation but deliver us from evil."

P: *Don't let us be fooled by outward appearances, but free us from whatever interferes with our life's true purpose.*

NARRATOR: It has always seemed strange to me that we need to ask God not to lead us into temptation. Why would a loving and holy God do that anyway? After the original Aramaic was written down in Greek and translated into English, this could well be a mistranslation. At any rate, the original meaning is: Don't let us be seduced by surface appearances. This might include the things that make us upset and keep us from concentrating on things that are most important. It might mean materialism or even disconnection from the source of Life when we "play God" and try to meet all the needs around us on our own power rather than God's power: that is, "burn-out."

"Evil" might better be translated as "unripeness," failing to move on toward our true purpose which is becoming united with God's purpose. To move beyond surface appearances and more toward "ripeness" or maturity of faith, we need God's grace, God's wisdom and God's power.

Hymn: "God of Grace and God of Glory"

Part Seven

L: "For Thine is the kingdom and the power and the glory forever. Amen."

P: From You is born all power, breath, beauty, songs – may You always be the Wise Source from which our actions spring. In faith and trust, Amen.

NARRATOR: This is a line that has been added to the prayer in keeping with the closing of traditional Jewish prayers. It summarizes the main themes of the prayer and completes it with a note of joy! It expresses abundance within the body of Christ, the kin-dom. It speaks not of God as a power over but as a power with us and within us. It speaks of unity of all the peoples of the earth; this unity (Shalom) also involves all nature and all planets in union with God as God makes everything and everyone whole in this very moment.

Closing Hymn/Prayer: "Forward Through The Ages" or other hymn of pilgrimage

SOURCE: Interpretation of the Aramaic Lord's Prayer is adapted from *Prayers Of The Cosmos* by Neil Douglas-Klotz, Harper and Row, Publishers, San Francisco, 1990, pp. 1-41.

A PATTERN FOR PERSEVERANCE

BELONGING
Our Father who art in heaven
Relationship with the
Creator/Birther and
creation: new beginnings

GREEN
PASTURES
Hallowed be thy Name.
Making a place for God's Name
to be honored in our lives;
feeding on God's Word

STILL
WATERS
*Thy kingdom come. Thy will be
done on earth as it is in heaven.*
Uniting our wills with God's will
by reflecting on the Word

RESTORING TO
RIGHT PATHS
Give us this day our daily bread
Daily transformation and renewal
through reliance on God for
everyday needs and insight

SAFE
SHEEPFOLD
*For thine is the kingdom and the
power and the glory forever.
Amen.* Eternal life with Christ;
abundant living here; peace;
justice; SHALOM!

TABLE IN
THE PRESENCE
OF ENEMY
*Lead us not into temptation, but
deliver us from evil.* Bring us to
maturity of faith in the midst of
struggles and opposition

VALLEY OF
THE SHADOW
*Forgive us our trespasses as
we forgive those who trespass
against us.* Receiving God's undeserved pardon; letting go of
strands we hold of others'
guilt and shame

The last book in Scripture, Revelation, was written near the end of the first century when Christians were persecuted for not worshipping the Roman emperor. In the midst of this persecution, John received a vision of encouragement to faithful Christians. Within the vision are frequent groupings of sevens: seven stars, seven lampstands, seven churches, seven seals, seven trumpets, seven bowls, etc. The number seven was a number of completeness.

In the midst of the seven lampstands (churches) stood the "Son of Man" who was dead but is alive forevermore. He gives a message for the seven churches. Read these messages, and note the strengths and weaknesses of each church. Are the problems inside or outside the churches?

Ephesus (2:1-7)
    Strengths: _____
    Weaknesses: _____

Smyrna (2:8-11)
    Strengths: _____
    Weaknesses: _____

Pergamum (2:12-17)
    Strengths: _____
    Weaknesses: _____

Thyatira (2:18-29)
    Strengths: _____
    Weaknesses: _____

Sardis (3:1-6)
    Strengths: _____
    Weaknesses: _____

Philadelphia (3:7-13)
    Strengths: _____
    Weaknesses: _____

Laodicea (3:14-22)
    Strengths: _____
    Weaknesses: _____

Which church (or combination of churches) is your church or study group most like? _____

What do you think Jesus would say to your church or study group? _____

The last book in Scripture, Revelation, was written near the end of the first century when Christians were persecuted for not worshipping the Roman emperor. In the midst of this persecution, John received a vision of encouragement to faithful Christians. Within the vision are frequent groupings of sevens: seven stars, seven lampstands, seven churches, seven seals, seven trumpets, seven bowls, etc. The number seven was a number of completeness.

In the midst of the seven lampstands (churches) stood the "Son of Man" who was dead but is alive forever-more. He gives a message for the seven churches. Read these messages, and note the strengths and weaknesses of each church. Are the problems inside or outside the churches?

Ephesus (2:1-7)
> ***Strengths:*** _Good works, patience, sound doctrine, steadfastness, hating evil_
> ***Weaknesses:*** _Loss of love; backsliding_

Smyrna (2:8-11)
> ***Strengths:*** _Spiritual endurance_
> ***Weaknesses:*** _None given_

Pergamum (2:12-17)
> ***Strengths:*** _Faithful endurance in midst of evil and persecution_
> ***Weaknesses:*** _Tolerance of false teaching_

Thyatira (2:18-29)
> ***Strengths:*** _Love, faith, service, patient endurance_
> ***Weaknesses:*** _Tolerance of unrepentant false prophetess_

Sardis (3:1-6)
> ***Strengths:*** _Commendation of the few who are faithful_
> ***Weaknesses:*** _Outward works but inner death_

Philadelphia (3:7-13)
> ***Strengths:*** _Faithful works; patient endurance_
> ***Weaknesses:*** _None given_

Laodicea (3:14-22)
> ***Strengths:*** _None given_
> ***Weaknesses:*** _Lukewarmness, spiritual poverty, blindness, etc._

Which church (or combination of churches) is your church or study group most like? _____

What do you think Jesus would say to your church or study group? _____

DAILY SCRIPTURE
READINGS • WEEK 51

THE **AWE REVERENCE WONDER** AT THE **NEARNESS HOLINESS BEAUTY** OF GOD = THE BEGINNING OF **WISDOM**

(PROVERBS 1:7A)

	HEBREW SCRIPTURE	NEW TESTAMENT	PSALM	PROVERBS
Day 1	Nahum 1:1-3:19	Revelation 8:1-13	136:1-26	30:7-9
Day 2	Habakkuk 1:1-3:19	Revelation 9:1-21	137:1-9	30:10
Day 3	Zephaniah 1:1-3:20	Revelation 10:1-11	138:1-8	30:11-14
Day 4	Haggai 1:1-2:23	Revelation 11:1-19	139:1-24	30:15-16
Day 5	Zechariah 1:1-21	Revelation 12:1-13:1a	140:1-13	30:17
Day 6	Zechariah 2:1-3:10	Revelation 13:1b-18	141:1-10	30:18-20
Day 7	Zechariah 4:1-5:11	Revelation 14:1-20	142:1-7	30:21-23

Personal Notes and Glimpses of Wisdom:

_____

_____

_____

_____

_____

_____

_____

_____

_____

"I wonder if keeping on keeping on could become a habit..."

SESSION 52 • WISDOM'S ULTIMATE VICTORY

The aim of this session is to glimpse John's vision of wisdom's ultimate victory.

MATERIALS NEEDED

Bibles
Hymnals
Accompaniment
Chalkboard or Newsprint
Completed Search Sheet 51
Completed Insights from Daily Scripture Readings For Week 51
Copies for each participant of:
    "Wisdom's Ultimate Victory Search"
    "Wisdom's Ultimate Victory, Illustration A"
    "Wisdom's Ultimate Victory, Illustration B
    Daily Scripture Readings For Week 52

▨ ASSEMBLING

This session marks the end of a journey through the Scriptures. This alone is cause for celebration and commendation! The theme of the Book of Revelation is also cause for celebration – for in the midst of all the physical, emotional, psychological and spiritual struggles of life, the Good Shepherd introduced at the beginning of this series emerges as the Worthy Lamb who has accomplished Wisdom's Ultimate Victory!

▨ THE APPROACH TO GOD   (5 to 10 minutes)

❧ *Sing a hymn* such as *"Victory In Jesus," "Holy, Holy, Holy," "Crown Him With Many Crowns,"* etc.

❧ *Offer a prayer* of thanksgiving for God's grace and wisdom which has led throughout this series. Invite participants to share particular items of thanksgiving. Option: Conclude the prayer with a chorus of the group's choice.

▨ ENCOUNTERING THE WORD   (40 to 45 minutes)

⇨ Using Search Sheet 51, invite participants' responses to the questions regarding the seven churches – problems inside or outside? Characterization of your church/group? Christ's message to your church/group? If time permits, you may wish to brainstorm ways of accomplishing Christ's call to your church/group.

⇨ *Write the word "apocalyptic" on chalkboard or newsprint.* Ask participants if they know its meaning. If not, describe it as a prophetic, poetic and visionary style of literature which makes use of imagery and symbolism. It is found in the ancient prophetic literature, especially Daniel. In John's writings, it was particularly useful in conveying spiritual realities during oppressive political regimes. Since "Babylon" was the ancient power which conquered Jerusalem, Jewish people could easily understand that it meant

"Rome." John's visions thus reminded Christians oppressed by Rome that God's power, although not always humanly visible, is far greater and will win the ultimate victory! This reminder gave Christians the encouragement and hope they needed to sustain a long and difficult struggle. Thus apocalyptic literature conveyed God's love and power, larger than any human empire – giving comfort and hope to faithful people.

Since Revelation is a book of visions, it was **not** intended to be interpreted as a timeline – a sequence of chronological events. Viewing the visions as parables and searching for the **one main point** is more helpful in interpretation.

⇨ *Distribute copies of "Wisdom's Ultimate Victory Search" and "Wisdom's Ultimate Victory, Illustration A."* Provide time for them to individually or corporately select "Seals" or "Trumpets," scan the passage, list the seven seals or trumpets and their meaning on the "search" page, write them in on Illustration A, and complete the five questions on the "search" page.

⇨ Provide time for sharing "main point" insights. *Distribute copies of "Wisdom's Ultimate Victory, Illustration B."* Allow time for participants to look it over, reflect on it and share what it means to them.

⇨ Emphasize the **Ultimate Victory** which John's visions assure for all believers. Read Revelation 21:1-8 and 22:1-7, 20, 21 together.

▨ GOING FORTH IN GOD'S NAME   (5 to 10 minutes)

❥ Read Romans 8:35-39 together.

❥ *Sing a hymn* of assurance and victory such as *"Blessed Assurance," "Victory In Jesus,"* etc.

Option: Participants who have faithfully completed "The Wisdom Series" have worked hard, read the entire Bible, learned and grown together. This is a time for joy and celebration. Invite participants to plan a celebration as a closing session.

End Note: It is the nature of the "Good News" to be shared. Those who have received insights from Scripture and the assurance of their **Ultimate Victory** in Christ Jesus need to "pass it on." Invite participants to make plans for ways to live and share the gift of God's love and shepherding. Those who are unsure or unready may wish to take a class in lifestyle evangelism. Be ready to provide it.

Wisdom's Ultimate Victory Search

As individuals, teams, or the group as a whole, select one of the following passages:

Revelation 5:1 – 8:1 (The Seven Seals)

Revelation 8:2 – 11:19 (The Seven Trumpets)

Briefly list the seven seals or seven trumpets and their meaning:

1. _____
   _____

2. _____
   _____

3. _____
   _____

4. _____
   _____

5. _____
   _____

6. _____
   _____

7. _____
   _____

Using "Wisdom's Ultimate Victory Illustration A," arrange the seals or trumpets in a circle. Then search for answers to the following questions:

1. What is the setting or scene the vision portrays?

2. What seems to be the main point of the vision?

3. How does the writer interpret the vision?

4. What do you think God may be saying to us or to "the church" through the vision?

5. What does the vision tell about God's love and power in our individual, corporate and universal struggles?

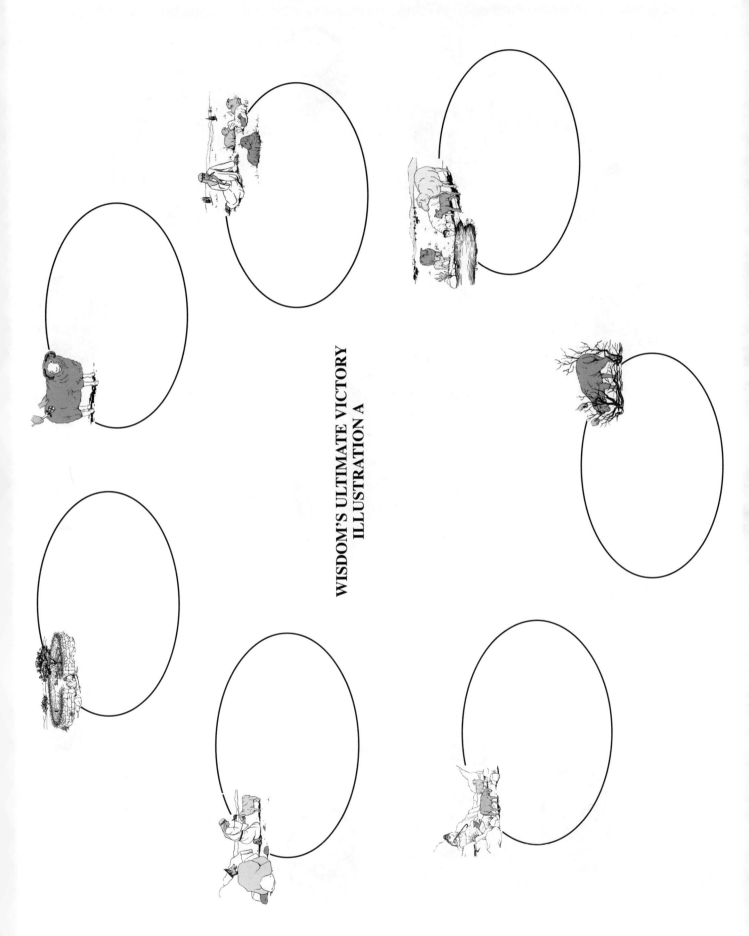

WISDOM'S ULTIMATE VICTORY
ILLUSTRATION A

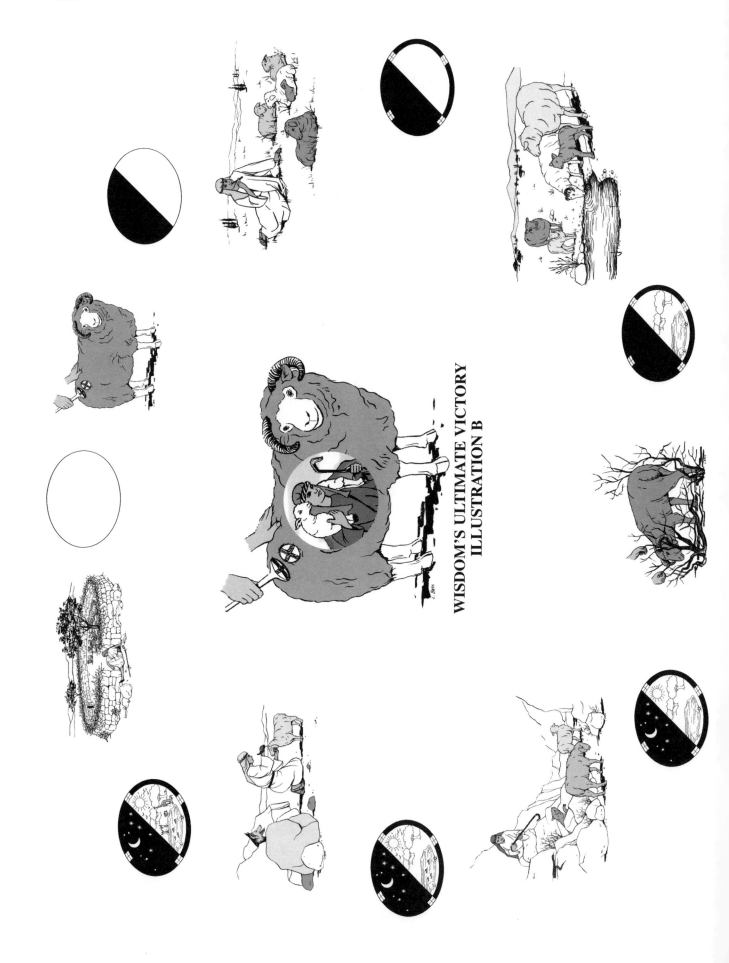

WISDOM'S ULTIMATE VICTORY
ILLUSTRATION B

DAILY SCRIPTURE
READINGS • WEEK 52

THE **AWE REVERENCE WONDER** AT THE **NEARNESS HOLINESS BEAUTY** OF GOD = THE BEGINNING OF **WISDOM**

(PROVERBS 1:7A)

	HEBREW SCRIPTURE	NEW TESTAMENT	PSALM	PROVERBS
Day 1	Zechariah 6:1-7:14	Revelation 15:1-8	143:1-12	30:24-28
Day 2	Zechariah 8:1-23	Revelation 16:1-21	144:1-15	30:29-31
Day 3	Zechariah 9:1-17	Revelation 17:1-18	145:1-21	30:22
Day 4	Zechariah 10:1-11:17	Revelation 18:1-24	146:1-10	30:33
Day 5	Zechariah 12:1-13:9	Revelation 19:1-21	147:1-20	31:1-7
Day 6	Zechariah 14:1-21	Revelation 20:1-15	148:1-14	31:8-9
Day 7	Malachi 1:1-2:17	Revelation 21:1-27	149:1-9	31:10-24
Day 8	Malachi 3:1-4:6	Revelation 22:1-21	150:1-6	31:25-31

Personal Notes and Glimpses of Wisdom:

"I wonder why a Shepherd would become a Lamb..."

BIBLIOGRAPHY

Adult Christian Education Foundation, The. <u>The Bethel Series</u>. Madison, Wisconsin: The Adult Christian Education Foundation, 1961, 1981.

Barker, Kenneth, Ed. <u>The NIV Study Bible</u>. Grand Rapids, Michigan: The Zondervan Corporation, 1985.

<u>Betty Crocker's New Picture Cook Book.</u> New York: McGraw Hill Book Company, Inc., c. 1961, General Mills, Inc.

Boogaart, Thomas A. Professor of Old Testament, Lecture Notes (1988) from "History Of Old Testament Traditions." Holland, Michigan: Western Theological Seminary.

Douglas-Klotz, Neil. <u>Prayers Of The Cosmos.</u> San Francisco: Harper & Row Publishers, 1990.

Eckstein, Yechiel, <u>What Christians Should Know About Jews and Judaism</u>. Waco, Texas: Word Books Publisher, 1984.

<u>Eerdman's Handbook To The Bible</u>. Edited by David Alexander and Patricia Alexander. Grand Rapids, Michigan: William B. Eerdmans Publishing Company, c. 1973, Lion Publishing, Icknield Way, Tring, Herts, England.

Erikson, Erik H. <u>Childhood And Society</u>. New York: W. W. Norton, 1963.

Fowler, James W. <u>Stages Of Faith</u>. San Francisco: Harper & Row Publishers, 1981.

Fowler, James W. <u>Weaving The New Creation (Stages Of Faith and the Public Church)</u>. San Francisco: Harper Collins, 1991.

Haley, Alex. <u>Roots</u>. Garden City, New York: Doubleday and Company, Inc., 1976.

<u>Holy Bible New Revised Standard Version</u>. New York: Oxford University Press, 1989.

How, William W. "O Word Of God Incarnate." (1867) <u>The United Methodist Hymnal</u>, Nashville: The United Methodist Publishing House, 1989.

Keller, Phillip. <u>A Shepherd Looks At Psalm 23</u>. Grand Rapids, Michigan: Zondervan (Daybreak Books), 1973.

Page, Charles R. II. <u>Jesus And The Land</u>. Nashville: Abingdon Press, 1995.

Phillippe, William R. <u>A Romp Through The Bible</u>. Evanston, Illinois: Wm Caxton LTD, 1987.

Rasmussen, Carl G. <u>The Zondervan NIV Atlas Of The Bible</u>. Grand Rapids, Michigan: Regency Reference Library, Zondervan Publishing House, 1989.

Stein, Robert H. An Introduction to the Parables Of Jesus. Philadelphia: The Westminster Press, 1981.

Stewart, Sonja M. and Jerome W. Berryman. Young Children And Worship. Louisville, Kentucky: Westminster/John Knox Press, 1989.

The Holy Bible, Authorized King James Version. Cleveland, Ohio: The World Publishing Company.

The One-Year Bible. Iowa Falls, Iowa: World Bible Publishers, Inc., c. Wheaton, Illinois, Tyndale House Publishers, Inc., 1985.

Trible, Phyllis. God And The Rhetoric Of Sexuality. Philadelphia: Fortress Press, 1978.

Wagner, C. Peter. Your Spiritual Gifts Can Help Your Church Grow. Ventura, California: Regal Books, 1982.

Wink, Walter. Transforming Bible Study. Nashville: Abingdon Press, 1980.

APPENDIX A

BOOKS OF BIBLE	SESSION	BOOKS OF BIBLE	SESSION
Genesis	2-8	Nahum	21
Exodus	9-12, 14	Habbakuk	21
Leviticus	13, 14	Zephaniah	21
Numbers	14	Haggai	21
Deuteronomy	14	Zechariah	21
Joshua	16	Malachi	21
Judges	17	Matthew	28-30, 34-37, 39,40,50,51
Ruth	24	Mark	29,31,35,39,40
1 Samuel	18,19	Luke	28,29,32,35-37,39,40
2 Samuel	19	John	29,33-35,39-40
1 Kings	19-21	Acts	41
2 Kings	20-22	Romans	42,43,48,50
1 Chronicles	19	1 Corinthians	43,44
2 Chronicles	20,22	2 Corinthians	44,50
Ezra	25	Galatians	45,48
Nehemiah	25	Ephesians	43,45
Esther	24	Philippians	45
Job	23,50	Colossians	45
Psalms	26	1 Thessalonians	46
Proverbs	(Daily)	2 Thessalonians	46
Ecclesiastes	—	1 Timothy	47
Song of Solomon	—	2 Timothy	47
Isaiah	21	Titus	47
Jeremiah	21	Philemon	47
Lamentations	21	Hebrews	48,50
Ezekiel	21	James	49
Daniel	21	1 Peter	43,49,50
Hosea	21	2 Peter	49
Joel	21	1 John	49
Amos	21	2 John	49
Obadiah	21	3 John	49
Jonah	21	Jude	49
Micah	21	Revelation	52

APPENDIX B

1. **Shepherd Wisdom** Psalm 23
2. **Creation Wisdom** Genesis
3. **More Creation Wisdom** Genesis
4. **The Wisdom of the Garden** Genesis
5. **Rebelling Against Wisdom** Genesis
6. **Wisdom's Cleansing Waters** Genesis
7. **Covenantal Wisdom** Genesis
8. **Patriarchal Wisdom** Genesis
9. **Shaping a Wise Leader** Exodus
10. **God's Saving Wisdom** Exodus
11. **The Law – Wisdom's Secrets** Exodus
12. **A Center for Wisdom and Glory** Exodus
13. **The Wisdom of God's Forgiveness** Leviticus
14. **Wilderness Wisdom** Exodus-Deuteronomy
15. **Wisdom's Journey** Psalm 23
16. **Wisdom's Conquest** Joshua
17. **Wisdom Through the Judges** Judges
18. **Wisdom In Crisis** 1 Samuel
19. **Wisdom In A United Monarchy** 1 & 2 Samuel, 1 Kings, 1 Chronicles
20. **Wisdom In A Divided Monarchy** 1 & 2 Kings, 2 Chronicles
21. **Prophetic Wisdom** 1 & 2 Kings, Isaiah through Malachi
22. **The Wisdom Of The Exile** 2 Kings, 2 Chronicles
23. **Wisdom In The Night** Job
24. **Women Of Wisdom** Ruth, Esther
25. **Restoration Wisdom** Ezra, Nehemiah
26. **Wisdom's Songs** Psalms

27. **Inter-Testamental Wisdom** 1 & 2 Maccabees
28. **Preparing Wisdom's Way** Matthew, Luke
29. **Wisdom's New Birth** Matthew, Mark, Luke, John
30. **Wisdom's Promise Fulfilled** Matthew
31. **Wisdom's Self-Giving Servant** Mark
32. **Wisdom's Seeking Savior** Luke
33. **Wisdom In Human Flesh** John
34. **Wisdom's Paradox** Matthew, John
35. **Wisdom's Secret Attitudes** Matthew, Mark, Luke, John
36. **Wisdom's Mysterious Growth Stories** Matthew, Luke
37. **Wisdom's Mysterious Love Stories** Matthew, Luke
38. **Wisdom's Mysterious Center** (General Bible Survey)
39. **When Wisdom Seemed Silent** Matthew, Mark, Luke, John
40. **Wisdom's Joyous Surprise** Matthew, Mark, Luke, John
41. **Wisdom's Power Unleashed** Acts
42. **Wisdom's Boundless Grace** Romans
43. **Wisdom's Gifts** Romans, 1 Corinthians, Ephesians, 1 Peter
44. **Living as Wisdom's People** 1 & 2 Corinthians
45. **Four Hymns Of Wisdom** Galatians, Ephesians, Philippians, Colossians
46. **Wisdom's Encouraging Words** 1 & 2 Thessalonians
47. **Pastoral Wisdom** 1 & 2 Timothy, Titus, Philemon
48. **Renewal Wisdom** Romans, Galatians, Hebrews
49. **Letters Of Everyday Wisdom** James, 1 & 2 Peter, 1, 2 & 3 John, Jude
50. **The Wisdom Of Suffering** Job, Matthew, John, Romans, 2 Corinthians, Hebrews, 1 Peter
51. **Persevering in Wisdom** Psalm 23, Matthew 6
52. **Wisdom's Ultimate Victory** Revelation

ORDER INFORMATION

COPY FREELY

ORDER FORM

The Wisdom Series — $49.95
Books may be returned for full refund – for any reason, no questions asked.

Shipping and Handling:
$4.95 for the first book, $3 for each additional book
Special rates available for quantity orders

Sales Tax:
Please add 6% for books shipped to Michigan addresses
Or Give Tax-Exempt Number _____

Payment:

___ Check or Money Order

___ VISA

___ MasterCard

Card Number _____   Expiration Date: _____

Name on Card:_____

Signature _____

Ship To: _____   Phone: _____

_____

_____

Fax Orders: (616) 588-7118

Telephone Orders: Call Toll Free: 1-888-399-3141, 8 a.m.-5 p.m. (Eastern time) weekdays

Postal Orders: Sheepfold Publishing
9268 Main St., P.O. Box 72
Ellsworth, Michigan 49729-0072, USA